SPECIMENS
OF
LANGUAGES OF INDIA

SPECIMENS OF LANGUAGES OF INDIA

G. CAMPBELL

DALTON*HOPKINSON*METCALFE
RAVENSHAW*EDGAR*CLARKE
TROTTER*LEWIN*BUTLER*POWER
HALLIDAY*LAMB*ALEXANDER*RIVER
ROWLATT*ENDLE*SKREFSEND*WHITLEY

GYAN

Published by

GYAN

Gyan Publishing House
5, Ansari Road
Daryaganj, New Delhi-110002
Phone: 011-47034999, 9811692060
E-mail: books@gyanbooks.com

Distribution Network
gyanbooks.com
India, USA, Canada, UK, Australia, France

ISBN : 978-81-212-3053-7 (PB)
First Published, 1874

2nd Impression 2020

Printed at: Gyan Press, Delhi.

Specimens of Languages of India
Author: G. Campbell

SPECIMENS

OF

LANGUAGES OF INDIA,

INCLUDING THOSE OF THE

ABORIGINAL TRIBES OF BENGAL,

THE

CENTRAL PROVINCES, AND THE EASTERN FRONTIER.

Calcutta:
PRINTED AT THE BENGAL SECRETARIAT PRESS.

1874.

SPECIMENS OF LANGUAGES OF INDIA,

INCLUDING THOSE OF THE

ABORIGINAL TRIBES OF BENGAL,

THE

CENTRAL PROVINCES, AND THE EASTERN FRONTIER.

For this collection of language-specimens, I am chiefly indebted to the officers now serving under me, and to those whom I formerly engaged in such work when I administered the Central Provinces. I have also obtained, for the purposes of comparison, specimens of the principal languages of other provinces, for which I am indebted to the kindness of friends and fellow-workmen with whom I have served in different parts of India. The Hon'ble R. Egerton has procured for me a most interesting and important collection of Punjab languages prepared by Messrs. Udney, Gladstone, Tucker, Hawkins, and others; and to the Hon'ble R. Dalyell I am indebted for a collection of the civilised Dravidian languages of Southern India. The Hon'ble A. Eden, Chief Commissioner of British Burmah, has been good enough to procure for me several of the languages of that country. The Political Agents in Khelat and Cashmere, Major Harrison and Mr. LePoer Wynne, have favoured me with the languages of those localities. The Mahratta and Guzratee specimens have been procured by Mr. Pedder, c.s., to whom my best thanks are due.

Collected as these specimens chiefly have been by working officers burdened with many duties, and without any prescribed system of transliteration or spelling, it is probable that most of them cannot pretend to scientific accuracy; but I have sought to make up for this by the number and variety of specimens of the less known languages, by which the various dialects may be compared and the forms may be checked and ascertained. It has also been impossible to examine them critically in passing through the press. My hope is that the abundant raw materials thus afforded will afford ample scope for the work of the scientific philologist. I trust that from the materials thus available, much scientific information and order may be educed by competent hands into which these language-specimens may find their way.

Meantime, I believe that already, from a mere rough comparison, much practical work in regard to the classification of people and tribes has been done, and may be done, even without scientific philology. The words and phrases have been selected with a view to test radical affinities, and already evident affinities may be traced, and the tribes may be classified better than has heretofore been possible. This was, in fact, the primary and official object of undertaking the work, and the justification of all the labour which it has involved. The many officers who have undertaken that labour so zealously and so well, may, then, be assured that from a practical as well as from a philological point of view their work is not without fruit. I tender to them my very best thanks.

In these provinces I may especially distinguish among many good workers, as having taken a large share in this compilation—

Colonel Dalton, Commissioner of the Chota Nagpore territories.
,, Hopkinson, Commissioner of Assam.
Mr. Metcalfe, Commissioner of Cooch Behar.
,, Ravenshaw, Commissioner of Orissa.
,, Edgar, Deputy Commissioner of Darjeeling.
Major Clarke, Deputy Commissioner of Luckimpore.
Lieutenant Trotter, Superintendent of Police, Durrung.
Captain Lewin, Deputy Commissioner of Chittagong Hill Tracts.
,, Butler, Political Agent, Naga Hills.
Mr. Power, C.S., Political Agent, Hill Tipperah.
,, Halliday, Magistrate of Tirhoot.
,, Alexander, Magistrate of Shahabad.
Colonel Lamb, Deputy Commissioner of Kamroop.
,, Bivar, Deputy Commissioner of Khasi Hills.
,, Rowlatt, Deputy Commissioner of Manbhum.
Revd. S. Endle.
,, L. Skrefsend.
,, A. Whitley.

I do not purpose to attempt here any comparisons of the languages shown. I have neither the time nor the ability to do so. Fortunately, the language-specimens were obtained before famine came upon us, and now that the printing is completed, I issue them with the briefest possible note. I will only mention one or two salient features in the classification of the non-Aryan tribes of these territories, which the specimens render self-evident.

It is very clear that most of the aboriginal tribes of the Central Provinces and several of those of Western Bengal (including in these latter the Dangars, Oraons of Chota Nagpore, Paharies of Rajmehal, and Khonds of Orissa) are radically allied to the Dravidians. Intermixed with these tribes, but speaking a language quite without affinity to the Dravidian tongues, are the tribes which I call Kolarian, forming a minority among the aborigines of the Central Provinces, but a great majority among those of Western Bengal. Throughout the western borders of Bengal, and all over the Chota Nagpore country, these people are very numerous and prolific, and form large, settled, and civilised communities among the best of Her Majesty's Indian subjects. Strange as it may seem, I believe that their very fully developed language has not yet been found to have any affinity with any other groups of language whatever, except with one now rapidly dying-out tongue, far away on the eastern side of the Bay of Bengal, the Mon or Talain of Pegu, with which some affinities are, I think, apparent.

The specimens numbered 9 and 10 make it clear that all the non-Aryan languages of the Darjeeling, Bhootan, and Nepalese Hills are of the Thibetan type.

In the border plains of Eastern Bengal, Assam, and Cachar, and the lower hills bounding these countries, we come on a group of tongues evidently very nearly allied to one another, and which show that a large number of tribes, extending, under very different conditions, over a wide extent of country, and known by different names, are in fact closely cognate. This fact is the more important, because a large part of the population of Eastern Bengal is universally recognised to be cognate to the tribes speaking these languages. This group comprises the Cooches and Meches of Cooch Behar the Sub-Himalayan Dooars and Goalpara, the Cacharees and Mekirs of Assam and Cachar, the Garos of the Garo Hills, and the Tipperahs of Hill Tipperah. Most of the civilized Cooches have lost their language, but all their traditions acknowledge their relationship to the Meches, who speak a language regarding which there can be no doubt. Under the name of Rajbunsees, Pullees, &c., people nearly allied to these form a large proportion of the population of the great districts of Rungpore and Dinagepore, as well as of Julpigoree, Goalpara, and parts of Assam. They are also found in the Dacca and Mymensing districts. Probably then these people form the main stock of the population of North-Eastern Bengal and Lower Assam, as well as of all the lower eastern hills.

Beyond these lower hills we have a great variety of tribes whose languages are very distinct from that of the Cacharees Garos Tipperahs &c., though those of the Kookees and other tribes (see the Looshai dialect and the Khumi of

Chittagong and Burmah, and also the Munipooree) are not without considerable traces of affinity to the above.

Going farther on this eastern frontier, we become involved in many languages, the affinities of which I cannot now attempt to trace.*

We have several specimens of civilised Shan languages in Upper Assam. The tribes to the north-east of Assam speak a set of languages the affinities of which I know not, but of which specimens are given. There was question whether the various tribes known to us as Nagas were really identical, or might not be found to comprise many dissimilar tribes. The language-specimens obtained from several different quarters show that all the Nagas speak a language substantially identical. The language of the Khasi and Jynteah Hills is substantially one, and a very peculiar one, apart from all these others. Several dialects of this language are given.

The comparison of languages of Burmah with several others enables us to trace the more or less remote connection of most of these with the languages of the south-eastern frontier of Bengal, and also the curious affinity between the old Pegu language and the Kolarian tongues of Western Bengal.

CALCUTTA,
The 20*th February* 1874.

G. CAMPBELL.

CONTENTS.

	PAGE.
1.—ARYAN LANGUAGES OF BENGAL, HINDUSTAN, AND THE BOMBAY TERRITORIES	2 to 21
2.—LANGUAGES OF THE PUNJAB AND NEIGHBOURING COUNTRIES	24 to 41
3.—DRAVIDIAN LANGUAGES OF SOUTHERN AND CENTRAL INDIA	44 to 57
4.—DIALECTS OF BEHAR	60 to 75
5.—ABORIGINAL LANGUAGES OF WESTERN BENGAL (KOLARIAN TYPE)	78 to 91
6.—FURTHER ABORIGINAL LANGUAGES OF WESTERN BENGAL (CHIEFLY DRAVIDIAN TYPE)	94 to 107
7.—ABORIGINAL LANGUAGES OF THE CENTRAL PROVINCES (KOLARIAN AND DRAVIDIAN)...	110 to 123
8.—FURTHER ABORIGINAL LANGUAGES OF THE CENTRAL PROVINCES (DRAVIDIAN, CHIEFLY GOND)	126 to 139
9.—THIBETAN AND BHOOTEA LANGUAGES	142 to 147
10.—COOCH BEHAR, DARJEELING (SIKHIM), AND NEPALESE LANGUAGES	150 to 165
11.—ASSAM LANGUAGES	168 to 186
12.—LANGUAGES OF THE TIPPERAH, CHITTAGONG, AND CACHAR FRONTIER	188 to 201
13.—FURTHER LANGUAGES FROM TIPPERAH AND CACHAR...	204 to 217
14.—LANGUAGES OF HILLS SURROUNDING ASSAM AND CACHAR	220 to 235
15.—LANGUAGES OF THE NORTH-EAST OF ASSAM	238 to 251
16.—DIALECTS OF NAGA TRIBES OF THE SEEBSAUGOR FRONTIER	254 to 269
17.—LANGUAGES OF THE KHASI AND JYNTEAH HILLS ...	272 to 283
18.—LANGUAGES OF BURMAH COMPARED WITH OTHERS ...	286 to 303

LIST OF WORDS AND PHRASES

SHOWING SOME OF THE

PRINCIPAL ARYAN LANGUAGES OF INDIA.

English.	Hindee.	Bengalee.	
		In common use.	*In use among the educated class.*
One ...	Ek, Ekgo, Ektho	Ek	Ek ... ...
Two ...	Do, Dogo, Dotho	Dui	Dui ... ...
Three ...	Tin, Tingo, Tintho	Tin	Tin ... ...
Four ...	Chár, Chárgo, Chártho	Chár	Chári ... ...
Five ...	Pánch Pánchgo, Pántho ...	Pánch	Pánch ... ...
Six ...	Chha, Chhau, Chhago, Chhotho ...	Chhai	Chhai ... ...
Seven ...	Sát, Sátgo, Sáttho	Sát	Sát ... ...
Eight ...	Ath, Athgo, Aththo	Át	Át, Ashto... ... ...
Nine ...	Nau, Naugo, Nautho	Nai	Nai ... ...
Ten ...	Das, Dasgo, Dastho	Das	Das ... ...
Twenty ...	Bis, Bisgo, Bistho	Bis, Kuri...	Bis, Kuri... ... ...
Fifty ...	Pachás, Pachásgo, Pachástho ...	Panchás	Panchás ... ...
Hundred ...	Sau, Sai, Saugo, Sautho ...	Ek sat, Sau	Ek sat, Sau ... ...
I ...	Main, Ham	Ámi, Mui...	Ámi ... ...
Of me ...	Merá, Hámár	Mor, Amár	Ámár ... ...
Mine ...	Merá, Hámár	Same as above	Same as above ... ...
We ...	Ham, Hamáni	Morá, Ámrá	Ámrá ... ...
Of us ...	Hamárá, Hamánikà, Hamsobinkaer	Modér	Ámáder, Ámádiger ... ..
Our ...	Hamara, Hamániká, Hamaráni ...	Same as "of us"	Same as "of us" ... ...
Thou ...	Tu, Tóu	Tui, Tumi	Tumi, Ápani ... ...
Of thee ...	Térá, Tohar, Tore	Tor, Tomár	Tomár, Ápanár ... ...
Thine ...	Tera, Tóhar, Teri		
You ...	Túm, Toháni	Torá, Tomrá	Tomrá, Ápanárá ... ...
Of you ...	Túmhárá, Tohanike, Tohár, Tohramkeir.	Toder, Tomáder	Tomádiger, Apanádiger ...
Your ...	Túmhárá, Tuhár, Tohánike ...		
He ...	Wuh	Sé	Tini ... ...
Of him ...	Uska, Okar	Tár	Táhár, Tahaúr ... ...
His ...	Uska, O-kar		
They ...	Wé, Ukani, Ohney	Tárá	Táhárá, Tahaúra ... ...
Of them ...	Unka, Uniká, Onkar	Táder	Táháder, Tahaúder ... ...
Their ...	Okoniká, Unkánhinká, Onkoror, Onhinikair.		

Mahrattee.	Guzerattee.	Oorya.	Assamese.	English.
Ek	Ek	Ek	Ek	One.
Don	Bé	Dui	Dui	Two.
Teen	Trina, traṇ	Tini	Tini	Three.
Chár	Chár	Chári	Chári, Sari	Four.
Pánch	Pánch	Páncha	Páúch	Five.
Sahá	Chha	Chhaa	Chhai, Soi	Six.
Sát	Sát	Sáta	Sát, Hát	Seven.
Áth	Áṭh	Atha	Ath, At	Eight.
Now	Nav	Naa Na	Na	Nine.
Dahá	Das	Dasa	Dah	Ten.
Vis	Vis	Kodie	Kuri	Twenty.
Pannas	Pachás	Panchása, Pachás	Panchás, Pansas	Fifty.
Shambhar	Sò	Sata, Sae	Eksa, Ha	Hundred.
Mi	Hún	Ámbhe, Áme, Muhi	Mai	I
M. F. N.				
Singular.—Majha, Majhi, Majheṇ	Márú	Ámbhára, Ámar, Mohar.	Mor	Of me.
Plural.—Majhay, Majhya, Majhiṇ	Márú	Ámbhara, Ámar, Mohar.	Mor	Mine.
Amhi	Amé	Ámbhemáne, Ámemáne.	Ami	We.
Singular.—Amcha, Amchi, Amchaiṇ	Amárú	Ámbhamánankar, Ámamánankar.	Amálokar	Of us.
Plural.—Amchéy, Amcheya, Amchiṇ	Amárú	Ámbhamánankar Ámamánankar.	Amalokar	Our.
Túṇ	Tún	Ápana, Tumbhe, Tume Tu.	Tumi, Tai, Apuni	Thou.
Tújha, Tújhi, Tújhaiṇ	Tárú	Ápanankar, Tumbhara, Tumar, Tor.	Tomár, Teor	Of thee.
Tujhay, Tújheya, Tújhiṇ	Tárú	Ápanankar, Tumbhara, Tumar, Tor.	Tomar, Apanár	Thine.
Tùmhi	Tamé	ÁpanamáneTumbhemáne, Tumemáne.	Tumi, Tomolák	You.
Tùmchá, Tumchi, Tùmchaiṇ	Tamárú	Ápanamánankar, Tumbhamánankar, Tumamánankar.	Tomar, Tomálokar	Of you.
Tumchay, Tumcheya, Tumchiṇ	Tamárú	Ápanamánankar, Tumbhamanankar, Tumamánankar.	Tomalokar, Tomar	Your.
Tó	Té	Se	Sé, Teo	He.
Teáchá, Teáchi, Teácheṇ	Té hé nú	Táhánkar, Tánkar, Táhára, Tar.	Teor, Tár	Of him.
Teáchey, Teáchaya, Teáchin	Té hé nú	Táhánkar Tánkar, Táhára, Tar.	Teor, Tar	His.
Téy, Téa, Tíṇ	Té ó	Semáne	Téobilak, Séheta	They.
Teánchá, Teánchi, Teáncheṇ	Té hé manú	Semánankar	Teobilakar, Sihatar	Of them.
Teánchey, Teánchayá, Teánchin	Té hé manú	Semánankar	Teobilakar, Tahatar	Their.

English.	Hindee.	Bengalee.	
		In common use.	*In use among the educated class.*
Hand ...	Hát, Banah	Hát	Hasta ... ...
Foot ...	Páon. Gód	Pá	Pá, Pada ... ...
Nose ...	Nák, Násika	Nák	Nák, Násiká ... ...
Eye ...	Ankh, Nayana	Chok	Chokhu, Nayana ... ...
Mouth ...	Múh, Múkh, Muṅh	Múkh	Badan, Múkh ... ...
Tooth ...	Dánt, Dantán	Dant	Danta ... ...
Ear ...	Kán	Kán	Karna, Kán ... ...
Hair ...	Bál, Kesha	Chul	Kesh, Chul ... ...
Head ...	Sír, Mantha, Mur	Máthá	Mastuck ... ...
Tongue ...	Jabán, Jibh, Jiba	Jib	Jihba ... ...
Belly ...	Peth, Lod	Pét	Udar, Pét... .. ...
Back ...	Pith	Pít	Pristha, Pít ... ...
Iron ...	Lohá	Loá	Lohá ... ...
Gold ...	Soná, Subarna	Soná	Suarna, Suburna ... ...
Silver ...	Nophra, Chándee	Rupá	Roupya ... ...
Father ...	Báp, Pitá	Báp, Bábá	Pitá ... ...
Mother ...	Má, Mayè, Mátá, Mátari ...	Má	Mátá ... ...
Brother ...	Bhai, Bharátá	Bhái	Bhrátá ... ...
Sister ...	Bahín	Bún	Bhogini ... ...
Man ...	Mánush, Ádmi	Mánus	Manusya ... ...
Woman ...	Áurat, Meraru	Meye mánus	Strilok ... ...
Wife ...	Áurat, Joru, Meraru, Stri ...	Mág	Potni, Stri ... ...
Child ...	Ler-ká, Pútrú, Bachha	Chhele	Santán ... ...
Son ...	Beta, Put	Betá	Putra, Sut, Janaù ... ...
Daughter ...	Lerki, Beti, Mayewan	Meye	Kanya, Duhita ... ...
Slave ...	Gu-lám, Naphar	Dás	Dás ... ...
...	... ...	... ...	... ...
Cultivator ...	Chási, Kisán	Chásá	Krisak ... ...
Shepherd ...	Bheríhārā, Bágál, Gauri, Bhoredar...	Rákhál	Rákhál, Meshpálak ... ...
God ...	Bhaga-wán	Debtá, Ishuar	Ishuar ... ...
Devil ...	Bhút, Asur	Bhut	Bhut, Pishách ... ...
Sun ...	Súrúj	Sujjee	Surjya, Dibákar ... ...
Moon ...	Chánd, Chandar-ma	Chánd	Chandra ... ...
Star ...	Tárá	Tárá	Nakhyatra ... ...

Mahrattee.	Guzerattee.	Oorya.	Assamese.	English.
Hāt	Háth, Báju, Acshar, Daskat.	Hasta, Háta ...	Hat	Hand.
Páe	Pag, Ek játa nu máp	Páda, Páhula Páhun-da, Khoja.	Bhari	Foot.
Nák	Nák	Násá, Náka ...	Nák	Nose.
Ḍolà	Ankha	Chakhyu, Akhi ...	Saku, Bhaku ...	Eye.
Tónd	Moho	Mukha, Muhau Páti, Tunda.	Mukh, Bet ...	Mouth.
Dant	Dañt	Danta, Dánta ...	Dát, Daut ...	Tooth.
Kan	Kán	Karna, Kána ...	Kán	Ear.
Keṉs	Bál, Nimálá, Vál ...	Kesa, Bála ...	Suli, Chuli... ...	Hair.
Dòkeṉ	Máthù	Mastaka, Munda ...	Mur	Head.
Jibh	Jibha	Jihwá, Jibha ...	Jibhá, Jíbá ...	Tongue.
Pót	Pét	Udara, Peta ...	Pet	Belly.
Path	Piṭh. Baiḍo, Vánso...	Prustha, Pithi ...	Pithi	Back.
Lokhand	Lohodhu ...	Louha, Luhá ...	Lo	Iron.
Soneṉ	Sonu	Swarna, Suná ...	Hon, Son	Gold.
Rupeṉ	Rúpu	Roupya, Rupá ..	Rúp	Silver.
Báp	Bápa	Pita, Bápa, Bábá ...	Bopae	Father.
Ai	Má, Bá ...	Máta, Má ...	Ai	Mother.
Bháú	Bhaé, Báṉdu ...	Bhrátá, Bhái ...	Bhái, Kakái ...	Brother.
Bahiṉ	Behen	Bhagini, Bhauni ...	Bhain	Sister.
Púrush, Manúshyă	Máṉas	Manusya, Manisa Manasa, Purusa, Minipa.	Manuh, Munih ...	Man.
Baekó, Stri	Báyadi, Strî ...	Stri, Strilá, Tilá, Máikinia.	Tirota, Maiki ...	Woman.
Baeko, Patni	......	Bhárjyá, Bhárijá Máipa.	Ghaini, Tirota ...	Wife.
Múl	Chhokro ...	Bálaka, Pilá ...	Tara, Soali... ...	Child.
Múlga, Púttra	Dikro, Chhokro ...	Putra, Pua ...	Po, Pitek ...	Son.
Mulgi, Kanyā	Dikri, Chhokri ...	Kanyá, Jhia, Jhna ...	Ji or Jik	Daughter.
Gulám, Dás...	Gúlám	Dása, Poilá ...	Golám, Tigerábundi, Bahatia.	Slave. (Mas.)
....	......	Dási, Poili, Poiláni...	......	Do. (Fem.)
Shetkari	Khedut... ...	Chási, Chasá, Tasá...	Khetiak	Cultivator.
Dhangar	Bharváḍ, Rabári ...	Chhelirakhá, Chhelia	Gorakhia, Rakhia ...	Shepherd.
Dev	Parméçvar, Isvar ...	Iswara, Prabhú ...	Ishwar, Gohai ...	God.
Bhút, Saitān	Bhút, Prét, Pisách...	Bhuta	Bhút	Devil.
Súraj	Súraj	Súrjya ...	Bénli, Huruj ...	Sun.
Chandra, Chánd	Chandrmá ...	Chandra, Chánda, Jahna.	Jou	Moon.
Chāndni, Naksatra, Tārā ...	Táro	Tárá, Nakhyatra, Tará.	Tará	Star.

English.	Hindee.	Bengalee.	
		In common use.	*In use among the educated class.*
Fire ...	Ág	Águn	Agni ... ...
Water ...	Páni	Jal, Páni	Jal ... ...
House ...	Ghar, Geh	Ghar, Bári	Báti, Griha ... ...
Horse ...	Ghorá, Gharwa	Ghorá	Ghotak, Ghorá, Ashwa ...
Cow ...	Gáe	Gai-garu	Gábhi ... .
Dog ...	Kút-ta	Kúkúr	Kúkúr ... ...
Cat ...	Bil-li	Berál	Birál ... ...
Cock ...	Murng	Kukura	Kukura ... ...
Duck ...	Páti haus, Chakwi	Hánsh	Pátihangsa ... ...
Ass ...	Gad-dha	Gádá	Gardhaba... ... ...
Camel ...	Unt	Ut	Ut, Ustra... ... ...
Bird ...	Panchhi, Pakhern	Pákhi	Pákhi, Pakhyi ... ...
Go ...	Jáná, Jou	Jáon	Jáwá, Goman karan ... ...
Eat ...	Kháná, Khou, Khá, Khali ...	Kháwá	Áhár, Bhokyun karau ...
Sit ...	Baithná, Baith	Basa	Basa karau ... ..
Come ...	Auná, Aó	Asá	Asa, Ágamun karan ... ...
Beat ...	Márná, Már...	Thengán	Márá ... ...
Stand ...	Kháráhoná, Khárá	Dárán	Dárán ... ...
Die ...	Marun, Marjo, Muá	Mará	Mará ... ...
Give ...	Dená, De	Deo-a	Deo-a ... ...
Run ...	Daurna, Dour	Douran	Douran ... ...
Up ...	Upar	Upar	Upar ... ...
Near ...	Nagich, bhir-lag	Káchhé	Nikate ... ...
Down ...	Nich, Henthe	Talaye	Nichè, Nimne ... ...
Far ...	Dúr, Pállá	Dúr	Dúr ... ...
Before ...	Agé	Agè	Agra, Purbe ... ...
Behind ...	Pichhé, Pichu	Páche	Paschát ... ...
Who ...	Kíon	Kè	Kè ... ...
What ...	Kiya	Ki	Ki ... ...
Why ...	Káhe, Kiáho	Kèna	Kijanya ... ...
And ...	Áúr	Ár	Ebang ... ...
But ...	Le-kin, Magar	Kintú	Kintú ... ...
If ...	Agar, Jaún, Jo	Jadi	Jadyapi ... ...
Yes ...	Hán	Áchhá	Hán ... ...
No ...	Neh	Ná	Ná ... ...
Alas ...	Há-e	Há-e	Há-e, Áhá ... ...
A father ...	Ek-báp, or ego báp	Ek báp	Ek pitá .. ..

Mahrattee.	Guzerattee.	Oorya.	Assamese.	English.
Vistu	Devtá	Agni, Niáṅ, Jui ...	Jui	Fire.
Pani	Páṇí, Jal ...	Jala, Pani ...	Pani	Water.
Ghar	Ghar, Kholdú ...	Gruha, Ghara ...	Ghar	House.
Ghóra	Ghodo	Aswa, Ghodá ...	Ghorá	Horse.
Gáe	Gáya	Gáhbi, Gái ...	Garu	Cow.
Kúttra	Kútro	Kukkura ...	Kukur	Dog.
Mānjar	Baládi, Mini ...	Birádi, Bilái, Pusi ...	Mekurí, Berali ...	Cat.
Kombarra (Komra)	Múrgo, Kúkḍo, Margaḍo.	Kukkuta Kukudá ...	Kukurá	Cock.
Badak	Batak	Bataka, Patihangsa, Kujihangsa.	Patihah	Duck.
Gādhav	Gadheḍu ...	Garddabha, Gadha...	Gadha	Ass.
Unt	Unt	Ostra, Ota ...	Ut	Camel.
Pākhrúṇ	Pakshi, Pankhi ...	Pakhyi, Chadái ...	Sarái	Bird.
Já	Já	Jáa, Já... ...	Já, Jáo, Baul ...	Go.
Khá	Khávú, Khá, Jamavú	Kháa, Khá ...	Khá, Kháo... ...	Eat.
Bais (Imperative Mood) ...	Beś, Beśvu ...	Basa, Bas, Ba ...	Bah, Boha	Sit.
Yé	Ava	Asa, A... ...	Ah, Aha	Come.
Már	Márvu, Már, Tipvú, Thokvú.	Mára, Pita ...	Mar, Márá	Beat.
Ubha-Ubhi-Ubhaiṇ, Rahá ...	Ubhárevu, Besṇi ...	Phiá Chhidá, Ubhá...	Theádá, Thiádiá, Theoha	Stand.
Mar	Marijávú ...	Mara ...	Mar	Die.
Dé	Apa, Apvú ...	Dia, De ...	De, Dia	Give.
Dháoṇ	Doda, Doḍvu, Násvu	Dhán Danda, Dhanda	Lar, Lara	Run.
Var	Upar	Upara	Upar, Opao ...	Up.
Javal, Zawal	Pásé	Nikata, Pákha Pása	Osar	Near.
Kháliṇ	Niche, Heṭhal-hethe	Tala	Pal	Down.
Dúr	Dúr, Aghu, Chhété...	Dúra, Dhúra Antara	Nilog durai ...	Far.
Purheṇ, Purvin, Samor... ...	Agáu, Mohoágal ...	Púrba, Aga ...	Agui, agot, ag ...	Before.
Māgaiṇ	Pachhádi, Pachhal...	Páschát, Pachha ..	Pissot, pasot, pisfále ...	Behind.
Kón, Jo	Koṇ	Ki, Kie (interrogative) Je (relative).	Kori (interrogative), jee (relative).	Who.
Kāy?	Sú, or Çu ...	Kana, Ki, Kisa ...	Ki (interrogative), ji (reltive).	What.
Káṇ	Kém, Sáwáste ...	Kipán, káhinki ...	Kia, kelei	Why.
Āni	Ané-tathá ...	Ebang, Au Auri, O	Aru	And.
Pan, Parantú	Paṇ-parantú ...	Kintu, Mátra, Puni...	Kintu	But.
Jar	Jo, To, Agar ...	Jadi, Jebe ...	Jadi	If.
Hóe	Há	Hán, Han, Hui ...	Hai, or era ...	Yes.
Náhiṇ	Nahi	Ná, N̄áhin ...	Nahai or néi ...	No.
Arréy, Háe-háe	Arere, Háe-háe ...	Ahá, Háhá ...	Hai-hai	Alas.
Báp	Ekbáp	Ekapitá, Ekabápa ...	Ejon bopai, bopai eta ...	A father.

English.	Hindee.	Bengalee.	
		In common use.	*In use among the educated class.*
Of a father ...	Bápká, or ki, or keir	Ek báper	Ek pitár ... ...
To a father ...	Báp-ko, or báp kone	Bápke	Pitáke ... ...
From a father.	Báp-se	Ek báp thái	Pitá haete ... ...
Two fathers ...	Do-báp	Dui báp	Duipitá ... ...
Fathers ...	Báp log, Bapán	Bábárá	Pitásakala ... ...
Of fathers ...	Bábá-logká, Bápsabki, Bápankeir ...	Bápdèr	Pitáder, Pitasakaler ... ...
To fathers ...	Bábá sab ká, or ki, or ke ...	Bápdigake	Pitá digaké, Pitásakalete ...
From fathers ...	Báp-sab-se	Bápder tháí	Pitáder haeté, Pita sakala haete ...
A daughter ...	Eik-larki, beti, or chhokre ...	Ek méyé	Ek kanyá... ... ...
Of a daughter .	Larki-ká, or keir	Ek méyèr	Ek kanyar ... ...
To a daughter.	Larkiko, or ke	Ek méyéte, or ke	Ek kanyate, or ke .. ...
From a daughter.	Larki se	Ek méyér thái	Ek kanya hoite ... ...
Two daughters .	Do larki	Dui méyé...	Dui kanya ... ...
Daughters ...	Larkiaǔ, Betisabó, Betin ...	Méyéra	Kanyagan ... ...
Of daughters ...	Larkioǔká, or Betin keir ...	Méyéder	Kanyader ... ...
To daughters ..	Larkioǔko, Beti sabko ...	Méyé subke	Méyédigake, kanyadigake ...
From daughters	Larkioǔ se, Beti sub-se ...	Méyéder tháí	Kanyader haete ... ...
A good man ...	Eik bhálá, or bés, or achhá mánoosh	Ek bhála lók	Ek uttum manusya ... ...
Of a good man.	Eik bhálá, or bés, or achhá mánoosh-ká, or ki, or ker	Ek bhála lokér	Ek uttum manusyer ...
To a good man.	Eik bhálá, or bés, or achhá mánooshká or ko	Ek bhála lok ke, or te ...	Ek uttum manusya ke, or te ...
From a good man.	Eik bhálá ádmi sen, or se ...	Ek bhála lok thai	Ek uttum manusya haeté ...

Mahrattee.	Guzerattee.	Oorya.	Assamese.	English.
Bápá chá, chi, chain ... ... Bápá chày, cheya, chin... ...	Bápno	Ekpitár, Ekabápár...	Bopáir-bopekar ...	Of a father.
Bapa-lā	Báp páse, Bap kane	Ekapitáku, Ekabápaku.	Bopai lai, bopekalai ...	To a father.
Bapa pásún...	Bápná taraf thi ...	Ekapitátháru, Ekbápatháru.	Bopair perá ...	From a father.
Dow bāp	Bé báp	Duipitá, Duibápa ...	Duijon bopar, duta bopek	Two fathers.
Báp	Báp	Pitámáne, Bápánáne	Bopai bilok, bopekhat, bopai sakul.	Fathers.
Bapán—Chá-chi-chain ... ... *Bapán*—Chay-cheya-chin ...	Bápno	Pitámánánkar, Bápamánankar.	Bopai bilakar, bopekhater, bopai sakaler.	Of fathers.
Bapan-lā	Báp páse, Bap kane, Bàpne.	Pitámánanku Bápamánanku.	Bopai bilakolai bopek hatalai, bopai sakalak lai	To fathers.
Bápán pá sún	Bápná taraf thi ...	Pitámánankatháru, Bápamánankatháru.	Bopai bilakar pera, bopekhater pera, bopai sakaler pera.	From fathers.
Múlgi	Ek dikri ...	Eka kanyá, Gotie jhia, Jhiatie.	Ejani ji	A daughter.
Múlgi—Cha, chi, chen ... *Múlgi*—Chay, cheya, chin ...	Dikrinú ...	Eka kanyár, Gotie jhiar, Jhiatira.	Ejani jir	Of a daughter.
Múlgi—Lā-sa-ten	Dikri páse, dikri kane, dikri taraf.	Eka kanyáku, Gotie Jhiaku, Jhiatiku.	Ejani jilai ji, ejani lai ...	To a daughter.
Múlgi pá sún	Dikri taraf thi, dikri páse thi, dikri kanethi.	Eka kanyátháru, Gotie jhiatháru.	Ejani jir hera ...	From a daughter.
Don Múlgyā	Be dikri ...	Dui kanyá, Dui jhia-Jhia dioti.	Dui jani ji	Two daughters.
Múlgyá	Dikrio	Kanyámáne, Jhiamáne, Jhiagudie.	Jihát, jihilak ...	Daughters.
Múlgyán—Cha, chi, chen ... *Múlgyán*—Chay, cheyá, chin ..	Dikrionú ...	Kanyámánankar, Jhiamánankar, Jhiagudinkar.	Jihatar, jibilaker ...	Of daughters.
Múlgyán—La, sa, ten-ná ...	Dikrio ne, dikrio pase, dikrio taraf.	Kanyámánanku, Jhiamánanku, Jhiagudinku.	Jihatalai	To daughters.
Múlgyán pá sún	Dikrio taraf thi ...	Kanyámánankatháru, Jhiamánankatharu, Jhiagudinkatharu.	Jehater pera, jibilaker pera.	From daughters.
Changla manúshyā	Ek sáru máṇas ...	Eka or jane uttam loka, Bhadrolokutie, Bhalamanusiatie.	Ejon bhal manuh, haj manuh egraki, bhal manuha eta.	A good man.
Tsangaley manushya—Cha, chi, chen *Tsangaley manushya*—Chey, chayá, chin.	Sárá máṇas nu ...	Eka or jane uttum lokar, Bhadrolokar, Bholamanusiar.	Ejon bhál mánuher, haj manuh egrakir, bhal manuha eta.	Of a good man.
Tsangaley manushya—La, sa, ten... *Tsangaley manushya*—La, sa, ten, na	Sárá máṇasne-taraf-pá se.	Eka uttam lokaku, Bhadra lokutiku, Jane bhalamanusiaku.	Bhál mánuh holai, haj manuh egrakilai, eta bhal mánuhalai.	To a good man.
Tsangaley manushya—Pá, sún ...	Sárá máṇas taraf thi	Eka uttam lokatháru, Eka bhadra lokatháru, Jane bhala manusiatháru.	Bhál mánuher pera, haj manuh egrakirpera, eta bhál mánuhar perá.	From a good man.

English.	Hindee.	Bengalee.	
		In common use.	*In use among the educated class.*
Two good men.	Do bhále mánoosh	Dui bhála lok	Dui uttum manusya ... ...
Good men ...	Bhále mánoosh log, Bés log ...	Bhála lok sab	Uttum manusya sakal ...
Of good men ...	Bhále mánooshoù ká, or ker ...	Bhála lok der	Uttum manusya sakaler ...
To good men ...	Bhále mánooshoù kú	Bhála lok subke, or tc ...	Uttum manusya diga ke, or te ...
From good men	Bhále mánooshoù sen, or se ...	Bhála lok der thai	Uttum manusya diger haete ...
A good woman	Eik-bhálá áurat, Eik bés merárú ...	Ek bhála mági	Ek uttum strilok ... ...
A bad boy ...	Eik-kharáb-larká, Eik dingar larká...	Ek kháráp chhokrá	Ek manda bálak ... ...
Good women ...	Bhále áuratoù, Bés merárún ...	Bhála mágirá	Uttum strilokerá ... ...
A bad girl ...	Eik-kharáb-larki, Ek dingar chokri	Ek kháráp chhuri	Manda báliká ... ...
Good ...	Achhá, Bés, Niman, Suthra ...	Bhála	Bhála, Uttam ... ...
Better ...	Usen-áchhá, Okra se bés	The same with the noun with which comparison is made in the ablative case.	
Best ...	Ba-hut, or anek áchhá, Sub se bés ...	The same with noun in ablative and all prefixed to it	
High ...	Uchá	Ochu	Uchchya ... ...
Higher ...	Unsen-uchá, Okráse uchá ...	The same as in "better" and "best."	......
Highest ...	Sub-sen-uchá, Sub se uchá ...		
A horse ...	Eik ghorá	Ek ghorá	Ek ghorá, Ashwa ... ...
A mare ...	Eik ghuri, or ghori	Ek ghuri	Ek ghuri, Ghotokee ... ...
Horses ...	Ghorá sab, Ghorewan	The plurals are formed by prefixing numerals or adjectives of number, as, several, many, &c.	
Mares ...	Ghuri sab, Ghorian	......	......
A bull ...	Eik sáñr, Bail, Bulad	Shaúrh	Shaúrh, Brisha ... ...

Mahrattee.	Guzerattee.	Ooryah.	Assamese.	English.
Dou Tsãngale manushyă ...	Be sárá máṇas ...	Dui uttam loka, Bhadra lokajodie, Bhala manusia duhen.	Dúijon bhál mánuh, Haj manuh dugaraki, duita bhal manuha.	Two good men.
Tsangaley manúshyă	Sárá máṇaso ...	Uttam lokamáne, Bhalamanusiajodi.	Bhál mánuh bilek, haj manuh bilak, bhál mánuha bor.	Good men.
Tsangaley manushyan—Chá, chi, cheṉ. *Tsangaley manushyang*—Chey, chaya chiṉ.	Sárá máṇaso nú ..	Uttam lokankar, Bhadra lokagudinkar, Bhalamanusiankar.	Bhál mánuh bilaker, haj manuh bilaker, bhal mánuha borar.	Of good men.
... ...	Sárá máṇso-pásetaraf-nè.	Uttamlokanku, Bhadralokanku, Bhalamanusianku.	Bhál mánuh bilákálai, haj manuh bilaklai.	To good men.
Tsangaley manushayang, pá, sún ...	Sárá máṇaso taraf thi	Uttam lokankatháru, Bhadra lokankatharu, Bhalamunsiankatháru.	Bhal manuh bilakarpera, haj manuh bilakarpera.	From good men.
Changli báekó	Sári báyaḍi ...	Eka uttom stri, Bhadra máipati, Bhalamáipatie.	Ejini bhal tirata, haj tirota egaraki, ejini bhol maike.	A good woman.
Wáet mulgá	Ek kharáb-naṭháro-khoto chhokaro.	Eka manda bálaka, Nákará pilátie, Nákará tokátár.	Ejon, or eta bia lorá ...	A bad boy.
Tshangalyā báeká	Sári báyadio ...	Uttam strimáne, Bhala maipe, Achhá maipigudie.	Bhal tirota bhilák, haj tirota bilak, chikon máikibor.	Good women.
Wáet mulgí	Naṭhári chhokri ..	Eka manda toki, Nákará takitáe.	Ejani beá soáli ...	A bad girl.
Tsáng—La, li, leṉ ... ... *Chang*—Ley, leya, liṉ	Sáru	Uttam, Bhala, Achhá	Bhál, Haj or Baru ...	Good.
Pekshán... *Hún* ... { tsangala, li, leṉ ... tsangaley, leya, liṉ ... }	Vadháre, Sáru ...	Apekhyákrutanttam, Pátháru bhala or Achhá.	Bara bhál, Barut koi baru aru bhál.	Better.
Sarván Peksa ... *Sarván Hún* .. { tsangala, li, len tsangaley, leya, liṉ. }	Sárámán, Sáru ...	Atiuttam, Bese ...	Uti bhál, uti baru bhalat kai bhál.	Best.
Unch	Unchú	Uchcha, Uncha ...	Okha ...	High.
Pekshā ... *Hún* ... } Unch	Vadháre Unchú ...	Apekhyákrutauchcha, Tátháru uncha.	Bar okha, aru okhará ...	Higher.
Sarván Pekshā *Sarvan Hún* ... } Unch	Unchá mán únchú ...	Atiuchcha, Bháriuucha.	Uti okha, okhat kai okha	Highest.
Ghora	Ek ghoḍo ...	Eka aswa, Eka ghodá, Ghodátie.	Eta ghorá ...	A horse.
Ghori	Ghoḍi	Eka ghodi, Ghoditie	Ejani ghuri ...	A mare.
Ghorey	Ghoḍa	Aswa samuha, Ghodájáka, Ghodipala Ghodigudáe, Ghodigudáka.	Ghorabor, ghora bilak...	Horses.
Ghodyā	Ghoḍio	Ghodi samuha Ghodijáka, Ghodipala Ghodigudáe, Ghodigudáka.	Ghuribor, maiki ghora, Ghuribilak.	Mares.
Bail	Akhlo-Sanḍ ...	Eka sandha, Sandhutáe.	Ek bhatara, Hár ...	A bull.

English.	Hindee.	Bengalee.	
		In common use.	*In use among the educated class.*
A cow ...	Eik gái	Gái	Gábhi ... ...
Bulls ...	Bhot sakal, Sab sáñr	The plurals are formed as in "horse," "mare."	... ...
Cows ...	Gái sakal, Gáian	......	......
A dog ...	Eik kuttá	Ek kukur	Ek kukur ... ...
A bitch ...	Eik kutti	Kheñki	Kheñki, Kukuri ... ...
Dogs ...	Kuttá sakal, Kutaun	Kukur guno	Kukur sakal ... ...
Bitches ...	Kut-ti sakal, Kuttian	Kheñki guno	Kheñki sakal ... ...
A he goat ...	Bak-rá	Pañtha, Chhágal	Páñthá, Aja, Chhágal... ...
A female goat	Bakri	Páñthi	Páñthi, Chhági ... ...
Goats ...	Bakrisakal, Bakryán	Chhágul guno	Páñthá sakal, Chhágal sakal ...
A male deer ...	Harin	Hariñg	Harin, Mriga ... ...
A female deer	Harini	Medi hariñg	Harini, Mrigee ... ...
Deer ...	Harin	Hariñg guno	Harin sakal, Mriga sakal ...
I am ...	Ham-huñ or hé	Ámi áchhi	Ámi áchhi ... ...
Thou art ...	Tum-ho, or Tuñhae	Tui áchhis, Tumi áchho ...	Tumi áchho, ápni áchhen ...
He is ...	Un-he-hoeñ, Wuhhae ...	Sè áchhé	Tini áchhen ... ...
We are ...	Ham-log-hen, Hamani haiñ ...	Morá or ámrá áchhi	Ámrá áchhi ... ...
You are ...	Tum-log-ho, Tuhani hae ...	Torá or tomrá áchho... ...	Tomrá áchho, Ápnárá áchhen ...
They are ...	Unlog-hen, Ukani hath ...	Tárá achhè	Táhárá áchhe, Táhárá áchhen ...
I was ...	Ham or maiù thá, or hali, or rahin	Ámi chhilám	Ámi chhilám ... ...
Thou wast ...	Tum-thá, or Tun halen, or rahe ...	Tui or tumi chhile	Tumi chhilé, Ápni chhilen ...

Mahrattee.	Guzerattee.	Oorya.	Assamese.	English.
Gáe	Gáya	Eka gái, Gáitáe ...	Garu ejani, Ejani gai gara.	A cow.
Bail	Ákhál	Sandha or sendha samuha, Sandhapala Sandhagudáe Sandhagudáka, Sandhajáka.	Bhatara, bhatara, bhatara gavubor bilak.	Bulls.
Gaí	Gáyo	Gái samuha, Gaigu dáe, Gáigudáka, Gáipala, Gaijáka.	Garu bilak, gai garu bilak garu bor.	Cows.
Kuttrā	Kutro	Eka kukkura, Kukkuratáe.	Eta kukur	A dog.
Kuttri	Kutri	Eka kukkuri, Eka máikukkura máikukkuratáe.	Ejani maiki kukur kukur jáni.	A bitch.
Kuttrey	Kuttra	Kukkura samuha, Kukkuragudáe kukkura gudáka.	Kukur bilak, kukur bor	Dogs.
Kuttryā	Kuttrio... ...	Kukuri samuha máikukkuragudáe,máikukkuragudáka.	Maiki kukur, bor or bilak	Bitches.
Bakrā	Bakro	Eka chhága, Eka bodá, Eka andirá chheli bodatie.	Eta Matá ságali ...	A he goat.
Sheli	Bakri	Eka chhági, Eka chheli, Eka máichheli máichhelitáe.	Ejani maiki sagale, sagali egani.	A female
Bakarin	Bakran ...	Chheli samuha, Chhelipala, Chheligudáe, Chheligudáka.	Ságali bilak ...	Goats.
Haran	Káliar	Eka mruga, Mirigagutáe.	Eta máta páhu, matá páhu etá.	A male deer.
Harani	Harni	Eka mruguni, Maimirigagutáe.	Ejani macki pahu, páhu ejáni.	A female deer.
Haran	Harina	Mrugagudáe, Mirigapala.	Pahu bilak... ...	Deer.
Méán hain, mi āhen	Hun chhun ...	Ámbhe achhu, Áme achhu, Mu achhi.	Mui hai, or asa, mai achho.	I am.
Tu áhes	Tu chhe-u ...	Tumbhe achha. Tume achha, Tu achhu.	Tumi or te har or ha, apuni achhó.	Thou art.
To áhey	Te chhe ...	Se achhauti Se achhi.	Teo hae or áse he áchhe	He is.
Āmhi āhon	Ame chhie ...	Ámbhemáne achhu, Ámemáne achhu.	Ami háe or ase, ami achho	We are.
Tumhi áhá	Tame chho ...	Tumbhemáne achha, Tumemáne achha.	Tumlok hai or tohát ho or tumlok ase, tumi achha.	You are.
Tey, tyātin,—á het	Teó chhe ...	Semáne achhanti ...	Teolok or tehat hae or teuhilák ase or achhe.	They are.
Mhi—hoton hoti, hoten... ...	Hun hato ...	Ámbhe thilu, Áme thilu, Mu thili ...	Moi asilo, moi áchhilo...	I was.
Tún—hotas hotis hotens ...	Tu hato ...	Tumbhe thila, Tume thila, Tu thilu.	Tumi or tei ásilá or asile, or tumi ásila, apuni áchhili.	Thou wast.

English.	Hindee.	Bengalee.	
		In common use.	*In use among the educated class.*
He was ...	Wuh-thá, or Unne-the, U halye, or rahe.	Sè chhila	Tini chhilen ... ...
We were ...	Ham-log-the, halan or rahin ...	Morá or ámrá chhilám ...	Ámrá chhilám ... ...
You were ...	Tum-log-the, Tohani hola, or rahi ...	Torá or tomrá chhile	Tomrá chhilé, Ápnárá chhilen ...
They were ...	Wé-the, Ukani halan, or rahath ...	Tárá chhila	Táhárá chhila, Táhárá chhilen ...
Be ...	Hoeñ, Ho, Hae	Tháka	Hai ... ...
To be ...	Sen, Hanyá, Honá	Haite	Haite ... ...
Being ...	Hote, Hañyte, Harete	Thákiá	Hao-á ... ...
Having been ...	Ho-kar, Hogale	Thákiá	Haí-á ... ...
I may be ...	Maiṅ or ham-ho-sek-ta, Ham hun-hoti.	Ámi hate-pári	Ámi haite pári ... ...
I shall be ...	Maiṅ or ham-hogá, Hamhun hoeb...	Ámi ha-ba	Ámi haiba ... ...
I should be ...	Merá-honá uchit, Hamrá howéke chahi.	Ámi hatám	Ámi haitám, Ámár hao-á uchit ...
Beat ...	Már, Pitn	Márá	Márá ... ...
To beat ...	Márná, Pitna	Márte	Máritè ... ...
Beating ...	Mare, Pityte	Marte	Marité, Maritéché ... ...
Having beaten	Mar-kar, Pitkar	Méré	Máríá ... ...
I beat ...	Maiṅ or bam maren, Ham pitahi, Ham márit hán.	Ámi márí...	Ámí mári ... ...
Thou beatest ...	Tum máro, Tum pita halin, Tum márithá.	Tui or tumi máro	Tumi máro ... ...
He beats ...	Wuh mártá hai, U pita hye, U márit hath.	Sé márchhé	Tini máritéchhen ... ...
We beat ...	Ham log máreñ, Ham hani pitahi. Hamni márithain.	Morá mári	Ámrá mári ... ...
You beat ...	Tum log máro, Tuháni pituhahak, Tun máritha.	Torá or tomrá máro	Tomrá máro, Ápnárá máren ...
They beat ...	Un log márte, Ukani pitá huth, Usub márit huth	Tárá márè	Táhárá máren ... ...
I am beating ...	Maiṅ or ham márta hun, Ham pityt hi.	Ámi márchhi	Ámi máritechhi ... ...
I was beating...	Maiṅ or ham márta thá, Ham pitahali or rahin.	Ámi marchhilám	Ámi máritechhilám ... ...
I had beaten ...	Maiṅ or ham márá tha, Ham pitalial hul, Ham márli rahi.	Ámi méréchinu	Ámi máriáchhilám ... ...

Mahrattee.	Guzerattee.	Oorya.	Assamese.	English.
To hotā	Té hato	Se thile, Se thilá	Teo ásila, se achili	He was.
Amhi hoton	Amé hatá	Ámbhemáne thilu, Ámemáne thilu.	Ami ésilo, ami achilo	We were.
Tumhi—hotā	Tamé hatá	Tumbhemáne thila, Tumemáne thila.	Tomolák ásila or tohat asili, tumi achila	You were.
Té hotey tya hotyatin hotin	Teó hatá	Semáne thile	Teolok or tehat ásilo, or teobilak ásila, teobilak achlila.	They were.
Hó, *as*	Thá	Hua	Hoá, haba	Be.
	Thavánu	Hebáku	Habaloi	To be.
Hot asat	Tháya chhe	Hebára	Hoat, hae, haipelai	Being.
Höun, asun	Tháyu chhe	Hoikari	Hoat, haigai, haipelai	Having been.
Mi ăsen	Hun thá u	Ámbhe hoipáru, Áme hoiparu, Mu hoipáre.	Mai habaparu	I may be.
Mi hoin, miasén	Hun thá iś	Ámbhe hebu, Áme hebu, Mu hebi.	Mai hauni	I shall be.
Min whaven, min asáven	Hún thávánó	Ámbhar hebára uchita, Ámar hebára uchita Mohar hebáku uchita.	Mai haba pao, or lagibo	I should be.
Mār	Tip mára	Mára Pita	Mar	Beat.
Māranen	Márvu	Máribáku Pitibáku	Maribalai	To beat.
Mārit	Mára	Máruchhi, Pituchhi	Mari, morat marichhe	Beating.
Mārun	Máre lu	Márikari, Pitikari	Marat mari etai, mara hai pelai.	Having beaten.
Mi—mariton maritei marateu	Hún márù chhún	Ámbhe or Áme maru or pitu, Mu máre or pite.	Moi máro or maricho	I beat.
Tun—maritos marites martens	Tu máre chhe	Tumbhe or Tume mára or pita, Tu máru or pitu.	Tumi márá or Tei márá apuni marichho.	Thou beatest.
To marito	Té máre chhe	Se máranti or pitanti, Se máre or pite.	Teo mare or márichhe	He beats.
Amhi mariton	Hamé márie chhie	Ámbhe or Ámemáne máru or pitu.	Ami maro, ami marichho	We beat.
Túmhi maritán	Tame máro chho	Tumbhe or Tumemáne mára or pite.	Tomolake márá or Toboti márá, tumi marichha.	You beat.
Té, tya, tin—maritāt	Téo maré chhe	Semáne máranti or pitanti.	Teobilak máre sibali márichhé.	They beat.
Mi marit áhen	Hún márù chhùn	Ámbhe or Áme maruchhu or pituchhu, Mu maruchhi or pituchhi.	Moi mariáso, moi márichho	I am beating.
Mi marit—hoton hotin hoten	Hún márto hato	Ámbhe or Áme maruthilu or pituthilu, Mu máruthilu or pitithili.	Moi mariasilo, mai márichilo.	I was beating.
Mi—marila hota, marili hoti, marilen hoten, marila hotay marilya hotya, marilin hotin.	Me máro hato	Ámbhe or Áme marithilu or pitithilu, Mu márithili or pitithili.	Moi márilo or moi máre ásiloo, moi marielo.	I had beaten.

English.	Hindee.	Bengalee.	
		In common use.	*In use among the educated class.*
I may beat ...	Maiṅ or ham mársektehe, Ham pitun, Ham márbo.	Ámi márte pári	Ámi márite pári ... ...
I shall beat ...	Ham máregá, Ham petbye, Ham máráh.	Ámi márbo	Ámi máribo ... ...
I should beat...	Merá or hamárá márná uchit. Hamrá pítaki chahi or márki chahi.	Ámi mártem	Ámár márá uchit ... ...
I am beaten ...	Maiṅ or ham már kháyáhe, Ham pital jáeb, Ham márel geli.	Ámáké méréchhe	Ámáke máriáchhe ... ...
I was beaten ...	Maiṅ or ham már kháyáthá, Ham pital gelihal, Ham márelgel rúhin.	Ámáke méréchhila	Ámáke máriáchhila ... ...
I shall be beaten	Maiṅ or ham már khaenge, Ham pital jáeb, Ham márel gayali.	Ámáke márbe	Amáké márbe ... ...
I go ...	Maiṅ or ham jáy, Ham jáhi, Ham jáethe.	Ámi jái	Ámi jái ... ...
Thou goest ...	Tum jáo, Tun jáhen, Tum jáethu ...	Túmi jáo, Tui já, ...	Tumi jáo, Ápni ján ... ...
He goes ...	Wuh or un ne játe hen, U jáhye, U jáet haith.	Sè jái	Tini ján ... ...
I went ...	Maiṅ or ham giá thá, Ham gili, Ham gali hal.	Ámi gichlem	Ámi giáchhilám ... ...
Thou wentest...	Tum giáthán, Tun gelen, Tun gila ...	Tumi gichhilé	Tumi giáchhile ... ...
He went ...	Wuh or un né gaithe, U gélye, U gaele	Sè gichhila	Tini giáchhilen ... ...
Go ...	Já neka, Jo or chal ja	Já, Jáo	Jáoá ... ...
Going ...	Já te hen, Jaite, Jaliber ...	Já-e	Jáiá ... ...
Gone ...	Giá, Chal gelye, gel	Geche	Giáchhe ... ...
What is your name?	Tumhárá kiá nám, Tohár ká náuṅ hai	Tomár nám ki	Ápanár nám ki ... ...
How old is this horse?	Eah ghorá ketná rojka or kituk din ke hai.	E ghorár bayash kata ...	E ghoráti ka butsorer ...
How far is it from here to Kashmir?	I' hañ se Kásmir ketná dur ...	Ekhán theke Kashmir kata dúr ...	Ekhán haete Kashmir kata dur ...
How many sons are there in your father's house?	Tumhárá báp ká gharme ketne larke hein, Turá bápki geh kee betá hathu.	Tomár bápèr ghare ka jan chhele áchhe.	Tomár pitár bátitte kaiti putra santán áchhe.

Mahrattee.	Guzerattee.	Oorya.	Assamese.	English.
Mikadāchit marin, mala maranyas harkat náhi.	Hún máru ...	Ámbhe or Áme máripáru or pitipáru, Mui máripáre or pitipáre.	Moi márila para mae masibaparo.	I may beat.
Mi marin	Hún máriś ...	Ámbhe or Áme máribá pitiba, Mu máribi or pitibi.	Moi marim... ...	I shall beat.
In mārāven	Hún máriś ...	Ámbhar or Ámar máribara or pitibára uchita Mora máribáku or pitibáku uchita.	Moi máribá páo or lagibo maiimarila hate. ...	I should beat.
Mi marila játon, mi marla gelon, mi mārali geli.	Hun maráyo or mane maro.	Ámbhe or Áme máda or pitá kháichhu, Mu máda or pitákháichhi.	Mok márile or máre ...	I am beaten.
Mi marla ge lon hoton, mārali geli hoti, ,mi marila jat hoton mé márli jat hoti.	Hun maráyo hato ...	Ámbhe or Áme máda or pitákháithilu, Mu máda or pitakháithili.	Mok márile, or marisila mae márishalo.	I was beaten.
Mi marilá jáin, márali jáin, marilen jáen.	Hun maráiś ...	Ámbhe or Áme máda or pitákhibu, Mu máda or pitákháibi.	Mok maorilá, mae maraban.	I shall be beaten.
Méja—Ton, tin, ten	Hun ján chhu ...	Ámbhe or Ámeján, Mu jae.	Moi jao	I go.
Túja—Tos, tais, tens	Tú jáechhé ...	Tumbhhe or Tume Jáa Tu Jáu.	Tumi balá or jaé, or tái ja, apuni gaichhe.	Thou goest.
To jato	Te jáe chhé ...	Se Jánti Se Jáe ...	Teo jai, or gaisa ...	He goes.
Mi gelon, gelin, gelen	Hun gayó ...	Ámbhe or Áme jáithulu, Mu jáithili.	Moi galo, mae gailo ...	I went.
Tún gelās, gelis, gelens... ...	Tú gayó ...	Tumbhe or Tume jáithila, Tu jáithilu.	Tumi gala, apuni gaichili	Thou wentest.
Ton gelá	Té gayó ...	Se jáithile Se jaithilá	Teo gal	He went.
Já	Já javu ...	Jáa ...	Bal, ja	Go.
Jāt	Jato	Jáuchhi ...	Jao, gai, jain ...	Going.
Gelela, geleli, gelalen, gelale, gelelyā, gelelin.	Gayeló	Gála ...	Gal	Gone.
Tújhen nāo kayáhey ? ...	Tamáru náma śú ? ...	Tumbha náma kana or ki, tuma náma ki To ná kana.	Tumar nam ki ? Tumar ki náo ?	What is your name ?
Ha ghora kiti warshyā chá áhey ...	Á ghodó ket lá varas no chhe.	Eghodá kete barsara.	Eito ghorrar kiman basar hoise, Ei ghora kiman bars paichhe.	How old is this horse ?
Ethun Káshmir kiti dúr áhey ? ...	Ahi yánthi Káśmir ket eu dur tháe ?	Káshmir ethária kete antara ? Káshmir etháru kete dúr or dhura.	Iár para Kásmir oloi kiman duroi ? Iar para Kásmir lai kiman dur ?	How far is it from here to Kashmir ?
Tujhe bapache gharant kiti múl age āhet ?	Tamárá báp ná ghar, mán ketea chhokrá chhe ?	Tumbha pitanka gruhare kete putra achhanti, tu bapa ghare kete putra achanti ?	Tumar baprar ghavat reita putck ase, or kiman lora áchhe ?	How many sons are there in your father's house ?

English.	Hindee.	Bengalee.	
		In common use.	*In use among the educated class.*
I have walked a long way to-day.	Maiṅ or ham áj bahat dúr phirá hi, Ham áj bari dúrla phirti haijo or phirul hai.	Ámi áj badda hátiáchhi, Aj ámi khub beriáchhi.	Adya ámi anèk bhromon koriáchi
The son of my uncle is married to his sister.	Hamár cháchera bhái okár bahinse beahul naiye or behul ghaile.	Ámár khúrthutho bhái tár búnkó bió karéchhé.	Ámar pitrèbya putrér sahit táhár bhagnír bibáha haiáchhe.
In the house is the saddle of the white horse.	Saphed ghorá ka khugir ghár me hai, Ujor ka ghorwake khúgiria úghurwá menhye.	Sádá ghorár jin ghore áchhe ...	Same as column 3 ... ...
Put the saddle upon his back.	Uska pithpar khugir kaso, Okra pith par khogir kas	Uhár pitè jin dáo	Same as column 3 ...
I have beaten his son with many stripes.	Maiṅ or ham uska or unka larká ko korá se bahút mará hai, Ham okhar betáke korá se bari már márli hai.	Ámi taár chhélé ké badda bet merechhi.	Táhár chhélé ke ámi anèk betrághát kariáchhe
He is grazing cattle on the top of the hill.	Us páhár ke chonthi par Gáe Baicl chará tá hai, U ápan gáe goru páhárwa chonthi par churawa hai.	Páhárer churár upar se pál charáchhe.	Parbater churár upar tini go mésh poshur pál charáitéchhen.
He is sitting on a horse under that tree.	Wuh-darkhat ke niche ghoraki uparbaithá hai, Ughora pur churhah rukh taru hai.	Oi gáchher taláye se ghorár upar basa raechhe.	Oi brikher talaye tini ghorár upar basiá rahiáchhen.
His brother is taller than his sister.	Uská or unká bahin se uská or unká bhái bara hai, Okar bhahi okar bahin se larma hai.	Uhár bhái uhár bun cheyethe lumbá.	Uhár bhrátá uhár bhagnir apekhyá lumbá.
The price of that is two rupees and a half.	Uska kimat áráhi rupiá, Okar dám áráhi rupiá hai.	Uhár dám árái táká	Uhár mulya árái táká ...
My father lives in that small house.	Merá or hámáre báp us chhotá ghar mé rahet hen, Hámár báp u chhotká gharwa me rahai huth.	Oi chhota ghare ámár báp tháken	Same as column 3 ...
Give this rupee to him.	Uska or unko iah rupiá tho deo, I rupyá okrá dé dé or unko dahin.	Ta ke ei táká tá dio	Ei tákáti táhákó dío ... ...
Take those rupees from him.	Unsab rupiá unke nuzdik se leo, Usab rupiá okrá se lili.	Or tháe oi táká guno neo ...	Táhár nikat hoite táká gulin lao ...
Beat him well and bind him with ropes.	Usko or unko áchhi tarap se máro áur rasi dekar báṅdho, Okrá khúb már áur rase se bándh.	Okó bhála kore máro ár darí diá bándho.	Uhákó dari diá bándhiá khub máro
Draw water from the well	Kuá se páni uthao, Kuánse páni bhár	Kuá thékó jal tol	Kupa hoite jal tol ... ...
Walk before me	Mere or hamáre samhne phiro, Hamráse águ chal iá bul.	Ámár ágé chala, or jáo ...	Ámár agré chala, Ámár sanmukhe beráo.

Principal Aryan Languages of India.—(Continued.)

Mahrattee.	Guzerattee.	Oorya.	Assamese.	English.
Aj mi pushkal chalalon... ...	Hun ája aghú bahú chálo.	Ajiambhe bahuta bhramana kariachhu, Mu áji bahuta bulilini or chalilini.	Mái áji bahu dur phuri ahilo. Aji moi ohale khini furilo. Aji moi bunbat furilo.	I have walked a long way to-day.
Mājhyā chulatyachey mulāchen ti chey bahinishin lagn jhalen āhen.	Márá káká no chhocro teni bena ne par nelo chhe.	Ambba dádánka r· tratánka bhaunku bibáha hoiachhanti, Mo dádi puatá bhauniki báhá hoi achhi.	'eor bhanickar logut mor dadair putekar bia hal, or karáli.	The son of my uncle is married to his sister.
Pāndrey ghodiā chen khogir gharānt áhey.	Dholá ghodá nu jina gharmán chhe.	Dhobalá or dhalághodára sája ghare bhitore achhi.	Baga ghorar talisa ghorite ase. Hai baga ghorar jinta, hai ghorete ase. Ghorar bhitarat thaká jin khanbaga ghoratar hayne.	In the house is the saddle of the white horse.
Tya che pathi var khogir thév ...	Ghodá upar jina mándo.	Táhá pithire saja bhida or kasa.	Tar pithete talisa bandha, *or* jinta paro, *or* de.	Put the saddle upon his back.
Mi tyaché mulās pushkal phatkey marile.	Men tená chhokrá ne ghaná phatká márá.	Tánka putraku ambhe aneka betragháta kariachhu, Tápuakumu bahuta bádeiachhi.	Moi teor putek ke kebatao betere kob marilo. Moi tar putek ke bohut kob marilo. Tar putekak mai mai bahut kob marichho.	I have beaten his son with many stripes.
To tya tekri che mathya var guren chárit áhe.	Te dhor dúngrini tocha upar charáve chhe.	Se páháda upare gotha charáuchhi.	Teo parbater uperat garu saraise. Si parbator tin gat garu charaichhe.	He is grazing cattle on the top of the hill.
To tya jhara khalin ghodya var basala áhey.	Pelá jhád tale ghodá upar te betho chhe.	Se brukhya tale aswa upare basichhanti. se gachha mule ghodá upare basichhi.	Teo gasar talate ghorar uthi ase or bahiase.	He is sitting on a horse under that tree.
Tya cha bhan tya che bahini pekshyā unch áhey.	Teni bena ná kara tan teno bhái úncho chhe.	Tánka bhrátá tánka bhaganitháru uchcha. Tá bhái tá bhauni tháru dengá.	Peor bhanickat koi teur bhäck okha par bhack. Tar bhanickat koi dighol. Tar kakáck tar bhaniyek kai okh.	His brother is taller than his sister.
Tya chi kimat arish rupaye áhey ...	Pelá ni kimat adi rupiá chhe.	Táhára mulya adhái tanká, Tá mula adhái tanká.	Tar Mol dah mahá. Hatar dar du taka aru ek adheli. Tar dam du taka ek adhuli hai.	The price of that is two rupees and a half.
Majha bap tyā lāhan gharant rāhato	Máro báp pelá nána ghar man rahe chhe.	Ambha pitá se khyudra ghare bása karanti, Mo bápa se sána ghare rahichhi.	Mor bopai hauto haru gharate thake. Mor bopái seito saru gharet thake.	My father lives in that small house.
Ha rupayā tyas dé ...	A rupio tehené á po	E tankáti tánku dia, E tanká táku de.	Ei rup taka tenk de, ei taka tenk dia, ei rup taká ták dibi.	Give this rupee to him.
Te rupaye tya pasun gha ...	Teni páse thi pelá rúpiá lo.	Se tanká tánkatháru nia, Se tanká táthu ne.	Han rup keitaka teur pera an, han bilak taka teur pera loo.	Take those rupees from him.
Tyas tsangala marun dorini bándh	Te ne sári pethe mári dora vab bándho.	Tánku or táku áchhá kari mari dandire bandha or bandhe.	Tak bhálkoi már áru ták jarire bandh. Tak bhalkui maribi áru jariri bandhi thubi.	Beat him well and bind him with ropes.
Vihirintún páni kadh ...	Kúvá man thi páni káhá do.	Kuaru páni or jala kádha.	Pat nadar panitola, nádar purá páni tol	Draw water from the well.
Majhyá pudhen tsál ...	Mári ágal chál ...	Ambba agare chála, Mo áge ja.	Mor agate fur ..	Walk before me.

English.	Hindee.	Bengalee.	
		In common use.	*In use among the educated class.*
Whose boy comes behind you?	Kiske larká tumhára pechheh áotáhe, Kekar pútrú torá páchhee lagal áwa han, or Kokei larká tohárá pecha áho.	Tomár pechhané kár chhélé asechhe?	Tomár paschát káhár bálak ási téchhe?
From whom did you buy that?	Kiske nikut tum ottho mol liá hai, or U kekrá se ton mole lili háin.	Káhár thác túmi íhá kinéchho? ...	Káhár nikat haete tumi ihá kineáchh?
From a shop-keeper of the village.	Gáoñke dokándár se, Gáuñ ke ek dokándár sé.	Gáńer ek dokándárer thae ...	Grámer ek dokándárer nikaté

Principal Aryan Languages of India.—(Concluded.)

Mahrattee.	Guzerattee.	Oorya.	Assamese.	English.
Túmche magun koṇa chā múlgayet á hey?	Tamári páchhal ko no chhokro áve chhe?	Káhá pilá tumbha pachhare asuachhi? Ká pilá to pachhe asuchhi?	Tomar pasat kar lorá ahisi? Tor páchhát kar lora áhichhe?	Whose boy comes behind you?
Tún kona pásún teṇ vikat ghét ālen?	Tamé pélú koni páse-thi, vechá tú lidhú?	Táhá tumbhe káhá-tháru kraya kala, Tá tu káháthu ki-nilu?	Heito tumi kar pera kenila, kár pará seito kini lali?	From whom did you buy that?
Gáonā chá eká dukāndárá pasun ...	Te gamná dukánḍár páse thi.	Egrámara jane doká-nitháru, Egánra jane dokanithu.	Gáot pobar dia manuh etar pera hik hon, gao dokaner pera, gáor eta beparir pera.	From a shop-keeper of the village.

PUNJAB LANGUAGES.

English.	Punjabee of Lahore.	Punjabee of Mooltan.	Cashmeeree.	Pushtoo of Kohat.
Numerals.				
One	Ek	Hik	Ak	Yo
Two	Do	Ḍú	Zeh	Dwah
Three	Tin, Trai	Trai	Treh	Dhre
Four	Char	Chár	Tsōr	Tslor
Five	Panj	Panj	Pánts	Pindza
Six	Cheeh, chhe	Chih	Shĭh	Speg
Seven	Sat	Sat	Săt	Awah
Eight	Ath	Ath	Aṭh	Atah
Nine	Naw	Nau	Nauh	Anah
Ten	Das	Dáh	Dăh	Las
Twenty	Bis, bih	Bíh	Wúh	Shil
Thirty	......	......	Treuh	......
Fifty	Panjáh	Panja	Pantsăh	Pindzos
Hundred	Sáw	Sau	Hăth	Sil
Pronouns.				
I	Main	Maiṅ	Bú	Zah
We	Nam, assi	Assáṅ	Assi (the last *i* hardly pronounced.)	Mú (whattak múg̣)
Thou	Tu	Túṅ	......	Ta
You	Tum, tusi	Tussáṅ	......	Tású
He	Wah, oh	U'h	......	Ag͟ha*
They	We, ah	U'hé	Tĭm	Ag͟ha*
Of me	Mera	Méḍá-ḍí ḍí	Miŭn	Emá (khatt-demá)
Of us	Sada	Assáḍá ḍí ḍí	Sōn	Emú (khatt-demú)
Of thee	Tera iwada	Téḍá-ḍí-ḍé	Chōn	Tá (or, less frequently, etá *or* detá.)
Of you	Tumrhara	Tussáḍa ḍí ḍé	Tŭhŭn	Tású (*or* detasú *or* etasú.)
Of him	Oh da	Uṅḍá ḍí ḍé	Tĭmsŭn	Ag͟ha (or, in full, de ag͟ha.)
Of them	Unhunda	Unháṅḍá-ḍí ḍe	Tĭhŭn	Ag͟ho (or de ag͟ho)
Mine	Mera	Méḍá ḍí ḍé	Minúnĭ	......
Our	Sada	Assáḍá-ḍí-ḍé	Sōni	......
Thine	Tera	Teḍá-ḍí-ḍé	Chánuĭ	......
Your	Twada	Tussáḍá-ḍí-ḍé	Tŭhŭndŭĭ	......
His	Ahda	Unḍá ḍí ḍé	Tĭmsŭndŭĭ	......
Their	Unhanda	Unhanḍá ḍé di	Tĭhŭndŭĭ	......
Hand	Hath	Hăth	Atha	Lás
Foot	Pair	Per	Kŭr	Pk͟ha

* Spelt by Bellew and Raverty "Hagha". The transliteration of this and other words and particles, *e. g.*, "po" for "pa," "de" for "da" (sign of genitive), "da" for "dai" (="is"), "I starga" for "starga," "I spín" for "spin," "werkawul" for "warkawul," "wele" for "wale," "shpeg" for "shpag," "wílár" for "wular," &c., has been carefully adapted to represent the local pronunciation of the district, and must not be considered wrong, although it may be at variance with the ordinary authorities, whose spelling is generally based on the pronunciation of the Peshâwar and Yusufzai country. The same remark applies to what may appear to be inaccuracies in other respects, all of which, however, may be trusted as faithfully representing the local usage.

Languages.

Pushtoo of Dera Ismail Khan.	Brahui of Dera Gazee Khan.	Brâhui of Khelat.	English.
Yo ...	Asit ..	Āsĭt ..	One.
Dwah ...	Irat ..	Erŭt ..	Two.
Dre ...	Musit ..	Mōōsĭt ..	Three.
Chalor ...	Chár ..		Four.
Pinzah ...	Panch ..		Five.
Spaj ...	Shash ..		Six.
Awah ...	Haft ..		Seven.
Atah ...	Hasht ..		Eight.
Nah ...	Noh ..	In the Bhahui language there are only the three numerals given; from four upwards Persian is used.	Nine.
Las ...	Dá ..		Ten.
Shil ...	Bíst ..		Twenty.
......	......		Thirty.
Panzas ...	Panjáh ..		Fifty.
Sil ...	Sad ..		Hundred.
Zah ...	I ..	E ..	I.
Muj ...	Nan ..	Nn ..	We.
Ta ...	Ní ..	Nēē ..	Thou.
Tású ...	Núm ..	N m ..	You.
Haghah-dá ...	E (this), hame (that) ..	O ..	He.
Haghah-doí ...	Da, hame ..	Afŭk ..	They.
Zma ...	Kaná ..	Kŭnna† ..	Of me.
Zmuj ...	Naná ..	Nŭnnā ..	Of us.
Stá ...	Ná ..	Nā ..	Of thee.
Stású ...	Numá ..	Nōōmtā‡ ..	Of you.
Da haghah ...	Ená, hamená ..	O,nā ..	Of him.
Da hagha ...	Dáná, hamená ..	O ftā ..	Of them.
......	Kaná ..	K nnā ..	Mine.
......	Naná ..	Nnn ā ..	Our.
......	Ná ..	Nā§ ..	Thine.
......	Numá ..	Noomā ..	Your.
......	Ená, hamená ..	Dānā ..	His.
......	Dáná, hamená ..	Oaftā ..	Their.
Las ...	Dú ..	Dōō ..	Hand.
Pohah ...	Nath ..	Nŭt ..	Foot.

† The Brahuis express "of me" with the word given, which however literally rendered means "mine."
‡ "Ta" is used to express the genitive plural, "na" singular.
§ Used also to express genitive singular.

English.	Punjabee of Lahore.	Punjabee of Mooltan.	Cashmeeree.	Pushtoo of Kohat.
Nose	Nakh	Năk	Nast	Peza
Eye	Ankh	Akh	Uchh	Istarga
Mouth	Munh	Munh	A'as	Khula
Tooth	Dand	Dănd	Dand	Ghákkh
Ear	Kan	Kăn	Kan	Ghweg
Hair	Bál	Vál	Mast	Wekkhta
Head	Sír	Sir	Luk	Sar
Tongue	Zaban jibh	Zabán-jibh	Zeo	Zhiba
Belly	Peth	Dăhăḍ	Yadd	Geḍa
Back	Pith	Kanḍ	Tharr	Sh
Iron	Lohá	Lóhá	Shastur	Ospana
Gold	Seoná	Sona	Son	Srazar
Silver	Chándi	Chándí, rupá	Raf	Spínzar
Father	Pro	Bap, babu (Hindus—pin, bhan).	Mol or bab	Plár
Mother	Ma	Má, ammáṅ (used by children).	Máj	Mor
Brother	Bharár	Bhirá, bhaya	Boi	Wror
Sister	Bahin	Bhaën, kaki (used by children).	Biniah	Khor
Man	Manukh	Mard, munas	Mahini	Saṛai
Woman	Túni	Trímat	Zanana	Kkhadza
Wife	Bahti	Trímat-zal, kaṅwár	Kolái	Kkhadza (khatt; artína)
Child	Munda-Bâl	Níngar	Shur	Bachai
Son	Putr	Pútr	Nichu	Dzwá-e
Daughter	Dhi	Dhí	Kúr	Lúr
Slave	Palak	Ghulám, banah, golah	Tsowz	Mure-ai
Cultivator	Kastkar, Halwah	Rahiráh, ráhak, valú váh.	Láganai wol	Sharík (*i.e.*, if not himself proprietor of the land he cultivates. A "khudkásht" is called Zamíndár).
Shepherd	Gudheria, charhwal	'Ayálí ájrí	Gabaroch (patrol, if the flock is large).	Shpún
God	Permasur	Khuda, Alláh, Sachá, Ral.	Dai	Khudá-e
Devil	Shaitan	Shaitán (always with daín "the execrable" after it.)	Shaitán	Shaitán
Sun	Sooraj	Sigh, súraj	Aith	Nmerstarga (or, in connection with an unmistakeable context, simply Istarga; nmer, by itself, = sunshine).
Moon	Chand	Chandar, chan	Zun	Spogma-í (khatt-shpogma-í) a somewhat rare word, for moon is "úngí."

Languages.—(Continued.)

Pushtoo of Dera Ismail Khan.	Brahui of Dera Gazee Khan.	Brahui of Khelat.	English.
Súnclah pazah ...	Bámus ...	Bā,mo͞oz ...	Nose.
Stargah ...	Khan ...	Khūn ...	Eye.
Khulah ...	Mon ...	Bā ...	Mouth.
Ghásh ...	Dandán ...	Dŭntān ...	Tooth.
Ghwaj—ghwej ...	Khaf ...	Khŭf ...	Ear.
Veshtah ...	Phuzha (sing.), phuzhghak (plur.)	Pe͞esh, koh, ...	Hair.
Sar ...	Kátum ...	Kā, to͞om ...	Head.
Zibah, jibah ...	Duví ...	Do͞oee ...	Tongue.
Nas ...	Pid ...	Fĭd ...	Belly.
Shá, chattah ...	Baj ...	Bŭdge (sounded as the English substantive).	Back.
Aspaná ...	Alun ...	Ahe͞en (corruption of Persian).	Iron.
Sara zar ...	Khísun ...	Khe͞e,so͞om ...	Gold.
Spín zar ...	Chandi ...	Seam (sounded like the English substantive).	Silver.
Plár ...	Báwá ...	Bā, wā ...	Father.
Mor ...	Lumá ...	Lo͞omā ...	Mother.
Wror ...	Ilum ...	E,to͞om ...	Brother.
Khor ...	Ir ...	Eerr ...	Sister.
Merah, saraí ...	Narína ...	Á, ré ...	Man.
Shazah, shajah, shidzah ...	Taífa ...	Zā, e, fā ...	Woman.
Ditto ditto ...	Arwat ...	Ar,wăt ...	Wife.
Zankai, warkáchi, palak ...	Chuna ...	Cho͞onŭkā ...	Child.
Zae ...	Már ...	Mār ...	Son.
Lúr ...	Massir ...	Mŭs,se͞er ...	Daughter.
Marujai ...	Mé ...	Māy ...	Slave.
Ráhak ...	Langarvahok ...	Zémĭndār ...	Cultivator.
Ajú, rammewál ...	Kurkhálfok ...	Chōpān or Shāōbān ...	Shepherd.
Khudá, Alláh ...	Khudá ...	Kho͞odā ...	God.
Shaitán ...	Shaitán ...	Shăĭtān ...	Devil.
Nmar ...	Dé ...	Dé ...	Sun.
Spogmai ...	Tuwé ...	To͞o, bé ...	Moon.

English.	Punjabee of Lahore.	Punjabee of Mooltan.	Cashmeeree.	Pushtoo of Kohat.
Star	Tara	Tárah	Távăk	Istorai
Fire	Ag	Bhá, ăgh	Nár, zŭng	Or
Water	Pani	Pání, jal	Pōŭi	Obo (sometimes, but rarely, "obe").
House	Ghar	Ghar, túgá, sáhal (thatched house).	Gărh Sháĭ	Kor
Horse	Ghora	Ghóṛá	Gŭr	A's (khatt—yás)
Cow	Go	Gáṅ (*Hindus.*—gáú.) (*Jat.*—dahgí, vaharkí.)	ŏ Gá	Gẖwá
Dog	Kutta	Kutta	Hún	Spai
Cat	Billi	Billi	Brōr	Písho
Cat, female	......	......	Breur (*eu* as in French.)	......
Cock	Kukur	Kukaṛ	Kăkŭr	Chirg
Hen	......	......	Kŏkĭr	......
Drake	......	......	Bătŭk	......
Duck	Batakh	Badak, batak	Bătĭck	Battah, or battaka
Ass	Kata	Gadóṅ, khótah	Khăr	Kẖar
Camel	Uth	Uṭh, máhrá (riding camel).	U'nt	U'kkh
Bird	Chiria	Pakhí	Wŭdăwŭn	Murgẖai
Go	Ja	Vanjh, jul, já	......	Tlal
To go	......	......	Gătsŭn	......
Eat	Kha	Kha	......	Khuṛal
To eat	......	......	Khĭĭn	......
Sit	Bith	Bahi	......	Kenástal, or Kkkhenástal.
To sit	......	......	Bĭhŭn	......
Come	A	A'	......	Rátlal, or rágẖlal
To come	......	......	Yŭn	......
Beat	Mar	Már, kúṭ	......	Wahal
To beat	......	......	Láyŭn	......
Stand	Khora (khala) ho	Khará thí, khaṛ vanjh.	......	Wudredal
To stand	......	......	Wŭdănĭ rōzŭn	......
Die	Mar	Mar	......	Mral
To die	......	......	Marŭn	......
Give	De	Déh	......	Werkawul
To give	......	......	Diŭn	......
Run	Daur Bhaj	Dṛuk vanjh	......	Zgẖaledal (Po munḏo tlal, or munḏa kawul are the expressions in general use.)
To run	......	......	Dōrŭn	......

Pushtoo of Dera Ismail Khan.	Brahui of Dera Gazee Khan.	Brahui of Khelat.	English.
Storai ..	Istár ...	Is, tārā ...	Star.
Or ..	Khákhár ...	Khā, khŭr ...	Fire.
Obáh ..	Dír ...	Dēēr ...	Water.
Kor ..	Urá ...	O,orā ...	House.
As ..	Hulí ...	Núr, rēān (Persian) ...	Horse.
Ghwá ..	Dagi ...	Dŭggēē ...	Cow.
Spai ..	Kuchak ...	Kōōchūk ...	Dog.
Pishai ..	Pishí ...	Pĭshēē ...	Cat.
......	......	......	Cat, female.
Charg ..	Bángo ...	Bāngh, go ...	Cock.
......	......	......	Hen.
......	......	......	Drake.
Da obo chargah ..	Hanj ...	Hŭnj ...	Duck.
Khar ..	Bísh ...	Bēēsh ...	Ass.
U'sh ..	Huch ...	Hōōch ...	Camel.
Marghah ..	Ginjishk ...	Ginjishk ...	Bird.
Lársah ..	Hiningna ...	Hĭn, nŭk ...	Go.
......	......	......	To go.
Khorah ..	Iragna ...	Kōōn or Kōōnūk ...	Eat.
......	......	......	To eat.
Kshenah ..	Tulingna ...	Thōōlt ...	Sit.
......	......	......	To sit.
Raisah ..	Banigna ...	Bŭr, rŭk ...	Come.
......	......	......	To come.
Wahah ..	Khalingna ...	Khŭlt ...	Beat.
......	......	......	To beat.
Wadrejah, tamsah ..	Bashmarína ...	Sŭl ...	Stand.
......	......	......	To stand.
Marsah ..	Káingna ...	Kāi, hĭssā ...	Die.
......	......	......	To die.
Warkah ..	Thisuna ...	Eté ...	Give.
......	......	......	To give.
Washirejah, tashtah ..	Hilgharna ...	Dōdĭng ...	Run.
......	......	......	To run.

English.	Punjabee of Lahore.	Punjabee of Mooltan.	Cashmeeree.	Pushtoo of Kohat.
Up	Uti	U'te, útáṅh, ú par	Peth	Pás *or* porta.
Near	Nera	Néré, kólóṅ	Năhătăl	Nizẖde
Who	Kown (who?), gora (who.)	Kaun	Kŭs	Tsok
And	Or	Hór, bĭyá	Bĭh	O
Yes	Hau	A'h, áíṅ, áhó	Adăh	Ho, *or* hau
Down	Hethau	Jhiká, talé, héthánh	Bŭn	Kúz
Far	Dur	Móklá, paṛé, dúr	Dúr	Lire
What	Ki	Kihṛá	Kĭáh	Tsa
But	Por	Par	Yān kănĭkă	Magar
No	Nah	Náhíṅ, náh, nahíṅ, násé, nimí (agreeing with a singular subject), nisé (agreeing with a plural subject.)	Năh	Nah
Before	Agu	Agé, agáṅh, agúṅ	Bărnōth	Wṛánde
Behind	Pichhe magar	Pichúṅ	Păth	Wrusto
Why	Kyun	Kiúṅ	Kĭáazăh	Wele
If	Jekur	Jekar, jékadáháṅ	Yŭdwai	Ka
Alas!	Amsos (áfsos)	Afsós, Armán, Hariáni	Háĭ	Hai hai
A father	Pro	Báp	Ak mōl	Plár
Of a father	Pro da	Báp ḍá ḍí ḍé	Akĭs mál sŭnd	De plár
To a father	Pro nu	Báp, kúṅ	Akĭs málĭs	Plár ta
From a father	Pro te	Bap, kannúṅ	Akĭs málĭs nĭshĭ	De plár na
Two fathers	Do pro	Dú bap	Zŭh mál	......
Fathers	Pro	Bápáṅ	Málĭ	Plárán, *or* Plárúna
Of fathers	Pron da	Bápáṅ ḍá ḍí ḍé	Málĭn hŭnd	De plárúno
To fathers	Pron nu	Bápán kúṅ	Săthá málĭn	Plárúno ta
From fathers	Pron te	Bápán kannúṅ	Málĭn nĭshĭ	De plárúno na
A daughter	Dhi	Dhí	Ak kúr	Lúr
Of a daughter	Dhi da	Dhí ḍá ḍí ḍé	Akĭs kúrĭ hŭnd	De lúr
To a daughter	Dhi nu	Dhí kúṅ	Akĭs kúrĭ	Lúr ta
From a daughter	Dhi te	Dhi kannúṅ	Akĭs kúrĭ nĭshĭ	De lúr na
Two daughters	Do dheyau	Ḍu dhiriṅ	Zŭh kúrĭ	......
Daughters	Dheyau	Dhíríṅ	Kúrĭ	Lún̲r̲a
Of daughters	Dheyau da	Dhíríṅ ḍá ḍí ḍé	Kúrĭn hŭnd	De lun̲r̲o
To daughters	Dheyau nu	Dhíríṅ kúṅ	Kúrĭn	Lún̲r̲o ta
From daughters	Dheyau te	Dhíríṅ kánnúṅ	Kúrĭn nĭshĭ	De lún̲r̲o na
A good man	Chunga manukh	Changá ádmí	Ak rút măhnú	Kk̲h̲a saṛai

Languages.—(Continued.)

Pushtoo of Dera Ismail Khan.	Brahui of Dera Gazee Khan.	Brahui of Khelat.	English.
Portah	Burya	Bōōrzā	Up.
Nizde	Khurk	Khōōrk	Near.
Tchok	Derus	Dāre	Who.
O	(Wanting)	Pain (pronounced like the English substantive *pain.*)	And.
Ho	Han	Hā	Yes.
Kshatah	Shef	Shaif (*Shain shaip* pronounced as *sha* in *shade*).	Down.
Lare	Mur	Mōōrr	Far.
Tchah	Antse	Ūñt	What.
Magar	Lekin (rare)	Wallé	But.
Yá	Kapar	Āhā	No.
Mukh ta, vránde	Mokábil	Mōné	Before.
Shá ta	Phazáe	Pŭd	Behind.
Wale	Ante	Unlé	Why.
Ki, kah	Agé (rare)	Āga	If.
Ahá	Hoe hoe	HiHi *or* Āhbōōēē	Alas!
Yo plar	Báwa	Bāwā	A father
Da plár	Báwa na	Bāwānā	Of a father.
Plár ta	Báwé	Bāwā é	To a father.
La plár dzakhah	Báwaghan	Bāwā, ān	From a father.
Dwa plárah	Irra báwa	Eēērā bāwā ghāk (*Eerat* used in adj. form *Eera*).	Two fathers.
Plárah	Báwa	Bāwā ghāk	Fathers.
Dapláro	Báwaghatá	Bāwā ghātā (kin *ghak* dropped).	Of fathers.
Plaro ta	Báwaghante	Bāwā ghātú (ditto)	To fathers.
La plaroh dzakh	Báwaghantián	Bāwā ghātē ān (ditto)	From fathers.
Lúr	Massir	Mūs, sēēr	A daughter.
Da lúr	Massir na	Mussēērîka	Of a daughter.
Lúr ta	Massiré	Museeré	To a daughter.
La lúr dzakhah	Massiran	Mus, sēēr ān	From a daughter.
Dwe lúrnah	Irra massir (o)*	Eērā Mŭssēērĭk (*Eera* adj. form of *erut.*)	Two daughters.
Lúrnah	Massiro	Mussēērîk	Daughters.
Da lúrno	Massinta	Mussēérikta	Of daughters.
Lúrno ta	Massinte	Mussēērikté	To daughters.
La lúrno dzakh	Massintian	Mussēērík tíān	From daughters.
Yo shah sarai	Jawán narína	Jowānō Ārré	A good man.

* *N.B.*—When numerals to any amount are used, it appears to be optional to add "o" or not to the noun. "O" appears to be used to make the plural nominative, but it appears to be used everywhere irregularly.

English.	Punjabee of Lahore.	Punjabee of Mooltan.	Cashmeeree.	Pushtoo of Kobat.
Two good men ..	Do chunga manukh	Ḍú change ádmí ..	Zeh rit măhneo ...	......
Good men ..	Chunga manukh ..	Changé ádmíáṅ ..	Rit măhneo ...	Kkha saṛí ...
Of a good man ..	Chunga manukh da	Change ádmí ḍá, ḍí, ḍé.	Akis ritis măhnú shnd.	De kkha saṛí ...
Of a good woman ..	......	......	......	De kkhe kkhadze ...
To a good man ..	Chunga manukh me	Changé ádmí kúṅ..	Akis ritis măhnuis ..	Kkha saṛí ta ...
From a good man ..	Chunga manukh te	Changé ádmí kannún	Akis ritis mahnevis nishi.	De kkha saṛína ...
Of good men ..	Chunga manukhan da.	Changé ádmíáṅ ḍá, ḍí, ḍe.	Ritin mahneon hund	De kkho saṛíyo ...
Of good women ..	......	......	......	De kkho kkhadzo ...
To good men ..	Chunga manukhun me.	Changé ádmíáṅ kuṅ	Ritin măhnevin ...	Kkho saṛíyo ta ...
From good men ..	Chunga manukhun te.	Change ádmíáṅ kannúṅ.	Ritin mahnevin nishi.	De kkho saṛiyo na ...
A good woman ..	Chungi tuni ..	Changí trímati ..	Ak nits zanána ...	Kkhá kkhadza ...
Good women ..	Chungi tuniyan ..	Changíáṅ trímatáṅ	Nitsăh Zănána ...	Kkhe kkhadze ...
A bad boy ..	Bura munda ..	Bhágá chóhar ..	Ak rándăh nicheú...	Kharáb úrkai ...
A bad girl ..	Buri kaori ..	Bhágí chóhir ..	Ak rándăh kúr ...	Kharába úṛkí ...
Good ..	Chunga ..	Changá ..	Nit (*or*) ján (*or*) zăhăr.	Kkha (fem: kkhá) ...
Better ..	Bahut chunga ..	Then changa (as the thing with which the comparison is made in the ablative case) *and* ún ín kannúṅ changa né (that is, "better than this.")	Săthá rŭt ...	De agha nakkha (than that).
Best ..	Sarah nal chunga..	Sabh kannúṅ changá, sabh de nál changá.	Amōh rut ...	Deṭolo na kkha ...
High ..	Ucha ..	Ucha ..	Thŭd ...	Dhíng, uchat, lwaṛ (less common).
Higher ..	Bahut ucha ..	(See "better") ..	Tsŭr, săthá, thŭd ...	(Same as "better") ...
Highest ..	Sarah nal ucha ..	Sabh kannún ucha, sabh dé nál uchá.	Amóh thŭd ...	Ditto ...
A horse ..	Ghora ..	Ghóṛá ..	Ak gŭrr ...	A̓s (khatt. yás) ...
A mare ..	Ghori ..	Ghóṛi ..	Ak gŭr ...	A̓spaŭ ...
Horses ..	Ghora ..	Ghóṛe ..	Gŭrri ...	A̓súna ...
Mares ..	Ghoriyan ..	Ghóríáṅ ..	Gŭré ...	A̓spe ...
A bull ..	Gau ka sandh ..	Dánd ..	Ak dánd or hăkŭr...	Ghuṯskai ...
A cow ..	Gow ..	Vahaṛki ..	Ak gáo orăk haŭr...	Ghwá ...
Bulls ..	Goka sandh ..	Dánd ..	Dánd ...	Ghuṯskí (*or*) ghwá-e
Cows ..	Gaiyan ..	Vaharkíáṅ ..	Gáo ...	Ghwá ...
A dog ..	Kutta ..	Kuttá ..	Ak hún ...	Ispai ...
A bitch ..	Kutti ..	Kuttí ..	Ak húin ...	Ispa-í ...

Pushtoo of Dera Ismail Khan.	Brabui of Dera Gazee Khan.	Brabui of Khelat.	English.
Ḍwa shah sarí ...	Jera jawan (o) narịna ...	Eēradōwānō Ārréik (*reik* pro. like sub. *rake.)*	Two good men.
Shah sari ...	Jawáno naríno ...	Jōwānō Ārréik ...	Good men.
Dasho sari ...	Jawán narína (se)* na ...	Jōwānō Ārré, nā ...	Of a good man.
......	......	......	Of a good woman.
Shah sarí ta ...	Jawán narína (se) ...	Jōwānō Arré é ...	To a good man.
La shah sarí dzakhah ...	Jawán narínághan ...	Jōwānō Arré ān ...	From a good man.
Da sho saro ...	Jawáno narínaghán ta ...	Jōwānō Arréikta ...	Of good men.
......	......	......	Of good women.
Sho saro ta ...	Jawánághan narínaghán te	Jōwānō Arréik,té ...	To good men.
La sho saro dzakhah ...	Jawánaghan narínaghán tiar	Jōwānō Arréik tēān ...	From good men.
Yawah shah shajah ...	Jawano zaíf ...	Shŭr, rō zāēfā ...	A good woman.
She shaje ...	Jawáno zaífo ...	Shŭr, rō zāēfā ghāk ...	Good women.
Bad halak ...	Gandah már ...	Gŭndō mār ...	A bad boy.
Badah jinkáí ...	Gandah massir† ...	Gŭndō mus, sēēr ...	A bad girl.
Shah ...	Jawán‡ ...	Jōwān ...	Good.
Der shah ...	Ditto ...	Jōwān ṭēēr ...	Better.
Tar waro shah ...	Ditto ...	Koŏtan jown ...	Best.
Chig ...	Burza ...	Mōōr, ghōōn ...	High.
Der chig ...	Ditto ...	Mōōrghōōn tēēr ...	Higher.
Tar waro chig ...	Ditto ...	Gir,rān mōōrgkōōn ...	Highest.
Ás ...	Niriyan ...	Nŭrrēān ...	A horse.
Áspahgh ...	Mádián ...	Hōōllēē ...	A mare.
Ásúnah ...	Niriyan ...	Nŭrrēānk ...	Horses.
Áspe ...	Mádián ...	Hōōllēēk ...	Mares.
Sán, ghwaij'ái (bull or ox)	Kárígár ...	Khrās ...	A bull.
Ghwá ...	Dagi ...	Dŭggēē ...	A cow.
Ghwayi ...	Kárígáro ...	Khrāsk ...	Bulls.
Ghwá ...	Dagio ...	Dŭggēēk ...	Cows.
Spai ...	Naráz ...	Kōōchŭk ...	A dog.
Spaí ...	Hand ...	Madō kōōchuk§ ...	A bitch.

* No reason can be given for this (*se*) it does not occur in words of similar termination.
† *N.B.*—The indefinite article is wanting.
‡ None of the degrees of comparison by inflexion, like Urdu.
§ No separate word for bitch; *mado*, female, always prefixed.

English.	Punjabee of Lahore.	Punjabee of Mooltan.	Cashmeeree.	Pushtoo of Kohat.
Dogs ..	Kutte ...	Kutté ..	Hún ...	Ispí ..
Bitches ..	Kuttiyan ...	Kuttiáṅ ..	Húnieh ...	Ispa-í ..
A he-goat ..	Bakora ...	Bakrá ..	Ak tsáwăl ...	Psa ..
A female goat ..	Bakri ...	Bakrí ..	Ak tsáwăj ...	Bza ..
Goats ..	Bakriyan ...	Bakré, bakríáṅ ..	Tsáwăjeh ...	......
He-goats ..	......	......	......	Psúna ..
She-goats ..	......	......	......	Bze ..
A male deer ..	Heran ...	Haran ..	Ak rús ...	Lakka shiwai (a "buck" or leader of a herd, narkakkh.)
A female deer ..	Hirni ...	Haraní ..	Ak rús kăt ...	Lakka shiwá-í ..
Deer ..	Hirúyan ...	Haran, haraníáṅ ..	Rús ...	Lakkashiwí and a-í (masc. & fem.)
I am ..	Main háu ...	Main háṅ *or* hun ..	Bú chŭs ...	Zah yam ..
Thou art ..	Tu hai ...	Túṅ hé ..	Tsh chúk ...	Ta e ..
He is ..	Oh hai ...	Uh hé ..	Sú chŭk ...	Ag̱ha da ..
We are ..	Assi háu ...	Assáṅ haiṅ *or* hissé	As chih ...	Mú yú ..
You are ..	Tun ho ...	Tussaṅ ho ..	Túih chúh ...	Tású ya-í ..
They are ..	Oh hain ...	Uhé hin ..	Tim chih ...	Ag̱hadí (masc. & fem.)
I was ..	Main sau ...	Main ham ..	Bú asús ...	Zah wum ..
Thou wast ..	Tu sa ...	Túṅ han ..	Tsŭh ásúk ...	Ta we ..
He was ..	Oh sa ...	Uh háí ..	Sú ás ...	Ag̱ha wuh (fem. ag̱ha wa.)
We were ..	Assi sa ...	Assáṅ hásé ..	As ás ...	Mú wú ..
You were ..	Tusi sa ...	Tussáṅ hávé *or* hávi	Tŭih ásuăh ...	Tású wa-í ..
They were ..	Oh sa ...	Uhé hann ..	Tim ás ...	Ag̱ha wu (masc.) ag̱ha (fem.)
Be ..	Ho ...	Thí ..	Ás ...	Wu sha *or* keg̣a* ..
To be ..	Hona ...	Thíoná ..	Ásăn ...	Kedal ..
Being ..	Hata ...	Thíndá ..	Ásán ásan ...	Kedún (or more commonly in the fem. form kedana).
Having been ..	Hoka ...	Thíndá hóiyá ..	Ásit ...	Kedalai or shiwai* ..
I may be ..	Main howan ...	Main thíoáṅ ..	Bú hikŭh ásit ...	(Wanting)† ..
I shall be ..	Main hanga ...	Main hóṡáṅ *or* thíoáṅ	Bú ásăk ...	Za ba yam ..
I should be ..	Main un chuhi da	Main thíndá (rarely hondá.)	Mi gŭtsăh ásun ...	Za ba wum ..
Beat ..	Már ...	Már ..	Láyé ...	Wu waya ..
To beat ..	Márná ...	Máran ..	Lăyăn ...	Wayal‡ ..
Beating ..	......	Maréndá ..	Lá'yăn ...	Wayún *or* wayana ..
Having beaten ..	Márke ...	Maréndá hóiyá ..	Láyith ...	Wayalai ..
I beat ..	Main márdan ...	Maiṅ marĕndá háṅ	Bú láyis ...	Zah wayam ..
Thou beatest ..	Tu márda hai ...	Túṅ maréndá hé ..	Tsŭh láyăk ...	Ta waye ..
He beats ..	Oh márda hai ...	Uh maréndá hé ..	Sú lá'yăn ...	Ag̱ha wayí ..
We beat ..	Assi márde hain ...	Asṡáṅ marénde hain	As láyós ...	Mú wayú ..

* These forms come directly from the verb "shwal," which, like "kedal,"=*to become*. There are no equivalents in the language for "be," "to be," "being," and "having been," in the sense of simple existence.

† Third person, he may be = ag̱ha ba wi.

‡ This verb is properly "wahal," but in this district is pronounced (and has therefore been spelt) exactly the same as "wayal"=*to say*.

Languages.—(Continued.)

Pushtoo of Dera Ismail Khan.	Brahui of Dera Gazee Khan.	Brahui of Khelat.	English.
Spí ...	Narazo ...	Kōōchŭk kāk ...	Dogs.
Spaí ...	Hando ...	Mādō kōōchŭk kāk ...	Bitches.
Vaz ...	Math ...	Dŭgghŭr ...	A he-goat.
Vza ...	Heth ...	Hait ...	A female goat.
Vze ...	Matho, Hetho ...	Mailt‖ ...	Goats.
......	......	......	He-goats.
......	......	......	She goats.
Nukhtsír ...	Narásk ...	Khŭzzŭm ...	A male deer.
Nakhtsírah nakhsérunah ...	Máda ásko ...	Mādō khŭzzŭm ...	A female deer.
Nakhtsire ...	Narásko, Máda ásko ...	Khŭzmāk ...	Deer.
Zah yam ...	'I uth ...	Āréit ...	I am.
Tah ye ...	Ní us ...	Āréis ...	Thou art.
Haghah dai ...	E é§ ...	Āré ...	He is.
Muj yú ...	Nan un ...	Aréin ...	We are.
Tású, yást, yástah ...	Num ure ...	Aré ré ...	You are.
Haghah dí ...	Dá o§ ...	Āreer ...	They are.
Zah wum ...	I asut ...	Us, sōō, tā ...	I was.
Tah we ...	Ní asus ...	Us, sōōs ...	Thou wast.
Haghah wuh (fem. wah) ...	E as ...	Us ...	He was.
Muj wú ...	Nan asun ...	Us, sōō, nā ...	We were.
Tású, wáast, wástah ...	Num asun ...	Us, sōō, ré ...	You were.
Haghah wú ...	Dá asur ...	U, ssōōrāh ...	They were.
Sa ...	Mabo ...	Mŭr, rŭck ...	Be.
Swal ...	Maning ...	Mŭnningh ...	To be.
Kedún ...	(Wanting) ...	Mŭrrōke ...	Being.
Kedalai ...	Maré ...	Mŭs, sōō, ne ...	Having been.
Zah wusam ...	'I maréu ...	Mur, réwur¶ ...	I may be.
Zah ba sam ...	I maréva ...	Mŭrrōte ...	I shall be.
Zah wusam ...	'I marév ...	Mŭs, sōōnōōt ...	I should be.
Wawahah ...	Khalbo ...	Khŭlt ...	Beat.
Wahal ...	Khallingna ...	Khŭlling ...	To beat.
Wáhah ...	(Wanting) ...	Khŭltissā ...	Beating.
Wahalai ...	Khalkut ...	Khŭlkōō, né ...	Having beaten.
Zah wawaham ...	'I khaleva ...	Khul, lé wŭt, tā ...	I beat.
Tah wawahe ...	Ní khalesa ...	Khŭllingŭttēē, use ...	Thou beatest.
Haghah wawahí ...	E khalek ...	Khullāiktur ...	He beats.
Muj wawahú ...	Nan khalena ...	Khullinguttee yoon ...	We beat.

§ Used as an affix.
‖ *Mail* pronounced as in English, with a terminal sound of *t*.
¶ "Wur" appears to be the best way of writing the termination of words ending in *w* or *wh*.

English.	Punjabee of Lahore.	Punjabee of Mooltan.	Cashmeeree.	Pushtoo of Kohat.
You beat ...	Tusi márda ha ..	Tussáṅ maréndé ho	Túïh láyós ..	Tású waya-í ...
They beat ...	Oh márda hain ..	Uhe maréndá hin. .	Tïm láyïnās ..	Agha wayí ...
I am beating ...	Main márde hau ..	Maiṅ maréndá hán	Bú láyăn chús ..	Zah wayam ...
I was beating ...	Main márda sa ..	Main maréndá hám	Bú láyăn ásās ..	Má wayalu ...
I had beaten ...	Main márchuk sa ..	Maiṅ máriá hé ..	Mï láyós ..	Má wayalai wuh ...
I may beat ...	Main máran, main mára janda hun.	Maiṅ máráṅ ..	Bú hïkăn, lăyit mávit	Zah wu wayam ...
I shall beat ...	Main máranga ..	Main marésaṅ ..	Bú láyé ..	Zah ba wu wayam ...
I should beat ...	Main un márna ..	Main marísaṅ, main máríá baisáṅ.	Mi gütseh láy h ..	Zah ba wu wayam ...
I am beaten ...	Main nu már pie ..	Main mária bainda hán.	Bú tsüs lágimăt ..	Zah wayalai kegam....
I was beaten ...	Mainuo már pie sa.	Main máríá bainda hám.	Bú ásús láinámăt ..	Zah wu wayalai shwam
I shall be beaten ...	Main un márpanaya chahi de.	Main marísaṅ, main mária baisáṅ.	Bú gălseh, láinámăt mavah.	Zah ba wu wayalai sham.
I go ...	Maiu janda hau ..	Main, ainda hán ..	Bú gătsăh ..	Zah dzam ...
Thou goest ...	Tu janda hai ..	Tun vaindá hé ..	Ts h gătsăh ..	Ta dze ...
He goes ...	Oh janda hai ..	Uh vaindá hé ..	Sú gütsán chúh ..	Agha dzí ...
I went ...	Main gaya si ..	Main giá ..	Hú gós ..	Zah láṛam ...
Thou wentest ...	Tu gaya si ..	Tun giá ..	Tsüh gókh ..	Ta láṛe ...
He went ...	Oh gaya se ..	Uh giá ..	Sú gás ..	Agha láṛu ...
Go ...	Ja ..	Vanjh ..	Găts ..	Dza or Láṛsha (imp.)...
Going ...	Janda ..	Vaindá ..	Gătsăh ..	Tlana ...
Gone ...	Gaya hua ..	Giá ..	Gás ..	Tlalai ...
What is your name?	Twárá nam ki? ..	Tédá ná keh hé? ..	Túih kyáh chúh náo?	Tá núm tsa da or Num de tsa da?
How old is this horse?	Ghora kinniyan borayanda hai?	Kittí umar dá ghóṛa hé?	Imis (of this) güri-săuz (horse) waihs (age) kyáh (what) chúh (is)?	Dá ás de tso kalo da, or ba wi=Urdu "hogá."
How far is it from here to Kashmir?	Eto Kashmir tani kinna purdah hai? (kitna dur.)	Kashmír iṭháóṅ kitté pandh hé?	Ité pitt (from this place). kătsáh (how) dúr (far) chuh (is) · Kăshír (Kashmir)?	Dalta na Kashmír tsomra lire da?
How many sons are there in your father's house?	Tra prodeghar luchkinna putr hai?	Tédé báp dé ghar kitté pútr hin?	Tühündio mális săndé (in) găré (house) kătyáh nichen chih?	Tá plár kara tso dzáman dí?
I have walked a long way to-day.	Main aj bara paindah kitá.	Main aj bahú pandh kítá hé.	Az (to-day) kúr (made) mé (I) săthá (very) dur (far) ťáú (to) sair (journey).	Má nan ḍer mazal kiṛai da.
The son of my uncle is married to her sister.	Mera chachi da put ohda bahin nal byahaya.	Médé cháché dé pátr ne uṅdi bhaen nál parnéiá kítá hé.	Miánis (my) pitrsănd (uncle of) nichen (son) kúr (made) tăs (that) zănáná (woman) hăwzé (of) biniă (sister) süét (with) néthărr (marriage).	De aghe khor de má trazwí kiṛí da.

Languages.—(Continued.)

Pushtoo of Dera Ismail Khan.	Brahui of Dera Gazee Khan.	Brahui of Khelat.	English.
Tású wawahuí ...	Num khalere ...	Khŭllingŭttēē aoré ..	You beat.
Haghah wawahí ...	Dá khalera ...	Khŭllingŭttēē ārēēr ..	They beat.
Zah waham ...	'I khaligatiut ...	Khŭllé wŭttā ..	I am beating.
Mú wáhah ...	'I khaligatiasut ...	Khŭlk kōōtā ..	I was beating.
Má wahalai wuh ...	'I khalkuta ...	Khŭlk sōōt ..	I had beaten.
Zah wawaham ...	'I khaleva ...	Khŭléwŭr ..	I may beat.
Zah ba waham ...	'I khaleva ...	Khŭlōte ..	I shall beat.
Zah ba waham ...	'I khaleva* ...	Khŭlk kōōtā† ..	I should beat.
Zah wahalai kijam ...	......	Khŭlōke mŭrréwŭr ..	I am beaten.
Zah wahalai kedam ...	......	Khŭlke mŭs'sōōt ..	I was beaten.
Zah ba wahalai kejam ...	......	Khŭlōke mārōte ..	I shall be beaten.
Zah dzam ...	'I káwa ...	Hinning, gŭt,tēē yōōt ..	I go.
Tah dze ...	Ní kása ...	Kāssā‡ ..	Thou goest.
Haghah dzí ...	E káik ...	Hinning, gŭttū yeh ..	He goes.
Zah láram ...	'I hinát ...	Hinnūt ..	I went.
Tah láre ...	Ní hinás ...	Hinnās ..	Thou wentest.
Haghah láraí ...	E hiná ...	Hinnā ..	He went.
Lársah wardzah ...	Hin ...	Hinnk ..	Go.
Talah ...	(Wanting) ...	Hinnōkē ..	Going.
Talalai ...	Hínán ...	Hinnān, né ..	Gone.
Stá núm tchahdai ? ...	Ná pindéri ? ...	Nā pin ŭn,tŭs,sū ? ..	What is your name ?
Daghah ás tchomrah umr lari ?	Dá hulíná umar akhási ...	Dāh nŭrrēān nā ākhās, ōōmur āré ?	How old is this horse ?
La daghahdzí dzakhah Kashmír tchomrah lare dai ?	Dá ká Kasmír akham muré ?	Dāhkā Cāshmir ākhŭs mōōré ?	How far is it from here to Kashmir ?
Stá da plár pa kor kshitcho zaman di ?	Ná háwáná uráti akham máro ?	Nā bāwā, nā, bōrātēē ākhŭs mākō ?	How many sons are there in your father's house ?
Zah nan der lare pale larama.	I annoi piáda báz pandh karen uth ?	Inó, e, bāz pēāda, hin, nā nōōt	I have walked a long way to-day.
Zmú da trah zoe da haghah la khor sarah wadah karai dai.	Kaná ilná már ena irna are	Kŭnnā illé, nā mār ōnā, ēēr, to, brāhm kŭrré né.	The son of my uncle is married to her sister.

* Passive Voice wanting.
† Same as "I was beating," and only distinguishable by the general meaning of the sentence.
‡ *Hinning, guttee yoos* might be used, but would not be understood.

English.	Punjabee of Lahore.	Punjabee of Mooltan.	Cashmeeree.	Pushtoo of Kohat*.
In the house is the saddle of the white horse.	Chitta ghora di kathi ghar bich paihui hai.	Baggé ghóṛé ḍá sang ghar hé.	Gărăs (house) mauz (in) chŭh (is) chithis (white) gŭrisŭnd (horse of) káth (saddle).	De ispín ás zín po kor kkkhe da.
Put the saddle upon his back.	Oh do pith uti kathi páo.	Undé kanḍ uté sanj rakh.	Tăs (of that) zih (his) tharr (back) peth (on) kath (saddle) lad (put).	Agha po shá zín keda
I have beaten his son with many stripes.	Main ne ohde putr un kunihi karamara.	Main úndé pútr kúṅ bahu charíáṅ (kau nail) katiá hé.	Mi lŏé (stroke) tamsŭndis (of that man's) nicheuis (son) săthá (many) kămchih (stroke).	Má de agha dzwá-e po ḍero guzárúno wayalai da.
He is grazing cattle on the top of the hill.	Oh tibhi uti mal charanda paya hai.	Uh pahárí úté choakhar kúṅ charíndá hé.	Tămi (that) bălăkkis (of the hill) tăngis (top) peth (on) chŭh (is) sú (he) tív (sheep) gópăn (quadruped) gásăh (grass) kháwáṅ (feeding).	Agha de ghra po sir mál starawí *or* "piyáyí".
He is sitting on a horse under that tree.	Us boota de hitan oh ghora uti charah hua hai.	Uh darakht talé ghóṛé úté chariá hóiyá hé.	Sú chŭh gúris (horse) peth (on) tăth (that) kúlis (tree) tăl (beneath) bihit (sitting).	Agha po ás swor de aghe wane lánde wilár (*lit.*, "standing") da.
His brother is taller than his sister.	Oh da bharar ohdi bhain nalow bunha hai.	Undá bhirá apní bhaen kannúṅ lamba hé.	Tăsăṅd (his) bói (brother) chŭh (is) tăsăuzé (his) biniăh (sister) hăndi (of) kothăh (than) tud (high).	De agha wror de agha khor na úchat da.
The price of that is two rupees and a half.	Oh da mul dhai rupiya hai.	Un dá mól dhai rupíyá hé.	Tămik (of that) mŏl (price) chŭh (is) zăh (two) rúpiăh tăh (and) aith ánă.	De agha bai'a dwah níme rupa-í dí.
My father lives in that small house.	Mera prous chhoto jeh ghar bichrahuda.	Médá báp chótí júgé vich báhnda hé.	Miún mól chŭh tăli (that) gărăh (home) hăne (little) mănz rózáṇ (abiding).	Emá plár po agha waṛúki kor kkkhe osí.
Give this rupee to him.	E rupiya un nu dede.	Th rúpíyá ún káṅ ḍeḍe.	Imah rúpiăh dih timis.	Dá rúpa-í agha ta werka.
Take those rupees from him.	Oh rupiya us to lile	Uh rúpíyá ún kannúṅ ghin ghin.	Timăh (those) rúpiăh hih (take) tăs (from him).	Agha rúpa-i de agha na wákhla.
Beat him well and bind him with ropes.	Un nu bura maro or russeyan nal banno.	Un kúṅ changí tarah már karáiṅ rassí nál badh.	Tăs (him) láé wárăh (good) páthin (manner) bih (and) găndú (bind) răzé (ropes) suet (with).	Agha kkha wu waya o puṛiyo sara wu taṛa.
Draw water from the well.	Kui bichho pani kadho.	Khúh bíchóṅ páné chik.	Kréré (well) mŭnz kăd (draw) póiṅ.	Kúhi na obo wu bása
Walk before me ...	Mera age age chal	Meḍé agé chal jul	Mi (me) brónth (before) hărouth pakh (move).	Emá po wṛánde wṛánde drúma (Urdú "chal").

* Note.—The equivalents of the English words and phrases noted in this column throughout are entered in the Roman character and transliterated in the Jonesian method.

The following transliteration has been used for the letters peculiar to the Pakkhta alphabet in accordance with Bellew:—

Dz or Ts = ځ G. = ږ Kkh (pronounced by the Khattaks "sh") = ښ and Nr = ڼ or نړ (ړ — r, and is nearly the same as the Urdu ڑ)

Languages.—(Continued.)

Pushtoo of Dera Ismail Khan.	Brahui of Dera Gazee Khan.	Brahui of Khelat.	English.
Pa kor kshi da spín ás zín dai.	Uráti phihuna hulína zen...	Oōrā nā, thŭrtēē-pēhōōn nŭrrēan, na, zeen aré.†	In the house is the saddle of the white horse.
Da haghah pa shá bándi zín kshejdah.	Zene namena bajáe tighbo	Nŭrrēan, nā, bŭjā-zēēn shāgh.‡	Put the saddle upon his back.
Da haghah zoe padero satto sarah má wahalai dai.	Hamena mare 'I báz kurat khalkunuth.	Onā, maré, e bāz shēēp, ānk khŭlkonōōt.	I have beaten his son with many stripes.
Da ghrah pa sar bándi mál píáí.	Mashana zí hae kuré hamé khwahfera.	O-mŭshnā, zēēā, mal, khwafing, gŭttēē é.	He is grazing cattle on the top of the hill.
Tar haghe wune láude pa ás bandi spor walur dai.	Halí ná zehae sowaré hamen darakhtána keraghan.	O, é, dŭrukht, nā, kēērgŭt hŭr, rēā nāthōō, sooné.	He is sitting on a horse under that tree.
Da haghah wror la khpule khor dzakhah chig dai.	Hamenai ílum hamená irán hurze.	O, nā, etōōm, ōnā ēērā moorgoon, é.	His brother is taller than his sister.
Da haghah kímat dwá níme rúpaí dí.	Hamena báhá do ném rupié	Onā, bāhā, ērŭt nēēm rōōpaí āré.	The price of that is two rupees and a half.
Zmá plár pa haghah kam kor kshi tamkají.	Káná hawa chunka uráti túlik.	Bāwā kŭnnā, é, chōōnŭkā ōrātee, thōōlik.	My father lives in that small house.
Dághah rúpai haghah ta warkah.	Handá rúpaie hamo etibo	Dāh, rōōpāi, ōdé, été ..	Give this rupee to him.
Haghah rúpaí la haghah dzakhah yosah.	Hamo rupí te hamoran halbo.	É-rōōpāi, érān, hŭlt ..	Take those rupees from him.
Daghah shah wawahah as pa pariyo sarah e watarah.	Od báz khalbo, rezat tavbo	Odé jōwān, khŭlt, raiz, tōtuf	Beat him well and bind him with ropes.
La haghah kúhí dzakhah obah wakajah.	Dúnán dír kasheho ..	Dōōnān, dēēr, kush ..	Draw water from the well.
Zmá pa mukhah wa kwajah	Kaná monáti piáda maho..	Kunnā monuttēē, khuré ..	Walk before me.

† *Thwi* is meant to express sound of *pers-th*.
‡ The Brahuis always use the word *sung*, which includes all horse accoutrements.

English.	Punjabee of Lahore.	Punjabee of Mooltan.	Cashmeeree.	Pushtoo of Kohat.
Whose boy comes behind you?	Tera pichhe kida putr aunda hai?	Teḍé píché kainḍá bál ándá hé?	Kóhund nichen chuh tŭhé păth (behind) yúán (coming)?	Tá po wrusto de chá úṛkai rádzí?
From whom did you buy that?	Oh ki de kal mul leya hai?	Uh kaiṅ kannúṅ mol ghida hé?	Kas (whom) nishi (from) hitŭl (bought) tsih (you) sú (that)?	Agha de chá na po bai'e ákhistai da?
From a shop-keeper of the village.	Us pind do hati wale kalow.	Vastí ḍé kirár kannún.	Aké gámekis (of village) wánăh (shop) wális (keeper) nishi (from).	De kilí dúkándár na . .

Languages.—(Concluded.)

Pushtoo of Dera Ismail Khan.	Brahui of Dera Gazee Khan.	Brahui of Khelat.*	English.
Da chá zaukai pa tá pise raizi?	Diná már ná randat barek?	Nā, pŭddŭttēē, dinnā, mār bŭnninggŭttēē yēh?	Whose boy comes behind you?
Tá la chá dzakhah haghah pirodai dai?	Odera nal kus? ...	Dhēr, ān, é, girrā, hŭl-kōōnōōs?	From whom did you buy that?
La yo hatuiál da kali dza-khah.	Tatti na philan bakhálan halkut.	É, wustee, nā, dhōōkāndā, ān. (*Bukhal*, "buniah" is used, not *dhookanda*).	From a shop-keeper of the village.

* The accentuation "in the words and phrases in this column throughout is almost entirely the same as in Latin. Short and long marks —, v, a final accented—is sounded "ar;" e with acute accent as in French.

DRAVIDIAN LANGUAGES

OF

SOUTHERN INDIA.

English.	Tamil.	Malayalum.	Telugu.
Numerals.			
One ...	On-ru ...	Onna ...	Va-ka-ti ...
Two ...	I-ran-du ...	Raṇḍa ...	Ren-du ...
Three ...	Mún-ru ...	Mûnna ...	Mú-du ...
Four ...	Nán-gu or Ná-lu ...	Nâla ...	Ná-lu-gu ...
Five ...	Ain-thu ...	Anja ...	Ai-thu ...
Six ...	Á-ru ...	Aṛa ...	Á-ru ...
Seven ...	É-lu ...	Ézha ...	É-du ...
Eight ...	Ettu ...	Eṭṭa ...	E-ni-mi-thi ...
Nine ...	On-ba-thu ...	Onbadha ...	Thom-mi-thi ...
Ten ...	Path-thu ...	Pattha ...	Pa-thi ...
Twenty ...	I-ru-pa-thu ...	Iruvadha ...	I-ru-vai ...
Fifty ...	Aim-ba-thu ...	Ambadha ...	É-bhai ...
Hundred ...	Nú-ṛu ...	Nûṛa ...	Nú-ru ...
Pronouns.			
I ...	Nán ...	Nyân ...	Né-nu ...
Of me ...	En-nu-dai-ya ...	Endê ...	Ná-yok-ka ...
Mine ...	En-na-thu ...	Endêdha ...	Ná-thi ...
We ...	Nám ...	Nyanngal ("ng" as in sing).	Ma-na-mu ...
Of us ...	Nam-mu-dai-ya ...	Nyangaludê ...	Ma-na-yok-ka ...
Our ...	Nam-ma-thu ...	Nyangaludêdha ...	Ma-na-thi ...
Thou ...	Ní ...	Nî ...	Ní-vu ...
Of thee ...	Un-nu-dai-ya ...	Nindê ...	Ní-yok-ka ...
Thine ...	Un-na-thu ...	Nindêdha ...	Ní-thi ...
You ...	Nír ...	Ninngal ...	Mí-ru ...
Of you ...	Um-mu-dai-ya	Ningaludê ...	Mí-yok-ka ...
Your ...	Um-ma-thu ...	Ningaludêdha ...	Mí-thi ...
He ...	A-van ...	Avan ...	Vá-du ...
Of him ...	A-va-nu-dai-ya ...	Avandê ...	Vá-ni-yok-ka ...
His ...	A-va-na-thu ...	Avandêdha ...	Vá-ni-thi ...
They ...	A-var-gal ...	Avar (masc.), ava (neuter)	Vá-ru ...
Of them ...	A-var-ga-lu-dai-ya ...	Avarudê ...	Vá-ri-yok-ka ...
Their ...	A-var-ga-lu-thu ...	Avarudêdha ...	Vá-ri-thi ...
Hand ...	Kai ...	Kei ...	Che-yi ...
Foot ...	A-di, (or) Pá-tham ...	Kâl ...	Pá-tha-mu (or) A-du-gu
Nose ...	Múk-ku ...	Mûkka ...	Muk-ku ...
Eye ...	Kaṇ ...	Kaṇṇa ...	Kan-nu ...
Mouth ...	Váy ...	Vây ...	Nó-ru ...

Canarese.	Toda (Neilgherries.)	Badaga (Neilgherries.)	English.
Ondu ...	Vodd ..	Vondu ..	One.
Eradu ...	Ed ..	Yeraḍu ..	Two.
Múru ...	Muḍu ..	Muru ..	Three.
Nálku ...	Nanku ..	Nalku ..	Four.
Aidu ...	Uj ("ü" as in German) ..	Eídu ..	Five.
Áru ...	Ār ..	Āru ..	Six.
Elu ...	Yṭeu ..	Ylen ..	Seven.
Entu ...	Yett or eṭṭ ..	Yeṭṭu ..	Eight.
Ombhattu ...	Onpad ("d"=th) ..	Vombhattu ..	Nine.
Hattu ...	Pad ..	Hattu ..	Ten.
Ippattu ...	Eppad ..	Ippattu ..	Twenty.
Ai-vattu ...	Eivad ..	Eivattu ..	Fifty.
Núru ...	Vodd núr ..	Nuru ..	Hundred.
Nánu ...	Ān ..	Nā ..	I.
Nannannu ...	Yenna ..	Yenna ..	Of me.
Nannadu ...	Yennadu ..	Yennadu ..	Mine.
Návu ...	* Ém, ām ..	* Yengla, angla ..	We.
Namma ...	* Yemma, namma ..	*Yenga, anga ..	Of us.
Nammadu ...	......	......	Our.
Nínu ...	Ni ..	Ni ..	Thou.
Ninna ...	Ninna ..	Ninna ..	Of thee.
Ninnadu ...	Ninnadu ..	Ninnadu ..	Thine.
Nívu ...	Niv ..	Ningla ..	You.
Nimma ...	Nimma ..	Ninga ..	Of you.
Nimmadu ...	......	......	Your.
Avanu ...	Adum ..	Ava ..	He.
Avaṇadu ...	Adun ..	Avana ..	Of him.
Avana ...	......	......	His.
Avaru ...	Adum ..	Avaka ..	They.
Avara ...	Adun ..	Avakara ..	Of them.
Avaradu ...	......	......	Their.
Kai ...	Kei ..	Kei ..	Hand.
Adi (or) Páda ...	Kāl ..	Kālu ..	Foot.
Múgu ...	Mituff ..	Muku, mugu ..	Nose.
Kaṇṇu ...	Kaṇṇ ..	Kaṇṇu ..	Eye.
Báyi ...	Bāi ..	Bāi ..	Mouth.

*Em, yemma is used when the person spoken to is not included ; ám if the person is included. The same is the case with yengla and angla in Badaga.

English.	Tamil.	Malayalum.	Telugu.
Tooth ...	Pal ...	Palla ...	Pal-lu ...
Ear ...	Ká-thu ...	Cheni ...	Che-vi ...
Hair ...	Ma-yir ...	Rômam, talanârā ...	Ven-tru-ka ...
Head ...	Tha-lai ...	Tala ...	Tha-la ...
Tongue ...	Nák-ku ...	Nâva ...	Ná-lu-ka ...
Belly ...	Va-yi-ru ...	Vayaṟa ...	Ka-du-pu ...
Back ..	Mu-thu-gu ...	Mudhuga ...	Ví-pu ...
Iron ...	I-rum-bu ...	Irumba ...	I-nu-mu ...
Gold ...	Pon ...	Swarnam, pon ...	Ban-gá-ru ...
Silver ...	Vel-li ...	Velli ...	Ven-di ...
Father ...	Tha-gap-pan ...	Achchan ...	Than-dri ...
Mother ...	Tháy ...	Amma ...	Thal-ḷi ...
Brother ...	Sa-gó-tha-ran ...	Udapirannavan ...	Sa-hó-tha-ru-du ...
Elder brother ...	......	......	......
Younger brother ...	......	......	......
Sister ...	Sa-gó-tha-ri ...	Udapirannaval ...	Sa-ho-tha-ri ...
Elder sister ...	......	......	......
Younger sister ...	......	......	......
Man ...	Ma-ni-than ...	Manushyan-ân ...	Ma-ni-shi ...
Woman ..	Stri ...	Stri, pen ...	Stri ...
Wife ...	Pen-dát-ti ...	Chârya-keṭṭiyval ...	Pen-dlá-mu ...
Child ...	Ku-lan-dai ...	Kutti, kidâwa ...	Bid-da ...
Son ..	Ma-gan ...	Magan ...	Ko-má-ru-du ...
Daughter ...	Ma-gal ...	Magal ...	Ko-már-the ...
Slave ..	A-di-mai ...	Aiḍma ...	Bá-ni-se ...
Cultivator ...	Pa-yir-i-du-ki-ra-van ...	Krishi-khâran ...	Vya-va-sá-ya-mu-ché-yu-vá-du.
Shepherd ...	I-dai-yan ...	Aṭṭukâran ...	Gol-la-vá-du ...
God ...	Ka-da-vul ...	Deivam ...	Thé-vu-du ...
Devil ...	Pi-sá-su ...	Pishâcha ...	Pi-sá-cha-mu ...
Sun ...	Sú-ri-yan ...	Sûryan ...	Sur-yu-du ...
Moon ...	San-thi-ran ...	Chandran ...	Chan-thru-du ...
Star ...	Nat-chath-thi-ram ...	Nakshatram ...	Nat-cha-thra-mu ...
Fire ...	Ne-rup-pu ...	Tî ...	Nip-pu ...
Water ...	Thaṇ-ṇír ...	Vellam ...	Níl-lu ...
House ...	Ví-du ...	Vîda ...	Il-lu ...
European house ...	......	......	......
Horse ...	Ku-thi-rai ...	Kudhira ...	Gur-ra-mu ...
Cow ...	Pa-su ...	Pashu ...	Á-vu ...

of Southern India.—(Continued.)

Canarese.	Toda (Neilgherries.)	Badaga (Neilgherries.)	English.
Hallu ...	Parzh ...	Hallu ...	Tooth.
Kivi ...	Kev ...	Kivi ...	Ear.
Kúdulu ...	Mir ...	Kudalu, meiru ...	Hair.
Tale ...	Madd ...	Mande, tale ...	Head.
Nálige ...	Nāv ...	Nalange ...	Tongue.
Hotte ...	Bir ...	Hoṭṭe ...	Belly.
Bennu ...	Uf ...	Bennu ...	Back.
Kabbiṇa ...	Kabban ...	Kabbuṇa ...	Iron.
Chinna (or) Honnu ...	Chinna ...	Chinna ...	Gold.
Belli ...	Bilti ...	Belli ...	Silver.
Tan-de ...	Enin ...	Appa, tande ...	Father.
Táyi ...	Av ...	Ave, tai ...	Mother.
Sahódara ...	......	......	Brother.
......	Enon etud ...	Aṇṇa ...	Elder brother.
......	Enon kinnud ...	Tamma ...	Younger brother.
Sahódiri ...	......	......	Sister.
......	Akka ...	Akka ...	Elder sister.
......	Enorvet kukh ...	Tange ...	Younger sister.
Manushya ...	Āl ...	Ālu ...	Man.
Hengasu ...	Kukh ...	Heṇṇu ...	Woman.
Hendati ...	Kaṭṭvodi kukh ...	Heṇḍaru ...	Wife.
Magu (or) Kúsu ...	Popan ...	Kusu ...	Child.
Maganu ...	Makh, kin makh ...	Maga ...	Son.
Magalu ...	Tüj makh ...	Magalu ...	Daughter.
Dasa (or) Gulám ...	......	......	Slave.
Ságuvalidára (or) Sédyagára.	Vokali khan ...	Vokaliga ...	Cultivator.
Kuruba ...	Āḍu kāran ...	Āḍukāra ...	Shepherd.
Dévaru ...	Dér ...	Devaru ...	God.
Pisáchi (or) Bhúta ...	Etud put (great Devil) ...	Pishachi ...	Devil.
Surya ...	Birzh ...	Hattu ...	Sun.
Chandra ...	Tiggal ...	Tingalu ...	Moon.
Nakshatra (or) Chuk-ke.	Min ...	Minu, nakisatra ...	Star.
Benki ...	Diḍd, nerp ...	Penki, kichchu nerpu ...	Fire.
Níru ...	Nir ...	Niru ...	Water.
Mane ...	Ārzh ...	Āle ...	House.
......	Koat (fortress) ...	Bangale ...	European house.
Kudure ...	Kadare ...	Kudure ...	Horse.
Góvu (or) Hasa (or) Akalu	Danam ...	Dana ...	Cow.

English.	Tamil.	Malayalum.	Telugu.
Dog ...	Náy ...	Nây ...	Kuk-ka ...
Cat ...	Pú-nai ...	Pûcha ...	Pil-li ...
Cock ...	Sé-vał ...	Pûvankkorhi ...	Pun-ju ...
Duck ...	Vath-thu ...	Târâva ...	Bá-thu ...
Ass ...	Ka-lu-thai ...	Kanhudha ...	Gá-di-the ...
Camel ...	Vot-tai ...	Oṭṭagam ...	Von-te ...
Bird ...	Pat-chi ...	Pakshi ...	Pat-chi ...
Go ...	Pó ...	Pôga ...	Pó ...
Eat ...	Sáp-pi-du ...	Tinnuga ...	Thi-nu ...
Sit ...	Vut-ká-ru ...	Irikkuga ...	Kúr-chó ...
Come ...	Vá ...	Varuga ...	Rá ...
Beat ...	A-di ...	Adikkuga ...	Kot-tu ...
Stand ...	Nil-lu ...	Nilkkuga ...	Ni-lu-vu ...
Die ...	Sá-vu ...	Châvuga ...	Chá-vu ...
Give ...	Ko-du ...	Kodukka, taruga ...	Yiy-yi ...
Run ...	O'-du ...	Oduga ...	Pa-ru-geth-thu ...
Up ...	Mé-lé ...	Mîdhe ...	Pai-na ...
Down ...	Kí-lé ...	Tâzhê ...	Kin-tha ...
Before ...	Mun-né ...	Munbe ...	Mun-thu ...
Near ...	Kit-ta ...	Adukkê ...	Thag-gi-ra ...
Far ...	Thú-ram ...	Agalê ...	Thú-ra-mu ...
Behind ...	Pin-né ...	Pinbe ...	Ve-nu-ka ...
Who ...	Ar ...	Ara ...	Ye-va-ru ...
What ...	En-na ...	Endha ...	Yé-mi ...
Why ...	Én ...	Endhakoṇḍa ...	Yé-la ...
And ...	Vum ...	Um-um ...	Nnu ...
But ...	A'-nál ...	Engil, ennâl ...	A-yi-thé ...
If ...	A'l ...	Engil ...	Thè (or) Pat-cha-man-thu
Yes ...	A'm ...	Adhê uvva ...	A-vu-nu ...
No ...	Il-lai, (or) Al-la ...	Illa, alla ...	Lé-thu (or) ká-thu ...
Alas ...	Ai-yó ...	Kashtam, ayyo ...	Ay-yó ...
A father ...	Tha-gap-pan ...	Achchan ...	Than-dri ...
Two fathers ...	I-ran-du Tha-gap-pa-nar	......	Ith-tha-ru Than-dru-lu ...
Father's ...	Tha-gap-pan-már ...	Achchanmâr ...	Than-dru-lu ...
Of a father ...	Tha-gap-pa-nu-dai-ya ...	Achchandê ...	Than-dri-yok-ka ...
Of fathers ...	Tha-gap-pan-má-ru-dai-ya	Achchanmârudê ...	Than-dru-la-yok-ka ...
To a father ...	Tha-gap-pa-nuk-ku ...	Achchanna ...	Than-dri-ki ...
To fathers ...	Tha-gap-pan-má-ruk-ku...	Achchanmârkka ...	Than-dru-la-ku ...
From a father ...	Tha-gap-pa-ni-li-run-thu	Achchanilninna ...	Than-dri-nun-chi ...

Canarese.	Toda (Neilgherries.)	Badoga (Neilgherries.)	English.
Náyi ...	Nāi ..	Nai ..	Dog.
Bek-ku ...	Kotti ..	Kotti ..	Cat.
Hunja ...	Huja ..	Hunja, huva ..	Cock.
Báthu ...	Bāt ..	Sime batu ..	Duck.
Katte ...	Klatte ..	Klatte ..	Ass.
Onṭe ...	Voṭṭe ..	Voṭṭe ..	Camel.
Pakshi (or) Hakki ...	Belṭ ..	Hakkilu ..	Bird.
Hogu ...	Atfo, Atpo ..	Hogu, po ..	Go.
Unnu ...	Tinn ..	Tinnu ..	Eat.
Kútu-kollu ..	Neshkir ..	Kuli ..	Sit.
Bá ...	'tva, itvā ..	Ba ..	Come.
Hodi ...	Pui ..	Hui ..	Beat.
Nillu ...	Nellu ..	Nillu ..	Stand.
Sá-yu ...	Keṭṭ fo ..	Keṭṭ hogu ..	Die.
Kodu ...	Tā, koḍu ..	Ta, ko ḍu ..	Give.
O'du ...	Voḍu ..	Voḍu ..	Run.
Méle ...	Mok ..	Mele ..	Up.
Kelige ...	Erg, nerzhg ..	Kelage, klia ..	Down.
Munde ...	Muddk, muchche ..	Munde, Munche ..	Before.
Hattara (or) Samipa ...	Kekhuri ..	Sāre, vottura ..	Near.
Dúra ...	Batkhi ..	Dura ..	Far.
Hinde ...	Pindalk ..	Hinde ..	Behind.
Yáru ...	Ario ..	Yāru ..	Who.
Énu ...	......	......	What.
Yatakké ...	Et? ..	Yéka ..	Why.
Mattu ...	U affixed to the foregoing noun.	U ..	And.
Ádare ...	Āle ..	Āle ..	But.
Re (affix) ...	Ārzh or narzh ..	Re (annexed to the verb)	If.
Houdu ...	Ha ..	Haudu ..	Yes.
Illa ...	A ..	Illa ..	No.
Ayyó ...	Āh! ..	Āyo! ..	Alas.
Tan-de ...	Enin ..	Tande ..	A father.
Ibbaru tan-de-ga-lu ...	......	......	Two fathers.
Tan-de-ga-lu ...	......	Tandeglo ..	Fathers.
Tandeya ...	Enin ..	Tandea ..	Of a father.
Tandegala ...	......	......	Of fathers.
Tandege ...	Ening ..	Tandega ..	To a father.
Tandegalige ...	......	......	To fathers.
Tandeyinda ...	Eninedd ..	Tandeinda ..	From a father.

English.	Tamil.	Malayalum.	Telugu.
From fathers ...	Tha-gap-pan-má-ri-li-run thu.	Achchanmârilninna ...	Thun-dru-la-nun-chi ...
A daughter ...	Ku-má-rath-thi ...	Magal ...	Ko-már-the ...
Two daughters ...	I-ran-du ku-má-rath-thi-gal.	......	Ith-tha-ru ko-már-the-lu
Daughters ...	Ku-má-rath-thi-gal ...	Magalugal ...	Ko-már-the-lu ...
Of a daughter ...	Ku-má-rath-thi-yi-nu-dai-ya.	Magaludê ...	Ko-már-the yok-ka ...
Of daughters ...	Ku-má-rath-thi-ga-lu-dai-ya.	Magalugaludê ...	Ko-már-the-la yok-ka ...
To a daughter ...	Ku-má-rath-thik-ku ...	Magalkka ...	Ko-már-the-ku ...
To daughters ...	Ku-má-rath-thi-ga-luk-ku	Magalugalkka ...	Ko-már-the-la-ku ...
From a daughter ...	Ku-má-rath-thi yi-li-run thu.	Magalilninna ...	Ko-már-the nun-chi ...
From daughters ...	Ku-má-rath-thi-ga-li-li-run-thu.	Magalugalilninna ...	Ko-már-the-la nun-chi ...
A good man ...	Nal-la ma-ni-than ...	Nalla manushyan ...	Man-chi ma-ni-shi ...
Two good men ...	I-ran-du nal-la ma-ni-thar-gal.	......	Ith-tha-ru man-chi ma-nush-yu-lu.
Good men ...	Nal-la ma-ni-thar-gal ...	Nalla manushyar ...	Man-chi ma-nush-yu-lu...
Of a good man ...	Nal-la ma-ni-tha-nu-dai-ya.	Nalla manushyandê ...	Man-chi ma-ni-shi yok-ka
Of good men ...	Nal-la ma-ni-thar-ga-lu-dai-ya.	Nalla manushyaruḍê ...	Man-chi ma-nush-yu-la yok-ka.
To a good man ...	Nal-la ma-ni-tha-nuk-ku	Nalla manushyanna ...	Man-chi ma-ni-shi-ki ...
To good men ...	Nal-la ma-ni-thar-ga-luk-ku.	Nalla manushyarkka ...	Man-chi ma-nush-yu-la-ku.
From a good man ...	Nal-la ma-ni-tha-ni-li-run-du.	Nalla manushanilninna...	Man-chi ma-ni-shi nun-chi.
From good men ...	Nal-la ma-ni-thar-ga-li-li-run-du.	Nalla manushyarilninna	Man-chi ma-nush-yu-la nun-chi.
A good woman ...	Nal-la stri ...	Nalla strî ...	Man-chi stri ...
Good women ...	Nal-la stri-gal ...	Nalla strîgal ...	Man-chi stri-lu ...
A bad boy ...	Ket-ta pai-yan ...	Chîttha kutti ...	Ched-da pil-la-ká-ya ...
A bad girl ...	Ket-ta pen ...	Chîttha peṇ-kuṭṭi ...	Ched-da pil-la ...
Good ...	Nal-la ...	Nalla ...	Man-chi ...
Better ...	A-thi-ka nal-la ...	(*a*)	Mik-ki-li man-chi ...
Best ...	Ma-há nal-la ...	......	Ma-há man-chi ...
High ...	Vu-yarn-tha ...	Uyarnna ...	Po-du-gai-na ...
Higher ...	A-thi-ka vu-yarn-tha ...	......	Mik-ki-li po-du-gai-na ...
Highest ...	Ma-há vu-yarn-tha ...	......	Ma-há po-du-gai-na ...
A horse ...	Ku-thi-rai ...	An-kudhira ...	Gur-ra-mu ...
A mare ...	Pet-tai ku-thi-rai ...	Peṇ-kudhira ...	Á-da gur-ra-mu ...

(*a*.) There is no comparative and superlative in Malayalum. "This is *better* than that" is expressed by, "If you look at that this is good."

of Southern India.—(Continued.)

Canarese.	Toda (Neilgherries.)	Badaga (Neilgherries.)	English.
Tandegalinda ...	......	......	From fathers.
Magalu (or) Kumárte ...	Kukh, tüj makh ...	Heṇṇu, magalu ..	A daughter.
Ibbaru kumártegalu ...	......	......	Two daughters.
Kumártegalu ...	......	Heṇṇu makkalu ..	Daughters.
Kumárteya ...	......	......	Of a daughter.
Kumártegala ...	......	......	Of daughters.
Kumártege ...	......	......	To a daughter.
Kumártegalige ...	......	......	To daughters.
Kumárteyinda ..	......	......	From a daughter.
Kumártegalinda ...	......	......	From daughters.
Obba ollé manushyanu ...	Ulle āl ...	Volle āl ..	A good man.
Ibbaru olle manushyaru.	......	......	Two good men.
Ollé manushyaru ...	The same as in the singular.	Volle āluglo ..	Good men.
Ollé manushyana ...	......	......	Of a good man.
Ollé manushyara ...	......	......	Of good men.
Ollé manushyanige ...	......	......	To a good man.
Ollé manushyarige ...	......	......	To good men.
Ollé manushyaninda ...	......	......	From a good man.
Ollé manushyarinda ...	......	......	From good men.
Ollé strí (or) Hengasu ...	Ulle kukh ...	Volle heṇṇu ..	A good woman.
Ollé strīyaru (or) Hengasaru.	As in the singular ...	Volle heṇgla ..	Good women.
Ketta huduga ...	Holāivi makh ...	Keṭṭa huḍuga ..	A bad boy.
Ketta hudugi ...	Holāivi kukh ...	Keṭṭa heṇṇu ..	A bad girl.
Ollé ...	Ulle ...	Aduninda volle ..	Good.
Adakinta ollé ...	Adunedd ulle ...	Adumuda volle ..	Better.
Ellakinta ollé ...	Ellaedd ulle ...	Yellainda volle ..	Best.
Yettara ...	Nila ...	Udda ..	High.
Adakinta yettara ...	......	......	Higher.
Ellakinta yettera ...	......	......	Highest.
Kudure ...	Kadare ...	Ganḍu kudure ..	A horse.
Heṇṇu kudure ...	Caret ...	Hêṇṇu kudure ..	A mare.

English.	Tamil.	Malayalum.	Telugu.
Horses ...	Ku-thi-rai-gal ...	An-ku-dhiragal ...	Gur-ra-mu-lu ...
Mares ...	Pet-tai ku-thi-rai-gal ...	Peṇ-kudhiragal ...	Á-da-gur-ra-mu-lu ...
A bull ...	Ri-sha-bam ...	Kâla ...	Vru-sha-bha-mu ...
A cow ...	Pa-su ...	Pashu ...	Á-vu ...
Bulls ...	Ri-sha-ban-gal ...	Kâlagal ...	Vru-sha-bha-mu-lu ...
Cows ...	Pa-suk-kal ...	Pashukkal ...	Á-vu-lu ...
A dog ...	Náy ...	Nây ...	Kuk-ka ...
A bitch ...	Pet-tai náy ...	Paṭṭi ...	Á-da kuk-ka ...
Dogs ...	Náy-gal ...	Nâykkal ...	Kuk-ka-lu ...
Bitches ...	Pet-tai náy-gal ...	Paṭṭigal ...	Á-da kuk-ka-lu ...
A buffalo ...	......	......	......
Male buffalo ...	......	......	......
A he-goat ...	Áṇ vel-lá-du ...	An-âḍa ...	Mé-ka pó-thu ...
A female goat ...	Peṇ vel-lá-du ...	Penn-âḍa ...	Á-da mé-ka ...
Goats ...	Vel-lá-du-gal ...	Aḍugal ...	Mé-ka-lu ...
A male deer ...	Áṇ mán ...	An-mân ...	Mo-ga jin-ka ...
A female deer ...	Peṇ mán ...	Pen-mán ...	Á-da-jin-ka ...
Deer ...	Mán-gal ...	Mângal ...	Jin-ka-lu ...
I am ...	Nán I-ruk-ki-rén ...	Nyân âgunnu ...	Né-nu-vun-ná-nu ...
Thou art ...	Ní I-ruk-ki-ṛáy ...	Nî „ ...	Ní-vu vun-ná-vu ...
He is ...	A-van I-ruk-ki-ṛán ...	Avan „ ...	Vá-du vun-ná-du ...
We are ...	Nán-gal I-ruk-ki-ṛóm ...	Nyanugal „ ...	Mé-mu vun-ná-mu ...
You are ...	Nín-gal I-ruk-ki-ṛír-gal...	Ninggal „ ...	Mí-ru vun-ná-ru ...
They are ...	A var-gal I-ruk-ki-rár-gal	Avar „ ...	Vánd-lu vun-ná-ru ...
I was ...	Nán i-run-thén ...	Nyân âyirnnnu ...	Né-nu vun-ti-ni ...
Thou wast ...	Ní i-run-tháy ...	Nî „ ...	Ní-vu vun-ti-vi ...
He was ...	A-van I-run-thán ...	Avan „ ...	Vá-du vun-de-nu ...
We were ...	Nán-gal I-run-thóm ...	Nyangal „ ...	Mé-mu vun-ti-mi ...
You were ...	Nín-gal I-run-thír-gal ...	Ningal „ ...	Mí-ru vun-ti-ri ...
They were ...	A-var-gal I-run-thár-gal	Avar „ ...	Vánd-lu vun-di-ri ...
Be ...	I-ru ...	Aguga ...	Vun-du ...
To be ...	I-ruk-ka ...	Aguwân ...	Vun-da ...
Being ...	I-ruth-thal ...	(*)	Vun-du-ta ...
Having been ...	I-run-thu ...	......	Vun-di ...
I may be ...	Nán I-ruk-ka-lám ...	......	Né-nu vun-da-vach-chu-nu
I shall be ...	Nán I-rup-pen ...	......	Né-nu vun-thu-nu ...
I should be ...	Nán I-ruk-ka-vé-ṇum ...	......	Né-nu vun-da-va-la-si-na-thi ...
Beat ...	A-di ...	Aḍikkuga ...	Kot-tu ...

* Context is required—"*being* afraid"; "this *being* the case"; "my *being* present"; "the state of *being*," &c., all require to be rendered differently.

Canarese.	Toda (Neilgherries.)	Badaga (Neilgherries.)	English.
Kuduregalu ...	......	......	Horses.
Heṇṇu kuduregalu ...	......	......	Mares.
Gúli ...	Danam ...	Hori ...	A bull.
Hasa (or) Ákalu ...	Hori ...	Dana ...	A cow.
Gúligalu ...	......	......	Bulls.
Hasagalu ...	......	......	Cows.
Náyi ...	Caret ...	Nāi ...	A dog.
Hṇṇeu náyi ...	Nāi ...	Heṅṇu nāi ...	A bitch.
Náyigalu ...	......	......	Dogs.
Hṇṇeu náyigalu ...	......	......	Bitches.
......	Er ...	Yemme ...	A buffalo.
......	Esht ...	Kona ...	Male buffalo.
Hóta ...	......	......	A he-goat.
Méké ...	......	......	A female goat.
Hótagalu ...	......	......	Goats.
Gandu hulle (or) Jinke	......	......	A male deer.
Heṇṇu hulle ...	......	......	A female deer.
Hullegalu (or) Jinkegalu.	......	......	Deer.
Id-dhéne ...	Ān erzhkeni ...	Nā iddene ...	I am.
Id-dhí ...	Ni erzhchi ...	Ni iddare ...	Thou art.
Id-dháne ...	Adum erzhchi ...	Ava iddane ...	He is.
Id-dhéve ...	Ām (ém) erzhkemi ...	Yengla iddeneo ...	We are.
Id-dhíri ...	Niv erzhchi ...	Ningla iddāri ...	You are.
Id-dháre ...	Adum erzhchi ...	Avaka iddāra ...	They are.
Id-denu ...	Ān erzhpini ...	Nā idde ...	I was.
Id-di ...	Ni erzhchi ...	Ni iddi ...	Thou wast.
Id-danu ...	Adum erzhchi ...	Ava idda ...	He was.
Id-devu ...	Ām erzhkemi ...	Yengla iddeo ...	We were.
Id-diri ...	Nív erzhchi ...	Ningla iddi ...	You were.
Id-daru ...	Adum erzhchi ...	Avaka iddaru ...	They were.
Iru ...	Eru ...	Iru ...	Be.
Ira (or) Iralikke ...	Era ...	Ira ...	To be.
Iruvike (or) Iróṇa ...	Erzhaivi ...	Iruva ...	Being.
Iddu ...	Eddu ...	Iddu ...	Having been.
Nánu ira bahudu ...	Caret ...	Nā ira bahudu ...	I may be.
Iruvenu ...	Caret (*a*) ...	......	I shall be.
Nánu iratakkadu ...	Caret ...	Caret ...	I should be.
Hodi (or) Badi ...	Pui ...	Hui ...	Beat.

(*a*.) There is neither in Toda nor in Badaga a future tense; they use the present tense for it with adverbs of time. The Badagas have the 2nd person singular futures, which they use for the 2nd person singular and plural in a strong imperative sense.

English.	Tamil.	Malayalum.	Telugu.
To beat ...	A-dik-ka ...	Aḍippân ...	Kot-ta ...
Beating ...	A-dith-thal ...	Adichcha koṇḍirikkunnu	Kot-tu-ta ...
Having beaten ...	A-dith-thu ...	Aḍichchiṭṭa ...	Kot-ti ...
I beat ...	Nán a-dik-ki-ṛen ...	Nyân aḍikkunnu ...	Né-nu kot-tu-thá-nu ...
Thou beatest ...	Ní-a-dik-ki-ṛáy ...	Nî „ ...	Ní-vu kot-tu-thá-vu ...
He beats ...	A-van a-dik-ki-ṛán ...	Avan „ ...	Vá-du kot-tu-thá-du ...
We beat ...	Nán-gal a-dik-ki-ṛóm ...	Nyangal „ ...	Mé-mu kot-tu-tha-mu ...
You beat ...	Nín-gal a-dik-ki-ṛir-gal...	Ningal „ ...	Mí-ru kot-tu-thá-ru ...
They beat ...	A-var-gal a-dik-ki-ṛár-gal	Avar „ ...	Vá-ru kot-tu-tha-ru ...
I am beating ...	Nán a-dith-thuk-koṇ-di-ruk-ki-réṇ.	Nyân adikkunnuṇḍa ...	Né-nu kot-tu-thun-ná-nu
I was beating ...	Nán a-dith-thuk koṇ-di-run-thén.	Nyân adikkugayâyirunnu	Né-nu kot-tu-thú-un-ti-ni
I had beaten ...	Nán a-dith-thi-run-thén...	Nyân adichchirunnu ...	Né-nu kot-ti-vun-ti-ni ...
I may beat ...	Nán a-dik-ka-lôm ...	Inikka adikkugayum âm	Né-nu kot-ta vach-chu-nu
I shall beat ...	Nán a-dip-pén ...	Nyân adikkum ...	Né-nu kot-tu-thu-nu ...
I should beat ...	Nán a-dik-ka-vét-ṇum ...	Nyân adikkêndadhâṇa ...	Né-nu kot-ta-va-la-si-na-thi.
I am beaten ...	Nán a-dik-ka-pa-du-ki-ṛen.	Nyân adikkappeḍunnu ...	Né-nu kot-ta-ba-du-thá-nu
I was beaten ...	Nán a-dik-ka-pat-tén ...	Nyân adikkappeṭṭu ...	Né-nu kot-ta-ba-di-thi-ni
I shall be beaten ...	Nán a-dik-ka-pa-du-vén	Nyân adikkappedum ...	Né-nu kot-ta-ba-du-thu-nu
I go ...	Nán pógi-ṛén ...	Nyân pôgunnu ...	Né-nu pó-thá-nu ...
Thou goest ...	Ní pógi-ráy ...	Nî „ ...	Ní-vu pó-thá-vu ...
He goes ...	A-van pó-gi-ṛán ...	Avan „ ...	Vá-du pó-tha-du ...
We go ...	......	......	......
You go ...	......	......	......
They go ...	......	......	......
I went ...	Nán pó-nén ...	Nyân pôyi ...	Né-nu pó-thi-ni ...
Thou wentest ...	Ní po-náy ...	Nî „ ...	Ní-vu pó-thi-vi ...
He went ...	A-van pó-nán ...	Avan „ ...	Vá-du pó-yi-ná-du ...
We went ...	......	......	......
You went ...	......	......	......
They went ...	......	......	......
Go ...	Pó ...	Pô (Imperative.) ...	Pó ...
Going ...	Pó-thal ...	Pôgunnuṇḍa-pôyikondi-rikkunnu.	Pó-vu-ta ...
Gone ...	Póy ...	Pôyippôyi ...	Pó-yi ...
What is your name? ...	Vun pe-yar en-na? ...	Nindê pêr endha ...	Ní pé-ru yé-mi?
How old is this horse? ...	In-tha ku-thi-raik-ku eth-tha-nai va-ya-su?	I kudhirêkka etra vayass-âyi.	I gur-rá-ni-ki va-ya-su-en-tha?

Canarese.	Toda (Neilgherries.)	Badaga (Neilgherries.)	English.
Hodilikke ...	Puiya, puiya ...	Huiya ..	To beat.
Hodiyuvike ...	Puiyāivi ...	Huiyuva ..	Beating.
Hoḍidu ...	Puidu ...	Huidu ..	Having beaten.
Hoḍiyutténe ...	Puikeni ...	Huidene ..	I beat.
Hoḍiyuttí ...	Puichi ...	Huidare ..	Thou beatest.
Hoḍiyuttáne ...	Puichi ...	Huidana ..	He beats.
Hoḍiyuttéve ...	Puikemi ...	Huideneo ..	We beat.
Hoḍiyuttíri ...	Puichi ...	Huidāri ..	You beat.
Hoḍiyut-táre ...	Puichi ...	Huidāra ..	They beat.
Hoḍiyut-tid-dhéne ...	......	......	I am beating.
Hoḍiyut-tid-denu ...	......	......	I was beating.
Hoḍidu-id-denu ...	......	......	I had beaten.
Nánu hoḍiya bahudu ...	Caret ...	Nā huiya bahudu ..	I may beat.
Hoḍiyuvenu ...	......	......	I shall beat.
Nánu hoḍiyatakkadu ...	......	......	I should beat.
Hoḍiyal paḍutténe ...	Caret ...	......	I am beaten.
Hoḍiyal-paṭṭenu ...	......	......	I was beaten.
Hoḍiyal-paḍuvenu ...	......	......	I shall be beaten.
Hógut-téne ...	Ān pokeni* ...	Nā hone ..	I go.
Hóguttí ...	Poki ...	Ni hore ..	Thou goest.
Hóguttáne ...	Poki ...	Ava hona ..	He goes.
......	Pokemi ...	Yengla honeo ..	We go.
......	Poki ...	Ningla hādāri ..	You go.
......	Poki ...	Avaka hādāra ..	They go.
Hódenu ...	Poki fichpini ...	Avaka hode ..	I went.
Hóde (or) Hódi ...	Poki fichi ...	Avaka hodi ..	Thou wentest.
Hódanu ...	Poki fichi ...	Avaka hoda ..	He went.
......	Poki fichpimi ...	Avaka hodeo ..	We went.
......	Poki fichi ...	Avaka hodi ..	You went.
......	Poki fichi ...	Avaka hodaru ..	They went.
Hógu ...	Atfo ...	Hogu ..	Go.
Hógutta ...	Poaivi ...	Hoguva ..	Going.
Hógi ...	Poi ...	Hogi ..	Gone.
Ninna hesaru énu ...	Ninn per exna ?	Ninna hesaru yenu ..	What is your name?
I kuduregе yeshtu varusha	I kadareg yett kvār udi.	I kuduregа yeja varija ātu	How old is this horse?

* This verb is irregular in Toda and Badaga.

English.	Tamil.	Malayalum.	Telugu.
How far is it from here to Kashmir?	Iv - vi - dath - thirk - kum-Kash-mi-rath-thirk-kum ev-va-la-vu thu-ram?	Ividê-ninna Kashmîr-illêk-ka etra dûram uṇḍa.	Ik-ka-di-ki Kásh-mi-ra-mu en-tha thú-ra-mu?
How many sons are there in your father's house?	Vun-nu-dai-ya tha-gap-pa-nar vít-til eth-tha-nai ku-má-rar-gal i-ruk-ki-ṛár-gal?	Nindê achchandê vîttil etra ân-makkal uṇḍa.	Ní than-dri intló en-tha-ru ko-mál-lu vun-ná-ru?
I have walked a long way to-day.	In-draik-ku ne-dun-thú-ram na-dan-thén.	Nyân inna adhigam vazhi nadannirikkunnu ("dh" aspirate).	Né-du ba-hu thú-ra-mu na-di-chi-ná-nu.
The son of my uncle is married to her sister.	En-nu-dai-ya má-man ma-gan a-va-lu-dai-ya than-gai-yai vi-vá-gam sey-thu-koṇ-dán.	Endê ammâmandê magan avaludê udalpirannavale kalyânam kazhichchirik-kunnu.	Ná má-ma ko-má-ru-du thá-ni sa-hó-tha-ri-ni pen-dlá-de-nu.
In the house is the saddle of the white horse.	Vít-ti-lé vel-lai ku-thi-rai sé-ṇam i-ruk-kị-ṛa-thu.	Vella kudhirayudê jîni vîttil uṇḍa.	Int-ló thel-la gur-ra-pu jí-ni vun-na-thi.
Put the saddle upon his back.	A-thin mél sé-ṇath-thai-kat-tu.	Jîniye avandê-puṛattha iḍuga.	Thá-ni mí-tha jí-ni-ni kat-tu.
I have beaten his son with many stripes.	A-va-nu-dai-ya ma-gan-nai a-né-ga a-di a-dith-thén.	Nyân avandê magane valare adi aḍicchirik-kunnu.	Vá-ni ko-du-ku-nu chá-lá theb-ba-lu kot-ti-ná-nu.
He is grazing cattle on the top of the hill.	Ma-lai vuch-chi-yil a-van má-du - meyth - thu-koṇ-di-ruk-ki-ṛan.	Kunnindê mugalil avan kannagale mêyikkunnu.	Kon-da mé-tha pa-su-vu-lu mé-pu-thun-ná-du.
He is sitting on a horse under that tree.	A-van ku-thi-rai-mél vut-kán-thu-koṇ-du an-tha-ma-rath-thin kél i-ruk-ki-ṛan.	A maratthindê chumaṭṭil avan oru kudhira puṛat-tha irikkunnu.	Vá-du á chet-tu-kin-tha gur-ra-mu mí-tha kúr-chun-di vun-ná-du.
His brother is taller than his sister.	A-va-nu-dai-ya sa-gó-tha-ran a-va-nu-dai-ya sa-gó-tha-ri-yai vi-da vu-ya-ram.	Avandê sahôdaran avandê pengalêkkâl uyaram-ullavan-âgunnu.	Vá-ni sa-hó-tha-ru-du vá-ni sa-hó-tha-ri kan-té po-du-gu-gá vun-ná-du.
The price of that is two rupees and a half.	A-thin vi-lai i-ran-du-rai-rú-pay.	Adhindê vila raṇḍara uruppiga âgunnu.	Thá-ni kha-rí-thu ren-dun-na-ra rú pá-yi.
My father lives in that small house.	En tha-gap-pa-nár an-tha sin-na vít-til vá-sam-paṇ-ṇu-ki-ràr.	Endê achchan â cheriya vîttil pârkkunnu.	Ná than-dri á chin-na int-ló vá-sa-mu chés-thá-du.
Give this rupee to him ...	A-va-ruk-ku in-tha rú-pá-yai ko-du.	I uruppiga avanna koduk-ka.	I ru-pá-yi-ni a-tha-ni-ki im-mu.
Take those rupees from him.	A-va-ri - dath - thi - li-run-du an-tha ru-páy-ga-lai ván-gik-kol.	I uruppigagate avandê-vakkal ninna edukka.	A-tha-ni-vath-tha-nun-chi á rú pá-yi-la-nu puch-chu-kom-mu.
Beat him well and bind him with ropes.	A-va-nai nan-dráy a-dith-thu ka-yit-rál kat-tu.	Avane nallavaṇṇam aḍich-cha kayaragal-koṇḍu keṭ-ṭuga.	Váṇ-ni bá-gá kot-ti thál-la-thó kat-tu.
Draw water from the well	Ki-ṇat-ri-li-run-thu thaṇ-ṇír sén-thu.	Kinattil-ninna vellam kôra.	Bhá-vi-ló níl-lu ché-thu...
Walk before me ...	E-nak ku mun na-da ..	Endê-munbil nadakka ...	Ná-ku mun-thu na-du-vu
Whose boy comes behind you?	Yá-ru-dai-ya vé-laik-ká-ran vun pin-nál va-ru-ki-ṛán.	Nindê-pinnil varunnadha ârudê chekkan âgunnu.	E-va-ri pa-ni-vá-du ní vem-ba-di vas-thá-du?
From whom did you buy that?	Yá-ri-dath-thi-li-run-thu a-thai ván-gi-náy!	Adhine ni ârudê-vakkal-ninna vilakka vângi.	Thán-ni e-va-ri vath-tha kon-ti-vi?
From a shop-keeper of the village.	Vúr ka-daik-ka-ra-ni-dath thi-lé.	Grâmatthilê oru pîdiga-kâranil-ninna.	Grá-ma an-ga-di-vá-ni-vath-tha.

Canarese.	Toda (Neilgherries.)	Badoga (Neilgherries.)	English.
Illinda Kashmírige yeshṭu dúra.	Ittedd Kashmirg upamai badkhiya.	Illinda Kashmirug a yeja duravo.	How far is it from here to Kashmir?
Nimma tandeya maneyalli yeshtu gandu makkalu iddáre.	Atte nimmenin ārzhulg yett makh udi.	Alli nimma appana maneo yeja makk alu.	How many sons are there in your father's house?
I hottu bahala dúranaḍade	Ini badkhiedd naḍed verzhpini.	Indu durainda naḍedu bande.	I have walked a long way to-day.
Nanna mávana maganu avala sahódiriya magalannu maduve mádi kondanu.	Yenn enin perud makhadun enorvet kukh kaṭṭchi.	Yenna doḍḍappana maga avla heṇṇa kaṭṭiddane.	The son of my uncle is married to her sister.
Bilí kuduréya jínu maneyalli ide.	Bilṭi kadare jin koaṭulg udi.	Billi kudure jinu maneolge unṭu.	In the house is the saddle of the white horse.
Adakke jínu kattu ..	Jin adun uf mok iḍu.	Jiṅu aduna bennuna mele hāku (iḍu).	Put the saddle upon his back.
Avana maganige bahala dabbe hodoale.	Ān adun makh upāmādi puidpini.	Nā avana magana ghaṭṭiagi huidubiṭṭe.	I have beaten his son with many stripes.
Beṭṭada méle danavannu meyisut-tid-dáne.	Diṭṭ mok adum er kāṭchi.	Dittuna mele ava yemme kāṭina.	He is grazing cattle on the top of the hill.
Ámarada kelage kudure méle kútid-dháne.	Adum ā men erk kadare mok ershchi.	Ava ā morada kelage kudure mele kulidana.	He is sitting on a horse under that tree.
Avana sahódaranu avana sahódiriginta uddavágiddáne.	Adun enon tann enor vet kukhedd ni-lamāiudi.	Avana aṇṇa tanna akkainda udda āgiddane.	His brother is taller than his sister.
Adara kraya eradúvare Rúpáyi.	Adun bele eḍ aḍa kās.	Aduna bele yeraḍu are rupei.	The price of that is two rupees and a half.
Áchikka maneyalli nanna tande vása máduttáne.	Yenn enin ā kinnud ārzhulg udi.	Yenna appa ā kunna maneo iddane.	My father lives in that small house.
Avanige í rupáyi kodu ..	I kās aḍug koḍu ..	I rupei avaniga koḍu. . ..	Give this rupee to him.
Árú páyigalanna avaninda tegadukó.	Ākās adunedd yettu ..	Ā rupei avaninda tegi ..	Take those rupees from him.
Avananna chennági hoḍadn huggadinda kaṭṭu.	Adum upāmai puidu haggaedd kaṭu.	Avana channagi huidu haggainda kaṭu.	Beat him well and bind him with ropes.
Bháviyinda níru sédu ..	Pāedd (from the stream) nir yettu.	Hallainda niru yettu ..	Draw water from the well.
Nanna munde naḍi ..	Yenna muddk naḍe ..	Yenna munde naḍe ..	Walk before me.
Nanna hinde yára huḍuga baruttáne.	Āran makh yenn pindalk or boddehya farzhchiya.	Yara maga yenna hinde bannana vo?	Whose boy comes behind you?
Adannu yárinda belege konḍukonḍe?	Āredd adum yett farzhiya (or baddehya?)	Yārinda aduna yetti konḍya.	From whom did you buy that?
Gramada angaḍiyavaninda	Uru aggadi karaedd yett baddpini.	Uruna angadi karaninda konḍu konḍe.	From a shop-keeper of the village.

DIALECTS OF BEHAR.

English.	Vernacular of Patna.	Vernacular of Gya.	Vernacular of Champarun.	Vernacular of West Tirhoot.
Numerals.				
One ..	Ek, ekgo, ektho ...	Ek ...	Ék, égó, éktho ...	Ek ..
Two ..	Do, dogo, dotho ...	Dú ...	Dú, dúgó, dúthó ...	Dú ..
Three ..	Tín, teengo, teentho.	Tín ...	Tín, tíngo, tínthō...	Tín ..
Four ..	Chár, chárgo, chártho.	Chár ...	Chár, gandá, chártho.	Chár ..
Five ..	Pánch, Páūchgo, Pánchtho.	Pánch ...	Pánch, gáhi ...	Pánch ..
Six ..	Chhah, chhago, chhatho.	Chhau ...	Chhau ...	Chau ..
Seven ..	Sát, sátgo, sáttho	Sát ...	Sát ...	Sát ..
Eight ..	A't, átgo, áttho ...	A't ...	A'th ...	A'th ..
Nine ..	Nau, naugo, nautho.	Nau ...	Nau ...	Nau ..
Ten ..	Das, dasgo, dastho	Das ...	Das ...	Das ..
Twenty ..	Bis, bisgo, bistho.	Bis or Kôri ...	Bis, kóri ...	Bis ..
Fifty ..	Pachás, pachásgo, pachástho.	Pachás ...	Pachás ...	Pachás ..
Hundred ..	Sau, saugo, sautho	Sau ...	Sau ...	Sau ..
Pronouns.				
I ..	Ham ...	Ham ...	Ham ...	Ham ..
We ..	Hamne ...	Hamáni ...	Hamni ...	Ham ..
Thou ..	Tou ...	Tou ...	Tún ...	Ten ..
You ..	Tuhne ...	Tohani ...	Tohni ...	Túm ..
He ..	O ...	U ...	U, haú ...	U' ..
They ..	Ohney or wahny	Ukani ...	Uhéisabh ...	U' sab ..
Of me ..	Hammar, hamar more.	Hamar ...	Hanmar ...	Hamar ..
Of us ..	Homrohni kair ...	Hamani ke ...	Hamni ké ...	Hamar ..
Of thee ..	Tore, tohar, tohār	Tore ...	Tohar ...	Tor ..
Of you ..	Tohrohnikaér, toh-lagnikāir.	Tohani ke ...	Tohani ké ...	Tohar ..
Of him ..	Okar ...	Okar ...	Okar, unkar ...	Okar ..
Of them ..	Onkar or wonhoni-tāir.	Ukanhin ke ...	Unhamké, uhén sabh kè.	U'nká ..
Mine ..	Hammar, hamar ...	Hamar ...	Hammar ...	Hamrá ..
Our ..	Hamrohnikáér ...	Hamani ke ...	Hamni ke ...	Hamrá ..
Thine ..	Tere ...	Tore ...	Tóhar ...	Tohar ..
Your ..	Tohar ...	Tohani ke ...	Tohaniké ...	Tobrá ..
His ..	Okar ...	Okar ...	Okar, unkar ...	Unka ..
Their ..	Onkor, or onhini-káir.	Unkanhin ke ...	(The same as "of them.")	U'nká sab ..

Vernacular of East Tirhoot.	Vernacular of West Purneah (Hindee).	Vernacular of East Purneah, (Bengali).	English.
Ek ...	Ek ...	Ek ...	One.
Du ...	Du ...	Dúi ...	Two.
Tín ...	Tín ...	Tín ...	Three.
Chár ...	Chár ...	Chár ...	Four.
Pánch ...	Pánch ...	Pánch ...	Five.
Chhau ...	Cha ...	Cha ...	Six.
Sát ...	Sát ...	Sát ...	Seven.
Áth ...	Áth ...	Áth ...	Eight.
Nau ...	Nau ...	Nau ...	Nine.
Das ...	Das ...	Das ...	Ten.
Bis ...	Bis ...	Bis ...	Twenty.
Pachás ...	Pachás ...	Pachás ...	Fifty.
Sa ...	......	Sáu ...	Hundred.
Ham ...	Hamain ...	Hami ...	I.
Ham ...	Hamralog ...	Hamrá ...	We.
Tou ...	Tohani ...	Túi ...	Thou.
Tousah ...	Tohrarke ...	Tomra ...	You.
Hun, wah ...	Uni ...	Oha ...	He.
Hunka lokani ...	Unsab ...	Ora ...	They.
Hamra ...	Mera ...	Hamar ...	Of me.
Hamrá ...	Hamrasabhoke ...	Hamsar ...	Of us.
Tohar ...	Tohrai ...	Tor ...	Of thee.
Tohrasah ...	Tohrasabke ...	Tomsar ...	Of you.
Hunka ...	Okrake ...	Okar ...	Of him.
Hunka sabhak ...	Hemkasabhooke ...	Usar ...	Of them.
Hamrá ...	Mera ...	Mor ...	Mine.
Hamrá ...	Hamrásabhooke ...	Hamsar ...	Our.
Tohar ...	Tohrarke ...	Tor ...	Thine.
Tohrasah ...	Tohar ...	Túir ...	Your.
Hunka, sah ...	Okar ...	Ohar ...	His.
Hunka sabhak ...	Okarsabhuke ...	Osar ...	Their.

English.	Vernacular of Patna.	Vernacular of Gya.	Vernacular of Champarun.	Vernacular of West Tirhoot.
Hand ..	Hat ...	Hat ...	Hát, kar* ...	Hát ...
Foot ..	Gor ...	Gor ...	Gór, paón, pair ...	Gór ...
Nose ..	Nák ...	Nák ...	Nák ...	Nák ...
Eye ..	Nayan *or* ankh ...	Ankh ...	Ánkh, nayan, netra†	Ankh ...
Mouth ..	Mûh ...	Munh ...	Múnh, múkh ...	Múnh ...
Tooth ..	Dánt ...	Dánt ...	Dánt ...	Dánt ...
Ear ..	Kán ...	Kán ...	Kán ...	Kán ...
Hair ..	Bár, *or* kes ...	Kes ...	Bál, kes, churke ...	Bál, bár ...
Head ..	Murh, *or* kapár ...	Máthá ...	Máth, máthá, múri, kapár.	Máth, múr, sir ...
Tongue ..	Jibh, jeeh ...	Jibh ...	Jibh ...	Jibh ...
Belly ..	Pet, *or* lod ...	Pet ...	Pet ...	Pet ...
Back ..	Pith ...	Pith ...	Pitti ...	Pith ...
Iron ..	Lohá ...	Lohá ...	Lohá ...	Lohá ...
Gold ..	Soná ...	Soná ...	Soná, soharan ...	Soná ...
Silver ..	Chándi, *or* rupa ...	Chándi ...	Cháni, rúpá ...	Chándi ...
Father ..	Bappa, *or* bap ...	Báp (in Nawada sub-division they say dádá.)	Báp, pita ...	Báp ...
Mother ..	Mahtári, *or* mae ...	Mae ...	Mái, já, maiyá, jawá, mahtáre.	Máye ...
Brother ..	Bhayia, *or* bhai ...	Bhái ...	Bhái, sahodar ...	Bhái ...
Sister ..	Bahin *or* bahni ...	Bahin ...	Bahin ...	Bahin ...
Man ..	Admi ...	Admi ...	Admi, marad, manukh.	Marad ...
Woman ..	Mehráru, *or* jenauri.	Mehráru ...	Mehrárú ...	Mehrárú ...
Wife ..	Mahar, kabíla, mehráru, janána.	Maug, joru, *or* bekti (in Nawada sub-division they say "janiouri.")	Jórú, kabilá, gharkélóg, gharni, janáná.	Jorú ...
Child ..	Larika, butru, bachchá.	Bútrú ...	Lariká, nanhká ...	Lariká ...
Son ..	Betá, pût, larika ...	Beta ...	Betá, lariká ...	Betá ...
Daughter ..	Beti, *or* mayewan...	Betí ...	Bèti, larki, dhíá ...	Beti ...
Slave ..	Ponibhar ...	Nafar ...	Ghulám, nafar ‡ ...	Gúlám ...
Cultivator ..	Girhast, kisan, jata,	Kisán ...	Kisán, girhast, khetáetá.	Girhast ...
Shepherd ..	Bhorihar ...	Gauri ...	Charwáh ...	Churwáhá ...
God ..	Parmeshar, *or* bhagwán.	Bhagwán ...	Rám, isar, parméshar, bhajoán.	Bhagwan, purmeshár
Devil ..	Malechh, *or* paret...	Bhút ...	Bhút, páret ...	Bhút ...
Sun ..	Sûraj ...	Suraj ...	Súraj ...	Súraj ...
Moon ..	Chandya, chandrawan.	Chánd ...	Chanarmáú, chánd	Chánd ...
Star ..	Tárágan ...	Táregan ...	Tárá, tarígan, johní	Táregan ...

* Borrowed from Sanscrit. † Borrowed from Sanscrit. ‡ Both borrowed from Persian.

Behar.—(Continued.)

Vernacular of East Tirhoot.	Vernacular of West Purneah (Hindee).	Vernacular of East Purneah (Bengali).	English.
Hát ...	Hát ..	Hát ..	Hand.
Gor ...	Gor ..	Páon ..	Foot.
Nák ...	Nák ..	Nák ..	Nose.
Ankhi ...	Ankh ..	Ankh ..	Eye.
Munh ...	Muh ..	Mukh ..	Mouth.
Dánt ...	Dánt ..	Dánt ..	Tooth.
Kán ...	Kán ..	Kán ..	Ear.
Kes ...	Kesh ..	Chul ..	Hair.
Math ...	Math ..	Matha ..	Head.
Jibh ...	Jiha ..	Jibha ..	Tongue.
Pet ...	Pet ..	Pet ..	Belly.
Pitha ...	Pith ..	Pith ..	Back.
Lohá ..	Loho ..	Lúhá ..	Iron.
Soná ...	Soná ..	Soná ..	Gold.
Rupa ...	Rúpó ..	Rupa ..	Silver.
Bap ...	Bapau ..	Bap ..	Father.
May, matari ...	Maiyo ..	Mái ..	Mother.
Bhái ...	Bhaya ..	Bhai ..	Brother.
Bahin ...	Bahin ..	Bahin ..	Sister.
Marad ...	Manukh ..	Admi ..	Man.
Mehraru ...	Janáná ..	Mágí ..	Woman.
Joru, bekat ...	Kabila, joroo ..	Mág ..	Wife.
Larika ...	Bacha, nunu ..	Betá ..	Child.
Betá ...	Betá ..	Betá ..	Son.
Beti ...	Beti, lerhki ..	Chua ..	Daughter.
Bahia ...	Naphur ..	Gulám ..	Slave.
Girhast ...	Kisán ..	Girhast ..	Cultivator.
Charbáha ...	Churwáha ..	Rakhwál ..	Shepherd.
Parmesar ...	Isar, Bhagwán ..	Khoda ..	God.
Malechh ...	Paret ..	Saitan ..	Devil.
Suraj ...	Suraj ..	Suraj ..	Sun.
Chanarma ...	Chandarmá ..	Chand ..	Moon.
Táregan, Tárá ...	Taringán ..	Tárá ..	Star.

English.	Vernacular of Patna.	Vernacular of Gya.	Vernacular of Champarun.	Vernacular of West Tirhoot.
Fire ..	Aggin ...	Ág ...	Ág, ágin ...	Ág ..
Water ..	Jal ...	Páni ...	Páni, jal ...	Páni ..
House ..	Ghar ...	Ghar ...	Ghar ...	Ghar ..
Horse ..	Ghorá, *or* charwa...	Ghorá ...	Ghórá ...	Ghorá ..
Cow ..	Gow, goru, gya, gai.	Gái ...	Gái ...	Gáye ..
Dog ..	Kutta, *or* kukkur	Kukur, *or* kutta	Kuttá, kúkúr ...	Kúttá ..
Cat ..	Bilai ...	Billi ...	Biláyi ...	Bilái ..
Cock ..	Murga ...	Múrga ...	Múrúgá ...	Múrgá ..
Duck ..	Háns ...	Batak ...	Batak ...	Batak ..
Ass ..	Gadhá ...	Gadhá ...	Gadhá ...	Gadhá ..
Camel ..	Uat ...	Unt ...	Unt ...	U'nt ..
Bird ..	Pakháru, *or* chiryu	Chiryu ...	Chiriyá, pachhi, chiráí.	Chirái ..
Go ..	Ja, *or* já ...	Ja ...	Jáh, jain, ja ...	Jáo ..
Eat ..	Kha, khá, khále ...	Kha ...	Kháh, jenwah, bhojan.	Kháu ..
Sit ..	Bayath ...	Baith ...	Baithah, baithén, baithú.	Baitha ..
Come ..	Ao ...	Ao ...	Áwah, áin, áiljáo ...	Áu ..
Beat ..	Már, pit, dangáo ...	Már pit ...	Mara, marin, pito	Máro ..
Stand ..	Kharáho oh *or* poriho oh.	Khará ho ...	Kharárahe, thárh rahén, tharáhóin.	U'tho ..
Die ..	Marjá, muwa, margái.	Mar ...	Marah, marná, múh	Máro ..
Give ..	Do, *or* de ...	Tha ...	Dah, déná, dén, dénhín.	Deo ..
Run ..	Daur, dowg ...	Daur ...	Daur, daurná ...	Bhágo, *or* daúro ..
Up ..	Upar ...	Upre ...	Upar ...	U'par ..
Near ..	Nagich, *or* bhir ...	Nagich, *or* Bhiri ...	Neari,' negché, lagé, lagle, sataleē.	Bhir ..
Who ..	Kaun, *or* ki ...	Kaun, *or* ke ...	Ke, kasan ...	Kaun ..
And ..	Aur ...	Aúr ...	Aúr, á ...	Aúr ..
Yes ..	Achchhá, bes, bhalái, hán.	Hán ...	Han, hun ...	Haṉ ..
Down ..	Nichai, *or* hāintha	Henthe ...	Niché, nichú, taré	Nichá ..
Far ..	Dur, pallá ..	Dúr, *or* pallá ...	Dúr, tána, baré, tán	Dúr ..
What ..	Ká ...	Ká ...	Ká, kyá ...	Kyá ..
But ..	Magar, ki ...	Mudá ...	Lekin,* magar ...	Magar ..
No ..	Nā, nái, nahi ...	Na ...	Na, nahin ...	Na ..
Before ..	Pahle, *or* áge ...	Agú ...	Pahilí, áge, peshtar	Agá ..
Behind ..	Pichhu, pichhan ...	Pichhú ...	Pichhé páchhe ...	Pichha ..
Why ..	Kahai, *or* kâhai lâg	Káhe ...	Káhé ...	Kahá ..
If ..	Agar, *or* bhala ...	Joun ...	Jóṇ, agar † ...	Agar ..

* Borrowed from Persian. † Persian.

Behar.—(Continued.)

Vernacular of East Tirhoot.	Vernacular of West Purneah (Hindee).	Vernacular of East Purneah (Bengali.)	English.
Ágí ...	Ág ...	Ágin ...	Fire.
Páni ...	Jal ...	Páni ...	Water.
Ghar ...	Girhee ...	Ghar ...	House.
Ghorá ...	Ghorá ...	Ghorá ...	Horse.
Gái ...	Gou ...	Gái ...	Cow.
Kunkur ...	Kukur ...	Kuttá ...	Dog.
Bilái, bilári ...	Bilái ...	Billi ...	Cat.
Ghari ...	Murag ...	Múrgá ...	Cock.
Batak ...	Chinya batak, bat ...	Háns ...	Duck.
Gadaha ...	Gadha ...	Gadhá ...	Ass.
Unt ...	Unt ...	Ot ...	Camel.
Chirái ...	Chirhái ...	Chiriya ...	Bird.
Ja ...	Jáo ...	Já ...	Go.
Kha ...	Jainio ...	Kháo ...	Eat.
Baitha ...	Bais ...	Baith ...	Sit.
Aiba ...	Ao ...	Aei ...	Come.
Mára ...	Márah ...	Máro, Már ...	Beat.
Khiurahoi ...	Thark ...	Khará ...	Stand.
Mara ...	Moral, murl ...	Márei ...	Die.
Da ...	De, diya ...	Deo ...	Give.
Daura ...	Dogal, doral ...	Daur ...	Run.
Upar ...	Upar ...	Upar ...	Up.
Laga ...	Ligich ...	Nagij ...	Near.
Ka ...	Kai, ki ...	Kaié ...	Who.
Aur ...	Aur ...	Aur ...	And.
Bes ...	Hán ...	Hán ...	Yes.
Nicha ...	Nich ...	Nichu ...	Down.
Dur ...	Dur ...	Dúr ...	Far.
Ka ...	Kithik ...	Ki ...	What.
Takhun ...	Matōr ...	Maj ...	But.
Na ...	Nehi ...	Nahi ...	No.
Pahila ...	Agtain ...	Agat ...	Before.
Pachha ...	Pachhu ...	Pichhu ...	Behind.
Kaha ...	Kethelai ...	Kiso ...	Why.
Jakhan ...	Agar ...	Maj ...	If.

English.	Vernacular of Patna.	Vernacular of Gya.	Vernacular of Champarun.	Vernacular of West Tirhoot.
Alas! ..	Apsose ...	Háe ...	Háh, aháha ..	Hái ...
A father ..	Ego bap ...	Ek báp ...	Báp, bapsí ..	Ek báp ...
Two fathers ..	Do bapan ...	Dú báp ...	Dú báp, dú bapsí ..	Dú báp ...
Fathers ..	Bapan ...	Báp sab ...	Báplog ..	Báb sab ...
Of a father ..	Ego bápkaér ...	Ek báp ké ...	Bápké ..	Ek báp ká ...
Of fathers ..	Bápan kaér ...	Báb sab ke ...	Bápanké ..	Báp sáb ká ...
To a father ..	Ek báp kane ...	Ek báp ke ...	Egó báp sé ..	Ek báp ko ...
To fathers ..	Bapan ke ...	Báb sab ke ...	Báp log, *or* bápan sé	Báp sab ko ...
From a father ..	Ek báp sa ...	Ek báp ke ...	Báp kéhán sé, bap sé	Ek báp se ...
From fathers ..	Bápan se ...	Báp sab ke ...	Bápan sé ..	Báp sab se ...
A daughter ..	Chhokri, beti, kanyá, chhonri.	Ek beti ...	Ek larkì, ego chhonúri, ego chhokri, nauhké.	Ek beti ...
Two daughters ..	Do beti ...	Dú beti ...	Dugo bitiá, dugo chhaunrí.	Dú beti ...
Daughters ..	Chhokrain, betin ...	Beti sab ...	Chanuṛi sa ..	Beti sab ...
Of a daughter ..	Ek Betián ker ...	Ek beti ke ...	Chhaunṛí ké ..	Ek beti ka ...
Of daughters ..	Betián ker ...	Betí sab ke ...	Chhanṛiuḥ ké ..	Beti sab ká ...
To a daughter ..	Ek beti ke ...	Ek betí ko ...	Chhaunṛi ké ..	Ek beti ko ...
To daughters ..	Betian ka ...	Beti sab ko ...	Chhaunṛi ké ..	Beti sab ko ...
From a daughter ..	Ek beti se ...	Ek beti sa ...	Chhaunṛí ka, *or* sé	Ek beti se ...
From daughters ..	Betián se ...	Beti sab se ...	Chhaunṛhú ká, *or* sé	Beti sab se ...
A good man ..	Ek bhalá ádmi ...	Ek bés ádmi (the word "murad" is also used for ádmi).	Ek bhal manus, *or* ego bhala ádmí, ego néman admí.	Ek achhá ádmi ...
Of a good man ..	Ek bhala admi ker	......	Bhalá admi ké ..	Ek achha ádmiká ...
Of good men ..	Bhala ádmi ker ...	......	Bhala ádmín ké ..	Achhá ádmi sab ...
Two good men ..	Do bhala ádmi ...	Du bes ádmin ...	Dú bhalá ádmi, dú néman ádmi.	Dú achha ádmi ...
Good men ..	Bhala ádmi sab ...	Bes ádmin ...	Bhalá manus, néman ádmí.	Achha ádmi sab ká ...
To a good man ..	Ek bhala ádmi ka...	Ek bes ádmin ke ...	Ek bhalá ádmí ké..	Ek achha ádmiko ...
To good men ..	Bhala ádmi ke ...	Bes ádmi ko ...	Bhala ádmin ké ..	Achha ádmi sab ko ...
From a good man..	Ek bhala admi se	Ek bes ádmi se ...	Bhala ádmi sé ..	Ek achho ádmi se ...
From good men ..	Bhala ádmi se ...	Bes ádmi se ...	Bhala ádmín sé ..	Achhá ádmi sab se ...
A good woman ..	Ek achchha mehraru.	Ek bes mehárú ...	Ek achha mehrarú, néman mehrárú, bhalí manús.	Ek niman mehrárú ...
Good women ..	Bhala mehraru sab.	Bes merúrún ...	Achha mehrárú bhalí manus.	Nemun mehrarú sub
A bad boy ..	Ek joban larka ...	Ek dingár lariká ...	Kharáb* lariká, challi lariká barúá, laríká	Ek nikamá lariká ...
A bad girl ..	Ek joban chakri ...	Ek dingar chhokri	Kharáb larki, kharáb chhaunṛi.	Ek nikummi lariki ...

* Borrowed.

Behar.—(Continued.)

Vernacular of East Tirhoot.	Vernacular of West Purneah (Hindee).	Vernacular of East Purneah (Bengali).	English.
Há ...	Haye ...	Oe ...	Alas!
Ek bap ...	Ek bap ...	Bap ...	A father.
Du go báp ...	Do bap ...	Bapgala ...	Two fathers.
Bápsab ...	Bápsabhok ...	Bápe saber ...	Fathers.
Ek bápak ...	Bápok ...	Baper ...	Of a father.
Unaaek bapak ...	Sab bápok ...	Bap saber ...	Of fathers.
Bápkane ...	Bápek log ...	Bápke ...	To a father.
Bápak, báp sabka hai ...	Báp sabhok log ...	Báp sabke ...	To fathers.
Ek bápse ...	Ek pápse ...	Bápase ...	From a father.
Báp sabse ...	Báb sabse ...	Bap sabse ...	From fathers.
Ek beti ...	Ek beti ...	Chua ...	A daughter.
Du go beti ...	Duithor beti ...	Dui larki ...	Two daughters.
Beti sab ...	Lerkisab ...	Chuar ...	Daughters.
Ek beti ke ...	Lerkik ...	Chuar ...	Of a daughter.
Sab beti ke ...	Lerki sabke ...	Chua sabke ...	Of daughters.
Ek beti kane ...	Beti log ...	Larkiko ...	To a daughter.
Sab beti kane ...	Sab beti log ...	Larki sabbki ...	To daughters.
Ek beti se ...	Ek beti se ...	Chua se ...	From a daughter.
Sab beti se ...	Beti sabse ...	Chua sabse ...	From daughters.
Ek nek loge ...	Ek nek ádmi ...	Bhala ádmi ...	A good man.
Ek nek loguk ...	Nek ádmike ...	Nek ádmike ...	Of a good man.
Nek loge sab. ...	Achha ádmi saber. ...	Bhala manuser ...	Of good men.
Dunik loge ...	Duigot nek ádmi ...	Dui acha ádmi ...	Two good men.
Nek lognik ...	Sablog nek ...	Bhala manus ...	Good men.
Ek nek logeka ...	Ek achha ádmi ke ...	Nik ádmi lag ...	To a good man.
Nek lognika ...	Achha sab ádmi ke ...	Bhala manús ke lag ...	To good men.
Ek nek loge sa ...	Ek nek ádmi se ...	Bhala ádmi se, bhala manús se.	From a good man.
Nek lognisa ...	Achha ádmi sabse. ...	Nek ádmi sabse, bhala mánus se.	From good men.
Ek nek mehraru, *or* mag ...	Ek nik maugi ...	Ek bhala maugi ...	A good woman.
Nek mehraru sab, *or* mag sab.	Nik maugi sab ...	Achha maugi sab ...	Good women.
Ek adhlah larika ...	Adlaha beta ...	Bedhang beta ...	A bad boy.
Ek adhlah lariki ...	Ek adlahi beti ...	Ekta bedhang beti ...	A bad girl.

English.	Vernacular of Patna.	Vernacular of Gya.	Vernacular of Champarun.	Vernacular of West Tirhoot.
Good ..	Bhal, or bhala ..	Bes, Bhalá, Niman, suthar.	Nik, achha, bésho*	Acha, nimun ...
Better ..	Nuinan bhala, nek, achchhá.	To express comparative degree the word "Okra se" is prefixed before the positive degree.	Achha, nek, besh*	Nimun se nimun ...
Best ..	Bhalsa bhal, or nek sa nek.	To express superlative degree the word "sab se" is prefixed before the positive degree.	Ditto* ..	Sab se nimun ...
High ..	Unch, or dhewo ..	Unch ..	Uṇch ..	U'nchá ...
Higher ..	Bor oonch ..	This is expressed by prefixing "okra se"	Ditto† ..	U'nchá se únchá ...
Highest ..	Burgo oonch, or dher oonch.	This is expressed by prefixing "sab se' se"	Ditto† ..	Sub se únchá ...
A horse ..	Ego charwá ..	Ek ghorá ..	Ghoṛá ..	Ek ghorá ...
A mare ..	Ekgo tatooani, or ghori.	Ek ghori ..	Ghorí ..	Ek ghori, ...
Horses ..	Dher ghorá, or charwá.	Ghorwán ..	Ghoṛá, ghorán ..	Ghorá sab ...
Mares ..	Dher ghori ..	Ghorián ..	Ghoṛí ..	Ghori sab ...
A bull ..	Ego sanr ..	Saṇdh, byl, barad..	Sáṇdh ..	Ek sánrh ...
A cow ..	Ekgo goru, or gau, or gái.	Gái ..	Gái, asar, gaú ..	Ek gáye ...
Bulls ..	Dher sanr ..	Sab sándh, *or* sab-báil, *or* sab-barud.	Sándh ..	Sánrh sab ...
Cows ..	Dher goru ..	Gayán ..	Gái sabh, gáe-lag, gáu sabh, gáiyán.	G ye sab ...
A dog ..	Ego kukur, or kutta.	Kutta, or kukur ..	Kutta, kúkur ..	Ek kúttá ...
A bitch ..	Ego kutti ..	Ek kutti ..	Kutti, pílli ..	Ek kutti ...
Dogs ..	Dhair kookoor, koottaw sab.	Kutwon ..	Kutwá sabh ..	Kúttá sub ...
Bitches ...	Dher kutti ..	Kuttyan ..	Kuttiá ..	Kutti sab ...
A he-goat ..	Ego patru, *or* khassi.	Ek khasi, *or* botu..	Khasi, chhir ..	Ek bakrá ...
A she-goat ..	Ego bakri, or chheri	Bakri, or páthi ..	Bakri ..	Ek bakrai ...
Goats ..	Dhair bakri, or patthi, or chheri.	Bakaryan ..	Pathrú ..	Bakrá sab ...
Female goats ..	......	......	......	Bukri sub ...
A male deer ..	Ego harná ..	Ek harná ..	Harna ..	Ek harin ...
A female deer ..	Ego harni ..	Ek harni ..	Harni ..	Ek harni ...
Deer ..	Harin ..	Harin ..	Harin ..	Harin sab ...
I am ..	Ham hi ..	Ham hi ..	Ham háni, ham haín	Ham hain ...
We are ..	Hamrahni, or hamni he.	Hamani hi ..	Hamniháni ..	Hamni hain ...
Thou art ..	Tou hay ..	Tún hán ..	Túnhára, raúáṇ hain	Tú ha ...

* There is no distinction of Degree. † No distinction of Degree.

Behar.—(Continued.)

Vernacular of East Tirhoot.	Vernacular of West Purneah. (Hindee.)	Vernacular of East Purneah, (Bengallee.)	English.
Nek, *or* bes ...	Nek ..	Achhá ...	Good.
Nekose nek ...	Bhalaso bhala ..	Bhalaso bhala ...	Better.
Tahu san nek ...	Maha nek ..	Sabse acha ...	Best.
Unch ...	Unch ..	Unch ...	High.
Ohuse unch ...	Osse unch ..	Osse unch ...	Higher.
Sab sau unch ...	Sabse unch ..	Sabse unch ...	Highest
Ek ghora ...	Ek ghora ..	Ghora ...	A horse.
Ek ghori ...	Ek ghori, Bachari ..	Ghori, Bacheri ...	A mare.
Ghorá sab ...	Ghorá sab ..	Ghorala ...	Horses.
Ghori sab ...	Ghori sab ..	Ghorila ...	Mares.
Ek sán ...	Ek shár, dhakur ..	Ako, áriá ...	A bull.
Ek gai ...	Ek gai ..	Ekta gái ...	A cow.
Sándh sab ...	Dhakur sab ..	Akooah ...	Bulls.
Gái sab ...	Gái sab ..	Gáila ...	Cows.
Ek kukur ...	Ek kuttá ..	Ekta kuttá ...	A dog.
Ek kutti ...	Ek kutti, ek pilli ..	Ekti kuti, ekti pilli ...	A bitch.
Kukur sab ...	Kuta sab ..	Kutala ...	Dogs.
Kutti sab ...	Kutti sab ..	Kutila ...	Bitches.
Ek khassi ...	Ek batu, ek pátha ..	Bakra, patha ...	A he-goat.
Ek bakri ...	Ek bakri ..	Bakri ...	A she-goat.
......	Bakra sab ..	Bakrala ...	Goats.
Bukri sab ...	......	......	Female goats.
Ek harin ...	Ek harná ..	Ekta narharin ...	A male deer.
Ek harini ...	Ek harni ..	Madi harin ...	A female deer.
Harin sab ...	Harna, harni ..	Harná, hárni ...	Deer.
Ham chhi ...	Hama che ..	Hamichi ...	I am.
Ham sab chi ...	Hamralok chi ..	Ohá che ...	We are.
Ton chhah ...	Tuhe cho ..	Tuhichis ...	Thou art.

English.	Vernacular of Patna.	Vernacular of Gya.	Vernacular of Champarun.	Vernacular of West Tirhoot.
You are ..	Tou sab hay ...	Tuhani ha ..	Tohniháralı ...	Tohni hu ...
He is ..	O hi ...	U′ hye ..	U há, uhán ráharen	U′ hai ...
They are ..	Osab hat ...	Akani hath ..	Unhani háré ...	U′ sub huth ...
I was ..	Hom rohi, hom hali, hom haloon...	Ham hali ..	Ham rahlin, ham rahén.	Ham rahin ...
Thou wast ..	Toiu holin ...	Tun halen ..	Tún rala ...	Toú rahe ...
He was ..	O hal ...	U halye ..	U rahí ...	U′ rahe ...
We were ..	Hom rohni holi, ham sab holi.	Hamani halún ..	Hamni háne, hamun ráhani.	Humin rohin ...
You were ..	Tohrohini hola ...	Tohani hala ..	Tohni hára ...	Tohin rohin ...
They were ..	O sab holau ...	U′kani halan ..	U sabh rahas ...	U′ sub rahath ...
Be ..	Hay, ho, oh ...	Hô ..	Raha ...	Hay ...
To be ..	Hoye ki ...	Howyá ..	Rahna ...	Hona hoet ...
Being ..	Hoet ...	Howyte ..	(No equivalent except when applied to other sentences.)	Hogah ...
Having been ..	Hoka ...	Hokur, *or* bhelápur	Ditto ...	......
I may be ..	Hom hooye ...	Hamhun hoti ..	Ham rahah ...	Ham hosakila ...
I shall be ..	Hom hoeb ...	Hamhun hoeb ..	Ham rahah ...	Ham hoyah ...
I should be ..	Hom hoeb ...	Hamrá howéke cháhi	Hamra rahá ké chahín.	Hameá hoye ke cháhi
Beat ..	Mara ...	Pit. The word 'már' is also used for "pit."	Máró, pitú ...	Mará ...
To beat ..	Danga wangay, maroin, peta gain.	Pite ke ..	Marna ...	Márna ...
Beating ..	Mar ...	Pityte ..	Már ...	Mareit hea ...
Having beaten ..	Mar ka ...	Pit ke ..	Marké ...	Marke ...
I beat ..	Ham mara hay ...	Ham pita hi ..	Ham márili ...	Ham marit hain ...
Thou beatest ..	Tain mara hain ...	Tún pita hahin ..	Tún márila ...	Tú marait ha ...
He beats ..	O maroihay ...	U pita hye ..	U márilá	U′ marit hath ...
We beat ..	Ham rohni marahy	Hamhani pitahi ..	Hamni marilí ...	Hamni marit hain ...
You beat ..	To sab mara hain...	Tuhani pitu hahak	Túhni márilá ...	Tou marit há ...
They beat ..	Oon kohni, or o sab marahat.	Ukani pita huth ..	U marilí ...	U′ subh marit huth ...
I am beating ..	Ham marrohli hay	Hum pityt hi ..	Ham márathani ...	Ham mareit hai ...
I was beating ..	Hom mara holi, hom mar rohli hol.	Hum pita hali ..	Ham marati rahin	Ham marti rahin ...
I had beaten ..	Hom marli hol ...	Ham pitalial hul ..	Ham márlí rahin ...	Ham marli rahi ...
I may beat ..	Hom maray ...	Ham pitun ..	Ham márín ...	Ham marho ...
I shall beat ..	Ham marah, hom marbo.	Ham pitbye ..	Ham márah ...	Ham marah ...
I should beat ..	Hom mara-kay chahli hol.	Hamrá pita ki cháhi.	Hamrá márná chá-hfn.	Humra mareke chahin
I am beaten ..	Ham mar khaili haye, ham pitoyli haye.	Ham pital jahi ..	Ham márkhailin ...	Ham maral gali ...

Behar.—(Continued.)

Vernacular of East Tirhoot.	Vernacular of West Purneah, (Hindee.)	Vernacular of East Purneah, (Bengallee.)	English.
Auban chhi	Toharah sab	Tora chis	You are.
Ubhathi	Uchot	Ohai ché	He is.
U sab chhathi	Usab che	Ora ché	They are.
Ham chhalahun	Hama chi	Hami chinu	I was.
Tou chhale	Tuha chala	Toe chilo	Thou wast.
U chhal	Uchála há	Oe chula	He was.
Ham sabh chhalown	Tora lok chala	Tora chile	We were.
Tou sab chhalah	Hamra sub chelo	Hamra chinu	You were.
U sab chhalah	U sab chalo	Ura chilo	They were.
Ho	Hóae	Bhelah che	Be.
Hohaka	Hóáto	Hamatane	To be.
Hoit santa	Hóá chae	Háche	Being.
......	Bhaelche	Habár tane	Having been.
Ham hou	Hama sakub	Hamipari	I may be.
Ham hoeb	Ham hohib	Hámi hámu	I shall be.
Hamra hamab chahi	Ham hoek jog che	Hámi habo sakhe	I should be.
Mara	Már	Mara	Beat.
Marwa	Marba kurtai	Marbartane	To beat.
Marait santa, marik	Marlok che	Máre che	Beating
......	Marló	Markhate	Having beaten.
Ham-marai chhi	Ham marul	Hami marnu	I beat.
Tou marait chhai	Tu márló	Toh mari chis	Thou beatest.
U maraitany	U marlok	Oha mári chis	He beats.
Hamsabh maraichhi	Hamra subhu marul	Hamra marnu	We beat.
Ahan maraitchhiyik	Tohara sub marulcho	Tora mari chis	You beat.
U sub marat chathin	U sub marna che	Ora máriche	They beat.
Hamarait chhiyik	Hamra marlok	Hami marechi	I am beating.
Hammarait chhalon	Hamra marna chelo	Hami marichinu	I was beating.
Hammarait chhataik	Ham marul chul	Hami maria chinu	I had beaten.
Sait-ham-marban	Ham mara saka chi	Hami marbar pari	I may beat.
Ham-marah	Ham marub	Hami mármu	I shall beat.
Hamra marak chahi	Ham mara chi	Hámi marmu	I should beat.
Ham maral gelahun	Ham mar khail chi	Hami mar kha chi	I am beaten.

English.	Vernacular of Patna.	Vernacular of Gya.	Vernacular of Champarun.	Vernacular of West Tirhoot.
I was beaten ..	Hom mar khaili hol	Ham pital geli hal	Ham márkhailí rahin	Ham maral gil rahin
I shall be beaten ..	Hom mar khaeh ..	Ham pital jaeb ..	Ham már khaib ...	Ham maral jayah ...
I go ..	Hom jahi ..	Ham jahi ..	Ham jaib, ham jaín	Ham jáet he ...
Thou goest ..	Tom ja hoy ..	Tun já hain ..	Tún gála ...	Tou jait hu ...
He goes ..	O jahay ..	U jáhye ..	U jála ...	U′ jait hath ...
I went ..	Hom goyli hol ..	Ham geli ..	Hamgail rahín ...	Ham gali ...
Thou wentest ..	Tom gaylay hol ..	Tun gēlēn ..	Tún gail raha ...	Tou gelá ...
He went ..	O gail hol ..	U gelye ..	U gaelé ...	U′ gale ...
Go ..	Jo, ja ..	Jo, *or* chal ..	Jáh ...	Já ...
Going ..	Jagi ..	Jaitē ..	Jáná, ját ...	Jati bir ...
Gone ..	Gail ..	Chal gēlye ..	Gaílé, chal gaile ...	Gel ...
What is your name?	Tohor noo ka ho ..	Tohar ka nawn hon	Tohar nám ka ha, raur nám ka how.	Tohar náwn ká hai ...
How old is this horse?	Ye ghora koy boch-char ka ho.	Katek din ke i ghorwa hye.	I' ghorá ketna din ke hái.	E ghorá katek din ki hai.
How far is it from here to Kashmir?	Ej goon say *or* yaha-say Kashmeri katok dur hay.	Hián sē Kasmir kute dúr hai.	Ihán le Kashmir ketná (*or* keték) dur hátí.	Ehánse Kusmir ketek dúr haik.
How many sons are there in your father's house?	Tohra bap ka ghar mao katok beta hotho.	Turá báp kē ghar kai beta hathu.	Tohrá báp ká ghár mén kae lariká háṛé.	Tohrá bap ke ghar men kai larika haú.
I have walked a long way to-day.	Hom aj dhair door phiral hyn.	Ham áj bari dúr la phirli hē.	Aj ham bahut phirlin (*or* ghumhíṇ) hán.	Ham áj buhút phirli
The son of my uncle is married to his sister.	Homra chacha ka betáka upna bohin sa beahal gylhye.	Hamar chacherá bhai okar bahin se béahal haye.	Hamrá chachá kè betá okrá (*or* unhká) bahin sé biahal bá.	Hamar chacherá bhai okrá bahin se behal hai.
In the house is the saddle of the white horse.	Ujjar ghoraka khogir ghar mai hye.	Ujarká ghorwa ke khogiry a ú gharwa men hye.	Ghar mén, ejarká ghorá ké tang ("tekeg" borrowed) háté.	Ujar ghorá ke tang torha ghar men hai.
Put the saddle upon his back.	Khogirya okra phit pa dadahuk.	Okra pith par khogir kas.	Tangakrápith pár rákhah.	Tang okrá pith pur rakha.
I have beaten his son with many stripes.	Hom okra beta ka bahut marli hay.	Ham okar betá ke korá se bari mar marli hai.	Ham okrá betá ke kaṅk béṇt sé marlíhán.	Ham okrá betá ke korá se márli hai.
He is grazing cattle on the top of the hill.	Ooh pâhar or parbat ka upar gohair chara rohal hay.	U apan gáe gôrú páhárwá par charawa hye.	U mál jál pahár ká mathani par charawat háte (*or* ha).	U pahár pur gorú churwait hai.
He is sitting on a horse under that tree.	Oh ghora par pair tolay boithal hay.	U ghôrá par charhol rukh tare hye.	U gharápar charhal gachh ká níché há (*or* háṛí).	U′ ho pair tar ghorá per charhul hai.
His brother is taller than his sister.	Okra bhaye okra bahinsa bohut achcha lomba haik.	Okar bhái okar bahinise lamhar hye.	Okár bhái okrábahin sé lamhá (*or* lamhar) há.	Okar bhai okrá bahin se lama hai.
The price of that is two rupees and a half.	Okar mole aṛahi rupayea haik.	Okar dam arhái rupyá hye.	Okar dám arhái rupaiyá how (*or* dú rupaiya ego adhéli haw).	Oker dám arhái rupyáh hai.

Behar.—(Continued.)

Vernacular of East Tirhoot.	Vernacular of West Purneah, (Hindee.)	Vernacular of East Purneah, (Bengallee.)	English.
Ham maral gelchhalahun	Hamra marlok chol ...	Hami mar khaya chinu ...	I was beaten.
Ham maral jayali ...	Hamra marut ...	Hami mar khaba pie ...	I shall be beaten.
Hamjait chhi ...	Ham jaw ...	Hami jamu ...	I go.
Tojait cha ...	Túha já ...	Tui jie chis ...	Thou goest.
Ojaitahi ...	O'ho jak ...	Oha jache ...	He goes.
Hamgelahun ...	Ham gael che ..	Hami ganu ...	I went.
Tou gelai ...	Tuhé gaelchu ...	Tuh gela ...	Thou wentest.
O gel ...	O'hó gael ...	Ohae gel ...	He went.
Jah ...	Jo ...	Ja ...	Go.
Jait sauta ...	Jáe che ..	Jáche ...	Going.
Bhagel ...	Gael ...	Gael ...	Gone.
Tohar nam ki chhan, *or* aihauk ki nao ach.	Tuhur namki ...	Tornám ki ...	What is your name?
Ye churlea katek dinak ahi	Eau ghoraka katna umur	Eh ghóra kitna din ka chike.	How old is this horse?
Etai se Kasmir katek duri chhan.	E thamsa Kashmir katna dur che.	Ehán se Kashmir keta dur che.	How far is it from here to Kashmere.
Aihauk bapak gharmen katek larika ahi.	Tuhara bapuk ghurme katna larika chohu.	Keta beta chuah tor bapar ghorut.	How many sons are there in your father's house?
Ai-ham bahut ghumlahún	Aj ham bohut durtuk bululche.	Aj hami bahutdur berailgel chilo.	I have walked a long way to-day.
Hamar piti-auta-bhaik biah okra bahin sau chhaik.	Hamar chacha beta se okur bahin se beha bhel che.	Hamar chachar beta sé ohar bahin se beha bhol-chi.	The son of my uncle is married to her sister.
Ujur ghoraka tung turha ghur me achi.	Ghorma ugra ghoruker jin awcho.	Gharme ujra ghoraka char juma jin che.	In the house is the saddle of the white horse.
Ghorak tang tarhara okra pithpar rakha.	Okur pitpur jin dhuro ...	Ojin ohar pitath rakh ...	Put the saddle upon his back.
Ham okra chhawarik ka kora sau marlon.	Ham ókur betake korase bahoot marul chi.	Hami óhar beta ke kora nia bahut maria chi.	I have beaten his son with many stripes.
U paharah math parwal sab charbaiy achi.	Paharuk upore okar gai churao che.	U paharer upore gow charai che.	He is grazing cattle on the top of the hill.
......	U' gachoktor ghorapur baithul che.	Ohai úgachértale ghorar par battia chi.	He is sitting on a horse under that tree.
Okar bhay okra bahin sau bar chhaik.	Okur bhay awpun bahin se uch che.	O'har bhay apnar bahinsé uchachi.	His brother is taller than his sister.
Okar dam arhai rupaia chhaik.	O'kur dam araie rupaiea ...	Ohár dám araie taka ...	The price of that is two rupees and a half.

English.	Vernacular of Patna.	Vernacular of Gya.	Vernacular of Champarun.	Vernacular of West Tirhoot.
My father lives in that small house.	Homar bap chote ka ghar mai rohahay.	Hamar báp ú chhotka gharwá men raha hath.	Hamar báp hohi chhotka ghar mén rahílé.	Hamar báp ohi chhotka ghur me rahai huth.
Give these rupees to him.	Yeh rupea oonka dohun.	Í rupya okrá dēdē	Í rupayá unhká ké dah.	E rúpayá okra dedá...
Take those rupees from him.	Ooh rupeah onka sa lay loh.	U′ sob rupyá okrá sēlēlē.	Haú rupaewá unká se lelah.	U rúpya okra se lelá
Beat him well and bind him with ropes.	Mara okra achi tarah our russee sa bandh.	Okrá khúb már áúr jour sē bándh.	Okráké khub* mar á rassi sé bandh dé.	Okra bari már mára, aur rassi se bandho
Draw water from the well.	Kooyeau sa pani bhoroh.	Kuyán sē páni bhar.	Inará sé pani bhar	Indrá se páni bharo ..
Walk before me ...	Phiroh homra sojeh.	Hamrá se ágú chal yá búl.	Hamrá sójbá chal...	Hamrá sámnā phiro...
Whose boy comes behind you?	Kokar larka tohra pecha aoho.	Kēkar bútrú tora páchhu lagal áwa hon.	Tohrá pichhú kekar lariká áwat há.	Tohrá pichhá kakar lariká ahait hai.
From whom did you buy that?	Kekra saetun o mole lala hay.	U′ kekra sē ton mole lele hain.	Haú kékrá sé kinla háwé.	U′ tún kekra se mole lela hai.
From a shop-keeper of the village.	Gawa ka ekgo dukan dar *or* dukan wala sa.	Gáwn ke ek dokandár sē.	Egó gáon ka banian sé.	Gáwn ke banyáh se ...

Behar.—(Continued.)

Vernacular of East Tirhoot.	Vernacular of West Purneah, (Hindee.)	Vernacular of East Purneah, (Bengallee.)	English.
Hamar bap chhotka ghormen rahaichhathi.	Hamar bap u choto ghorme rahaie ché.	Morbap ú choto gharat ché	My father lives in that small house.
Yi rupiaïa unka daha ..	E taka okra dahuk ..	É taka ohak däo ...	Give this rupee to him.
O rupaia okra sau laleya..	E sub rupaian okrase lábo	É sub taka ohá sé lau ...	Take those rupees from him.
Okra khub maraho aur rassa men banhdaha.	Okra rasi se badhike khoob mare marhuk.	O'hak rasita bandiar khup mare mar.	Beat him well and bind him with rope.
Inar sau páni bharah ..	U' kuawse pani bhur ..	U' kuansepani bhur ...	Draw water from the well.
Hamra agu chalah ..	Chul hamar awgoo ..	Hamaragu chul ...	Walk before me.
Tora pachhu kekur larika, *or* chhowra awai chhaik.	Kakur beta tuhur pichu awbeh chó.	Kahar beta tor pachu asache.	Whose boy comes behind you?
Okra ton kekra sau mol lelahai.	U' too kakra la kinul chehi	Tui ú kahar lági kinlo ...	From whom did you buy that?
Ehi dahatak ek dokandar sau.	U' gawo ker dokani se ..	U'gair dokani sé ...	From a shop-keeper of the village.

ABORIGINAL LANGUAGES

OF

WESTERN BENGAL.

(Kalarian type)

English.	Sonthalee of Sonthal Pergunnahs.	Sonthalee of Midnapore.	Sonthalee of Bancoorah.	Sonthalee of Maunbhoom.
Numerals.				
One ..	Mit' ..	Mit ...	Mid ...	Mi ..
Two ..	Bārea ..	Bāreā ...	Bariya ...	Bareya ..
Three ..	Péa ..	Pe'ā ...	Péia ...	Peya ..
Four ..	Pnéa ..	Poneā ...	Pănia ...	Poneya ..
Five ..	Moṛé . ..	Mane' ...	Moré (gatáng) ...	Moṛe ..
Six ..	Turui ..	Turui ...	Turui (do) ...	Turui ..
Seven ..	Eae ..	Ai ...	Eyai ...	Eyáe ..
Eight ..	Irāl ..	E-rāl ...	Iral ...	Irál ..
Nine ..	Āré ..	Āré ...	re ...	Are ..
Ten ..	Gel ..	Gale ...	Gel ...	Gel ..
Twenty ..	Mit'-isi ..	Isi, bārgale ...	Bārgel ...	Mi isi ..
Thirty ..	....	....	Pé-gel ...	....
Forty ..	....	....	Tăn-găl ...	....
Fifty ..	Bar-isi-gél ..	Bār-isi-gale, mané'-gale, yālā sai.	Moré-gel ...	Baresi gel ..
Hundred ..	Moṛe-isi ..	Sai, manéisi, gale-gale.	Moré-ishí ...	Mi sai ..
Pronouns.				
I ..	In ..	Ing ...	I ...	Ing ..
We ..	A-le-a-bon, a-b ..	Āli, āb, āban ...	Āle ...	Ale or aban ..
Thou ..	Am ..	Ām ...	I-i ...	Am ..
You ..	A-pe ..	Apé ...	Āpé ...	Ape ..
He ..	Ach' (ai:) ..	Uni, ini, nui, huni, hāṅi nāi, ni.	Uni-ena ...	Uni ..
They ..	A-ko ..	Unko, onko, néko, énko, hānko, nāko, āko, noko.	Unko ...	Unko ..
Of me ..	In-ren, or' *reak'..	Ingréā, ingā, ingrén ingréni, ingi.	I-ya ...	Ingya ..
Of us ..	Ale-ren, or rea ..	Ālreā, āléā, ālriāng, ālrén, āléi.	Ale-ya ...	Aleya ..
Our ..	Ta-le ..	Ditto ditto ...	....	Aleya ..
Of thee ..	Am-ren, or reak'..	Āmréā, āmāh, āmré-ni, āmrén.	Āmā ...	Ama ..
Thine ..	....	Ditto ditto ...	....	Ama ..
Of you ..	Ape-ren, or rea ..	Āpiréā, āpéāh, āpéré āng, āpérén āpéréni, āpéi.	Āpeā ...	Apeya ..
Your ..	Ta-pe ..	Ditto ditto ...	....	Apeya ..
Of him ..	Ach'-ren, or reak'..	Uniréā, uniā, uni-rén, unirôni, unie.	Unia ...	Uniya ..
His ..	Ta-e ..	Ditto ditto ...	....	Uniya ..

Bhumij of Maunbhoom.	Kol or Kor of Singbhoom.	Juangs of Orissa Jungles.	English.
Moyon	Miad	Mi, mui	One.
Bariyá	Bár-eá	Ambar	Two.
Apiya	Á-piá	Sgota	Three.
Uponiya	Upuniá	Gudami	Four.
Moreyá	Moyá	......	Five.
Turiya	Tur-iá	......	Six.
Aiya	Iyá	......	Seven.
Iráliya	Irliá	......	Eight.
Areya	Á-vá	......	Nine.
Geleya	Gel	......	Ten.
Mo hisi	His-sí	......	Twenty.
......	......	......	Thirty.
......	......	......	Forty.
Barhisi geleya	Bár-his-sí-gel	......	Fifty.
More hisi	Mi-sa	......	Hundred.
Ing	Ingoráing	Aing, ain	I.
Ale	Ál-le	Ainje	We.
Am	Ám	Am	Thou.
Ape	Áp-pe	Apaú, Hain	You.
Ini	Ái or áyo	Ain	He.
Ako	Áko	Sadaîside-kira	They.
Ingya	Ingá or áingná	......	Of me.
Aleya	Álle-á	......	Of us.
Aleyá	Álleá	......	Our.
Ama	Ám-á	......	Of thee.
Ama	Ám-ā	Hiasíbsa, Ara	Thine.
Apeya	Áp-pe-á	......	Of you.
Apeya	Áp-peá	......	Your.
Aiaga	Ái-á	......	Of him.
Aiaga	Ini or ní	Ai, Ara	His.

English.	Sonthalee of Sonthal Pergunnahs.	Sonthalee of Midnapore.	Sonthalee of Bancoorah.	Sonthalee of Maunbhoom.
Of them	Ako-ren, or reak'	Unkôréā, unkôā unkôe, unkôréni.	Ankoa	Unkuya
Their	Ta-ko	Ditto ditto	....	Unkuya
Mine	Tin	....	....	Ingya
Thy	Ta-m	....	....	....
Hand	Ti	Ti	Ti	Ti
Foot	Jaṅga	Jāng, kātā	Jānga	Subti
Nose	Mu	Mu	Niyădā-mu	Muh
Eye	Met'	Mét	Me	Men
Mouth	Mocha	Machā	Neocha	Mocha
Tooth	Data	Data	Data	Data
Ear	Lutur	Lutur	Lotur	Lutur
Hair	Up'	Up	Up	Up
Head	Boho	Baha	Boho	Boho
Tongue	Alaṅ	Ālāng	Alang	Alang
Belly	Lach'	Laie	Lai	Laie
Back	Dea	Déā	Déhā	Deyá
Iron	Meṛhet'	Mínéhén	Mehiri	Meṛheṇ
Gold	Sona	Shanā	Sonai	Samanum
Silver	Rupa	Rupā	Rupa	Rupa
Father	Apa, baba	Bāba, āpā, bā	Bāhā	Apuing' um, át
Mother	Eṅga, ayo	Ekhā āio	Aio	Aiyo, eṅgat
Brother	Boiha, bokot	Bak, baiha, dādā	Rokain	Boiha
Sister	Mis-cra	Misérā, dāie, ājing	Misrai	Miseraing, ám, at
Man	Herel	Lar, mauti	Herél	Hoṛ
Woman	Maejiu	Maiju, āimai	Ai-mai	Kuri
Wife	Era, aimai	Bāhu, érā	Ara-gumke	Bahu
Child	Gidra	Gidrā, lidi letka, gedrāng, hapan.	Gidra	Gidra
Son	Koṛa-hopon	Kôrāhapan, han, kāré	Hapani	Hopon
Daughter	Koṛi-hopon	Hapanérā, kurigidrā kurihapan.	Hapanerāi	Hoponera
Slave	Guti	Kabaj	Kirienkadiai	Guti
Cultivator	Siok'-ich'	Chāshi	Chaskānay	Ariyat
Shepherd	Gupi	Verigoopie, māhārā	Merome gupakana	Chirigupi
God, a god	Thakur, boṅga	Singbakhia, thakur, chāndôbakhia, isar.	Sing-bungā	Siṅg boṅga
Devil	Maraṅ-buru	Mārābuk, lita, bāiri	Bhut	Boṅga
Sun	Ber-sin-chando	Singchāndô, bérā	Sing-bunga	Siṅg chando
Moon	(Ninda) chando	Indā chāndô	Chando-bunga	Chando
Star	Ipil	Ipil	I-pil	Ipil
Fire	Seṅgel	Shékél, rutni	Singal	Singel

of Western Bengal.—(Continued.)

Bhumij of Maunbhoom.	Kol or Kor of Singbhoom.	Juangs of Orissa Jungles.	English.
Akoya ..	Áko-á ..	......	Of them.
Akoya ..	En-koá ..	......	Their.
Ingya ..	Ingá ..	Ainja ..	Mine.
......	......	......	Thy.
Ti ..	Tí ..	Etiri, Alakti ..	Hand.
Talka ..	Ká-tá ..	Alag-ging, ipúg ..	Foot.
Muh ..	Mú-tá ..	Matai ..	Nose.
Men ..	Met ..	Emade, emar ..	Eye.
Mocha ..	A ..	Mukare, masare ..	Mouth.
Dáta ..	Dán-tá ..	Gani ..	Tooth.
Lutur ..	Lútúr ..	Sutude, sutur ..	Ear.
Up ..	Up ..	Inuta ..	Hair.
Bo ..	Bo ..	Bokan ..	Head.
Alang ..	Áláng ..	......	Tongue.
Lái ..	Lyi ..	......	Belly.
Deya ..	Doi-á ..	......	Back.
Mere ..	Med ..	Arlahar ..	Iron.
Samrum ..	Samom ..	......	Gold.
Rupa ..	Rúpá ..	......	Silver.
Aba ..	Áp-pú ..	Baare, ba ..	Father.
Má ..	Eng-á ..	Buinge, buin ..	Mother.
Hágá ..	Báo ..	......	Brother.
Misi ..	Mís-sí ..	......	Sister.
Horo ..	Ho ..	......	Man.
Kuri ..	Kúi ..	......	Woman.
....	Erá ..	......	Wife.
Hon ..	Siti-á ..	......	Child.
Hon ..	Hon ..	......	Son.
Hon kuri ..	Hon-erá ..	......	Daughter.
Dhangar ..	Dás-sí ..	......	Slave.
Chásá ..	Sitán-ho ..	Pasar ..	Cultivator.
Medi gopi ..	Gú-pí ..	......	Shepherd.
Sing bongá ..	Sing-Bongá ..	......	God.
Bonga ..	Bon-gá ..	Mesainke ..	Devil.
Sing bonga ..	Síngí ..	......	Sun.
Chando ..	Chán-du ..	......	Moon.
Ipil ..	I-píl ..	......	Star.
Sengel ..	Sen-gel ..	Selaide ..	Fire.

English.	Sonthalee of Sonthal Pergunnahs.	Sonthalee of Midnapore.	Sonthalee of Bancoorah.	Sonthalee of Maunbhoom.
Water ..	Dak' ..	Dāh, raté, mādam, bādla.	Da ..	Da ...
House ..	Aṛ-ak' ..	Arā, kumbā, ghāri, kuriā.	Ora ..	Oṛa ...
Horse ..	....	Sādam ...	Sadam ..	Sadom ...
Cow ..	Gai ..	Gaie ...	Gai ..	Dangri ...
Dog ..	Setak' ..	Sétā ...	Seta ..	Setá ...
Cat ..	Pusi ..	Pusi ...	Pushi ..	Pusi ...
Cock ..	Saṇḍi ..	Sandi ...	Sim-sāri ..	Sim ...
Duck ..	Geḍe ..	Geré ...	Hāns ..	Geṛe ...
Ass ..	Gadha ..	Gādha ...	Gadha ..	Gádhá ...
Camel ..	Uṭ ..	Unth ...	Unt ..	Unt ...
Bird ..	Cheṛe ..	Chéné ...	Cheure ..	Cheṛe ...
Go ..	Sen, chala ..	Chala, tārām ...	Ma-chalame ..	Du ...
Eat ..	Jom ..	Jummé-ben-pé ...	Ma-jamme ..	Jome ...
Sit ..	Daṛup' ..	Durupmé-ben-pé ...	Madarúm-mé ..	Duṛupme ...
Come ..	Hejuk' ..	Délā ...	Mahejúm-me ..	Delá ...
Beat ..	Dal ..	Dālmé-ben pé ...	Madalum-me ..	Daleme ...
Stand ..	Tiṅgun ..	Tôkhôn mé benpé ..	Ma-tengun-me ..	Tigunme ...
Die ..	Gujuk' ..	Laham ...	Coj-enna ..	Gujugme ...
Give ..	Em ..	Den, ema ...	Den-é-mum-me ..	Denho ...
Run ..	Nir, daṛ ..	Ďéd, pid gāu ...	Ma-dam-me ..	Daurame ...
Up ..	Chetan ..	Chat, chétān ...	Chat ..	Chot ...
Near ..	Sor ..	Shôr ...	Sore ..	Sur ...
Who? ..	Okae? chele? ..	Akay ...	Okay ..	Okai ...
And ..	Ar, ado ..	Chétna ...	Ar ..	Ar ...
Yes ..	He ..	Hôe, hén ...	He ..	Hi ...
Down ..	Latar ..	Tatar, féd ...	Latar ..	Latar ...
What? ..	Chet'? ..	Chét ...	Chat ..	Ched ...
Far ..	Saṅgin ..	Shākhing, Fārāk ...	Sangina ..	Sanginre ...
But ..	Men-khan ..	Menkhān ...	Kinta ..	Mentuk ...
No ..	Baṅ ..	Bāngā, bāng, enhen	Bang ..	Alo, bang ...
Before ..	Laha, maṛaṅ samaṅ	Tāhāré, shamāngré	Samang ..	Laha ...
Behind ..	Tayom ..	Tāghmaré ...	Taenam ..	Tainam ...
Why? ..	Chedat'? ..	Chédang ...	Cheday ..	Cheya ...
If ..	Khan ..	Hāpen, khān ...	Haping ..	Khan ...
Alas! ..	Haere! ..	Hāi ...	Hay-hay	Uh ...
A father ..	Apa ..	Baba ...	Baha-tiny ..	Mitang apát ...
Two fathers ..	Apa-kin ..	Baréa babā, bābā tékin.	....	Apatikin ...
Fathers ..	Apa-ko ..	Bābātekô ...	Baha-teko ..	Apateko ...
Of a father ..	Apa-ren ..	Babāréā ...	Bahar-eya ..	Apát reya ...

Bhumij of Maunbhoom.	Kols or Kor of Singbhoom.	Juangs of Orissa Jungles.	English.
Da ...	Dá ..	Dagude, dak ..	Water.
Oṛa ...	Oá ..	Ingaree, inga ..	House.
Sadom ...	Sá-dam ..	......	Horse
Gái ...	Urí or gimdi ..	Gaire, arei ..	Cow.
Seta ...	Setá ..	......	Dog.
Pusi ...	Bil-li ..	Bileire, billi ..	Cat.
Sim ..	Sim ..	......	Cock.
Koṛo ...	He-de-ge ..	......	Duck.
Gadha ...	Gádá ..	......	Ass.
Uṅt ...	......	......	Camel.
Cheṛe ...	O-e ..	......	Bird.
Ju ...	Sen-men ..	Nona ..	Go.
Jomeme ...	Jum-men ..	......	Eat.
Dupme ...	Dúb-men ..	Dokana ..	Sit.
Ela ...	Hújú-men ..	......	Come.
Dalime ..	Tám-men ..	......	Beat.
Tegunme ...	Tingún-men ..	Pangana ..	Stand.
Gojome ...	Gajo-men ..	......	Die.
Da ...	Emi-men ..	Nidinga ..	Give.
Dauṛime ...	Nir-men ..	......	Run.
Chetan ...	Sir-má ..	......	Up.
Nare ...	Ja-pár ..	......	Near.
Okoi ...	A-koi ..	......	Who.
Oṛo ...	Au-da ..	......	And.
Hi ..	E-á ..	......	Yes.
Later ...	Su-bá ..	......	Down.
Chikana ...	Chiá ..	......	What.
Sanginre ...	Sáng-ing ..	......	Far.
Mento ...	Mendo ..	......	But.
Alo ...	Ká ..	......	No.
Aiya ...	Áirte ..	......	Before.
Taiyam ...	Doi-á ..	......	Behind.
Chiya ...	Chikan-mente ..	......	Why.
Jodim ...	Euredo ..	......	If.
Uh ...	He-gurí ..	......	Alas.
Moyonaba ...	Áp-pu ..	......	A father.
Abatakin ...	Áp-pu-king ..	......	Two fathers.
Apomtako ...	Áp-pu-ko ..	......	Fathers.
Apoteya ...	Áp-pu-á ..	......	Of a father.

English.	Sonthalee of Sonthal Pergunnahs.	Sonthalee of Midnapore.	Sonthalee of Bancoorah.	Sonthalee of Maunbhoom.
Of fathers ..	Apako-ren ..	Bābā tékoréā ...	Baha-tekoya ...	Apat reya ...
To a father ..	Apa-ṭhen ..	Bābā ...	Baha-emaye ...	Apáte (thin) ...
To fathers ..	Apako-ṭhen ..	Bābā tékô ...	Baha-teko-emakura	Apat kothen ...
From a father ..	Apa-khon ..	Bābā kan ...	Baha-tei-surnā ...	Apáthin khon ...
From fathers ..	Apako-khon ..	Bābā téko khan ...	Baha-teko-are ...	Apat kothen khon ...
A daughter ..	Hoponera ..	Hapan-erā ...	Mingotang ...	Kuri ...
Two daughters ..	Hoponerakin ..	Hapan-era-tékin ...	....	Kuri kin ...
Daughters ..	Hoponerako ..	Hapan-era-tékô ...	Dher-uteroko ...	Kuri ko ...
Of a daughter ..	Hoponera-ren ..	Hapan-erā iā ...	Hopon-aronya ...	Kuri reya ...
Of daughters ..	Hoponerako-ren ..	Hapan-era-téko réā.	Hopon-raeteko ...	Kuri koreya ...
To a daughter ..	Hoponera-ṭhen ..	Hapan erā ...	Ming-gote-emae ...	Kuri then ...
To daughters ..	Hoponerako-ṭhen..	Hapan era tékô ...	Jato-houre-emakura	Kuri ko then ...
From a daughter ..	Hoponera-khon ..	Hapan era khan ...	Mitta-hopon-erai-teko.	Kuri then khon ...
From daughters ..	Hoponerako-khon	Hapan erā téko réā	Addi-uteriko-hopon-eraiteko.	Kuri kothen khona ...
A good man ..	Bugi herel ..	Bôgé har ...	Wilta-bes-horkānā	Bes herel ...
Two good men ..	Bugi-herel-kin ..	Bôgé harkin ...	....	Bes herel kin ...
Good men ..	Bugi-herel-ko ..	Bôgé harkô ...	Addi-bes-karkana	Bes herel ko ...
Of a good man ..	Bugi herel-ren ..	Bôgé har-reā ...	Mittang-hogeher ...	Bes herel reya ...
Of good men ..	Bugi-herel-ko-ren..	Bôgé har tékoréā ...	Dhar-utar-hogeher	Bes herel koreya ...
To a good man ..	Bugi herel-ṭhen ..	Bôgé har ...	Oke-okay-minher...	Bes herel then ...
To good men ..	Bugi-herel-ko-ṭhen	Bôgé hartékô ...	Udi-uteriko-hogehor	Bes herel ko then ...
From a good man ..	Bugi herel-khon ..	Bôgé har-khan ...	....	Bes herel then khona
From good men ..	Bugi-herel-ko-khon	Bôgé har tékô khan	....	Bes herel ko khona ...
A good woman ..	Bugi maejiu ..	Bôgé māiju ...	Mintang-hoge-aimai	Bes era ...
Two good women ..	Bugi maejiukin ..	Bôgé maijukin ...	....	....
Good women ..	Bugi maejiuko ..	Bôgé māijukô ...	Dhe-utarako-aimai	Bes era ko ...
Of a good woman ..	Bugi maejiu-ren ..	....	....	....
To a good woman ..	Bugi maejiu-ṭhen..	....	....	...
From a good woman	Bugi maejiu-khon.	....	....	....
A bad boy ..	Baṛich' koṛa ..	Bāri-korā-hapan ...	Mittang-karahapon-harigia.	Bari koṛa ...
A bad girl ..	....	Bāri kuri hapan ...	Mittang-kuri-hapon-harriga.	Bari kuṛi ...
Good ..	Bugi ..	Bôgé ...	Bageay ...	Bugi ...
Better ..	Arho bugi ..	Unikhan bôgé ...	Inekonda-hese-bagi-ya.	Bugi geyá ...
Best ..	Sanam-khon bugi or bugi.	Jatakhan bôgé ...	Khube-bagia ...	Bugi geyai ...
High ..	Usul ..	Ushul ...	Usula ...	Usul ...
Higher ..	Arho usul ..	Unikhan ushul ...	Khub-usula ...	Usul geya ...

of Western Bengal.—(Continued.)

Bhumij of Maunbhoom.	Kols or Kor of Singbhoom.	Juangs of Orissa Jungles.	English.
Abatakoya ...	Áp-pu-ko-á ..	......	Of fathers.
Apote ...	Áp-pu-tár ..	......	To a father.
Apate tako ..	Áp-pu-ko-tar ..	......	To fathers.
Abata ...	Áp-pu-te ..	......	From a father.
Apomta kota ...	Áp-pu-ko-te ..	......	From fathers.
Kuṛi hon ...	Hon-erá .	......	A daughter.
Kuri hon kin ...	Hon-erá-king ..	......	Two daughters.
Kuri hon ko ...	Honerá-ko ..	......	Daughters.
Kuri hon reya ...	Hon-erá-á ..	......	Of a daughter.
Kuri hon koya ...	Hon-erá-kuá ..	.....	Of daughters.
Kuri hon thin ...	Hon-erá-tár ..	......	To a daughter.
Ḳurihon thin ...	Hon-erá-ko-tár ..	......	To daughters.
Kuri hon tate ...	Hon-erá-te ..	......	From a daughter.
Kurin hon ko tate ...	Hon-erá-ko-te ..	......	From daughters.
Bugin sepaṛet ...	Búgi-ho ..	......	A good man.
Bugin sepaṛet kin ...	Búgi-ho-king ..	......	Two good men.
Bugin sepaṛet ko ...	Búgi-ho-ko ..	......	Good men.
Bugin sepaṛet reya ...	Búgi-ho-á ..	......	Of a good man.
Bugin sepaṛet koya ...	Búgi-ho-kuá ..	......	Of good men.
Bugin sepaṛet thin ...	Búgi-ho-tár ..	......	To a good man.
Bugin sepaṛet ko thin ...	Búgi-ho-ko-tár ..	......	To good men.
Bugin sepaṛet tate ...	Búgi-ho-te ..	......	From a good man.
Bugin sepaṛet ko tate ...	Búgi-ho-ko-te ..	......	From good men.
Bugin kuri ...	Búgi-kúi ..	......	A good woman.
......	......	......	Two good women.
Bugin kuri ko ...	Búgi-kui-ko ..	......	Good women.
......	......	......	Of a good woman.
......	......	......	To a good woman.
......	......	......	From a good woman.
Etkan koṛa ...	Etká-koá ..	......	A good boy.
Etkan kuṛi ...	Etká-kui ..	......	A bad girl.
Bugi ...	Bugi ..	......	Good.
Oṛo bugi ...	Ená or áiá-te-bugi ..	......	Better.
Marang bugi ...	Sabe-te-bugi ..	......	Best.
Salangi ...	Sirmá ..	......	High.
Oṛo salangi ...	Ená-te-sirmá ..	......	Higher.

English.	Sonthalee of Sonthal Pergunnahs.	Sonthalee of Midnapore.	Sonthalee of Bancoorah.	Sonthalee of Maunbhoom.
Highest	Sanam-khon usal or usul uttar.	Jatakhan ushul	Adi-char	Usul geyai
A horse	Aṇḍia sadom	Sādam	Mit-gote-sadam	Sadom
A mare	Eṅga sadom	Ekhā sādam	Mit-enga-sadam	Sadom enga
Horses	Aṇḍia sadomko	Sādamkô	Dhar-uteroko-sadam	Sadom ko
Mares	Eṅga sadomko	Ekhā sādamkô	Dhar-uteroko-enga-sadam.	Sadom enga ko
A bull	Daṅgra	Bāiār	Mitta-enra	Saṛ
A cow	Gai	Gaie	Mitta-gai	Gai
Bulls	Daṅgrako	Bāiārkô	Dhar-uteroko enra	Sar ko
Cows	Gaiko	Gaiekô	Dhar-utároko-gai.	Gai ko
A dog	Setak'	Shéta	Mitta setta	Seta
A bitch	Eṅga setak'	Ekhā shéta	Mitta-enga-seta	Seta engá
Dogs	Setak' ko	Shétakô	Dher-uteroko-seta	Seta ko
Bitches	Eṅga setak' ko	Ekhā shétakô	Dher-uteroko-enga-seta.	Seta enga ko
A he-goat	Merom-aṇḍia	Badā, kasi	Mitta-gotan boda.	Meram boda
A female goat	Merom-eṅga	Ekhā méram	Mit-gotang-enga-merom.	Meram enga
Goats	Meromko	Méramkô	Marom	Meram ko
A male deer	....	Jhankār, aré	Mittang-enra	Jhankar jil
A female deer	....	Pasta	Mit-gotang-posta.	Posta enga
Deer	....	Jelkô	Iel	Jil ko
I am	Menana, or kanan	Ménāing geā	Ing-menāyā	Menaing or mena ingeya.
Thou art	Menama, or kanam	Ménāmā	Am-menāyā	Menama
He is	Menaea, or kanae	Ménāia	Uni-menāyā	Mena iya
We are	....	Ménāleā, baya	Ana-menaniā	Mena leya
You are	....	Ménāpéyā	Hape-menatia	Mena peya
They are	....	Ménākôyā	Unko-menākā	Mena koya
I was	Tahekonan	Tāhén kānāing	Ing-topekana	Tahen khaing
Thou wast	Tahekonam	Tāhén kānām	Hapep-tahekana	Tahen kanam
He was	Tahekanae	Tahén kānāé	Unko-tahekana	Tahen kanai
We were	....	Tahen kānālé-ba-ban.	Allele-tahekana	Tahen kanale
You were	....	Tahen kānāpé	Amem-tahekana	Tahen kanape
They were	....	Tahen kānākô	Amen-tahekana	Tahen kanako
Be	Hoyuk' mé	Houmé	Hona	Heju me
To be	Hoyuk'	Hô-u	Haea-kana	Hoju te
Being	Hoyuk'	......	Howu-kana	Huikate
Having been	Hoeakan-khan	Hailén khān	....	Huien khan
I may be	Hoyuk'-gi-chon	Hôik āing	Ing-haikoiy	Heju choing
I shall be	Hoyuk'-an	Hôu āi	Ing-hawniy	Heju aing

of *Western Bengal.*—(Continued.)

Bhumij of Maunbhoom.	Kols or Kor of Singbhoom.	Juangs of Orissa Jungles.	English.
Marang salangi ...	Sabe-te-sirmá .	......	Highest.
Sadom ...	Sá-dam ..	......	A horse.
Enga sadom ...	Engá-sá-dam ..	......	A mare.
Sadom ko ...	Sā-dam-ko ..	......	Horses.
Enga sadom ko ...	Engā-sā-dam-ko ..	......	Mares.
Ariya ...	Án-diá ..	......	A bull.
Gai ...	Gundi ..	......	A cow.
Aiya ko ...	Án-diá-ko ..	......	Bulls.
Gai ko ...	Uri-ko or gundi-ko ..	......	Cows.
Seta ...	Setá ..	......	A dog.
Enga seta ...	Engá-se-tá ..	......	A bitch.
Seta ko ...	Setá-ko ..	......	Dogs.
Enga seta ko ...	Engá-setá-ko ..	......	Bitches.
Meram boda ...	Ba-dá-merom ..	......	A he-goat.
Engameram ...	Enga-merom ..	......	A female goat.
Meramko ...	Merom-ko ..	......	Goats.
Sari jilu ...	Sán-di-ji-lu ..	......	A male deer.
Enga jilu ...	Engá-ji-lu ..	......	A female deer.
Jiluko ...	Ji-lu-ko ..	......	Deer.
Menagiya ...	Ing-min-ná ..	......	I am.
Menameya ...	Ám-min-ná ..	......	Thou art.
Menagiya ...	Aio-min-ná ..	......	He is.
Mena leya ...	Álle-min-ná ..	......	We are.
Menapeya ...	Áppe-min-ná ..	......	You are.
Menakoya ...	Áko-min-ná ..	......	They are.
Tai ken aing ...	Ing-tái-ken-ná ..	......	I was.
Tai kenam ...	Ám-tái-ken-ná ..	......	Thou wast.
Tai kenai ...	Aio-tai-ken-na ..	......	He was.
Tai kenale ...	Á-l-le-tái-ken-ná ..	......	We were.
Tai kenape ...	Áp-pe-tái-ken-ná ..	......	You were.
Tai kena ko ...	Áko-tái-ken-ná ..	......	They were.
Howa ome ...	Ha-bo-men ..	......	Be.
Howa ote ..	Habo-teá ..	......	To be.
Howa kate ...	Habo-tán-te ..	......	Being.
......	Habo-ked-te ..	......	Having been.
Howa okaing ...	Ing-habo-to-rán ..	......	I may be.
Howa oing ...	Ing-ha-boá ..	......	I shall be.

English.	Sonthalee of Sonthal Pergunnahs.	Sonthalee of Midnapore.	Sonthalee of Bancoorah.	Sonthalee of Maunbhoom.
I should be	Hoe-kok'-an	Hôik āing	Ing-asariga	Hui ko aing
Beat	Dal-mé	Dālmé	Dalengowa	Daleme
To beat	Dal	Dāl, dadāl	Dalanagowa	Dalete
Beating	Dadal, dal-ket-khan	......	....	Dal kate
Having beaten	....	Dālalé khān	....	Dalket khan
I beat	Dal et'-an	Dālāing	Ing-daleiya	Dale kanaing
Thou beatest	Dal-et'-am	Dālām	Amgi-dalema	Dale kanam
He beats	Dal-et'-ae	Dālé dāé	Umdo-haredalea	Dale kanai
We two beat	Dal-et'-a lin	....	....	....
You two beat	Dal-et'-aben	. ..	....	....
They two beat	Dal-et'-akin	....	....	....
We beat	Dal-et'-ale	Dālālé, dālāba, or dalaban.	Medalea	Dale kanale
You beat	Dal-et'-ape	Dālé dāpé	Apama-dalepa	Dale kanape
They beat	Dal-et'-ako	Dalé-dako	Unko-daleā	Dale kanako
I am beating	Dal-et'-kan-an	......	Ing-dalekadia	Tahen dale aing
I was beating	....	.....	Ing-dalekana	Dalekan tahen kanaing.
I had beaten	....	Dālakā déāie	....	Dale kade aing
We two are beating	Dal-et'-kana-lin	....	....	....
We are beating	Dal et'-kan-ale	....	....	....
I may beat	Dal-gi-chon	Dālké āie	Ing-dareiy	Dalo choing
I shall beat	Dal-an	Dālé āing	Ing-dalea	Ingging daleya
I should beat	Dal-ke-an	Ditto	Ing-dalakadiasangi	Ingging dalkeya
I am beaten	Dal-ochok'-kan-an	Dāl hôch ākānāing	Ing-dalarigi-mena	Dalocho kanaing
I was beaten	Dal-ocho-enan	Dāl hôch lénāing	Ing dalaregi-tahe-kana.	Dalocho enaing
I shall be beaten	Dal-ochok'-an	Dāl hôch āing	Ing-dagajri-y	Dalocho choing
I go	Senok' konan	Chalā āing	Ing-senkanai	Ing chala kanaing
Thou goest	Senok' konam	Chala kanām	Am-doma-chelame.	Amen chala kanam
He goes	Senok' konae	Chālā kanai	Uni-senpachay	Uni chala kanai
I went	Senenan	Senanieing	Ing-selenai	Ing chalamenaing
Thou wentest	Senenam	Chālān-enām	Am-dasanena	Amem chala · menam
He went	Senenae	Chālān-énāi	Cinida-sen-hena	Uni chala menai
Go	Sen	Chalāmé-ben-pé	Chatakana	Chala meya
Going	Senok'	Chalā kanā	Senkana	Chalau kate
Gone	Sen, or Senakan	Chālān-enā	Chata-ena	Chalau en khan
What is your name?	Chet' nutum-tama?	Chélé āmā	Am intumchele-ama	Apeya niutum che
How old is this horse?	Noi sadom do tin sermaren konae.	Nui-sadam-tin-shémā hauknā.	Nue-sadum terser-my-hujukana.	Niu sadom reya umur tina
How far is it from here to Kashmir?	Nondekhon Kashmir-te tin sangina	Naudé khana-Kashmir-tin-sakhéan.	Narakam-Kashmir tinsangi.	Nore khona Kashmir tina sangaya.

of Western Bengal.—(Continued.)

Bhumij of Maunbhoom.	Kols or Kor of Singbhoom.	Juangs of Orissa Jungles.	English.
Howa ko aing ...	Ing-hobo-honang ..	......	I should be.
Dalime ...	Tám-men ..	......	Beat.
Dalte ...	Tám-teá ..	......	To beat.
Dalkete ...	Tám-tán-le ..	......	Beating.
Dalkat koya ...	Tám-ked-te ..	......	Having beaten.
Dal jadi ing ...	Ing-tám-tánná ..	......	I beat.
Dal jadi am ...	Ám-tám-tánná ..	......	Thou beatest.
Dal jadiya ...	Ái-lám-tánna ..	......	He beats.
......	......	......	We two beat.
......	......	......	You two beat.
......	......	......	They two beat.
Dal jadi ale ...	Alle-tám-tánná ..	......	We beat.
Dal jadi ape ...	Áppe-tám-tánná ..	......	You beat.
Dal jadi ako ...	Áko-tám-tánná ..	......	They beat.
Tising dalieng ...	Ing-tám-tán-tánná ..	......	I am beating.
Aiking daljatai kenaing ...	Ing-tám tánná ..	......	I was beating.
Dalta diing ...	Ing-tám-kiá ..	......	I had beaten.
......	......	......	We two are beating.
......	......	......	We are beating.
Dalja koing ...	Ing-tám-dáiá ..	......	I may beat.
Inging dalmeya ...	Ing-tám-eá ..	......	I shall beat.
Inging daltaing ...	Ing-tám-honang ..	......	I should beat.
Dalechiya kanaing ...	Ing-tám-ing-tánná ..	......	I am beaten.
Dalichi jaing ...	Ing-tám-ing-kid-da ..	......	I was beaten.
Dalichi naing ...	Ing-tám-ing-ha-honá ..	......	I shall be beaten.
Ing senotanaing ...	Ing-sen-tán-ná ..	......	I go.
Amam senat anam ...	Ám-sen-tán-ná ..	......	Thou goest.
Ini senat anai ...	Ái-sen-tánná ..	......	He goes.
Ing senojanaing ...	Ing-sen-ked-dá ..	......	I went.
Amseno janam ...	Ám-sen-ked-dá ..	......	Thou wentest.
Ini senojanai ...	Ái-sen-ked-dá ..	......	He went.
Senome ...	Sen-men ..	......	Go.
Senojanate ...	Sen-tán-te ..	......	Going.
Senojana ...	Sen-ked-te ..	......	Gone.
Apeya niutum chikana ...	Ám-chi-kán-na-túm ..	......	What is your name?
Ni sadoma unur chiminang mena.	Ne-sá-dam-chi-min-den-rea-miná.	......	How old is this horse?
Kashmir niyate chiminang sangaya.	Ne-te-Kásh-mír-chimin-sán-ging-miná.	......	How far is it from here to Kashmir?

English.	Sonthalee of Sonthal Pergunnahs.	Sonthalee of Midnapore.	Sonthalee of Bancoorah.	Sonthalee of Maunbhoom.
How many sons are there in your father's house?	Apum oṛak're tinak' hopon menakoa?	Āpun arāre tinā kôrā-hapan-menā koeā. .	Am-apum-arara-tin-gotekaragidra.	Ape apum teko oṛare tina gidar hena koya.
I have walked a long way to-day.	Tehen adi sangen in sentaṛamket'a.	Tiheng-ari-sakhi-hung-tārām-akā dā.	Tehinda-ari-dara-ken-day.	Ing do tehenge aḍi sangiye chalau lena ingeya.
The son of my uncle is married to his sister.	Mamonren hopon oniren miseratit' ṭhene capla akana.	Uni-reni-miséra gogoing hapan bāplā-ākādiai.	Ingkaka-hapan-herer raeing-hapa-nera-bahukhedia.	Uni kuṛiren bokat kuṛi mamoing ha-pene bahuakadiyar.
In the house is the saddle of the white horse.	Poṇḍ sadomreak' palan oṛ ak're menak'a.	Pônda sād maréā lagām-arāré-ménā iā.	Por-sadam-araepa-tam mena.	Oṛare punar sadom reya palan menaya.
Put the saddle upon his back.	Deare palan lade ae me.	Uni-diāré lāgām-hargamé.	Unia-deiyara-patan-dahayine.	Palan uniya deyare lademe.
I have beaten his son with many stripes.	Hopontit' adi dal in dal akadea.	Uni reni-kôra hapan bādi-géing-dalké diā.	Uning-gidra-ing-ad-ing hapadar-akadia.	Ing do unirin hopon aḍing dalakadiya.
He is grazing cattle on the top of the hill.	Buru chot chotte gaie atin et'ko kana.	Uni-dukhi-chetanaré-gāie- gupi kānai.	Bure-chetanre-gay gupikana.	Unido buru chotre gupi kanai.
He is sitting on a horse under that tree.	Hana dare butare sadomre e dech' akana.	Anā dāré-butāré sādam chetanaré uni dudu pākānāi.	One-dare-tutari-sadam re-durube-kana.	Uni sadom chetanre durup katedare hutare menaiya.
His brother is taller than his sister.	Miseratit' khon, bokottit' e usula.	Uni-reni-misé rākhanā-baré-tégé usulai.	Uning-ajiterkhan bakter marranga.	Uniren bokat miserat khon hoi usulai.
The price of that is two rupees and a half.	Anareak' gonoṅ tet' do bartaka tala.	Anāreā ganang bara tākā tāla.	Uniradam-barataka-bar-sika.	Uniriya dám bar táká bar sika.
My father lives in that small house.	Apundo hana hopon hopon oṛak're e tahen kana.	Anā huding adāré āpuing né tahénā.	Ing-apui-ina-hird-ing-ara-re-tahena.	Ingrin apuing ona kuriyare menaiya.
Give this rupee to him.	Noa taka emae me.	Niā tākā uni-emāiémé.	Naiya-taka-uni-ema-yma.	Nauya taka uni emai-me.
Take those rupees from him.	Ma noako taka oni ṭhen khon ataṅ me.	Unithen khan-anā tākāko hata umé.	Uni-teikhan-taka-aguime.	Ona taka uni then kho-na aguime.
Beat him well and bind him with ropes.	Bugite dalepue or baberte tol kae me.	Āchhā dalé mé ār bārér té talé mé.	Unida-khub-dalkate barbartatabe.	Uni khup daleme ar taleme.
Draw water from the well.	Kui khon dak' lo agui me.	Kuin khana dā lârā kab mé.	Khuikhan-dalorak amme.	Kui khona da aguime
Walk before me ...	In samaṅ samaṅte (or laha la hate) chalak' me.	Ing tahālé chalé mi	Ing-nahartiachur-re.	Ingya lahate chalame
Whose boy comes behind you?	Okoeren koṛa hopon am ta gomte e he juk'kana?	Akai rini gidra āmtai mati dārāi kanā.	Antai namte-gidra darai-kana.	Okairin gidar ama taí omte heju kanai.
From whom did you buy that?	Ona do okoe ṭhen an kirin ket'a?	Akai ten anām kiring akādā.	Unida-akaite-kiring akardia.	Ona okaithen khona kiring kedam.
From a shop-keeper of the village.	Atoren mit' ṭaṅ dokan ṭhen.	Atoréni-balia thén...	Nowa-atarini-min-had dondarman-nendai.	Atureya baṛiya then kiringle aing.

Bhumij of Maunbhoom.	Kols or Kor of Singbhoom.	Juangs of Orissa Jungles.	English.
Apeya aba oṛare chiminang hanko mena.	Ámá-áp-puá-o-á-re-chi-min-kuá-hon-ko-miná.	......	How many sons are there in your father's house?
Tising aing esu during hanor ledaing.	Tising-sáng-ing-horáho-nar-bá-kid-ing.	......	I have walked a long way to-day.
Ingya mama honte kora en kuṛiya misite arandi taiya.	Impossible ...	......	The son of my uncle is married to his sister.
Puṛi sadoma palan oṛare mena.	O-á-re-pun-di-sá-dam-reá-pálán mi-ná.	......	In the house is the saddle of the white horse.
Palan aia deare ladime ...	Pá-lán-urui-men ...	......	Put the saddle upon his back.
Aiya hon esoing daltya ing	Iniá-hon-ing-purá-dán–dá-tám-kid-dá.	......	I have beaten his son with many stripes.
Ini buru chetanre gupitanai	Ái-buru-chetán-ṛe-uri-gupi-tán-ná.	......	He is grazing cattle on the top of the hill.
Sadom chetanre deya kanate daru subare menagya.	Ái-en-dá-ru-subá-re-sá-dam tár-duhen-ná.	......	He is sitting on a horse under that tree.
Aiya misite bokate koṛe salangi menagya.	Iniá-báo-iniá-missite-sá-lan-gi-miná.	......	His brother is taller than his sister.
Iniya dam bar taka bar sika	Ená-gonam-bár-táká-tá-lá-mi-ná.	......	The price of that is two rupees and a half.
Ingya aba huring oṛare menagya.	Ing-áp-pu-en-hu-ṛing-oá-re-táin-tán-ná.	......	My father lives in that small house.
Ne taka aike amaime ...	Ne-táká-ái-tár-emi-men ...	......	Give this rupee to him.
Ne taka aitate aguime ...	En-tá-ká-ko-di-te-idi-men..	......	Take those rupees from him.
Inike khup dalime bayar te tolime.	Ini-tám-men-bugi-auda-tol-men-bair to.	......	Beat him well and bind him with ropes.
Kuyate da aguime ...	Súd-te-dá-táur-ondong-men	......	Draw water from the well.
Ingya ayarte seneme ...	Air-ing-men ...	......	Walk before me.
Okoiya hon ingya taiomte hiju tanai	Okoiá-kuá-ámá-doiá-te-hujo-tán-ná.	......	Whose boy comes behind you?
Enjinis okai tare kiring ledam.	En-okoi-te-kiung-kid-ám ?	......	From whom did you buy that?
Hature bariya tare kiring le daing.	Hátu-re-á-do-kán-dái-te ...	......	From a shop-keeper of the village.

FURTHER LANGUAGES OF ABORIGINES

OF

WESTERN BENGAL AND BEHAR.

(Chiefly Dravidian)

English.	Moondari of Lohardugga.	Oorain of Lohardugga.	Rajmehalee of Rajmehal Hills.
Numerals.			
One ...	Miyad ...	Onṭa ...	......
Two ...	Bāria ...	Enṛ ...	......
Three ...	Apiā ...	Múnd ...	......
Four ...	Upunya ...	Nákh ...	......
Five ...	Moṇiān ...	Panche ...	......
Six ...	Turúya ...	Soe ...	......
Seven ...	Eyá ..	Satte ...	......
Eight ...	Iralya ...	Athe ...	......
Nine ...	Áreya ...	Nane ...	......
Ten ...	Gelya ...	Dase ...	......
Twenty ...	Míyad hisí ...	On bisol ...	......
Thirty ...	......	......	......
Forty ...	......	......	......
Fifty ...	Bár hisí gelya ...	Bís suṛ dase ...	......
Sixty ...	......	......	......
Seventy ...	......	......	......
Eighty ...	......	......	......
Ninety ...	......	......	......
Hundred ...	Moṇi hisí ...	Panche kuṛi ...	......
Thousand ...	......	......	......
Pronouns.			
I ...	Aiñ or Iñ ...	En ...	Ayn ...
We ...	Ale ...	Em ...	Aym ...
Thou ...	Am ...	Nín ...	Nín ...
You ...	Ape ...	Ním ...	Nín ...
He ...	Iní ...	Ás ...	Áh ...
They ...	Ako ...	Ár ...	Ahaber ...
Of me ...	Aiñya ...	Enghai ...	Aynkí ...
Of us ...	Alea ...	Emhai ...	Emsubki ...
Of thee ...	Amá ...	Ninghai ...	Ningkid ...
Of you ...	Apeá ...	Nimhai ...	Níngkid ...
Of him ...	Iniá ...	Ásgahí ...	Áhikíd ...
Of them ...	Akoá ...	Árgahí ...	Áhebkid ...
Mine ...	Same as above ...	Same as above ...	Aynkí ...
Our ...	......	......	Emsobkí ...
Thine ...	......	......	Ningkid ...
Your ...	......	......	Ningkid ...
His ...	......	......	Áhikid ...
Their ...	......	......	Ahebkid ...

Khond of Orissa.	Khond of Ganjam.	Dhangar of Shahabad.	Kharwar of Shahabad.	English.
Rande ..	Ek, randá, randi ...	Ek ...	Ek ..	One.
Rindi ..	Din, rendi ...	Dooee ...	Do ..	Two.
Munji ..	Tini, munji ..	Tini ...	Teen ..	Three.
Nálgi ..	Chári, náligi ...	Char ...	Char ..	Four.
Pánsu ..	Pánchu, sengi ...	Panch ...	Panch ..	Five.
Sa ..	Sa, sájigi ...	Chhuh ...	Chhuh ..	Six.
Sátu ..	Sátu, adgi ...	Sat ...	Sat ..	Seven.
Áthu ..	Atá ...	Ath ...	Aoth ..	Eight.
Nouñ ..	Naha ...	Nou ...	Nou ..	Nine.
Dasu ..	Dásá ...	Dus ...	Dus ..	Ten.
Kodeka ..	Kode ...	Bees ...	Bees ..	Twenty.
......	Kodedásá ...	......	....	Thirty.
......	Rikodi ...	......	....	Forty.
Rikodi ..	Rikodidássá ...	Puchas ...	Puchas ..	Fifty.
......	Tinikodi ...	......	....	Sixty.
......	Tinikodidasá ...	......	....	Seventy.
......	Chárikodi ...	......	....	Eighty.
......	Chári kodidásá ...	......	....	Ninety.
Pánsukodi ..	Pánch kodi ...	Sou ...	Sou ..	Hundred.
......	......	Hujar ...	Hujar ..	Thousand
Ánu ..	Anu ...	In ...	Ma ..	I.
Ámu ..	Ámu aju ...	Ain ...	Humunsubh ..	We.
Inn ..	Inu ...	Nain ...	Tor ..	Thou.
Iru ..	Iru ..	Umjateens ...	Toohunlog ..	You.
Ábánju ..	Eánju ...	As ...	Ao ..	He.
Abáru ..	Eáru ...	Arhoormur ..	Oologun ..	They.
Nádi ..	Nándá ...	Inga ..	Mor ..	Of me.
Mádi ..	Mándá ...	Inga ...	Humun subhke	Of us.
Nidi ..	Eri ...	Ninga ...	Tohar ..	Of thee.
Midi ..	Mindi ...	Ninga ...	Tohar ..	Of you.
Ebándi ..	Tránidi, enidi ...	Asgohee ...	Oonkur ..	Of him.
Ebaridi ..	Ewárdi ...	Arhoormus ...	Oonlogke ..	Of them.
Nadi ..	Nidi ...	Inga ...	Mor ..	Mine.
Madi ..	Mándi ...	Inga ...	Humar ..	Our.
Nidi ..	Nitárá ...	Ninga ...	Tohar ..	Thine.
Midi ..	Mindá ...	Ninga ...	Tohra ..	Your.
Ebandi ..	Yánidi ...	Asgohee ...	Oonkur ..	His.
Ebaridi ..	Trandí ...	Asgehee ...	Oonkur ..	Their.

English.	Moondari of Lohardugga.	Oorain of Lohardugga.	Rajmehalee of Rajmehal Hills.
Hand ...	Tí ...	Khekhá ...	Tetu ...
Foot ...	Káṭá ...	Khed ...	Kedu ...
Nose ...	Muṇ ...	Muṇí ...	Muied ...
Eye ...	Meṭ ...	Khan ...	Kánu ...
Mouth ...	Mochá ...	Bai ...	Toro ...
Tooth ...	Ḍáṭá ...	Pal ...	Palu ...
Ear ...	Lutur ...	Khebda ...	Kaiedbu ...
Hair ...	Ub ...	Chuṭí ...	Táli ...
Head ...	Bo ...	Kukk ...	Kuku ...
Tongue ...	Alañ or lee ...	Tatkhá ...	Tartay ...
Belly ...	Lai ...	Kúl ...	Kocho ...
Back ...	Deyá ...	Khokhá ...	Kokeh ...
Iron ...	Mened ...	Ṗanná ...	Lohá ...
Gold ...	Samarum ...	Soná ...	Soná ...
Silver ...	Rupá ...	Rupá ...	Chandi ...
Father ...	Apu ...	Tambas ...	Ábbah ...
Mother ...	Engá ...	Tangio ...	Áíáh ...
Brother ...	Hagá ...	Bháí ...	Báiáh ...
Sister ...	Misí ...	Tangḍí ...	Báí ...
Sister (younger) ...	......	......	......
Sister (elder) ...	......	......	......
Man ...	Hoṛo (generic), Koṛá ...	Met, álas (generic) ...	Málay ...
Woman ...	Kúṛí ...	Mukka ...	Peli ...
Wife ...	Kúṛí ...	Mukka ...	Dáni ...
Child ...	Hon ...	Khadd ...	Makkeh ...
Child (male) ...	......	......	......
Child (female) ...	......	......	......
Son ...	Kora hon ...	Tangdas; kukko khadd=boy.	Tengádeh ...
Daughter ...	Kúṛí hon ...	Tangda; kukkoe khadd=girl.	Tengádi ...
Slave ...	Dási (hired) ...	Ioṅkh (hired) ...	Keagapmolay ...
Cultivator ...	Kisán ...	Urbar ...	Kichháneh ...
Shepherd ...	Mahrá; gupitaní ...	Khapus ...	Charatru ...
God ...	Sing bonga=sun spirit ...	Dharme ...	Gosaín ...
Devil ...	Bonga (all malicious spirits)	Nád ...	Dindeh ...
Sun ...	Singi ...	Bíṛí ...	Beṟu ...
Moon ...	Chandu ...	Chando ...	Bilpu and chando ...
Star ...	Ipil ...	Binko ...	Bíndkeh ...
Fire ...	Sengel ...	Chich ...	Chichu ...
Water ...	Dáa ...	Am ...	Ámu ...

of Western Bengal and Behar.—(Continued.)

Khond of Orissa.	Khond of Ganjam.	Dhangar of Shahabad.	Kharwar of Shahabad.	English.
Káju ...	Káju, kagu ..	Kikkha ..	Hath ..	Hand.
Páádá ...	Kadu ..	Khid ..	Gor ..	Foot.
Mungeli ...	Mungeli ..	Mooeen ..	Nak ..	Nose.
Káunn ...	Kánu ..	Khun ..	Ankh ..	Eye.
Muñlm ...	Sudá ..	Bye ..	Moonh ..	Mouth.
Pálu ...	Pátka, pánu ..	Pull ..	Dant ..	Tooth.
Kriu ...	Kriu ..	Khebda ..	Kan ..	Ear.
Jendiri ...	Meranga, tlámerká	Chotee ..	Bar ..	Hair.
Hán ...	Tlán ..	Kookh ..	Kapar, moor..	Head.
Sándosi ...	Uángasy ..	Titkha ..	Jeebh ..	Tongue.
Tutu ...	Tutu ..	Kool ..	Pait ..	Belly.
Betta ...	Gándi, murenji ..	Maid ..	Peeth ..	Back.
Lahá ...	Luhá ..	Punna ..	Loha ..	Iron.
Suná ...	Suná ..	Sona ..	Sona ..	Gold.
Rupá ...	Rupá ..	Chandee ..	Chandee ..	Silver.
Ábbá ...	Ábá, tángi ..	Imbus ..	Bapoo ..	Father.
Iá ...	Áyá ..	Indeo ..	Muhtaree, Myya	Mother.
Támbesá ...	1*st* Dádá, 2*nd* ámbesá	Dodus ..	Bhaee ..	Brother.
......	Bái tángi ..	......	......	Sister.
......	......	Ingree ..	Baheenee ..	Sister (younger.)
......	......	Ingdye ..	Didya, Deedee	Sister (elder.)
Loku ...	Midenju, loku ..	Metus ..	Murd ..	Man.
Ásá ...	Ásá, midá ..	Mookkur ..	Mehraroo ..	Woman.
Mendhali ...	Kuduá, midiháli ..	Ingkhyne ..	Mahur ..	Wife.
Mida ...	Mídá ..	......	......	Child.
......	......	Kookoo, khuddur ..	Renga ..	Child (male.)
......	......	Kookee, khuddur ..	Rengee ..	Child (female.)
Mrienju ...	Mrienju ..	Jokhus ..	Bata ..	Son.
Mráu ...	Ápi budí ..	Pellar ..	Betee ..	Daughter.
Takimidá ...	Toki, midá ..	Balposle khuposkuw	Palpos ..	Slave.
Cháságátánju ...	Táságátánju ..	Nana, lugduw ..	Girhut ..	Cultivator.
Mendhiadáka ...	Adárnárai ..	Gurrereeas ..	Gurreree ..	Shepherd.
Penu ...	Panu ..	Dhurmeus ..	Bhugwan, Purmesir, Ram.	God.
Jálákara ...	Piduru ..	Nad ..	Bhoot ..	Devil.
Belápenu ...	Belá ..	Beeree ..	Soorooj ..	Sun.
Dánju ...	Dánju ..	Chundo ..	Chundurma ..	Moon.
Sukká ...	Suká, tárá ..	Beenko ..	Turye ..	Star.
Náni ...	Nádi ..	Chich ..	Agee ..	Fire.
Sira ...	Sidru ..	Urw ..	Panee ..	Water.

English.	Moondari of Lohardugga.	Oorain of Lohardugga.	Rajmehalee of Rajmehal Hills.
House ...	Oṛaá ...	Eṛpá ...	Addáh ...
Horse ...	Sádom ...	Ghoṛo ...	Ghoṛo ...
Cow ...	Gai ...	Gunḍi ...	Oyou ...
Dog ...	Setá ...	Allá ...	Áleh ...
Cat ...	Púsí ...	Berkha ...	Bergeh ...
Cock ...	Sánḍi ...	Kokoro ...	Chayok keṛu ...
Duck ...	Koṛo ...	Geḍe ...	Bátekeh ...
Ass ...	Gadhá ...	Gadhá ...	Gadagoṛo ...
Camel ...	Unṭ ...	Unṭ ...	Uñteh ...
Bird ...	Cheṇe ...	Oṛá ...	Puzu ...
Go ...	Senomeṅ (imp.) ...	Kalá (imp.) ...	Káláh ...
Eat ...	Iommeṅ ...	Oná ...	Lápá ...
Sit ...	Dubmeṅ ...	Okká ...	Okáh ...
Come ...	Elá ; hijumeṅ ...	Bará ...	Báṛáh ...
Beat ...	Dálmeṅ (imp.) ...	Laua ...	Bájíá ...
Stand ...	Tingunmeṅ ...	Ija-á ...	Eláh ...
Die ...	Goi (root) ...	Kheá (imp.) ...	Tádura ...
Give ...	Um ,, ...	Chiá ...	Kata ...
Run ...	Nir ,, ...	Bongá ...	Bongáh ...
Up ...	Sirma = sky ; chetan = upon	Merkha = sky ; minyá = upon	Maiñieh ...
Near ...	Náne ...	Hedde ...	Atgi ...
Who ...	Okoi ...	Ne ...	Ikkeh ...
And ...	Oṛo ...	Dará ...	Ádenteh ...
Yes ...	He ...	Ha-i ...	Añañ ...
Down ..	Latar ...	Kíya ...	Pichhi ...
Far ...	Sañíñ ...	Gechchha ...	Gichay ...
What ...	Chikan, chinaá ...	Endra ...	Indray ...
But ...	Mendo, batkam ...	Paṅheṅ ...	Jay, ze ...
No ...	Ká, bano ...	Mal-á ...	Málá ...
Before ...	Aiar ...	Mund ...	Ágdu ...
Behind ...	Táyom ...	Khokhá ...	Kokbazeh ...
Why ...	Chikaná mente, chia ...	Enderná ...	Indrik ...
If ...	—— re or —— re do ...	Je ...	Inken ...
Alas ...	Helaiya, háe, oh ...	Háe ...	Áiáreh, daíenuzi ...
A father ...	Apu ...	Tambas ...	Ortá ábbáh ...
Two fathers ...	Apukiñ ...	No dual (Iríb tambar=2 fathers.)	Jorer ábbáh ...
Fathers ...	Apuko ...	Tambar ...	Ábbassa eber ...
Of a father ...	Apuá ...	Tambas gahí ...	Ortá ábbákí ...
Of fathers ...	Apukoá ...	Tambar gahí ...	Ábbassebká ...

Khond of Orissa.	Khond of Ganjam.	Dhangar of Shahabad.	Kharwar of Shahabad.	English.
Iddu ..	Idd ..	Surpa ..	Ghur ..	House.
Godá ..	Godá ..	Ghoro ..	Ghora ..	Horse.
Gádikadi ..	Gáda ..	Gaed ..	Gae ..	Cow.
Nahuni ..	Náhudi ..	Alla ..	Kookoor ..	Dog.
Meo ..	Mea ..	Birkha ..	Bilar ..	Cat.
Kaju ..	Tadru ..	Cookro ..	Moorga ..	Cock.
Siropattá ..	Páná koská ..	Gerwa ..	Buttuck ..	Duck.
Gadu ..	Gadha, godá ..	Gudhed ..	Gudha ..	Ass.
Otu ..	Uta ..	Oontood ..	Oont ..	Camel.
Patá ..	Potá ..	Ora ..	Chirya ..	Bird.
Salmun ..	Sáju ..	Kula ..	Jah ..	Go.
Tinmun ..	Tunumu ..	Ona ..	Khah ..	Eat.
Kakumu ..	Kakasu ..	Okka ..	Bytha ..	Sit.
Bámu ..	Nárnu ..	Bura ..	Awa ..	Come.
Págámu ..	Bemu, sámu ..	Luwa ..	Marr ..	Beat.
Nilumu ..	Nilumu ..	Eja ..	Thura hokhuh	Stand.
Sátá ..	Sátá ..	Kichchus ..	Mooja ..	Die.
Simu ..	Siánárá ..	Chiya ..	De ..	Give.
Pinjámu ..	Gepá ..	Bonga ..	Koodo ..	Run.
Sendatá ..	Sendi ..	Mirkha ..	Oopray ..	Up.
Sadi ..	Ata ..	Hidday ..	Neara ..	Near.
Kimbai ..	Imbe, esti ..	Nay or Nidday ..	Ka ..	Who.
Ate ..	Atte ..	Orye ..	Aur ..	And.
Añ ..	Ana ana ..	Muno ..	Haw ..	Yes.
Nedá ..	Nede ..	Kiya ..	Hethay ..	Down.
Durá ..	Dura ..	Gichha ..	Door ..	Far.
Anna ..	Iná ..	Indra ..	Kahay, joy ..	What.
Ateká ..	Aná ..	......	Baki ..	But.
A, e ..	Ae ..	Mula ..	Naheen ..	No.
Káhe ..	Bele ..	Moondbhuray ..	Agaree ..	Before.
Dááná ..	Bia ..	Khokha ..	Puchharee ..	Behind.
Junádiki ..	Ináki, inádiki ..	Indur ..	Kahay ..	Why.
Esseká ..	Ehángá ..	Nalukhnuna ..	Saitke ..	If.
Aigo ..	Nárená ..	Pustoodeenkura, cheekha.	Ha, soch ..	Alas.
Ráábbá ..	Raábá ..	Onta embus ..	Ek bapoo ..	A father.
Riábbá ..	Ri ábáru ..	Doee embus ..	Doo bapoo ..	Two fathers.
Abbángáálbain ..	Abáru ..	Hurmur embus ..	Subhker bapoo	Fathers.
Raábbátári ..	Ra ábátárá ..	Onta embus gehee ..	Ek bapooke ..	Of a father.
Abbárutári ..	......	Koormur embus gehee	Subhkur bapoo ke.	Of fathers.

English.	Moondari of Lohardugga.	Oorain of Lohardugga.	Rajmehalee of Rajmehal Hills.
To a father ...	Apu te ...	Tambas ge ...	Orteh ábbok ..
To fathers ...	Apu kote ...	Tambar ge ...	Abbassebko ..
From a father ...	Apu te ...	Tambas gustí ...	Orteh ábbanteh ..
From fathers ...	Apu kote ...	Tambar gustí ...	Abbaseberinteh ..
A daughter ...	Kúṛí hon ...	Tangdá ...	Ortáh tengdí ..
Two daughters ...	Kúṛí honkiñ ...	No dual form ...	Jorertingadih ..
Daughters ...	Kúṛí honko ...	Tangdar ...	Tengadihseber ..
Of a daughter ...	Kúṛí honá ...	Tangdá gahí ...	Ortáh tengádikí ..
Of daughters ...	Kúṛí honkoá ...	Tangdar gahí ...	Tengadihseverki ..
To a daughter ...	Kúṛí honte ...	Tangdá ge ...	Orteh tengadík ..
To daughters ...	Kúṛí hon kote ...	Tangdar ge ...	Tengadihseverko ..
From a daughter ...	Kúṛí honte ...	Tangdá gustí ...	Orteh tengadinteh ..
From daughters ...	Kúṛí hon kote ...	Tandar gustí ...	Tengadiseverinteh ..
A good man ...	Bugin hoṛo ...	Nagad álas ...	Ortah eṛu málay ..
Two good men ...	Bugin hoṛo kiñ ...	(Irib nagad álar)—No dual	Jurer eṛu maler ..
Good men ...	Bugin hoṛoko ...	Nagad álar ...	Eṛu máler ..
Of a good man ...	Bugin hoṛoá ...	Nagad álas gahí ...	Ortah eṛu málekí ..
Of good men ...	Bugin hoṛokoá ...	Nagad álar gahí ...	Eṛu málerki ..
To a good man ...	Bugin hoṛo te ...	Nagad álas ge ...	Orteh eṛu málek ..
To good men ...	Bugin hoṛo kote ...	Nagad álar ge ...	Eṛu malerko ..
From a good man ...	Bugin hoṛo te ...	Nagad álas gustí ...	Orteh eṛu málenteh ..
From good men ...	Bugin ho o kote ...	Nagad álar gustí ...	Eṛu malerinteh ..
A good woman ...	Bugin kúṛí ...	Nagad mukka ...	Ortah eṛu pelé ..
Good women ...	Bugin kúṛíko ...	Nagad mukkar ...	Eṛu paylaír ..
A bad boy ...	Etkan koṛá ...	Maldan kukkos ...	Ortáh dográhá mákay ..
A bad girl ...	Etkan kúṛí ...	Maldan kukkoe ...	Ortáh dograhah makkí ..
Good ...	Bugin ...	Nagad ...	Eṛu ..
Better ...	—— te bugin ...	Adinti nagad (more good), ad hurminti nagad.	Gaṛa eṛu ..
Best ...	Sobente bugin, *i.e.*, of all ...	No superl. form of the word	Go tenteh eṛu ..
High ...	Sálangí ...	Mínyá ...	Mechge ..
Higher ...	{ No comparative and superlative forms. {	No comp. and superl. forms. { Add as above "adinti," "ad hurminti."	} Gaṛa mechge ..
Highest ...			} Getenteh mechge ..
A horse ...	Sáṇḍí sadom ...	Ghoṛo ...	Makond goṛo ..
A mare ...	Engá sadom ...	Ghuṛi ...	Makond páti goṛo ..

of Western Bengal and Behar.—(Continued.)

Khond of Orissa.	Khond of Ganjam.	Dhangar of Shahabad.	Kharwar of Shahabad.	English.
Raabbaki ..	Ábáriki ...	Onta embus gebee ..	Ek bapoo ke..	To a father.
Ábbárki ..	Ábariki ...	Koormur embus gehee	Subhkur bapoo ke.	To fathers.
Raábbáhátá ..	Abábahátá ...	Onta embus nijkuw ..	Ek bapoose ..	From a father.
Ábbárubáhátá ..	Ábárubáhátá ...	Koormur embus nijkuw.	Subhkur bapoose	From fathers.
Ramrán ..	Ra budi ápi ...	Onta khuddur ..	Ek betya ..	A daughter.
Riásámedá ..	Budi skátárá ...	Dooee khuddur ..	Doo betya ..	Two daughters.
Mranská ..	Budiská ...	Hoormur khuddur ..	Subh betya ..	Daughters.
Ramráutári ..	Buditárá ...	Onta khuddur gehee..	Ek betyeke ..	Of a daughter.
Mránskátári ..	Budi skátárá ...	Hoormur khudder gehee.	Subh betyake..	Of daughters.
Rámránki ..	Budini ...	Onta khuddur gehee..	Ek betyeke ..	To a daughter.
Mránskáni ..	Budiskániki ...	Hoormur khudder gehee.	Subh betyake	To daughters.
Rámránhátá ..	Budinibáhátá ...	Onta khuddur nijkuw	Ek betyasew..	From a daughter.
......	Budiskánibáhátá ...	Hoormur khudder nijkuw.	Subh betyunsew	From daughters.
Neggilokakurande ..	Negigátánju ...	Onta kuree metus ..	Ek bes murd..	A good man.
Rineggiloka ..	Negigátáruriáru ...	Dooee kooree metus..	Doo bes murd..	Two good men.
Neggilokungá ..	Negigátáru ...	Hoormur koree metus	Subh bes murd	Good men.
Neggilokutári ..	Negigátári ...	Onta koree metus gehee	Ek bes murdke	Of a good man.
Neggilokungátári ..	Negigátári ...	Doee koree metus gehee	Subh besmurdke	Of good men.
Neggiloku ..	Negigátániki ...	Onta koree metus gehee	Ek besmurdke	To a good man.
......	Negigátáriki ...	Doee koree metus gehee	Subh besmurdke	To good men.
Raanjunegiloku bahata.	Negigátánidái ...	Onta koree metus nijkuw.	Ek besmurdse	From a good man.
Neggilokunga-báhátá	Negigotáridái ...	Hoormur koree metus nijkuw.	Subh besmurdse	From good men.
Ranegiásá ..	Negi ásámidá ...	Onta koree mokkar..	Ek neek mehraroo.	A good woman.
Neggiásáská ..	Negi asámidángá ...	Hoormur koree mokkar.	Sub neek mehraroo.	Good women.
Kesárámida-rande ..	Dui ápa ...	Muha boorhus jokhus	Ek unaees renga	A bad boy.
Kesaramrairande ..	Dui budi ...	Muha boorhus khuddur	Unaees renga	A bad girl.
Negári ..	Negárá ...	Nebul ..	Bes ..	Good.
Dehanegar ..	Bala ...	Adint koree ..	Bes neemun ..	Better.
Negári ..	Askádengi ...	Adint bibi koree ..	Subhunse neek	Best.
Denga ..	Prisá ...	Michha ..	Oonch ..	High.
Debádeenga ..	......	Adint michha ..	Savae oonch..	Higher.
Debáui dengá ..	Prisátárá ...	Adint bibi michha ..	Subhunse ..	Highest.
Gadárande ..	Ra godá ...	Onta ghoro ..	Gora ..	A horse.
Tállágadárande ..	Ra táliglıodá ...	Boorhid ..	Ghorya ..	A mare.

English.	Moondari of Lohardugga.	Oorain of Lohardugga.	Rajmehalee of Rajmehal Hills.
Horses ...	Sáṇḍi sádom ko ...	Ghoṛo ...	Goro gáhindi ...
Mares ...	Engá sádom ko ...	Ghuṛi ...	Páti goro gahindí ...
A bull ...	Haḍá ...	Sánḍ ...	Makond sandeh ...
A cow ...	Gai ...	Gunḍé ...	Makond oyou ...
Bulls ...	Haḍáko ...	Sánḍ ...	Sand gahindí ...
Cows ...	Gai ko ...	Gunḍé ...	Oye gahindí ...
A dog ...	Sánḍí setá ...	Allá ...	Mákond áleh ...
A bitch ...	Engá setá ...	Kuṭṭì ...	Mákond páti áleh ...
Dogs ...	Sanḍí setá ko ...	Allá ...	Áleh gáhindí ...
Bitches ...	Engá setá ko ...	Kuṭṭí ...	Páti áleh gáhindí ...
A he-goat ...	Bakṛá ...	Eṛá ...	Mákond bokra bedí ...
A female goat ...	Engá merom ...	Buḍhí eṛá ...	Mákond páti bedí ...
Goats ...	Merom ko (generic) ...	Erá ...	Bedi gahindí ...
A male deer ...	Sánḍí jílu ...	Andiyá mák ...	Makond bakra chitra ...
A female deer ...	Engá jílu ...	Buḍhí mák ...	Makond páti chitra ...
Deer ...	Jílu ko ...	Mák ...	Chitra ...
I am ...	Aiñ menaiñyá ...	En raadan ...	Ainoo ...
Thou art ...	Am menameá ...	Nín raaddí ...	Ninoo ...
He is ...	Iní menaiyá ...	As raas (tali=it is) ...	Áhoo ...
We are ...	Ale menaleá ...	Nám raadat, em raadam ...	Aim sebem ...
You are ...	Ape menapeá ...	Ním raadar ...	Nin seber ...
They are ...	Ako menakoá ...	Ar raanar ("raí" with other than men).	Á seber ...
I was ...	Aiñ tainkenain ...	En rahachkan ...	Ain bechken ...
Thou wast ...	Am tainkenam ...	Nín rahachkai ...	Nin bechkeh ...
He was ...	Iní tainkenai ...	As rahachas ...	Á bechia ...
We were ...	Ale tainkenale ...	Nám rahachkat, em rahachkam.	Aim bechkem ...
You were ...	Ape tainkenape ...	Ním rahachkar ...	Nin chheber luchker ...
They were ...	Ako tainkenako ...	Ár rahachar ...	Á chheber luchia ...
Be ...	Akanmen ...	Maná ...	Uñuñ ...
To be ...	......	Manná ...	Menoti ...
Being ...	Akan ...	Manná ...	Menzáh ...
Having been ...	Jan ...	Manj kan ...	Menz kacharon ...
I may be ...	......	En manna ongon (I am able to be).	Ayn menoti parin ...
I shall be ...	Oá ...	En manon ...	Ayn menen ...
I should be ...	......	En manna ongdan (I was able to be).	Ayn menoti parien ...
Beat ...	Dálmen (2 p.s. imp.) ...	Laua ...	Bazéá ...
To beat ...	Dálteá ...	Launa ...	Bazoti ...
Beating ...	Dáltan ...	Laua ...	Bazuria ...

of Western Bengal and Behar.—(Continued.)

Khond of Orissa.	Khond of Ganjam.	Dhangar of Shahabad.	Kharwar of Shahabad.	English.
Gadángá ...	Godángá ..	Dher ghoro ..	Subh ghore ..	Horses.
Godátálingá ...	Táligodángá ..	Dher boorhid ..	Subh ghorya. .	Mares.
Shandakadirande ...	Randakodi ..	Addo ..	Burud ..	A bull.
Gádákadirande ...	Randá, gadukodi ..	Gaed ..	Gyea ..	A cow.
Shandakádingá ...	Kodingá ..	Dhir addo ..	Subh burdha. .	Bulls.
Pandákádinga ...	Gadungá ..	Dhir gaed ..	Subh gyeun ..	Cows.
Raná hundi ...	Ranáhudi ..	Alla ..	Kookoor ..	A dog.
Ranahuni ..	Ratálináhudi ..	Kootee alla ..	Pilly ..	A bitch.
Nahumingá ...	Náháká ..	Dher alla ..	Subh kookoor. .	Dogs.
Nahunigan ...	Tálináháká ..	Dher kootee alla ..	Subh pilroo ..	Bitches.
Bakadiadá ...	Odá ..	Bokka ..	Khusee ..	A he-goat.
Tálliaddá ...	Táli odá ..	Enra ..	Cher ..	A female goat.
Bakdiadángá ...	Adángá ..	Dher bokka ..	Subh khussee. .	Goats.
Ramiriga ...	Boda sitáli ..	Enrya ..	Chowrenga ..	A male deer.
Rasitáli ...	Talli sitáli ..	Boorhee ..	Bhoourlee ..	A female deer.
Mirigá ...	Sitáli ..	Dher enrya ..	Subh chowrenga subh bhoourlee.	Deer.
Ámunai ...	Ánu, Máin ..	Inhoraduw ..	Mahoon ..	I am.
Mumanji ...	Irumánjeru ..	Ninhoraday ..	Too howwa ..	Thou art.
Ebánju manenju ..	Ánjumanenju ..	Arhoraday ..	Ao how wus ..	He is.
Ámumanúa ...	Ámumánámu ..	Enhoraduw ..	Humun hyen ..	We are.
Irumassem ...	Inu manjí ..	Ninhoraday ..	Too howwa ..	You are.
Ebárugule ...	Árumáneru ..	Arhoradaw ..	Ao oubh how was.	They are.
Ámimassi ...	Ánu másse ..	Inhorum ..	Maruhloow ..	I was.
Inumassi ...	Inumánji ..	Ninhorum ..	Too ruhla ..	Thou wast.
Ebánjumásse ...	Zánjumásenju ..	Armoorhoraday ..	Aoruhla ..	He was.
Máiñgule massengu ...	Amumásámu ..	Emhorum ..	Humunke ruh-leen.	We were.
Irumasseru ...	Inu mánji ..	Ninhorum ..	Toow ruhlu ..	You were.
Ábárumáneru ...	Yáru máseru ..	Armoorhorum ..	Assubh ruhlun.	They were.
Imu ...	Mánba áná ..	Ho ..	Hokhus ..	Be.
Ábátangi ...	Mánbánda ..	Munaluggay ..	Hokheke ..	To be.
......	Mánba dái ..	Nulukh ..	Hoeke ..	Being.
Maseru ...	Mánbáteká ..	Kula ..	Hoke ..	Having been.
Ámuabá munámu ...	Ánumanbamui ..	Inhomunnun ..	Ma saed ruheen	I may be.
Amu ánámu ...	Anumaigiua ..	Inhoround ..	Maruhloow ..	I shall be
Máange ábásánjane...	Ánumai ..	Juroor kurke munnun	Majroor rahul hooch.	I should be.
Págámu ...	Sámu Bemu ..	Lowa ..	Murra ..	Beat.
Págátángi ...	Sápátengi ..	Lowarcha ..	Mareke ..	To beat.
......	Sahi ..	Lowchake ..	Mareke ..	Beating.

English.	Moondari of Lohardugga.	Oorain of Lohardugga.	Rajmehalee of Rajmehal Hills.
Having beaten ...	Dálkedte ...	Lauchkan ...	Bazúr káchrá ...
I beat ...	Aiñ dáli aiñ ...	En laudan ...	Ain bazen ...
Thou beatest ...	Am dáli am ...	Nín laudai ...	Nin bazurkeh ...
He beats ...	Iní dáli ai ...	Ás laudas ...	Ah bazuría ...
We beat ...	Ale dáli ale ...	Em laudam ...	Aim bazem ...
You beat ...	Ape dáli ape ...	Nám laudat ...	Nin bazah ...
They beat ...	Ako dáli ako ...	Ár launar ...	Achener bazer ...
I am beating ...	Ain dáltanaiñ ...	En laná lagdan ...	Ain bazeh behín ...
I was beating ...	Ain dáltan taikena ...	En laná lakan ...	Ain bazeh bíchken ...
I had beaten ...	......	En lauchkan rahachkan ...	Ain bazeh kochorken ...
I may beat ...	......	En lauongon (I am able to beat).	Ain bazoti paréin ...
I shall beat ...	Ain daléaiñ ...	En lauon ...	Ain bazoti maden ...
I should beat ...	......	....	Ain bazoti marmezeken ...
I am beaten ...	(No passive form) ...	(No passive form) ...	Ain bazurken ...
I was beaten ...	......	....	Ain bazur kocharken ...
I shall be beaten ...	......	....	Ain bazurenkoh ...
I go ...	Aiñ senoaiñ ...	En ká lagdan ...	Ain aiken ...
Than goest ...	Am senoam ...	Nín ká lagdai ..	Nin ekkeh ...
He goes ...	Iní senoai ...	Ás ká lagdas ...	Áh ekkí ...
I went ...	Aiñ senkenaiñ ...	En kerkan ...	Ain ekkeh kochorken ...
Thou wentest ...	Am senkenam ...	Nín kerkaí ...	Nin ekkeh kochorkeh ...
He went ...	Iní senkenai ...	Ás keras ...	Ah ekkeh kochoría ...
Go ...	Senomeñ ...	Kala ...	Kálá ...
Going ...	Senotan ...	Káná ...	Ekkeh behi ...
Gone ...	Senojan ...	Kálke ...	Ekkia ...
What is your name?...	Ama nutum chikaná ? ...	Ninghaí ender name ...	Ningki indor nameh ...
How old is this horse?	Ne sadom chimin sinua hobákaná.	I ghoṛo eyon chánantá tali	Yi goro iko páneh ...
How far is it from here to Kashmir.	Nea te Kashmír chiminañ sañiña.	Iyantí Kashmir gutí eyon gechchha raí.	Yí nonteh Kashmíreh iko chudí meníd.
How many sons are there in your father's house ...	Apumá oraá re chimin koṛá honko menákoá.	Nimbas gahí erpámí eyon jhan kukko khaddar raanar.	Ning aboki ádáno ikond maker behener.

Khond of Orissa.	Khond of Ganjam.	Dhangar of Shahabad.	Kharwar of Shahabad.	English.
Págá ...	Sábáuenju ..	......	Marke ..	Having beaten.
Ámupági ...	Ánusápimái ..	In lowa lugdun ..	Ma marho ..	I beat.
Irupagite ...	Inusápimánji ..	Ninlowa lugday ..	Too marut barra	Thou beatest.
Ebânjusáhápimá venju	Ánjusápimánenju ..	Askolowa lugdus ..	Ao marut ho. .	He beats.
......	Ámû sátá támu ..	Emholowa lugdun ..	Hamuw marut bareen.	We beat.
......	Inusátáti ..	Ninlondur ..	Toohun marut howwa.	You beat.
......	Árusátáteru ..	Arlonur ..	Aosub marut baruw.	They beat.
Ámupágimánuánu ...	Ánusápimái ..	Inguw loncher ..	Ma marut bareew.	I am beating.
Ámupágimásámu ...	Ánusápimáse ..	Inmar mokkuw ..	Ma marut ruhleew.	I was beating.
Ámupágámassamu ...	Ánu sáte ..	Injuroor lawa lewur. .	Ma marlay ruhleew.	I had beaten.
......	Ánu sapamuij ..	Inho luwuw ..	Ma marsakeela	I may beat.
Ámupágina ...	Ánusaiginá ..	Inlowunga ..	Marmarho ..	I shall beat.
Mángepágásángite ...	......	Injuroor lawunga ..	Ma juroor marho.	I should beat.
Ámusábi ...	Ánusápápáte ..	Ingunlonchus ..	Ma marul jat bareew.	I am beaten.
Ámu máddátinjámásámu.	Ánusápápánjámái. .	Ingunlonchus moonduw.	Ma marul jat ruhleew.	I was beaten.
Amu máddátinjinámu	Ánumádátuñ ..	Injuroor lawa mokkuw.	Ma juroor marul jaib.	I shall be beaten.
Ámu sabi ánusáin ...	Ánu sáiñ ..	Inkalugdun ..	Ma jaeebo ..	I go.
Iru sáju ...	Inusáji ..	Nunhokula ..	Too jat barra	Thou goest.
Ebanju sáji márenju. .	Iánjusásenju ..	Asaon ho kerus ..	Ao jat batey. .	He goes.
Ámumásse ...	Ánu sase ..	Inhokurkuw ..	Ma gyeleew ..	I went.
Inu másse ...	Inusási ..	Ninhokurkuw ..	Too gyela ..	Thou wentest.
Ebánju másse ...	Yánju sásenju ..	Asoonhokerus ..	Ao gyela ..	He went.
Sáju ...	Sáju sálámu ..	Kula ..	Jah ..	Go.
Sájimáne ...	Sájimane ..	Kulugduw ..	Jat bareew ..	Going.
Sásse ...	Sáse ..	Kowun ..	Jat ruhub ..	Gone.
Nipáddá áná ...	Nipádáinipádá ..	Indurneghi numay ..	Ka tohur nao ha.	What is your name?
Nigadágádiábáepe ...	Igodás sabudáájá máne.	Eyon olta oomur ghoro mano.	Ketna oomar re ghora ke howay.	How old is this horse?
Kásmir imbátáká esedurá.	Kásmira desa imbá tekás se duraáne.	Asle Keshmeer eyon gichhu mamo.	Ehwaw se Kushmir kateek door howay.	How far is it from here to Kashmir?
Miábbáedutárse Meiká máneru.	Ni ábá idutá ese srikamaneru.	Enluggay neembus kooeea kookoo khuddur.	Kutna beta tohra bap ke ghur me baruw.	How many sons are there in your father's house?

English.	Moondari of Lohardugga.	Oorain of Lohardugga.	Rajmehalee of Rajmehal Hills.
I have walked a long way to-day ...	Sisiñ aiñ asu sañiñá tein hijulená.	Inná en ḍher gechchhá kerkan.	Ain íneh ganṛi ganṛa haveh charach ken (or) Ain ineh dégaroh haveh choroch ken.
The son of my uncle is married to her sister.	Kakainyaá hon te koṛá iniá misé loo árandiakanai.	Eng kakasgahí tangdas gahí binja adígahí ṭangḍigane manjakí bü.	Eng dádá tengadek adí táng baíguni pelved menza.
In the house is the saddle of the white horse.	Oraá re punḍí sadomá jín mená.	Erpánú pandru ghoṛogahí khughir rai.	Yi, ádáno zínporo gorokí kokeno nanpo behí.
Put the saddle upon his back.	Niá ḍeyá re jín doimeṅ ...	Ádi gahí mednú khughir úiyá.	Navíkí kokeno kidpon oza.
I have beaten his son with many stripes.	Ain iniá hon koḍrá te isu hansakíya.	En asgahí tangdasín kodhem korrátí lauchkan beedan.	Ayn ahíkí tengaden peneth gañrí gañra bazken.
He is grazing cattle on the top of the hill.	Iní buru chetan re uri ko gupitanai.	Ás aḍdo mentaá lagdas partá meṅyá.	Aha pahar kornoh saoazen charatri kend kundí.
He is sitting on a horse under that tree.	En dáru súbá re iní sádom re dubakanai.	Ás ontá ghoṛonú ukkas beedas amannagahí múlínú.	Ahmon kolorno goro meche okí.
His brother is taller than his sister.	Inia hagá te iniá mísiáte sálangíakanai.	Ásgahí tangrís adígahí tangrinti mechchha raas.	Ah adí tang bainteh mechga
The price of that is two rupees and a half.	Ená réa gonoñ bár taká adalí mená.	Adígahí mullí aṛhái rupiya raí.	Nadiké kimoteh ádaitáká meneni.
My father lives in that small house.	Apúiñ en huḍiñ oraá re taintanai.	Embas hu sanní erpanú raadas.	Na ada mákono eng ábbá dokí.
Give this rupee to him	Ne taká umaimeṅ ...	I rupiyan ásge chiá ...	Yi takan, nahik chia ...
Take those rupees from him.	En taká ko iní táte agúimeṅ	Abṛá rupiyan ásgusṭi hoá ...	Ahi guni nao nao takan oúka.
Beat him well and bind him with rope.	Khúb dálímen oro baiar te tholimeṅ.	Ásín khob koda dará eptu-rú heá.	Nahin ehene baza adente gatath echekeroza.
Draw water from the well.	Kuán te dáa uruñemeṅ ...	Kubíntí am otharaá ...	Chuanteh ameh mulgá ...
Walk before me ...	Aiñya aiar re senomeṅ ...	Enghai mund gucha ...	Eng bahano choría ...
Whose boy comes behind you?	Okoiá koṛá hon amá tayomte hijutaná?	Nekhai tangdas nighai khokhánu bardas?	Nek tengadeh ningí kokok berí.
From whom did you buy that?	Ená am okoi tá tem kiriñlaá	Adín ním negusti khindkar (plural)?	Nek guni nadin kekkeh ...
From a shop-keeper of the village.	Hatu ren moyad dokanü tá te.	Padantá orot baṅiyas gustí	Na kekki bahond doka ninteh.

of Western Bengal and Behar.—(Concluded.)

Khond of Orissa.	Khond of Ganjam.	Dhangar of Shahabad.	Kharwar of Shahabad.	English.
Neamudebatre haginga mánámu.	Nenju ánu dehá páhári tákite.	A bether gichhcha koodoo'kun ke buruchkun.	Ma burdoor se aj sail kyle hyru.	I have walked a long way to-day.
Main kákumrienju táná angunibhiangitenju.	Nai koká mrijenju eri tánginisedu áhátenju.	Inka kusgay tungdus asgay tungdye asginay ing karrye.	Mor kara ke bete ke biyah oonkur buhine se bhyh ha.	The son of my uncle is married to her sister.
Mukágadá tári páláiu idumáde tamanne.	Su káligodátángín idutá mane.	Surpa jeen rye aeka pudro ghoro juhjeen.	Ghur men khogeer oojur ghora ke ha.	In the house is the saddle of the white horse.
Gadáshámu ...	I jini eánigándita itámu.	Ekade munja jeen luda	Khoogeer ke ohkur pith pur dhurra.	Put the saddle upon his beck.
Tánámi enjunianudeha págite.	Ánu eánumrini kidorudai dehásá te.	Tungdus koorkun kykdunda.	Ma oonkur beta ke kyik ghos murlayhyew.	I have beaten his son with many stripes.
Ásarukuiti tajan unjan kapáimánenju.	Eánjusoru, kuití kodi gáni solá tispámánenju.	Purta myan gaed myna lugay.	Ao mawasee toongur pur paharke charawat ba.	He is grazing cattle on the top of the hill.
Ámrábámmedá tágádá kuititá manunju.	Eánju ámránusáiti godátá kaksámánenju.	Enurtus ghoro rikkus ras mun moolee ijkus.	Ao ghora pur uswar bethe oo rookh ke ba.	He is sitting on a horse under that tree.
Tánáámbe satáná báitáká dengá.	Eáni dádá, eánitáugi kebe pidsámásenju.	Asgay tung dudus a dinty nuchhcha.	Okur bhaee sawae oonch banisbut okra baheen ke ba.	His brother is taller than his sister.
Erikriusitákárisuká ...	Erámotá, dosásuká áre.	Dam minjus arhaee rupya.	Mol okur arhaee rupya ba.	The price of that is two rupees and a half.
Máiábbáákagü dumá detá mánenju.	Náiábá kagári idutá máuenju.	Embus chotay surpa noradus.	Mor bap oo chhot ghur men ruhela.	My father lives in that small house.
Itákárandáebbani kisimu.	Itáká eánikisímu ..	Edbebun asgechiya.	Ee roopya ke okra keda.	Give this rupee to him.
Átákáibáin bábá tamuñ.	Átákángáeáni báhátáko dáum.	Adhebun asgoostay howa.	Ao roopya ke oonka se lela.	Take those rupees from him.
Ábánineggi giánái pagi, dorutá táhamu.	Eániki, balladengisáhámu, ate, i dorkádái tamu.	Askhoob luwa ipno asin beya.	Okra ke bhur jore mara our jorse okra ke banda.	Beat him well and bind him with ropes.
Kuántakási druka dámuu.	Kuátásidue belanue	Kobuntee amninda ..	Indara se panee bhar.	Draw water from the well.
Náin noki sallaum ...	náke nokámu ..	Inghay moond baharee gichha bokha moond kula bura.	Humra ugaree chul phir.	Walk before me.
Embarimidámi boatibáimáne.	Imberipagánju náibi ayájá mánenju.	Neekhay khidday ninghay bokha tintay hura lugmur.	Kehker larika tohra pichay awut ba.	Whose boy comes behind you?
Eri imberi bhábá kadditi.	Inu imberita, árákadá mánji.	Nesgoostay khind ke raday.	Kekara se toow okra kemol lele how ha.	From whom did you buy that?
Juátar ánju dokánibábá.	Náta bajáriatá kadá mánii.	Metus hunee angay goostay hoa.	Gano ke bunya se lele hyen.	From a shop-keeper of the village.

SPECIMENS

OF THE

ABORIGINAL LANGUAGES

OF THE

CENTRAL PROVINCES.

	TRIBES.				
	KOORKOOS.		MEHTO.	BYGAS OR BINJWARS.	
	Nimar.	Hoshungabad	Bilaspur.	Balaghat.	Mandla.
One	Mia	Mia	......	......	......
Two	Baria	Baria	......	Door	......
Three	Hapia	Aphia	......	......	......
Four	Oofoonia	Oofoonia	......	......	......
Five	Monoya	Monoya	......	Puch	......
Six	Toorooya	Toorai	......	Chaie	......
Seven	Ayeeah	Aie	......	......	......
Eight	Eelaria	Eelar	......	......	......
Nine	Area	Araie	......	......	......
Ten	Gél	Gul	......	......	......
Twenty	Esa	Eesa	......	......	......
Fifty	......	......	......	......	......
One hundred	Meeasuddie	Su	......	......	......
I	Eeng	Eeng	......	......	......
Of me	......	Yen	......	......	More
Mine	Eenja	Yan	......	......	More
We	Allay	Alay	......	Hame	......
Of us	......	Yen	......	Hamrá	More
Our	Allayja	Allay	......	......	......
Thou	......	Um	......	Tu	......
Of thee	......	Um Khun	......	Toor	......
Thine	......	Ama	......	......	......
You	......	Apay	......	Toom	......
Of you	......	Um Khun	......	Toomur	......
Your	......	Apay	......	......	......
He	Deeja	Hoojay	......	Oh	......
Of him	......	Deejun	......	Okúr	......
His	......	Deeja	......	......	......
They	Arkon	Hukoonay	......	......	......
Of them	......	Deejun	......	......	......
Their	......	Deeja	......	......	......
Hand	Tee	Tee	Teeth	......	......
Foot	Nanga	Nanga	Kuttath	Gode	......
Nose	Mon	Moo	Mooth	......	......
Eye	Med	Met	Maith	Ayekh	......
Mouth	Chaboo	Chaboo	Thoteth	Moo	......
Tooth	Teereen	Tiring	Tring	......	......
Ear	Lootoor	Lootoor	Lootoor	......	......
Hair	Op	Hoob	Oob	Choondee	Kesh
Head	Kupar	Dooing	Bho	......	......

TRIBES.					
PUNKA.	MEHRA.	KATYA.	RAJ GOND.	MARIA GOND.	
Mandla.	Mandla.	Narsinghpur.	Chanda.	Chanda.	
......	......	......	......	......	One.
......	......	......	......	......	Two.
......	......	......	......	......	Three.
......	......	......	......	......	Four.
......	......	......	......	......	Five.
......	......	......	......	......	Six.
......	......	......	......	......	Seven.
......	......	......	......	......	Eight.
......	......	......	......	......	Nine.
......	......	......	......	......	Ten.
......	......	......	......	......	Twenty.
......	......	......	......	......	Fifty.
......	......	......	......	......	One Hundred.
......	......	Mee	Nuna	Nunna	I.
More	More	Maja, Majee	Nawa	Nawa	Of me.
More	More	Maja, Majee	Nawa	Naiva	Mine.
......	......	......	Amot	Mummatoo	We.
More	More	Humche, Humchee	Mawa	Mawa	Of us.
......	......	Humche, Humchee	Mawa	Mawa	Our.
......	......	Too	Nimme	Mimma	Thou.
......	......	Toojha, Toojhee	Neewa	Neewa	Of thee.
......	......	Toojha, Toojhee	Neewa	Neewa	Thine.
......	......	......	Nimmet	Nimmutoo	You.
......	......	Toomche, Toomchee	Meewa	Meewa	Of you.
......	......	Toomche, Toomchee	Meewa	Meewa	Your.
......	......	Te	Wor, Wogoo	Bogoo, Hogoo	He.
......	......	Tacha, Tachee	Wana, Tana	Wana, Tana	Of him.
......	......	Tacha, Tachee.	Wona	Wona	His.
......	......	......	Hor	Woroo	They.
......	......	......	Hona	Wora	Of them.
......	......	......	Hona	Wora	Their.
......	......	......	Kin	Kinyoo	Hand.
......	......	......	Kal	Kaloo	Foot.
......	......	......	Mosar	Moshok	Nose.
......	......	Dor	Kuruk	Konda	Eye.
......	......	......	Todee	Toddee	Mouth.
......	......	......	Pulk	Pulloo	Tooth.
......	......	......	Kevee	Kevoo	Ear.
......	......	......	Kelk	Kelloo	Hair.
......	......	......	Tula	Tulla	Head.

	TRIBES.				
	KOORKOOS.		MEHTO.	BYGAS OR BINJWARS.	
	Nimar.	Hoshungabad.	Bilaspur.	Balaghat.	Mandla.
Tongue	Lang	Lang	Alung	......	......
Belly	Lai	Layee	Lai	......	......
Back	Patta Bhoree	Bhaodee	Tooteth	......	......
Iron	Lokhondo	Loh	Lohich	......	......
Gold	Sona	Sona	Souna	Soonna	......
Silver	Roopa	Chandi	Chandich	Chandee	......
Father	Aba	Awakur	Apoom	......	......
Mother	Mai	Mai	Egung	......	......
Brother	Dada	Bhaya, Dada	Wagum	Dada	......
Sister	Baie	Misee	Missim	Bai Nonee	......
Man	Koro	Koru	Munnai	......	Donka
Woman	Jupaie	Jufye	Eruth	Donkee	Donkee
Wife	Eanjupaie	Jufye	Erung	Dubkee	Loogaee
Child	Taunee	Tana	Lahee	Chawa	......
Son	Dhoki Kond	Kon	Helurhun	......	......
Daughter	Heerkon Kond	Koojye	Erahun	......	......
Slave	......	......	......	......	Jootha
Cultivator	Kirsan	Keersan	Hoorkoo	Kissar	......
Shepherd	Dhunkar	Gadanea	Mehrum mohoriah	......	Churwah
God	Gowaj	Gomuj	Bhugwan	Bhugwan	Naraindeo
Devil	Bhooto	Bhoot	Mara	Bhoot	Bhoot
Sun	Gomuj	Gomuj	Baér	Din	Soorujdeo
Moon	Chandniegoomai	Chand	Jone	Chand	Joodhaiwa
Star	Efil	Eefeel	Ipeel	Turaie	Taraiwa
Fire	Singél	Singul	Sengul	Aig	......
Water	Da	Dar	Dab	......	......
House	Oora	Oora	Orá	Ghur	......
Horse	Ghorgi	Goorgie	Ghore	......	......
Cow	......	......	Ooree	......	......
Dog	Cheeta	Seeta	......	Kookoor	Kookoor, Kootah
Cat	Meenoo	Meenoo	Ile	Bilwa	Beelar
Cock	Komba	Kooma	Sim	Kookdu	Morunga
Duck	Budduck	Buduk	Dabuk	Dubuk	Dubuk
Ass	Gudderee	Gudra	Gadhe	Gudha	......
Camel	Oont	Oont	Unthee	Oot	......
Bird	Teelit	Chisroj	Teetee	......	......
Go	Chineba	Senaja	Ibatum	......	......
Eat	Jomma	Jomeeja	Jum	......	......
Sit	Soobangu	Soobangija	Dooroop	......	......
Come	Hedjiba	Hirjay	Dum	......	......
Beat	Mondieja	Koomagai	Medai	......	......

PROVINCES LANGUAGES.—(*Continued.*)

TRIBES.					
PUNKA.	MEHRA.	KATYA.	RAJ GOND.	MARIA GOND.	
Mandla.	Mandla.	Narsinghpur.	Chanda.	Chanda.	
......	......	......	Wunjer	Wunjag	Tongue.
......	......	Pot	Peer	Potta	Belly.
......	......	......	Perreka	Mondko	Back.
......	......	......	Kuchee	Kuchee	Iron.
......	......	......	Sono	Sono	Gold.
......	......	......	Khooro	Khooro	Silver.
......	......	Dada	Babo	Minmal	Father.
Mohtaree	Mohtaree	Buhoo	Ava	Minya	Mother.
......	......	......	Tumoor	Tummogai	Brother.
......	......	......	Shelar	Helagai	Sister.
......	......	Log	Manial	Munkal	Man.
Donkee	Donkee	Logaee	Har	Anchurree	Woman.
Loogaee	Logaee	Bail	Mootte	Mootta	Wife.
......	......	......	......	......	Child.
......	......	Lekhoor	Murree, Meyar	Murree, Mugai	Son.
......	......	Andoor	Meeyar	Muyoree	Daughter.
Rootha, Balpose	Rootha, Balpose	......	......	......	Slave.
......	......	......	Kissan	Kuburkewar	Cultivator.
......	......	......	Koormar	Yeting-mehwah	Shepherd.
......	......	......	Pen	Penos	God.
......	......	......	Dinya	Dunjan	Devil.
......	......	......	Pordoo	Pordoo	Sun.
......	......	......	Nelenj	Lenjoo	Moon.
Taraiwa	Taraiwa	......	Hokko	Hookka	Star.
......	......	Istoo	Kis	Kissoo	Fire.
......	......	......	Yer	Yagoo	Water.
......	......	......	Lon	Lonoo	House.
......	......	......	Khora	Kora	Horse.
......	......	......	Moora	Moore	Cow.
Kookoor	Kookoor	......	Nui	Neiyoo	Dog.
......	......	......	Bilial	Pooshalee	Cat.
......	......	Komra	Ghoogootee	Gogooree	Cock.
......	......	......	Herema	Herma	Duck.
......	......	......	Gardee	Gardee	Ass.
......	......	......	Hootan	Ootoomee	Camel.
......	......	......	Pitte	Pitte	Bird.
......	......	Za, Zesin	Hum	Honnoo	Go.
......	......	......	Tin	Tinnos	Eat.
......	......	......	Ooda	Oodda	Sit.
......	......	......	Wura	Wayu	Come.
......	......	......	Pam, Jeem	Halsa, Pam	Beat.

	TRIBES.				
	KOORKOOS.		MEHTO.	BYGAS OR BINJWARS.	
	Nimar.	Hoshungabad.	Bilaspur.	Balaghat.	Mandla.
Stand	Tengneu	Tiginay	Churako	Thadruh	Thaira rohhy
Die	Gojuba	Gouj	Goiko	Murney	......
Give	Hukerja	......	Ewung	......	......
Run	......	Surubay	Nineerka	Bhugaoo	......
Up	Lee	Leeun	Rinko	Mey	......
Down	Otay	Etan	Dooroop	......	......
Before	Chova	Sootoogun	Aghere	......	......
Near	Meirja	Merun	Thaoen	......	Jorey
Far	Lanka	Utar	Turarim	......	......
Behind	Tawun	Tawun	......	Pachey	......
Who	......	Yae	Ame	......	......
What	Cho	Choee	......	......	......
Why	......	Chodeega	......	Kuelay	......
And	......	Aor	Aur	Ar	......
But	......	Pun	......	Pachoo	......
If	......	......	......	......	......
Yes	Thaka	......	Ho	Ho	......
No	Bung	Haibung	Bagin	Nahi	......
Alas	......	......	......	Arrura	Edaee
A father	......	Meea Dao	......	Baba	......
Of a father	......	......	......	Babako	......
To a father	......	Dao Khun	......	Babaley	......
From a father	......	Dao Tun	......	Babatey	......
Two fathers	......	......	......	......	......
Fathers	......	......	......	Baba	......
Of fathers	......	......	......	Babako	......
To fathers	......	......	......	Babaley	......
From fathers	......	......	......	Babatey	......
A daughter	......	Meea Eerkhoon	......	Betty	......
Of a daughter	......	......	......	Bettyko	......
To a daughter	......	Koonjye Khun	......	Bettyley	......
From a daughter ...	......	Koon Jat	......	Bettytey	......
Two daughters	......	......	......	......	......
Daughters	......	Ghoonick Eerkhoon	......	Betty	......
Of daughters	......	......	......	Bettyko	......
To daughters	......	......	......	Bettyley	......
From daughters	......	......	......	Bettytay	......
A good man	Awul Ja	Nigut Kora	......	Nik admi	......
Of a good man	......	......	......	Nik admiko	Ek bhala manoosh

TRIBES.					
PUNKA.	MEHRA.	KATYA.	RAJ GOND.	MARIA GOND.	
Mandla.	Mandla.	Narsinghpur.	Chanda.	Chanda.	
Tharrarowh	Tharrarowh	......	Nila	Nilla	Stand.
......	......	......	Sam	Ham	Die.
......	......	......	Sheem	Heem	Give.
......	......	......	Witta	Witta	Run.
......	......	......	Porro	Pogonoo	Up.
......	......	......	Sheer	Hirinoo	Down.
......	......	......	Moonne	Moonne	Before.
Lingha	......	......	Kuchool	Here	Near.
......	......	......	Luk	Jekoo	Far.
......	......	......	Puja	Peakke, Pinya	Behind.
......	......	......	Bor	Bogoo	Who.
......	......	......	Butee	Bota	What.
......	......	......	Baree	Barankoo	Why.
......	......	......	An	Un	And.
......	......	......	Muti	Mutee	But.
......	......	......	......	......	If.
......	......	......	Inge	Eiye	Yes.
......	......	......	Hille	Hille	No.
......	......	......	......	Aiyayo	Alas.
......	......	Dada	Babo	Minmal	A father.
......	......	Dada-chachee	Babona	Minmana	Of a father.
......	......	Dada-la	Babonee	Minmankoo	To a father.
......	......	Dada-lok	Babon agatal	Minman agatal	From a father.
......	......	......	......	......	Two fathers.
......	......	Dade	Babok	Minmalor	Fathers.
......	......	Dada-chachee	Babokna	Minmalona	Of fathers.
......	......	Dade-la	Baboknee	Minmalorkoo	To fathers.
......	......	Dade-lok	Babok agatal	Minmaloo agatal	From fathers.
......	......	Andoor	Meeyar	Minyaree	A daughter.
......	......	Andoor-chachee	Meeyarna	Minyareena	Of a daughter.
......	......	Andoor-la	Meeyaroon	Minyarkoo	To a daughter.
......	......	Andoor-lok	Meeyart agatal	Minyareen agatal	From a daughter.
......	......	......	......	......	Two daughters.
......	......	Andoor	Meeyarkoo	Minyaskoo	Daughters.
......	......	Andoor-chachee	Meeyarkna	Minyaskoona	Of daughters.
......	......	Andoor-la	Meeyarkoon	Minyaskoonkoo	To daughters.
......	......	Andoor-lok	Meeyark agatal	Minyaskoon agatal	From daughters.
......	......	......	Bes manial	Nehna munkal	A good man.
......	......	......	Bes maniana	Nehna munkana	Of a good man.

	TRIBES.				
	KOORKOOS.		MEHTO.	BYGAS BINJWARS..	
	Nimar.	Hoshungabad.	Bilaspur.	Balaghat.	Mandla.
To a good man	......	......	......	Nik admiley	......
From a good man ...	......	......	......	Nik admitay	......
Two good men	......	......	......	......	......
Good men	.....	......	......	Nik admi	Kool manoosh
Of good men	......	......	......	Nik admiko	......
To good men	......	......	......	Nik admilay	......
From good men	......	......	......	Nik admitay	......
A good woman	Awul japaie	Nigut jufye	......	Nik doukee	......
Good women	......	......	......	Nik donkee	......
A bad boy	Anda kond innil	Booro koon	Lahaie uraon	Kharah beta	......
A bad girl	Anda kottie innil	Boorokoojye	......	Kharah betty	......
Good	Awul	Nigut	Banne	Nik	......
Better	......	......	......	......	......
Best	......	......	......	......	......
High	......	......	Munnarung	......	......
Higher	......	......	......	......	......
Highest	......	......	......	......	......
A horse	Ghorgie	Ghoorgaie	......	......	......
A mare	......	......	......	......	......
Houses	......	Ghoorgaie	......	......	......
Mares	......	......	......	......	......
A bull	......	......	......	......	......
A cow	......	......	......	......	......
Bulls	Doobla	Doobla	......	......	......
Cows	......	......	......	......	......
A dog	Cheeta	Meea seeta	......	......	Ek kookoor
A bitch	......	Meea seetee	......	Kookree	Ek sitie
Dogs	......	Seeta	......	Kookar	Mooktey kookoor
Bitches	......	Seetee	......	Kookree	Gulley sitie
A he goat	......	Bookra	Merum	......	......
A female goat	......	Bookree	......	Chini	......
Goats	......	Bookra	......	......	......
A male deer	......	Heerna	......	......	Ek mriga
A female deer	......	Heernee	......	Hirni	......
Deer	......	Heern	......	......	......
I am	......	Eenj ja	......	Meyhoo	......
Thou art	......	Um ja	......	Tiahas	......

PROVINCES LANGUAGES.—(*Continued.*)

TRIBES.					
PUNKA.	MEHRA.	KATYA.	RAJ GOND.	MARIA GOND.	
Mandla.	Mandla.	Narsinghpur.	Chanda.	Chanda.	
......	......	......	Bes manieta	Nehna munkankoo	To a good man.
......	......	......	Bes maniat agatal	Nehna munkal agatal	From a good man.
......	......	......	......	......	Two good men.
......	......	......	Bes manelor	Nehenore munkalor	Good men.
......	......	......	Bes manena	Nehnore munkalora	Of good men.
......	......	......	Bes maneheta	Nehnore munkalorkoo	To good men.
......	......	......	Bes maniata agatal	Nehna munkalor agatal	From good men.
Ek uchi mehureea	......	Ek ucchi mehureea.	Bes har	Nehna ancharee	A good woman.
......	......	......	Bes hark	Nehna anchkoo	Good women.
......	......	Boora lakhoor	Aror pekah	Lagorpedal	A bad boy.
......	......	Boree andoor	Aror peree	Lago peree	A bad girl.
......	......	......	Bes	Nehna	Good.
......	......	......	......	......	Better.
......	......	......	......	......	Best.
......	......	......	Oonch	Dunkoo	High.
......	......	......	......	......	Higher.
......	......	......	......	......	Highest.
......	......	......	Khora	Potal kora	A horse.
......	......	......	Khoree	Tullo kora	A mare.
......	......	......	Khorang	Korang	Houses.
......	......	......	Khoring	Khorang	Mares.
......	......	......	Koora	Veja boroom	A bull.
......	......	......	Moore	Moore	A cow.
......	......	......	Koorang	Borok	Bulls.
......	......	......	Moorang	Mooreng	Cows.
Ek kookoor	......	......	Nin	Nuiyoo	A dog.
......	......	......	Totte	Totte	A bitch.
......	......	......	Nuyek	Niukoo	Dogs.
......	......	......	Totteng	Totteng	Bitches.
......	......	......	Bokra	Bokra	A he goat.
Ek chheree	......	Ek chheree	Hurre	Yettee	A female goat.
......	......	......	Bokrang	Bokrang	Goats.
......	......	......	Hurreng	Hurnalee	A male deer.
......	......	......	Kotra	Tulloor hurnalee	A female deer.
......	......	......	Hurna	Hurnaskoo	Deer.
......	......	Mee hoon	Nuna muntona	Nunna muntanoo	I am.
......	......	Too ás	Nime muntee	Nimma muntinee	Thou art.

	TRIBES.				
	KOORKOOS.		MEHTO.	BYGAS OR BINJWARS.	
	Nimar.	Hoshungabad.	Bilaspur.	Balaghat.	Mandla.
He is	......	Deeja	......	Oka ah	......
We are	......	Alayja	......	Hamey ah	......
You are	......	Umja	......	Tiaha	......
They are	......	Deeja	......	Okah	......
I was	......	Eeng dhan	......	Muyruhoo	......
Thou wast	......	Um dhan	......	Tirahas	......
He was	......	Dee dhan	......	Okarah	......
We were	......	Alay dhan	......	Humeyruhoo	......
You were	......	Apay dhan	......	Tirahey	......
They were	......	Dee dhan	......	Okruh	......
Be	......	Ja	......	Ah	......
To be	......	Ja	......	Aha	......
Being	......	Daboosye	......	......	......
Having been	......	Daeen	......	......	......
I may be	......	......	......	......	......
I shall be	......	......	......	Meho	......
I should be	......	......	......	......	......
Beat	......	Kooma khye	......	Mar	......
To beat	......	Kooma khye	......	Marna	......
Beating	......	Kookh maninee	......	......	......
Having beaten	......	......	......	......	......
I beat	......	Eeng kookh mao	Eng nedai	Mey mawhoo	......
Thou beatest	......	Um koolsh mao	......	Timarhus	......
He beats	......	Dee kookh mao	......	Or marha	......
We beat	......	Alay kookh mao	......	Hamay marut	......
You beat	......	Um kookh mao	......	Timarhu	......
They beat	......	Dee kookh mao	......	Ok marha	......
I am beating	......	......	......	May marutah	......
I was beating	......	Eeng kookhma dhan	......	Mey marha	......
I had beaten	......	Eeng kooma khuye	......	......	......
I may beat	......	......	......	May maroo	......
I shall beat	......	......	......	Mey marwo	......
I should beat	......	......	......	Mey marbo	......
I am beaten	......	......	......	Muley marhey	......
I was beaten	......	......	......	Muley marhus	......
I shall be beaten	......	......	......	......	......

PROVINCES LANGUAGES.—(*Continued.*)

TRIBES.					
PUNKA.	MEHRA.	KATYA.	RAJ GOND.	MARIA GOND.	
Mandla.	Mandla.	Narsinghpur.	Chanda.	Chanda.	
......	......	Te and	Wor muntoor	Wogoo muntogoo	He is.
......	......	......	Amoot muntorom	Mummatoo muntomoo	We are.
......	......	......	Nimet muntil	Nimmut muntiree	You are.
......	......	......	Hor muntor	Woroo muntoroo	They are.
......	......	Mee hutta	Nana mutan	Nunna muntan	I was.
......	......	Too hutta	Nime muttee	Nimma muttenee	Thou wast.
......	......	Te hutta	Wor muttor	Wagor muttor	He was.
......	......	......	Amot muttom	Mummatoo muttom	We were.
......	......	......	Nimet mutteel	Nimatoo mutteree	You were.
......	......	......	Hor mutter	Woroo muttoroo	They were.
......	......	......	Am	Amoo	Be.
......	......	......	......	......	To be.
......	......	......	......	......	Being.
......	......	......	Asee	Munjee	Having been.
......	......	......	Nuna ayana	......	I may be.
......	......	......	Nuna aykan	......	I shall be.
......	......	......	......	......	I should be.
......	......	......	Jeem or Pam	Pam or Halsa	Beat.
......	......	......	Jeeyana	Halskan	To beat.
......	......	......	......	......	Beating.
......	......	......	Jissee	Halsee	Having beaten.
......	......	......	Nana jintona	Nuna pakan or Halskan	I beat.
......	......	......	Nime jintonee	Nimma halstkin	Thou beatest.
......	......	......	Wor jintor	Wogoo halsintogoo	He beats.
......	......	......	......	Mummatoo halskom	We beat.
......	......	......	Nimet jintoneet	Mummatoo halstkeer	You beat.
......	......	......	Hor jintor	Woroo halsito	They beat.
......	......	......	Nunoojissore muntona	Nunna halshere muntan	I am beating.
......	......	......	......	Nunna halshere muntan	I was beating.
......	......	......	......	......	I had beaten.
......	......	......	Nuna jeeyana	......	I may beat.
......	......	Mee mare	Nuna jikan	Nunna halstkan	I shall beat.
......	......	......	......	Nunna halsantoroo	I should beat.
......	......	......	......	......	I am beaten.
......	......	......	......	......	I was beaten.
......	......	Mee marla jae	......	......	I shall be beaten.

	TRIBES.				
	KOORKOOS.		MEHTO.	BYGAS OR BINJWARS.	
	Nimar.	Hoshungabad.	Bilaspur.	Balaghat.	Mandla.
I go	......	......	Eng batun	May jathoo	......
Thou goest	......	......	......	Tijathus	......
He goes	......	......	......	Tijabey	......
I went	......	......	.. ...	Mey jamhoo	......
Thou wentest	......	......	......	Tijaruhus	Tooh gootho
He went	......	......	......	Tijarahey	Wuhgooruheh
Go	......	......	......	Ja	......
Going	......	......	......	......	......
Gone	......	......	......	......	......
What is your name? ...	Ama joomoo chodja	Uma joomoochoee	Amchi nau	Tor nao kahae	......
How old is this horse? ...	Ghorgie toto orsoja	Dee ghorga oomurchoee	Ghoro timun bachur	Oh ghoda kitna burikh ke haie	......
How far is it from here to Kashmir?	Inia tain Kashmir toto khat changain	Endaton Kashmir choee to utar ja	Kashmir hin mare timmin koss apoom ora timmin gota	Kashmir otey kutur door haie	......
How many sons are there in your father's house?	Ama aba kontey toto koja	Umadoo choee to kon koja	......	Tor babako ghud men kuttur beta haie	......
I have walked a long way to-day	Tani koratain khoob chunda keen	Ten eeng umatum ghuna atar olunja	Timmora mar wy kyam	Men aj atur door aha	......
The son of my uncle is married to her sister	Inia kuka kone hundija koney ikene	......	......	More doodh bhaie okey bety biha kuris	......
In the house is the saddle of the white horse	Oora talan poolum ghorgie khogir takha	Poolung ghorga khogir enee ora gun	Subbiaora khogeer oraree bhitur	Ghur men pundri ghodaka khogir haie	......
Put the saddle upon his back	Inia ghorgie pathan khogir dokey	Deeja bhaoree khogir dokhin	To be turri toltah khogeer	Wako pith men khogir dhurro	......
I have beaten his son with many stripes	Inia kontey chabuk ten khoob moonda kene	Deeja kon khin khoob bet koomakhnay	Bononum tanedai	Okur beta la khoob lukdee se marun	......
He is grazing cattle on the top of the hill	Budla ten junwur chacharaba	Hoojay kathree lyunchu churao	Oreeko charaya boroon	Dongur ke oopur gaie churut aha	......
He is sitting on a horse under that tree	Kooddey sung ghorgie ten koro choodba	Dee koru dee myaetun ghorgi lynn choojun	......	Rookh tuley ghoda men chudwut aha	......
His brother is taller than his sister	Inia dada ten inia bai ooncha hechkun	Deeja miseetun deeja bhytaoon chaja	......	Okur bhaie okur baie se ooncha aha	......
The price of that is two rupees and a half	Dija kimuto udia roopia taka	Deeja mola adhye roopeñja	......	Okur mole adhaie rupia aha	......

TRIBES.					
PUNKA.	MEHRA.	KATYA.	RAJ GOND.	MARIA GOND.	
Mandla.	Mandla.	Narsinghpur.	Chanda.	Chanda.	
......	......	Mee zata	......	......	I go.
......	......	Too zatoos	......	......	Thou goest.
......	......	Te zata	......	......	He goes.
Mai goyo	Maigoyo	Mee gelow	Nuna hattan	Nunna hattan	I went.
Too gotho	Too gotho	Too gelos	Nimme huttee	Nimma huttee	Thou wentest.
Wuh gotho	Wuh gotho	Te gela	Wor hattor	Wogoo hatogoo	He went.
......	......	Za, Zasen	Hun	Honnoo	Go.
......	......	......	......	......	Going.
......	......	......	Hattor	Hottoogoo	Gone.
......	......	Toojha nam kai ai	Nuva porol butee munta	Nuva porol batal munta	What is your name?
......	......	......	It korata win buchol munta	Idoo kora bu-choroo matri ata	How old is this horse?
......	......	......	Igdal Kashmir buchol luk munta	Intahee Kashmir buchoroo jekoo munta	How far is it from here to Kashmir?
......	......	Toojhe dada chee-ghureech kitte ek lekhoor ánd	Miwar babona lon buchol murk muntor	Miwa minmana lonoo buchoroo murkoo mun-tooroo	How many sons are there in your father's house?
......	......	......	Nend nunna welle luk suree toktan	Nendoo nunna wellejeekoo hur-ree taktanoo	I have walked a long way to-day.
......	......	......	Nawa kakana murrin wuna shelartora mur-mee ata munta	Nawa kakana murrinkoo tana helanoo murmee atoom	The son of my uncle is married to her sister.
......	......	......	Pandree korata khogeer lon munta	Pandree korata kogree lonoo soppo munta	In the house is the saddle of the white horse.
......	......	......	Tana perka kho-geer wata	Tana mondko porro kogree tasa	Put the saddle upon his back.
......	......	......	Wuna murri wele bete nuna hulstan munta	Wona mugainoo nunna jootile laoo hulsta munta	I have beaten his son with many stripes.
......	......	......	Wor mettaporro tala mehentor	Udoo kurgete tal-lawora kodang wogoomehe-chere muntor	He is grazing cattle on the top of the hill.
......	......	......	Wor khorat porro oottor murupoot muntor	Udoo murathedoo wogoo koraoo-chee munto	He is sitting on a horse under that tree.
......	......	......	Kuna tummoor wuna sheelar puxee oochmun-tor	Woono helankun-an wonoo tum-mogai dunkoo muntogai	His brother is taller than his sister.
......	......	......	Tana mol adai roopya munta	Tana mola ren-doon arda roo-pya munta	The price of that is two rupees and-a-half.

	TRIBES.				
	KOORKOOS.		MEHTO.	BYGAS OR BINJWARS.	
	Nimar.	Hoshungabad.	Bilaspur.	Balaghat.	Mandla.
My father lives in that small house	Inia aba samoora ten thadba	Yanada oohu sane ooragun doomao	......	More baba nanghur men ruht aha	......
Give this rupee to him ...	Ini roopia dijainiki	Deejun een roopea ekie	Mingota rupae angoya	Ye rupia okur de daro	......
Take those rupees from him	Deroopia diachlee	Deejatun deeropea lali	......	O rupia olo mangley	......
Beat him well and bind him with ropes	Khoob moonda kain dora tain tolekhey	Deekhun khoob kooma khai ranseetun tole koee	Bononum tenedai rupi tolai	Ola khoob maro aur doree la bhandhon	......
Draw water from the well ...	Baodi tain dakola lija	Kooatun daoday	Chimara dhaurai	A kooala pani hedo	......
Walk before me	Inia suman bo	Yan sootu gunbo	Enga aghurtain	More agey ho ...	......
Whose boy comes behind you?	Inia kone ajey baja taoo tain	Kayiakon amataon hujeo	Tayum durte awee durwa	Tor pacheg kakur beta awa	......
From whom did you buy that?	Amey thamey mola tain chawain	Ya dhureetun sawun	Kurra sojea aget	Ye kaha kani leni mol men	......
From a shop-keeper of the village	Digawa dookandar achawain	Gaon dookan daraton sawun	Gaon dokauru aget	A gaon ke muheratey	......

TRIBES.					
PUNKA.	MEHRA.	KATYA.	RAJ GOND.	MARIA GOND.	
Mandla.	Mandla.	Narsinghpur.	Chanda.	Chanda.	
......	......	Id nanh ghurree hamcha aie	Nawar babo hod hodla mundka ittog	Nawa minmal udoo hoodla lote mundka itton	My father lives in that small house.
......	......	Tella roopai oopida	Id roopya wuna sheem	Idoo roopya wonookoo hum	Give this rupee to him.
......	......	Taso roopai gheencho	Wor agdal id roopya yena	Won agatal aroo roopyong yena	Take those rupees from him.
......	......	......	Wuna nehna halssa un doreete doha	Wonoo nehna hulssee nodiane doha	Beat him well and bind him with ropes.
......	......	......	Ud choowata yer tenda	Udoo koohitayagoo toga	Draw water from the well.
......	......	......	Nawa moonne dayoo	Nawa moonne taka	Walk before me.
Kehker toorwa toomhar pichey aoout hai	Kehkur toorwa toomhar pichey aoout hai	......	Niwa puja wor murree wantor	Niwa puya bona mugai waitog	Whose boy comes behind you.?
......	......	Too koonche passe atalos	Wan agadal ud nime uttoor	Udoo nimma won agatal asee talo	From whom did you buy that?
......	......	......	Natinor dookandar agatal	Natena dookandar agatal	From a shop-keeper of the village.

FURTHER SPECIMENS

OF THE

ABORIGINAL LANGUAGES OF THE CENTRAL PROVINCES.

	TRIBES.					
	DHANGUR.	GOND TRIBES.				
	Bilaspur.	Narsingpur.	Chhindwarra.	Nagpur.	Balaghat.	Bhandara.
One	......	Oondee	Oondi	Orah oondu	Oondee	Oondi
Two	......	Rund	Rund	Rund	Rund	Rund
Three	......	Moond	Moond	Moond	Moond	Moond
Four	......	Laloo	Naloong	Naloong	Naloong	Naloo
Five	......	Saiyo	Seiyoong	Suyoong	Sayoong	Sunyugun
Six	......	Sarhoo	Saroong	Saroong	Sawa	Sadoom
Seven	......	Eroo	Yedoong	Eroong	Yeroo	Edoom
Eight	......	......	Urmoor	......	Armoor	Athum
Nine	......	......	Oonmah	......	Nubey	Nuoom
Ten	......	......	Pad	......	Pud	Dahoom
Twenty	......	......	......	......	......	......
Fifty	......	......	......	Tunnas	......	Punnasung
One hundred ...	......	......	Noor	Noor	Noor	Noor
I	......	Nunna	Anna	Ana	Nuna	Nunna
Of me	......	Náwá	Nawor, Nawa	Mawur	......	Ná-visee
Mine	......	Náwá	Nawor, Nawa	Mawur	......	Nawa
We	......	Ummut	Ammot	Amut	Amoat	Amote
Of us	......	Máwá	Mawor, Mawa	Mawa	Mawa	Ma-visee
Our	......	Máwá	Mawor, Mawa	Mawa	......	Mawa
Thou	......	Eema	Imma	Nee	Ima	Ime
Of thee	......	Niwá	Neewor, Neewa	Neewa	Neewa	Ni-see
Thine	......	Niwá	Neewor, Neewa	Neewa	......	Nee Ore
You	......	Eemat	Immat	Emat	Imat	Imat
Of you	......	Miwá	Miwor, Miwa	Neewa	Meewa	Wulle vise
Your	......	......	Miwor, Miwa	Neewa	......	Mee ore
He	......	Wor	Or	Hore	Oar	Oru
Of him	......	Woná	Onhor, Onha	Hona	Owa	Ena visee
His	......	Woná	Onhar, Onha	Hona	......	Hona
They	......	Wor	Ork	Hore	Oruk	Hudu
Of them	......	Worá	Orknor, Orkna	Hona	Odukna	Hona visee
Their	......	Worá	Orknor, Orkna	Hona	......	......
Hand	Thekkha	Kai	Kei	Kuee	Kaie	Kui
Foot	Khed	Kál	Kal	Kalk	Tal	Kalku
Nose	Mooi	Musurer	Mussor	Musoor	Musore	Musore
Eye	Khun	Kun	Kun	Kunk	Kunuk, Kuduk	Kuduku
Mouth	Bae	Toddee	Toodee	Todee	Toddy	Tondee
Tooth	Pul	Pul	Pul	Pulk	Pul	Oondee, Puluk
Ear	Khebda	Kou	Kuwee	Cawi	Kubee, Kouk	Kuvee
Hair	Choothee	Choothee	Chooting	Chotee	Choondee	Chootee
Head	Kook	Tulla	......	Tulla	Tala	Tula
Tongue	Tuthkha	Wunjur	Vunjur	Wanjair	Vunjur	Bunjhur
Belly	Kool	Peer	Peer	Peer	Peer	Peer

TRIBES.						
GOND TRIBES.						
Wardha.	Hoshangabad.	Seoni.	Jabalpur.	Mandla.	Sagar.	
Oondee	Oondee	Oondi	......	Oondee	Eykhlan	One.
Randa	Rund	Rund	......	Rund	Bu	Two.
Moonda	Moond	Moond	......	Moond	Trun	Three.
Nalunga	Naloo	Naloon	......	Naloo	......	Four.
Sayoong	Suyoon	Syoon	......	Saiwoo, Segh	......	Five.
Saroong	Saroon	Saroon	......	Saroo	Chho	Six.
Yedoong	Yaroo	Airoon	......	Eroo	......	Seven.
Yermood	Urmoor	Armoor	......	Aumore	......	Eight.
Navo	Oorma	......	......	Auma	......	Nine.
......	......	Pud	......	Pud	......	Ten.
......	......	......	......	......	Eekh	Twenty.
......	......	Udai veesa	......	......	Puchakh	Fifty.
Noora	......	Noor	......	......	Ko	One hundred.
Nana	Anna	Mumote	Ana, Nan	Nunna, Nowa	Hoon	I.
Nakoon	Nakoon	Másay	......	......	Mahoon	Of me.
Nawa	Nawa	Máwá	Nawal	Nawa	Maro	Mine.
Amoot	Ammutt	Nunah	Mam	Munna	Hoon	We.
Makoon	Nakoon	Nasay	......	......	Marhoon	Of us.
Mawa	Mawa	Náwáh	Ouna	Nawa	Markoon	Our.
Ema	Eemm	Eema	Ima	Imá	To	Thou.
Woan	Nikoon	Eemasay	......	......	Ta roon	Of thee.
Newa	Neewa	Neeya	......	Mowa	Tara	Thine.
Walai	Eemmut	Eemát	Ima	Ima	Too	You.
Nikoon	Nikoon	Eematsay	......	......	Tarhoon	Of you.
Meewa	Meewa	Neewah	......	......	Tarhoon	Your.
Wora	Wol	Ore, Udh	Hoe	Hore	Ulo, Anrey	He.
Waná	Oun	Oansay	......	......	Anho	Of him.
Wona	Ona	Oanah	Adandai	Hore	Inha	His.
Tai	Wol	......	Hoe	Hore	Ula	They.
Wansu	Oun	Oansay	......	......	Anhoon	Of them.
......	Ora	Oonah	Hukai	......	Inhoon	Their.
Kaya	Kyee	Kye	Kaik	Kai	Hath	Hand.
Kalk	Kal	Kal	Kal	Kal	Godo	Foot.
Masoor	Mussur	Mussoorh	Mussar	Musur	......	Nose.
Kadaka	Kankh	Kun	Kank	Kunk	Dora	Eye.
Todee	Toddee	Tooddy	Tuddi	Toodee	Bakon	Mouth.
Pulk	Pulk	Pulk	Palk	Puluk	......	Tooth.
Kawee	Koukh	Kuvee	Kouwi	Kowee	......	Ear.
Chootee	Choottee	Choontee	Chundi	......	Kekh	Hair.
Tala	Tulla	Thulla	Talla	Tulla	......	Head.
Wanajára	Bunjur	Vunjur	Vanjar	Wunjur	......	Tongue.
Peera	Peer	Peer	Pir	Dharr, Pir	Dimuroon	Belly.

	TRIBES.					
	DHANGUR.	GOND TRIBES.				
	Bilaspur.	Narsingpur.	Chhindwarra.	Nagpur.	Balaghat.	Bhandara.
Back	Medh	Mohto	Moorchool	Moorchool	Purrekee	Puraki
Iron	Purnoa	Kuchee	Cuchi	Kachee	Kuchu	Kuchchee
Gold	Souna	Sonoo	Sono	Sono	Soona	Sono
Silver	Chandia	Chandee	Chandee	Khooro	Khooro	Khooro
Father	Bung	Dadaharal	Dhas	Baho, Daoo	Daoo	......
Mother	Yangio, Aio	Ban	......	......	......	Buya
Brother	Dada, Engris	Tummoor	Tumoor	Tumboor	Tummoor	Tummoor
Sister	Engri, Didee	Seelar	Selar	Sailad	Salar	Bai, Tuka
Man	Alur	Mandrsal	Mánwál	Manwal	Manwal	Manuwa
Woman	Mukka	A'r, Maigoo	A'r	Myjoo	Myjo	Mayejo
Wife	Enghai	A'r	A'r	Myjoo	Nawa Myjo	Nawa Maejo
Child	Khuddur	Chhuwa	Chonwa	Chhuwa	Chawa	Suwa
Son	Engdus	Pergal, Murri	Murree	Muree, Toodal	Murree	Nawa Suwa
Daughter	Engdo	Perjee, Miar	Meear	Toodee	Pedgu	Toodiya
Slave	Jonkhur	Lorha	Burskalyal	......	......	Barpose
Cultivator	Oorba	Kisan	......	......	Kissan	Titintore
Shepherd	Era Khapuldus	Guderiya	Gadree	Sherkee	Dhungur	Sairkia, andore
God	Dhurmes	Bhugwan, Burradeo.	Ishwur	Pen	Kodopen	Pain
Devil	Nadh	Daito	Deitoor	Bhoot	Meerchook	Bhootu
Sun	Beeree	Soorujpen	Sooriyal	Din	Soorial	Soorya
Moon	Chundoo	Chundal	Chundurmal	Nulenj	Chundal	Nulunj
Star	Binko	Sookkoom	Sookoo	Sookoom	Sookumand	Channee
Fire	Chichi	Kiss	Kees	Kis	Kiss	Kis
Water	Um	Eer	Yer	Yeer	Err	Air
House	Erpá	Ron	Ron	Roon	Rone	Rone
Horse	Ghoro	Koda	Koda	Koda	Kodda	Koda
Cow	Owe	Talee	Mooda	Mooda	Mooda	Mooda
Dog	Allá	Nai	Nei	Nuee	Naye	Nue
Cat	Beerkhas	Beelal	Beelal	Beelal	Bilal	Beelal
Cock	Khaer	Gogotal, Gogoree	Gogotee	Ghogotee	Gogodee	Ghooghooti
Duck	Hunsagira	Bhuttuk	......	Buduk	Buduk	Buduck
Ass	Gadhe	Gádál	Gudhal	Gudha	Gudhal	Gudháll
Camel	Unthee	Oont	Ootoom	Hootoom	Woot	Hoot
Bird	Orá	Pitte	Pittee	Pitti	Pittay	Pukshi
Go	Káláin	Hun	Hun	Hun	Hund	Hán
Eat	Oná	Tin	Tin	Tin	Tin	Teen
Sit	Ookkuth	Oodda	Oodha	Ooda	Oodda	Ooda
Come	Bara	Wuree	Wuda	Wuda	Wuda	Buda
Beat	Kora	Jim	Jeem	Jim	Jeem	Gim
Stand	Elá, Ejá	Nihcheehun	Nita	Nila	Neila	Tédá

TRIBES.						
Gond Tribes.						
Wardha.	Hoshungabad.	Seoni.	Jubbulpur.	Mandla.	Sagar.	
Parakee	......	Moorchool	Murchur	Moorchul	Dondon	Back.
Kachee	......	Kuchee	Kachchi	Kunchi	Lokhund	Iron.
Sonoh	Sonna	Sono	Sunne	Sona	Khonoon	Gold.
Khooroh	Chandi	Chandee	Chandi	Chandee	Roopon	Silver.
Babadala	Daoo	Daoo	......	Babo	Bao	Father.
Avadu	Aabbul	......	......	......	Agya	Mother.
Tamoodal	Tummur	Bhyal	Bhayya	Daoo, Tunmoor	......	Brother.
Shelada	Sular	Sylar	Didi	Silar	......	Sister.
Manwal	Madoul	Manrsa	Mandsa	Munukh	Baoree	Man.
Myjoh	Ma	Myjoo	Naiju	Maijo	Marsee	Woman.
Madnuenah	Ask	Bungo	Mai	Yar	Bawun	Wife.
Toodala	Pedgul	Chuva	Chavva	Chowa, Murree	Cheeo	Child.
......	Murree	Murree	Marri	......	Cheeo	Son.
Toodu	Meeur	Myar	Miyar	Meyar	Chhoree	Daughter.
......	......	......	......	Jotha-Rootha	Uthor	Slave.
......	Keersan	Kissan	Neli	Koeethoor	Mand Kho	Cultivator.
Dhanakar	......	Gadree	Kopa	Cherkal	Dhunugur	Shepherd.
Pena	Bhugwan	Bhugwan	Deo	Bhugwan	Bhugwan	God.
Bhootal	Bhoot	Dano	Bhut	Ruksa	Bhoot	Devil.
Deina	Sooraj	Din	Din	Din	Dinnoo Chandr	Sun.
Nalainj	Chandrama	Chunda	Chanda	Chunda	Ratnoo Chandr	Moon.
Sookoom	Tara	Sookum	Sukkum	Thereya	Taro	Star.
Kees	Kis	Kis	Kis	Kis	Ag	Fire.
Yera	Aer	Air	Yer	Err	......	Water.
Rona	Rone	Roan	Roun	Rond	......	House.
Kodda	Kora	Koodda	Korá	Kora	Ghoro	Horse.
Mooda	Gai, Talee	Talee	Tali	Moora, Talee	Gao	Cow.
Nayee	Nayee	Nye	Nai	Nayek	Kootreyo	Dog.
Beelal	Bila	Bilar	Bilá	Billa	Bularee	Cat.
Bhagotu	Morgul, Koor	Gugoree	Gagori	......	Kookro	Cock.
......	Butuk	Dubuk	Dabak	Iree	Buduk	Duck.
Gadhal	Gadha	Gudhal	Gadha	Gadha	Gudheyroo	Ass.
Hoottoo	Oont	Oontoom	Unti	Aount	Oont	Camel.
Peetai	Pittay	Peetee	Pitte	Peetai	Chimuneyoo	Bird.
Hun	Hun	Hun	Hani	Hun	......	Go.
Teina	Tin	Thin	Tin	Tinda	Khaeylo	Eat.
Ooda	Oodda	Oodda	Uddá	Oodha	Besh	Sit.
Wada	Bura	Vurra	Wará	Wura	Aeoro	Come.
Jim	Jim	Jeem	Jim	Jeem	Mareena	Beat.
Neela	Leechheehun	Lichay munsane	Nillá	Neelum, Neecheemun	Oobhara	Stand.

	TRIBES					
	DHANGUR.	GOND TRIBES.				
	Bilaspur.	Narsingpur.	Chhindwara.	Nagpur.	Balaghat.	Bhandara.
Die	Kechus	Sum	Saoee hun	Satoor	Sasu	Satoo
Give	Chyá	Sim	Seem	Sim	Seem	Sim
Run	Bonga	Vitsee	Vita	Wita	Duyoo	Sódiá
Up	Choa	Purro	Purro	Puro	Purro	Puro
Down	Ookka	Turree	Khalwa	Nailee	Khaley	Ooda
Before	Heribar	Moonne	Moonee	Moone	Mooney	Moonne
Near	Heeribara	Dora	Kurroom	Kuroom	Kuchool	Kuchool
Far	Hari	Lukh	Lukh	Luk	Luk	......
Behind	......	Hulse	Pija	Puja	Puja	Puza
Who	Naen	Bor	Bor	Bore	Bor	Bore
What	Endra	Bud	Bang	Buda	Buttu	Buteande
Why	......	Barreekre	Baree	Bahoom	Badusaty	Bulyan
And	Aurchra	Ane	Oonday	Oh	Oondry	An, nu
But	......	Ugga	Oonday	Pur	Pun	Pur
If	......	......	Oonday	Tuh	Imma	Tu
Yes	Ho	Inge	Ingey	Ingee	Invgay	Hinge
No	Mulla	Hille	Hulle	Hille	Hilley	Hille
Alas	......	......	Hai Hai	Sos-lad-sos	Aruray	Hae
A father	......	Dada or Babo	Dhaoo	Babo	Daoo	Edoorbaba
Of a father	......	Dadata or Babbona	M. Dhaoonor Fem. Dhaoona	Babona	Daoona	Oondis Babana
To a father	......	Dadatoon or Babbotoon	Dhaoon	Babone	Daoon	Babana
From a father ...	......	Dadate or Babbote	Dhaoonseen	Babo Sin	Daoonsay	Baba Nigdal
Two fathers	......	Rund Dada	......	Rund Babo	......	Rundoo Baba
Fathers	......	Dada	Dhaoork	Wulene Babo	Daoong	Wule Baba
Of fathers	......	Dadana	M. Dhaoorknor F. Dhaoorkna	Wulene Babona	Daoongna	Wule baba vise
To fathers	......	Dadanoon	Dhaoorkoon	Wulene Babone	Daoongnaley	Wule Babano
From fathers	......	Dadani	Dhaoorkseen	Wulene, Babo Kikedal	Daoongnasey	Wule baba nigdal
A daughter	......	Pergee	Meear	Meeyan	Pedgee	Oondee Toodi
Of a daughter ...	......	Pergeeta	M. Meeanor F. Meeana	Meeyana	Pedgina	Toodi Na
To a daughter ...	......	Pergeetoon	Meean	Meeyan	Pedgitoon	Toodinu
From a daughter ...	......	Pergeete	Meeanseen	Meeya Hikedal	Pedgisay	Toodeenigdal
Two daughters ...	......	Rund Peking	......	Rund Meeyan	....	Rundu Toodee
Daughters	......	Peking	Meeark	Wulene Meeyan	Peking	Wuli Toodi
Of daughters ...	......	Pekina	M. Meearknor F. Meearkna	Wulene Meeyana	Pekinga	Wule Toodina
To daughters ...	......	Pekinoon	Meearkoon	Wulene Meeyan	Pekingtool	Wuli Toodi nu
From daughters ...	......	Pekine	Meeark Seen	Wulene Meeyan Hikedal	Pekingsay	Wuli Toodi Nigdal

TRIBES.						
GOND TRIBES.						
Wardha.	Hoshangabad.	Seoni.	Jabalpur.	Mandla.	Sagar.	
Sama	Sasut	Huneegay	Satur	Sathur sosee hunthur	Mareegyo	Die.
Shema	Sim	Seem	Sim	Situr, Seewur	Du	Give.
Weitha	Vichhihun	Soda	Vitta	Weetha	Murenchhoot	Run.
Porah	Purro	Purrote	Parro	Purroo	......	Up.
Nailee	......	Siddeen	......	Pulla	Heyt	Down.
Moonnai	Moonnee	Moonnay	Munne	Samoo	......	Before.
Kachool	Kurroom	Joray, Kurro	Gori	Mootus	Kunha	Near.
Luk	Luck	Lukoom	Valela	Luk	......	Far.
Paraku	Pijja	Pijja	Pachari	Pudja	Pachhey	Behind.
Boar	Bole	Bore, Boan	Boni	Bor	......	Who.
Butee	Buran	Buthee	Várá	Ka	Eyyoon	What.
......	Banko	Baran	Baga Váti	Bal	Eyyoon	Why.
Nah	Anee	Un	Tara	Aorey, un	Un	And.
Para	Pun	......	Tara	......	......	But.
......	......	......	Imá	Ath	......	If.
......	......	Yingay	Va-i-kam	Engey	Han	Yes.
Heilai	Hailay	Hillay	Hilliyan	Jhyn	Nuheen	No.
Arai	......	Aray Aray	Hay	Bah	Ureyrey	Alas.
......	Oondee Vollay	Daoo	Dada	Babo	Bao	A father.
......	Volluta	Daoonay	Dadana	Babola	Babanoon	Of a father.
......	Vollun	Daoonay	Dadan	Babola	Babanoon	To a father.
......	Vollutsay	Daoonsay	Dadanse	Babota	Baba Kunathoo	From a father.
......	......	Rund Daoo	Do Dada	Rund Babor	Bu Baba	Two fathers.
......	......	Vullay Daoo	Dada	Wulley Babor	Ghuna Baba	Fathers.
......	......	Vullay Daoonay	Dadana	Wulley Baborla	GhunaBaba Noon	Of fathers.
......	......	Vullay Daonay	Dadan	Wulley Baborla	Ghuna Baba Noon	To fathers.
......	......	Vullay Daoonsay	Dadanse	Wuelly Baborta	Ghuna Baba Hunathoo	From fathers.
......	Oondie Pergie	Pairgee	Miyar	Meyas	Chhoree	A daughter.
......	Pergina	Pairgeenay	Miyar Na	Meyasla	Chhoreenoon	Of a daughter.
......	Pergin	Pairgeenay	Miyaran	Meyasla	Chhoreenoon	To a daughter.
......	Pergisay	Pairgeensay	Miyaranse	Meyasta	Chhoree Kunathoo	From a daughter.
......	......	Rund Pairgee	Do Miyar	Rund Meyas	Bu Chhoree	Two daughters.
......	Mootkee Pergie	Vullay Pairgee	Miyar	Wulley Meyas	Chhoree	Daughters.
......	......	Vullay Pairgee	Miyarna	Wulley Meyasla	Chhoreenoon	Of daughters.
......	......	Vullay Pairgeenay	Miyaran	Wulley Meyasla	Chhoreenoon	To daughters.
......	......	Vullay Pairgeensay	Miyaranse	Wulley Meyasta	Choree Kunathoo	From daughters.

	TRIBES.					
	DHANGUR.	GOND TRIBES.				
	Bilaspur.	Narsingpur.	Chhindwara.	Nagpur.	Balaghat.	Bhandara.
A good man	Oruth Nagud Alus	Choko maurdsal	Chokho manwal	Changlo manwal	Beomanwal	Chokhut manwal
Of a good man ...	......	Choko maurdsana	Chokho manwanor	Changlo manwalna	Besmanwalla	Oondi chokhut manwalna
To a good man ...	......	Choko maurdsank	Chokho manwan	Changlo manwalkoon	Besmanwan	Oondi chokhut manwalnu
From a good man ...	......	Choko maurdsanal	Chokho manwan seen	Changlo manwal hikedal	Besmanwalsey	Oondi chokhut manwal nigdal
Two good men ...	Erib Nagud Alus	Rund choko manrdialor	......	Rund changlo manwal	......	Rundi chokhut manwal
Good men	......	Choko manrdsalor	Chokho manwalk	Wulene changlo	Besmanwaloodk	Wuli chokhut manwal
Of good men	......	Choko manrdsalora	Chokho manwalknor	Wulene changlo manwalna	Besmanwalookta	Wuli chokhut manwalna
To good men	......	Choko manrdsalork	Chokho manwalkoon	Wulene changlo manwal	Besman waloodkn	Wuli chokhut manwalnu
From good men ...	......	Choko manrdsaloral	Chokho manwalk seen	Wulene changlo manwal hikedal	Besman waeloodksey	Wuli chokhut manwalnigdal
A good woman ...	......	Chokoar	Chokhoar	Changlo myjoo	Besmyjo	Chokhut maezo
Good women	......	Chokoar	Chokho ask	Wulene changlo myjoo	Besmyjong	Wuli chokhut maezo
A bad boy	Oruth khuddus munjus	Boortor pergal	Boortor pedgal	Nadan toodal	Boorachaba	Chokhut todal hiledoo
A bad girl	......	Boorta pergee	Boortal pedgee	Nadan tooree	Booro pedgie	Oodi toodi chokhut hiledoo
Good	Nagud	Choko	Chokho	Changlo	Bes	Chokhut
Better	......	Udte choko	Tan seen chokho	Feda changlo	......	......
Best	......	Subrete	Subrot seen chokho	Feda changlo	......	......
High	Mechus	Ooncho	Dhongal	Dhongul	Kuddo	Oonch
Higher	......	Udte ooncho	Tan seen dhongal	Feda dhongal	......	......
Highest	......	Subte ooncho	Subrot seen dhongal	Feda dhongal	......	......
A horse	Enoto ghoro	Koda	Koda	Kodda	Kodda	Oondi koda
A mare	......	Ghooriya	......	Sittee kodda	Koddi	Oodi koda
Houses	......	......	Kodang	Wulene kodda	Koddang	Wule koda
Mares	......	Ghooriya	Kodang	Wulene sittu kodda	Kodding	Wulle koda
A bull	Enoto addo	Sanrd	Kooral	Koora	Korda	Konda
A cow	......	Talee	Mooda	Mooda	Mooda	Moodda
Bulls	......	Sanrk	Koorang	Wulene koora	Kodang	Wule konda
Cows	......	Talee	Moodang	Wulene mooda	Moodang	Wule moodda
A dog	Antaulla	Nai	Nei	Naee	Nayee	Oondi naee
A bitch	......	Sittee	......	Sittee naee	Sitte	Tote naee
Dogs	......	Naik	Neik	Wulene nai	Naik	Wule naee
Bitches	......	Sittee	......	Wulene sittee naee	Sitting	Wule naee
A he-goat	Era	......	Bukral	Bokdal	Bokdal	......

PROVINCES LANGUAGES.—*(Continued.)*

TRIBES.						
GOND TRIBES.						
Wardha.	Hoshangabad.	Seoni.	Jabalpur.	Mandla.	Sagar.	
......	Morrul kamonul	Base munoos	Asel manisa	Nugd manukh	Ushil manoosh	A good man.
......	......	Base munoosnay	Asel maursana	Nugd manukh la	Ushil manoosh ni	Of a good man.
......	......	Base munoosnay	Asel manrsa	Nugd manukhla	Ushil manoosh kaney	To a good man.
......	......	Base munoosay	Asel manrsanse	Nugd manukhta	Ushil manoosh kunathoo	From a good man.
......	......	Rund bais munoos	Do asel manrsa	Rund nugd manukh	Bu ushil manoosh	Two good men.
......	......	Vullay bais munoos	Asel manrsa	Wulley nugd manukh	Ghuna ushel manoosh	Good men.
......	......	Vullay bais munoosnay	Asel manrsana	Wulley nugd manukh la	Ushil manoosh ni	Of good men.
......	......	Vullay bais munoosnay	Asel manrsan	Wulley nugd manukh la	Ushil manoosh kaney	To good men.
......	......	Vullay bais munoosay	Asel manrsanse	Wulley nugd manukhta	Ushil manoosh kunathoo	From good men.
......	Kummool ma	Base maejoo	Asel maiju	Nugd maejookh	Ushil bawunee	A good woman.
......	......	Base vullay maejoo	Asel maiju	Wulle ynugd maejookh	Ushil ghun bawunee	Good women.
......	Boorotool pergul	Booruth toora	Buro perga	Nindruk murree	Khrab cheeo	A bad boy.
......	Boorotool meeur	Booruth tooree	Buri turi	Nindruk peergee	Boree chhoree	A bad girl.
Chokhota	Kamnah	Base	Asel	Nugd	Ushil	Good.
......	......	Sajro	......	......	Thoo ushil	Better.
......	......	Purssajro	Bahut asel	......	Sarey sey ushil	Best.
......	Pura	Ooncho	Unch	Dhanga	Oonchee	High.
......	......	Oorkoon ooncho	......	......	Thoo oonchee	Higher.
......	......	Puroor ooncho	Bura unch	......	Sarey sey oonchee	Highest.
Wanda kodda	Kora	Koodda	Kora	Koda	Ghoro	A horse.
Wandu koddee	......	Koodda	Kora	Ghoreea	Ghoree	A mare.
Kodan	Kora	Vullay koodda	Kora	Wulley koda	Ghuney ghorey	Houses.
Kodyan	......	Vullay koodda	Kora	Wulley ghoreea	Ghuna ghoree	Mares.
Wandu korrah	......	Koanda	Konda	Konda	Dhandho	A bull.
Wandu mooda	......	Tallee	Tali	Moora	Gaey	A cow.
Koorran	Konda	Vullay koanda	Konda	Wulley konda	Ghuna dhandho	Bulls.
Moodan	Puya	Vullay tallee	Tali	Wulley moora	Ghunee gaey	Cows.
Wandu nayu	Naie	Nye	Nai	Nyek	Kooturye	A dog.
Wandu kooteen	Naie	Sittee	Siti	Sitee	Kootree	A bitch.
Nayuk	Naye	Vullay nye	Nai	Wulley nyek	Ghuna kooturys	Dogs.
Kootuny	Naye	Vullay sittee	Siti	Wulley sitee	Ghunee kooturiyan	Bitches.
Bokral	Bookra	Bokral	Bukrai	Bukra	Bokro	A he-goat.

	TRIBES.					
	DHANGUR.	GOND TRIBES.				
	Bilaspur.	Narsingpur.	Chhindwara.	Nagpur.	Balaghat.	Bhandara.
A female goat ...	Boorhi eri	Yetee	Yetee	Etee	Yetti	......
Goats	......	Bukralor yeting	Bukralk	Wulene etee	Bokdaloodk	......
A male deer	......	Mirza	Mas	Kodral	Meergal	Mirgal
A female deer ...	......	......	Maok	Kodree	Hirna	Hurnee
Deer	Mak	Mirgalor	Maok	Wulene kodree	Mirgaloodk	Wule hurna
I am	......	Nunna aiatona	Anna andan	Ana mantona	Nuna andan	Nuna muntona
Thou art	......	Eema aiatonee	Imma andee	Ime mantinee	Immay andi	Imey muntona
He is	......	Wor aiator	Orándoor	To mantore	Or anddoor	Ohur muntore
We are	......	Umat aiatoram	Ammot andom	Amut mándá	Amot andom	Wule jhuna muntona
You are	......	Eemut aiatoreet	Immat andeet	Ime mantinee	Imet andit	Wule muntuna
They are	......	Wor aiator	Orkándoork	Hore mantore	Odk andoodk	Wule muntore
I was	......	Nunna huttan	Anna muthona	Ana mantore	Nuna muttona	Nuna muntona
Thou wast	......	Eema huttee	Imma muthonee	Eme mantona	Ima muttoni	Ime muntoni
He was	......	Wor huttor	Or muthor	Ore mantore	Or muttor	Hair muntore
We were	......	Amut hattam	Ammot muthorum	Amut muntore	Amot muttom	Wule jhuna mutodo
You were	......	Eemut hutteet	Immat muthoreet	Eme mantona	Imet mottonit	Wule jhum muntoda
They were	......	Wor huttor	Ork muthork	Hore muntore	Odk muttodk	Wule muntona
Be	......	Am	Am	Munda	Mun	Mund
To be	......	Aialle	Ayana	......	Mundina	Mundana
Being	......	Usse	Ayata	.. ...	......	Muttun
Having been	......	Usse koon	Asse koon	......	Muntton	......
I may be	......	Nunna aia paratona	Ayaka	Ana mantona	Nuna mundina	Nuna muntoria
I shall be	......	Nunna aika	Ayaka	......	Nuna mundka	Nuna hundaka
I should be	......	Nunna aia parandun	Ayata	......	Hadina munta	Nuna daka
Beat	......	Jeem	Jeem	Jim	Jeeana	Jim
To beat	......	Jeallee	Jeeana	......	Jitona	Jitun
Beating	......	Jisee	Jeeata	......	......	Jinake
Having beaten ...	......	Jisee koon	Jeseekoon	......	Jehseekoon	Jiskun
I beat	En louskan	Nunna jeealona	Anna jeeatona	Anna jika	Nuna jeeyatona	Nuna jitan
Thou beatest	......	Eema jeeatoni	Imma jeeatonee	......	Imey jeeyatoni	Ime jintoon
He beats	......	Wor jeeator	Or jeeator	......	Or jeeator	Hor jiantore
We beat	......	Umat jeeatoram	Ammot jeeatorum	Amut jika	Amot jeetoom	Amote jiantore
You beat	......	Eemut jeeatoreet	Immat jeeatoreet	......	Imet jiatonit	Wule jhun jiantond
They beat	......	Wor jeeator	Ork jeeatork	......	Odk jeeatodk	Hore jiantore

TRIBES.						
GOND TRIBES.						
Wardha.	Hoshangabad.	Seoni.	Jabalpur.	Mandla.	Sagar.	
Harrai	Bookree	Uttee	Iti	Cheerea	Bokre	A female goat.
Bakara loda	Bookra	Vullay bokral	Iti	Wulley Bukra	Ghunee bokree	Goats.
......	Heerna	Meergal	Chhigra	Kursal	Akhurree	A male deer.
......	Heernee	Heernal	Chhigra	Heronee	Hureyn	A female deer.
......	Heern	Vullay heernal meerga	Chhigra	Herona	Gunee hurn	Deer.
Nana mantonah	Anna hae	Mamoteandoom	Nan mandaka	Muma mundal	Hoon chhoon	I am.
Ema mantonee	Oomma hai	Eema aund	Iyar adur	Eema mundal	Too chhu	Thou art.
Wore mantore	Ol hai	Ud andoor	Had manda	Haur mundal	Ulo chhu	He is.
Amoot mantode	Ammut hai	Nuna undoom	Nan mandaka	Wulley muma mundal	Hoon chhoon	We are.
Emat muntodee	Oommut hai	Eemat aund	Iyar adur	Wulley eema mundal	Too chhu	You are.
Wora mantoda	Ol hai	Vullay aund	Hon manda	Wulley haur mundal	Ulo chhu	They are.
......	Una muttoona	Mumote mutona	Nana mandan	Nunna muttonee	Hoon huto	I was.
......	Oomma muttoona	Eema mutona	Ima ore mattoni	Ima muttonee	Too huto	Thou wast.
......	Ol muttool	Ud mutona	Hor mattur	Haur muttonee	Ulo huto	He was.
......	Ummut muttorum	Nuna mutona	Anave mandan	Wulley nuna muttonee	Hoon huto	We were.
......	Oommut muttool	Eemat mutona	Ima ore mattur	Wulley ima muttonee	Too huto	You were.
......	Ol muttool	Vullay mutona	Vale janamattur	Wulley haur muttonee	Ulo huto	They were.
......	Mundkee	......	......	Asee hut	Chhu	Be.
......	Mundkee	......	......	Asee hun	Hoon ulo huto	To be.
......	Awel	Iyar	......	......	......	Being.
......	Aseehut	Bunay masee	......	Seet	......	Having been.
......	......	Mumote assee	......	......	......	I may be.
......	......	Mumote aeeka	......	......	......	I shall be.
......	......	Makoon aee	......	......	......	I should be.
Jeem	Jim	Jeem	Jeem	Jeeond	Mar	Beat.
......	Jisibata	Jeeana	Jeem	Jeem	Marno	To beat.
......	Jea manool	Jeetakay	......	Jeyakun	Marto jaeych	Beating.
......	Jisi	Jeetay	......	......	Maren	Having beaten.
Nuna Jemtonah	Una jika	Mumote jeea toorum	Nana jiya tan	Nunna jeem	Hoon mareyt	I beat.
Eema jeemto nee	Oomma jiatool	Eema jeea thoonee	Ima jiti	......	Too mare chhoo	Thou beatest.
......	Oul jiatool	Ud jheea thoor	Hor jiyator	......	Ulo mare chhu	He beats.
Amoot jeemtodo	Ummat jiatool	Nuna jeea toorum	Nana jeyatan	......	Hoon maroon choon	We beat.
Emat jeemtodal	Oommut jiatool	Eemot jeca thonee	Ima jiti	......	Too mare chhoo	You beat.
......	Oul jiatool	Vullay jeea thoor	Hor jiyatur	......	Ulo mare chhu	They beat.

	TRIBES.					
	DHANGUR.	GOND TRIBES.				
	Bilaspur.	Narsingpur.	Chhindwara.	Nagpur.	Balaghat.	Bhandara.
I am beating	......	Nunna jeeatona	Anna jeeatona	Ana jika	Nuna jeeatona	Nuna jiantona
I was beating ...	......	Nunna jokdan	Anna jeendan	......	Nuna jiendan	Nuna jitar
I had beaten	......	Nunna jisee keitan	Anna jeetona	......	Nuna jeeamuntono	Nuna jisimunotona
I may beat	......	Nunna jeeapara-tona	Anna jeeka	Ana jika	Nuna jeyka	Nuna jeka
I shall beat	......	Nunna jeeaka	Anna jeeaka	......	Nuna jeyka	Nuna jeka
I should beat	......	Nunna jeea parandan	Anna jeeatona	......	Nuna jeyka	Nuna jeka
I am beaten	......	Nunna jesee aratona	Anna mar tin-datona	Makoon jit	Nakoori jeetoor	Nakoon jiantore
I was beaten	......	Nunna jesee matona	Anna martitan	......	Nakoon jitoor	Nakoon jhittore
I shall be beaten ...	......	Nunna jesee aika	Anna martindaka	......	Nakoon jeea noon	......
I go	En kala	Nunna hunda-tona	Anna hundatona	Ona huntona	Nuna hadeetona	Nuna hundaka
Thou goest	......	Eema hundato-nee	Imma hundatonee	......	Imay handitoni	Ime hun
He goes	......	Wor hundator	Or hundator	......	Or handatoor	Hore huntore
I went	......	Nunna hunji-tona	Anna hutan	Ana hunjee	Nun hatan	Nuna hatan
Thou wentest ...	......	Eema hunjitonee	Imma huteen	......	Imay hatoni	Ime hunti muntoo
He went	......	Wor hunjitor	Or hutoor	......	Or hatoor	Hore huttoore
Go	......	Hun	Hun	Hun	Hund	Hun
Going	......	Hunjee	Hunjode	......	Handina	Takintore
Gone	......	Hunjee koon	Hunjee koon	......	Hatona sasuhud	Huttoore
What is your name? ...	Nighendur na-men	Niwa buttee purol	Meewa pudol bang	Niwa buttee pudol	Niwo parole buti munda	Niwa nawa buti munda
How old is this horse?...	Eunn chanto ghoro	Ud koda ta but-tee oomr mun-data	Id koda buchale wursan na andoo	Hait koda buchale	Id kodda buchor oomurta mundar	Buchkul wursu munda koda
How far is it from here to Kashmir?	Istek Kashmir ai kosri	Yetal Kashmir bucho lukh mundar	Iggatal Kashmir toon buchale lukh andoo	Kashmir igedal buchale lukh munda	Ikdal Kashmir buchore lumbore munda	Buchul cose Kash-mir munda
How many sons are there in your father's house?	Nimbus erpaun enjhun khuddur rahnur	Niwa bubona rokhte bucho pekor munda-noor	Meewar dhaoon na rotte buchale murk andoork	Niwur babona roon buchale toodal mantore	Niwa daoona rotey buchore chabang mudang	Niwa babona rone buchul sava munda
I have walked a long way to-day	Inna niggeeha tooroo baruch kun	Nunna nend lukhtakee than	Nend anna lukh thaktona	Nend surde ana ajwule takta	Nunna naoo bul-ley lukkun dan batal	Nain wuli taksee watang
The son of my uncle is married to her sister	Enkakus tring dus is ge tun grin binjarus	Miwa kukka ta pergal yena selar te sung murming kiator	Nawor kaka nor mur ree tanha selan na mur-ming keetoor	Mawa kakator toodanee hona seladeen sung mudmee auntoo	Nawa kaka na murree wona se lang mudpee keetoor	Kakano murree suwa mudming kittore
In the house is the sad-dle of the white horse	Pandro ghorogi khogeer erpa-noo raee	Panduree koda ta zeem rote mundar	Pandree koda ta khogeer rotte andoo	Hud rot rupoo pandrial koda ta khogeer munda	Pundrie koda ta khogeer rotey muha	Pandhra kodang khogeer rotropo munda

TRIBES.						
GOND TRIBES.						
Wardha.	Hoshangabad.	Seoni.	Jabalpur.	Mandla.	Sagar.	
Emat jeitoor	......	Mumote jeea toorum	......	......	......	I am beating.
......	Una jeenun	Mumote jeea mutona	Nana jitan	......	Hoon mare ruheeto	I was beating.
......	Una jisi	Mumote jesaytee	......	......	Hoon mare ruheeto	I had beaten.
......	......	Mumote jeydoom	Inge ana jiyaka	......	Hoon mareech	I may beat.
......	......	Mumote jeydan	Nana kede jeka	......	Hoon mareech	I shall beat.
......	......	Makoon jeesee muttoor	Nana jevena	......	......	I should beat.
Nakoon jeetoor	......	Mumote jesee vatoom	Nak jitur	......	Hoon maro guyo chho	I am beaten.
......	......	Mumote jesee mutoorum	Nana mare hatten	......	Hoon mare ruheeto	I was beaten.
Nakoonjeeyanoor	......	Mumote maro daka	Nana mare daka	......	......	I shall be beaten.
Nanahantonah	......	Mumote hutha	Nana ve daka	Nunna hun	Hoonjaoonchhoon	I go.
Eema hantonee	......	Eema hutha	Ima hattur	Ima hun	Too jaey chhu	Thou goest.
......	......	Ud hutha	......	Haur hun	Uloja iruho chho	He goes.
Nana hattan	......	Mumote huttoor	......	Nunna hunhunjee	Hoon guyo	I went.
......	......	Eema, huttoor	Ima hattur	Eema hunhunjee	Too guyo	Thou wentest.
Wore huttoor	......	Ud huttoor	Hor hattur	Haur hunhunjee	Ulo guyo	He went.
Hun	......	Hun	Han	Hun	Jao	Go.
......	......	Hundatay	Hada tue	......	Jai ruho	Going.
......	......	Huttoor	Hattur	Hutur	Guyo	Gone.
Newa padodah buttee manda	Neea purool biha	Eemat buthee purool	Niybatti puror	Nya wutee purol mundol	Toro nam seeoo chey	What is your name?
Eed koddah bachal warona manda	Oul kora chaoomur buchon	Er kodda buchalay burusta atha	Id korabachale varsana manda	Koda purro teal mundol	Aghora kitna burukh noon chhu	How old is this horse?
Eegdul Kashmir bachal lukmanda	Egitul Kashmir buchon lakon day	Ekdatay Kusmeer buchalay lukoom-aund	Igra Kashmir buchalak kun	Kituk luk mundal Kashmir	Anhuto Kashmir sheeo	How far is it from here to Kashmir?
Newa babadala neeya bachore toodalod mantodo	Newa daoon rone bucho tooda loodhye	Neeya daootay roanthay buchalay chowa aundoor	Niy rutte dada chhavva bachale madanu	Keetek murree ima babala rond mundanoor	Tara bawun ghur men kitna chhiya chhey	How many sons are there in your father's house?
Nana wamd walai luknal taksee watal	Ned unna wulley luk kalkey kal wulleeton	Naind mumote purro lukoom taktoom	Sarri takina valela hanne na	Nunna wulley lukwurra atur nehr	Aj ghuna door gya	I have walked a long way to-day.
Nawa kakadala tamoodal shela deema madmeen keetoda	......	Mawa kakanoor murreenay tanoor sylanoor murmee keseethoor	Naur kaka marri selar maijee kitur marri	Nunna kakanur murree haursela adanoor moedo	Mara kukanoo chhiyo inhee buhun ko dajo bhuya chhu	The son of my uncle is married to her sister.
Pandree koddana ronakhogeer mandaya	Pandree korana khoogir edrouth hai	Eed roantay aund pundree kodda tay khogeer	Ad rot madan parrikora palecha mundal	Pudree kodatul pulaycha roun la mundal	Dwala ghoronee jeen ghur ma chhu	In the house is the saddle of the white horse.

	TRIBES.					
	DHANGUR.	GOND TRIBES.				
	Bilaspur.	Narsingpur.	Chhindwara.	Nagpur.	Balaghat.	Bhandara.
Put the saddle upon his back	Ghorohi mendhun khogeer heriloya	Wono mohchote zeen kussee keecheem	Tonna moorchoot purro khogeer irra	Hono pet puro-khogeer wata	Id khogiran ida ko dato parro disa	Khogeer purakhi mandi kikital tana kussi
I have beaten his son with many stripes	Assi khuddurin lanchkan	Nunna wona pergal toon wullee joktan	Anna onhor murreen wulle ko dang jeetan	Hona toadoo wulene gitoor	Nuna or chabutoor khoob lathi se jitan	Suwa toonrun korda wule gitani dan
He is grazing cattle on the top of the hill	Alus partaun owen minta alugdus	Dongur purro wor dhoral toon meatoor	Or mutta ta ehendit purrokondang taling mehtatoor	Hoodkeet puro hore dhore meh teen ta	Ad koddo ta puro mooda mahettor	Mundate dhore mehu sintore
He is sitting on a horse under that tree	Alus ghoronoo arik karadus	Wor koda purra murra turree ooddatoor	Or ad murrat khalwa kodat purro oodeetor	Hore muda tule kodat puro oochee muta	Ad mudda khaley koddatey oody tor	Mudat khalwa koda nititore
His brother is taller than his sister	......	Wona tummoor woona selar te ooncha aiator	Onhor tum moor onha selan seen dhongal andoor	Hona seladeen sin honatumboor dhongal munda	Ona tummooradina salarsay sojor mundah	Ona tumboor ona tuckapur se fudore mundah
The price of that is two rupees and a half	Idige moollee arhai rupae raee	......	Tanha mola adhai-roopeeang andoo	Hona kimut run roopa ath anna	Adena malo adhaie rupia munda	Ona kimut adeeeh rupuya munda
My father lives in that small house	Embus erpaun sunnee radus	Ud chuddor rote nawa dubbo mundatoor	Nawor dhaoo adchoodor rot te mundator	Mawa babohore choodoor rot rupo ruheemantore	Naoor daoo chidor rone mundat	Niwa babo hudchid rotropa munda
Give this rupee to him	Isguson rupae eron tun hoa	Wonk id kuldar seesee sim	Id roopeea on seem	Her roopaya horekoom sim	Id rupee ou sim	Id rupuya oon sisiwata
Take those rupees from him	......	Wonal iokuldar woya	Aon roopeeang on seem yena	Hore seem roopaye enut	Ona kuchoo dol waley rupeea cheha	Aoon rupuya turuksitura
Beat him well and bind him with ropes	Husin lowa epturn hea	Wonk wullee jeemane doree te doha	On wulle kodang jeeseekoon noonete dohat	Hore koom khoop gim nodhe koon doh chinwato	Oney nodaytey doda oondey khoob jeem	Khoop oon jim an dohochiroom
Draw water from the well	Chaata amum natga	Kooa te eer neehchee tulla	Kooa ta yer oomat	Koreetal err wule kim	Ad koowa tal yero thanda	Kooital viheer tunda olikim
Walk before me ...	Ghucha engauen ekote	Mawa moonne hun	Na moone thakat	Mawa moonee dut	Nawa mooney da	Nam oone da
Whose boy comes behind you?	Nekha khuddur bara engnur khon khanu	Mwa hulse bona pergal wunk tor	Meewa pija bonhor chonwa wayator	Bona tooda wantore nipuzie	Bona chawa niwa pujah wytor	Niya puda bugdore mantore .
From whom did you buy that?	Nagooste khindikai dadurkai	Eema bon iga tullo molattee	Immat tan bon seen molate yeteet	Bone hinda etenee	Imen id honi sya asti	O nigdul as tran
From a shop-keeper of the village	Puddatee dokantee imbuggee tooroo ondur kan	Nar ta dookandar te nunna molaltan	Natenor undi buniyan seen	Nate tal dookandar puro	Idna te doorwuni se	Hud gaonwa dookandar asetut

PROVINCES LANGUAGES.—*(Continued.)*

TRIBES.						
GOND TRIBES.						
Wardha.	Hoshangabad.	Seoni.	Jabalpur.	Mandla.	Sagar.	
Kaddana pura-kee khogeer kem	Tana moorchool khogir dasa	Thanay moor chootee khogeer doosay seem	Ad palecha adan purro tachchhi kasi kam	Peet ta purro pul-eecha kuse seem	Wa jeen chhuoo-pur churhee lu	Put the saddle upon his back.
Wuna toodan nana walai badgeen jeetan	Tana pergan bet khoob jitool	Mumote udteay toora toon buch-alay sooktee jeetoom	Unur marri jitan nanna	Nunna haur mur-eela khoob jeetun	Tina chhiya nu ghuna koera marya	I have beaten his son with many stripes.
Wore mattal parah kondan mehtantor	Ud puhar purro talee mehut toor	Ud dhore mhai-latoor phahartay	Chunri parro dhor meita ja ri	Kurrote purro dhoreal meh mundal	Ulo doongur pur dhorakh churai ruho	He is grazing cattle on the top of the hill.
Ad moda kho lai wore koddatar ootoor	Ud murra turree korat purro oottu	Ore kodatay ooehee antoor ore jharaysiree	Tui di kora te uddile mara sri	Murrate sinee kodate purro oodhtur	Ulo ghoro pur baitho chhu jharwa heyt	He is sitting on a horse under that tree.
Wuna toomoo-dal wana she-lad senoocho mantore	Oona selar tun sipudul tum-moor	Thainoor bhyal purote aund thainoor sylatay	Onor bhai than-gal madano mao selar	Haur selate tun-murdhanga mun-dal	Inho bhai inhe buhunee to oonchee budhu-jo	His brother is taller than his sister.
Wana keemat adeech roopya-na manda	Tana mola adhye roopea	Thana moal an-doorrund roopya urmoor aua	Adaina mol ran rupya our adha at	Hourla mola rund rupaya	Tinoo dam chhu urhaie roopya	The price of that is two rupees and a half.
Nowababo cho-too roon man-tore	Naha vulley cod-rontee	Mawa daoo mun-datoor ud choo-door roantay	Nava babo churur rote manda tour	Nunna babo chond rond la mudanoor	Mara baba ulo nuno ghur men ruhhey chhu	My father lives in that small house.
Eed roopaya wana washu shim	Roopea si siwata tan	Eed roopya ona seem	Yu rupya oun si-sun	Haur la rupea seem	Aroopya tino deyee du	Give this rupee to him.
Wana eegdal roopaya yena	Tan si roopea ench enut	Ud roopya oan-say aith	Yu rupya owne chhena	Haur ta rupaya it ka	Ulo kuntho tyo roopya leyeelo	Take those rupees from him.
Wona khoob jeem nah wona nodoitoor khoob	....	Ona khoob jeem un ruseetay dho cheem	Oun khub jim noune tain duha	Haur la khoob jeetun un nunte dohchee	Tina chunoo maro randho ko tina ban	Beat him well and bind him with ropes.
Doha ad koohee yertanda	Kooata ervinja	Koonwa tay air-nay cheem	Er kuan tal tanda	Seem kowata erl jute tundal	Dhee nakho koo-wa mutho panee churree to	Draw water from the well.
Nawa moonaida	Na mooney ta-kee	Dang mawa moo-nay	Nava samne taka	Nawa moonedah	Mara aga chal	Walk before me.
....	Onool pergul takee toolnee pucharee.	Bona chuwa vaya-noor neeya pijja	Won nur chhavo na pijja vandur	Oomur chowa mawa pudja-atur	Tara kiro akoo-noo chiyo awee ruho tho	Whose boy comes behind you?
Bona kareedal eema yettee	....	Bonatay eema ore mole ay tuttee	Ima vonna igral ete	Haur boneta mole etur	Takown kuntho mol tiyo	From whom did you buy that?
Natainore wa-neegdal yettal	....	Nataytay oondee dookandar tay	Nae dukandar tigral tattan nate	Narla dukandar ta	Ulo gam tho dookan tho mal liyo	From a shop-keeper of the village.

THIBETAN AND BHOOTEA LANGUAGES.

Thibetan and Bhootea Languages.

English.	Thibetan.	Bhootea of Changla (about Pongso and Dewangeeree).	Bhootea of Twang (to the north-east).	Bhootea of Lo (far to the east).	English.
One ..	Chik ..	Tur ..	Ti ..	Aken ..	One.
Two ..	Gni ..	Nik jin ..	Gnaie ..	Ani ..	Two.
Three ..	Sum ..	Tshum ..	Sum ..	Aone ..	Three.
Four ..	Zi ..	Pishi ..	Zi·blee ..	Assi ..	Four.
Five ..	Gnār ..	Gnah ..	Lenje ..	Anjo ..	Five.
Six ..	Tu ..	Kuhm ..	Pkarar ..	Aku ..	Six.
Seven ..	Dun ..	Yeu ..	Nis ..	Kanir ..	Seven.
Eight ..	Gyer ..	Zum ..	Ket ..	Pyeni ..	Eight.
Nine ..	Gu ..	Kun ..	Duju ..	Kyer ..	Nine.
Ten ..	Chutumba ..	Tsong ..	Chee ..	Adyin ..	Ten.
Twenty ..	Nishu ..	Ketur ..	Kalee ..	Nilang ..	Twenty.
Fifty ..	Napcho ..	Kaipedangsum ..	Kaipedangsum ..	Chani—arin ..	Fifty.
Hundred ..	Gyetumba ..	Kelenge ..	Kelenge ..	Angu ..	Hundred.
Hand ..	Lukti ..	Lang ..	La ..	Lab ..	Hand.
Foot ..	Kangpan ..	Nalong ..	Lemew ..	Lekpa ..	Foot.
Nose ..	Gnago ..	Nahu ..	Gua ..	Nung ..	Nose.
Eye ..	Mi ..	Ming ..	Melang ..	Nig ..	Eye.
Mouth ..	Kar ..	Kah ..	Kah ..	Kah ..	Mouth.
Tooth ..	Saw ..	Zom ..	Wa ..	Yechung ..	Tooth.
Ear ..	Namcho ..	Nah ..	Neblup ..	Nerong ..	Ear.

Hair	Tyah	Tsa	Krah	Tá	Hair.
Head	Gwah	Ah	Gwah	Dungpo	Head.
Tongue	Chi	Tse	Le	Rin	Tongue.
Belly	Tupa	Phalong	Kepa	Khopor	Belly.
Back	Gyup	Gyup	Gyup	Jyup	Back.
Iron	Chār	Chār	Lek	Chār	Iron.
Gold	Se	Ser	Shir	Ringya	Gold.
Silver	Mul	Mool	Mul	......	Silver.
Father	Apo	Papa	Apa	Abo	Father.
Mother	Ama	Ama	Ama	Annur	Mother.
Brother	Peun	Punar	Pun	Peunjar	Brother.
Sister	Singmo	Shomo	Namo	Bubma	Sister.
Man	Mei	Lang	Puibo	Milang	Man.
Woman	Pooma	Thu	Muibo	Phumoo	Woman.
Wife	Movi	Paksá	Movi	Nying	Wife.
Child	Tugoo	Kotta	Phucha	Auga	Child.
Son	Phu	Kotta	Shokpo	Ounga	Son.
Daughter	Phumo	Numi	Shoono	Neechar	Daughter.
Slave	Yeak pho	Yoh	Yoa	Kheur	Slave.
Cultivator	La	Thyenka	Lang	Kalayongla	Cultivator.
Shepherd	Lookzi	Shisa	Yeatta	No sheep	Shepherd.
God	Khla	Khla	Khla	Yuyu	God.
Devil	Dya	Háng	Hung	Aráng	Devil.
Sun	Mukpá	Sakhya	Sakhyá	Domuk	Sun.
Moon.	Dáw	La	La	Pholow	Moon.

Thibetan and Bhootea Languages.—(Continued.)

English.	Thibetan.	Bhootea of Changla (about Pongso and Dewangeeree).	Bhootea of Twang (to the north-east).	Bhootea of Lo (far to the east).	English.
Star	Kurmá	Kurmá	Kurmá	Takur	Star.
Fire	Mie	Mai	Mai	Ahmá	Fire.
Water	Chu	Rhiei	Sie	Echie	Water.
House	Khim also Khangbá	Kham	Kham	Ougu	House.
Horse	Ta	Thá	Thá	No horse	Horse.
Cow	Nong	Nong	Nong	Shapho	Cow.
Dog	Khie	Khie	Khie	Khie	Dog.
Cat	A'lu also Seemee	Chillá	Seemee	A'lu	Cat.
Cock	Phia also Chátee	Yulá	Khá	Porok	Cock.
Duck	Dámjá	Gualing	Yeachi	Satoom	Duck.
Ass	Punggoo	Pungboo	Pungboo	Sharak	Ass.
Camel	A'ma	A'ma	A'ma	No camel	Camel.
Bird	Peechoong	Peeácháng	Peeácháng	Phuthá	Bird.
Come	Showe	Phie also Oda	Shone	Em	Come.
Beat	Dung	Nyak	Tera	Dang	Beat.
Stand	Lung	Lung	Lángá	Godunglá	Stand.
Die	Seesung	Seesung	Seesung	Seechá	Die.
Give	Náung	Preesa	Phay	Dukoo	Give.
Run	Zook also Chung	Kee chaloo	Calá	A'mbojoo	Run.
Down	Du	Scuktsá	Scuktsá	Dunglá	Down.

Before	Heulá	Náná	Naskhá	Youcho	Before.
Far	Ringpho	Ringpho	Ringpho	Atho	Far.
Behind	Jalá	Soolá	Soolá	Kocheeka chálá	Behind.
What	Khá also Kurma	Zylo	Silo	Ogho	What.
Why	Káchaná	Seekyathoo	Seekyathoo	Banká banká toloo	Why.
But	Teunta	Zebregán	Zebregán	Heku	But.
If	Menná	Nálá	Nálá	Pungcholo	If.
Yes	Eeh	Haie	Haie	Aimba	Yes.
No	Mem	Mogo	......	Kámá	No.
Alas	Haye	Haye	Haye	Ápphie	Alas.
A father	Ápá chuk	Apathee	Apathee	Burook	A father.
Of a father	Ápothá neesá	Usoolá	Eyamáni	Leechabá	Of a father.
To a father	Ápotha neesjooni	Thogadee	Ápothagadhi	Leechee	To a father.
From a father	Ápochála	Ápasola	Apánama	Chabab	From a father.
A daughter	Pomee	Nimew	Purmew	Nijer	A daughter.
Of a daughter	Pomehi	Nimenki	Purmenki	Nijer-lackta	Of a daughter.
To a daughter	Pomoho la	Nimila	Purmen la	Nijer ka	To a daughter.
From a daughter	Pomonile	Nimi nitsen	Purmen ne ne	Nijer ani	From a daughter.
Two daughters	Pumoni	Nimai nitsen	Purmen nahee	Nijer ani	Two daughters.
A good man	Me le mu chi	Sharpa shimbutune	Mi lehu ni	Micha	A good man.
Of a good man	Mi limu ki	Mi depucha ki	Mi lihu ki ni	Alaber	Of a good man.
To a good man	Mi limu ki	Mi lepucha ki	Mi lihu ki ni	Mi alaki chak ub	To a good man.
From a good man	Mi di	Mi tebla ki	Mi pehu	Achi chabor	From a good man.
Good woman	Kermen zebu	Nimen tsarmu	Maibu lehutsho Maibu lehu	Nijer kaba	Good woman.
Good women	Kermen zebutso	Nimen tsarbuna	......	Nijer kapu ber	Good women.

Thibetan and Bhootea Languages.—(Concluded.)

English.	Thibetan.	Bhootea of Changla (about Pongso and Dewangeeree).	Bhootea of Twang (to the north-east).	Bhootea of Lo (far to the east).	English.
A bad boy ...	Pulcha dugrul ...	Kolā kembu ..	Skokpa lehu ...	Anju karuber ...	A bad boy.
A bad girl ...	Pumo chuk dobo ..	Nimen kyamba ..	Sho mu mauno shichilo ...	Niger alama ...	A bad girl.
Good ...	Yakpu ...	Tsarmu ..	Lehu ...	Kapu ...	Good.
High ...	Thimibu ...	Ringbu ..	Ringbu ...	Achaba ...	High.
Horse ...	Ta ...	Tai ..	Te ...	......	Horse.
Bull ...	Lung ...	Phadi ..	Phadi ...	Schepo ...	Bull.
Cow ...	Pha ...	Pa ..	Pa ...	Schena ...	Cow.
Dog ...	Chi ...	Ku ..	Chi ...	Chi pu ...	Dog.
Bitch ...	Chi mu ...	Kuma ..	......	Chi nu ...	Bitch.
Goat ...	Rapu ...	Ra ..	Ra ...	Yabeb ...	Goat.
She goat ...	Ra ma ...	Ramo ..	Ra mo ...	Nilu sichem ...	She goat.
What is your name? ...	Chen ming kan se ...	Tablá ming hang yah ..	Egu miang seng ya ju ...	Hooku bendu lala ...	What is your name?
How old is this horse? ...	Tade law kajee tsong ...	Ta lo gna umza ..	Te nim go-gaie en ...	......	How old is this horse?
How far is it from here to Lhassa?	Na la Láhssá kajee dogu en.	Hung Lhassa numja ..	A cho Lhassa go kajee ...	Lechi Lhassa atober ...	How far is it from here to Lhassa?
How many sons are there in your father's house?	Cha papa nungla peechu kajer en.	Tebla gu chimla kota lrup-thoru.	Apá ke chim ná pucha gona.	He kong aku ongoa donga	How many sons are there in your father's house?
I have walked a long way to-day.	Tering tha ringpu na youn ba en.	Thinutha ringpu na chaga	Tasu tha ringpu rasoen..	Adhoo pa cha tha siloo ...	I have walked a long way to-day.
The son of my uncle is married to his sister.	......	......	......	......	The son of my uncle is married to his sister.
In the house is the saddle of the white horse.	....	......	......	......	In the house is the saddle of the white horse.

Put the saddle upon his back.	Pheedi ga kyub ..	Thoro ga chaka ..	Ado godya ga ..	......	Put the saddle upon his back.
I have beaten his son with many stripes.	Peedu peecha gnennen seeboo dongba in.	Thoki kotha namu gnya	Ado pecha gnayi otho seepoo ter thang wain.	......	I have beaten his son with many stripes.
He is grazing cattle on the top of the hill.	Rilana palang dozen du ...	Rila pa dungdila ..	Rila pa guidur ..	......	He is grazing cattle on the top of the hill.
He is sitting on a horse under that tree.	Talá shunye shing ki ala do.	Tala chana dung bu alá chálá.	Tala chana shing dung oná gni.	......	He is sitting on a horse under that tree.
My brother is taller than his sister.	Gnye punda phida numule tho.	Thora tibla nima le zung	Otho shama otsa shamule tho.	......	My brother is taller than his sister.
The price of that is two rupees and a half.	Phide gang tiru cheda súm.	Thong nyet tiru pheda sum.	Otho ki ring tiru pheda sum.	......	The price of that is two rupees and a half.
My father lives in that small house.	Neka apa phina chun chong la de paing.	Hang apa chim chung zulálá.	Noku apo otho kim prin negna suhu in.	......	My father lives in that small house.
Give this rupee to him ..	Tiru de dila chin ..	Hang tiru thora pye ..	Otho tiru pesha pye ..	......	Give this rupee to him.
Take those rupees from him	Tiru phida duru kusoo ..	Thorgi tiru hang sta numb kar.	Otho tiru otso rota ..	......	Take those rupees from him.
Beat him well and bind with ropes.	Yepo dumg na tapher dum.	Chala galaleh yang thaper putsang yangda sing.	Thepu ter tong tek poi sing thany.	......	Beat him well and bind with ropes.
Draw water from the well	Jinua chu oh ..	Gom ni ri pye ..	Tsang pona chu chusa ..	......	Draw water from the well.
Walk before me ..	Nye ki dunla dor ..	Hongi nyela dong bila ..	Noka nosika gela ..	......	Walk before me.
Whose boy comes behind you?	Sui pacha jene yangi ..	Yege kotha kata lumu ..	Tui pacha shula rowdru ..	......	Whose boy comes behind you?
From whom did you buy that?	Disona newpa ..	Di hinge rupbo ..	Yege sune nyessu ..	......	From whom did you buy that?
From a shop-keeper of the village.	Eula tomla ..	Eula tomla ..	Eula tom lá ..	......	From a shop-keeper of the village.

COOCH BEHAR, DARJEELING, AND NEPALESE LANGUAGES.

English.	Mech.	Cooch.	Lepcha.
Numerals.			
One ...	Monohe ...	Gasak ...	Kot ...
Two ...	Mouneh ...	Dúi ...	Gyet ...
Three ...	Momthau ...	Tin ...	Sam ...
Four ...	Monbreh ...	Chárí ...	Phulee ...
Five ...	Monbah ...	Pánch ...	Phungo ...
Six ...	Mondoh ...	Chahí ...	Terok ...
Seven ...	Monchinee ...	Sát ...	Ka kyo ...
Eight ...	......	At ...	Ka kwo ...
Nine ...	......	Nau ...	Ka kyot ...
Ten ...	......	Das ...	Kati ...
Twenty ...	Thikon ...	Korí ...	Kha kot ...
Fifty ...	......	Panchás ...	Kha abungsum ...
Hundred ...	Bishabah socheh ...	Ek Sau ...	Kha phungon ...
Pronouns.			
I ...	Aug ...	An ...	Go ...
We ...	Jong ...	Nún ...	Koyu ...
Thou ...	Nooug ...	Ni ...	Ho ...
You ...	Noongcharo ...	Nirun ...	Hayu ...
He ...	Obehm anshee ...	Ua ...	Hoo ...
They ...	......	Ujaran ...	He yu ...
Of me ...	......	Aní ...	Kasusa ...
Of us ...	......	Núnni ...	Kyu sa ...
Of thee ...	......	Nini ...	Adosa ...
Of you ...	......	Nirunni ...	Hayusa ...
Of him ...	......	Uani ...	Hu soe a ...
Of them ...	......	Ujaranni ...	Hayu song sa ...
Mine ...	Augnee ...	......	Kasensa ...
Our ...	Jongnee ...	Núnní ...	Kayu pougsa ...
Thine ...	Noongnee ...	Nini ...	Ho sa ...
Your ...	Noongchinee ...	Nirunni ...	Hayu pongsa ...
His ...	Bissonee ...	Uani ...	Heu su ...
Their ...	......	Ujaranni ...	Hoyu pong sa ...
Hand ...	Nakhai ...	Chak ...	Kahok ...
Foot ...	Nathen ...	Jaten ...	Diang bok ...
Nose ...	Koontoong ...	Nakun ...	Tak nain ...
Eye ...	Mogon ...	Mukun ...	Anuk ...
Mouth ...	Khogah ...	Kakham ...	A bong ...
Tooth ...	Hathai ...	Pha ...	Apho ...

Nepalese.	Newar.	Limboo.	Magur.	English.
Ek ...	Chhee ...	Thik ...	Kat ...	One.
Don ...	Nusee, Gnee ...	Neche ...	Nis ...	Two.
Tin ...	Song ...	Soomse ...	Soom ...	Three.
Char ...	Pee ...	Lise ...	Booli ...	Four.
Panch ...	Gnya ...	Nase ...	Banga ...	Five.
Chpo ...	Khoo ...	Tookse ...	Chha ...	Six.
Sath ...	Neh ...	Noosee ...	Sath ...	Seven.
Ath ...	Chya ...	Ya-chhe ...	Ath ...	Eight.
Nao ...	Goon ...	Phangse ...	Naw ...	Nine.
Das ...	Sandho ...	Thibong ...	Das ...	Ten.
Bis ...	Sung sandho ...	Nebong ...	Bis ...	Twenty.
Pachas ...	Pee sandho ...	Phangip ...	Pachas ...	Fifty.
Sao ...	Goon sandho ...	Saw ...	Saw ...	Hundred.
Mo or hami ...	Jee ...	Inga ...	Gna ...	I.
Hame hero ...	Jee-ping ...	Anega ...	Kan koorik ...	We.
Timi ...	Chha ...	Khena ...	Nang ...	Thou.
Timi hero ...	Chha-ping ...	Khenee ...	Na koorik ...	You.
Teeyo (Tyo) ...	Wo ...	Khoona, Nakhen ...	Hos ...	He.
Une ...	Wo-ping ...	Khoonchhe ...	Hos koorik ...	They.
Mero or homro ...	Jee ta ...	......	......	Of me.
Hame hero ko ...	Jee mee ta ...	......	......	Of us.
Tero or tomro ...	Chhun ta ...	......	......	Of thee.
Timi hero ko ...	Chhu mee ta ...	......	......	Of you.
Usko ...	Wo-a-ta ...	......	......	Of him.
Uni ...	Wo-mee ta ...	......	......	Of them.
Mero or homro ...	Jee goo ...	Inga-in ...	Gnou ...	Mine.
Hame hero ko ...	Jee mee goo ...	Amga-in ...	Kanoong ...	Our.
Tero or tomro ...	Chhun goo ...	Khena-in ...	Nawo ...	Thine.
Timi hero ko ...	Chhu mee goo ...	Khene-in ...	Na koori koong	Your.
Teska ...	Wo-a-goo ...	Khoona-in ...	Hos koong ...	His.
Une ...	Wo-mee goo ...	Khoon chhi in ...	Hos koori koong.	Their.
Hatho ...	Laha pah ...	Hook taphe ...	Mihoot, hoot piak.	Hand.
Paitallo ...	Tooti palee ...	Lang daphe ...	Mihib ...	Foot.
Nak ...	Nha ...	Nebo ...	Mina ...	Nose.
An kha ...	Mee-kha ...	Meek ...	Mimik ...	Eye.
Mukh ...	Mhoo too ...	Moora ...	Minger ...	Mouth.
Dant ...	Wa ...	Ha, heboo ...	Misyak ...	Tooth.

English.	Mech.	Cooch.	Lepcha.
Ear ...	Khoma ...	Nakal ...	Anyor ...
Hair ...	Khanai ...	Khau ...	Achom ...
Head ...	Khoroh ...	Dhakam ...	At hiak ...
Tongue ...	Chhalai ...	Thelai ...	Ali ...
Belly ...	Oodai ...	Ok ...	Tabak ...
Back ...	Bikooug ...	Kúnjú ...	Achang ...
Iron ...	Shor ...	Loa ...	Panjuig ...
Gold ...	Shona ...	Sona ...	Zar ...
Silver ...	Roopa ...	Rupa ...	Kam ...
Father ...	Apha bipha ...	Awa ...	Abo ...
Mother ...	Aie, bima ...	Ame ...	Amo ...
Brother ...	......	Dada, bhai ...	Ing ...
Brother (elder) ...	Ada ...	......	......
Brother (younger) ...	Phongbai ...	......	......
Sister ...	......	Janau ...	Musing mo ...
Sitser (elder) ...	Abo ...	......	......
Sister (younger) ...	Binanaw ...	......	......
Man ...	Manshee ...	Murg ...	Maro-tagri ...
Woman ...	Hinjao ...	Magja ...	Thu ...
Wife ...	Bihi ...	Jugju, jiksai ...	Ain ...
Child ...	Bisha ...	Sasa ...	Akup ...
Son ...	Bisha hoowa ...	Mawa sasa ...	Tagri kup ...
Daughter ...	Bisha hinjao ...	Maju sasa ...	Tha u kup ...
Slave ...	Leng ...	Ghulam ...	Vith ...
Cultivator ...	Holwidan ...	Gam loinimurg ...	Khebu ...
Shepherd ...	Bromah laokar ...	Bhera rakwal ...	Thamchen nogbo ...
God ...	Batho modai ...	Rashan ...	Rem ...
Devil ...	Bhoot gotheechaw ...	Why ...	Mung ...
Sun ...	Shan ...	Rashan ...	Sechuk ...
Moon ...	Nokhabor ...	Ranrit, narek ...	Lavo ...
Star ...	Hathoorklee ...	Ramphut ...	Suhor ...
Fire ...	Wat ...	War ...	Mi ...
Water ...	Daee ...	Tíka tí ...	Ong ...
House ...	Naw ...	Nok ...	Li ...
Horse ...	Gorai ...	Ghora ...	On ...
Cow ...	Moshogai ...	Machú ...	Bik (biggu) ...
Dog ...	Chhaima ...	Koí ...	Kazen (kazu) ...
Cat ...	Maojee ...	Míyau ...	Aleu ...
Cock ...	Daw ...	Thak ...	Hickbu ...
Duck ...	Haugsho ...	Hansú ...	Dam byo ...
Ass ...	Gada ...	(Unknown) ...	Pangbu ...

Nepalese.	Newar.	Limboo.	Magur.	English.
Kan ...	Nhaipon ...	Nekho ...	Menakap ...	Ear.
Kesh ...	Sonh ...	Thagek yea ...	Misam ...	Hair.
Tanko ...	Chhon ...	Thagek ...	Mitaloo ...	Head.
Jiboo ...	Meh ...	Lesoth ...	Mekth ...	Tongue.
Bhunri or pet ...	Pooa ...	Sapok ...	Mitook ...	Belly.
Pith ...	Mha ...	Ek, ekshima ..	Mizang ...	Back.
Lohu ...	Noh ...	Phenje ...	Phalam ...	Iron.
Sun ...	Loon ...	Samyang ...	Gyo ..	Gold.
Chandi ...	Wo-ho ...	U-pah ...	Chandee ...	Silver.
Babu ...	Booba ...	Ambah, pa ...	Boi ...	Father.
Ama ...	Mang ...	Ammah, ma ...	Mai ...	Mother.
Daju or bhye ...	Kijah ...	......	....	Brother.
....	....	Am, Phoo ...	Daju ...	Brother (elder).
....	....	Anoosha ...	Bhai ...	Brother (younger).
Didui or bahini ...	....	......	....	Sister.
....	Tata ...	Anne ...	Dai ...	Sister (elder.)
....	Kenhe ...	Noosa ...	Banai ...	Sister (younger.)
Manchhi ...	Monoo ...	Gna me, Ambechha ..	Bharmi ...	Man.
Aye mye ...	Meesa ...	Men chhama ...	Mashto ...	Woman.
Sowas ni ...	Koloh ...	Ameith ...	Miya ...	Wife.
Chhoro chhori ...	Mochatha ...	Henjah ...	Lenjaja ...	Child.
Chhora ...	Kai ...	Asha, embechha ...	Lenja mija ...	Son.
Chhoree ...	Mha ...	Asha Menchhema ...	Mashto mija ...	Daughter.
Kamara ...	Cheo ...	Aiyoke ...	Myo ...	Slave.
......	Jamee ...	Kameikejopa ...	Hyami ...	Cultivator.
....	Phai jowa ...	Bhera gogumba ...	Gotala ...	Shepherd.
Bhugwan ...	Bhugwan ...	Bhagwan ...	Bhagwan ...	God.
Banjhakri ...	Bhooth ...	Bhooth ...	Bhooth ...	Devil.
Gham ...	Soorjoo ...	Nam ...	Namkhan ...	Sun.
Jun ...	Too Mila ...	Lab ...	Gya hot ...	Moon.
Tar a ...	Nugoo ...	Khes mikpa ...	Tooga ...	Star.
A go ...	Mee ...	Mee ...	Mhe ...	Fire.
Pani ...	Loh ...	Choоa ...	Dee ...	Water.
Gharo ...	Chhen ...	Him ...	Yim ...	House.
Ghora ...	Sonloh ...	On ...	Ghora ...	Horse.
Gye ...	San ...	Pith ...	Gnet ...	Cow.
Kukur ...	Khecha ...	Kocho, khyaba ...	Chu ...	Dog.
Biralo ...	Bhon, bhocha ...	Meongba, miong ...	Sootoo ...	Cat.
Bhala ...	Gongon ...	Ing wa ba ...	Gwa Chala ...	Cock.
Batak ...	Hai, hancha ...	Chookpa hans ...	Marcho hans...	Duck.
Gadha ...	Gadha ...	Gadha ...	Gadha ...	Ass.

English.	Mech.	Cooch.	Lepcha.
Camel ...	Oot ...	(Unknown) ...	Lamdong ...
Bird ...	Daosian ...	Thak ...	Pho ...
Go ...	Thang ...	Le ...	Non ...
Eat ...	Ja ...	Sa ...	Tha ...
Sit ...	Jo ...	Mosun ...	Gnán ...
Come ...	Foil ...	Ríanpai ...	Di ...
Beat ...	Shooio ...	Tok ...	Buk ...
Stand ...	Gosong ...	Kharaton ...	Lukding ...
Die ...	Thegar ...	Tilai ...	Mak ...
Give ...	Hort ...	Lahan ...	Bo le ...
Run ...	Khalang ...	Jar lei ...	Deung ...
Up ...	Gajaoo ...	Khara ...	Up long ka ...
Down ..	Gahayas ...	Kama ...	Chil ...
Before ...	Thoong joong ...	Age ...	Han ...
Near ...	Khateh ...	Kandik ...	Athal ...
Far ...	Gajanas ...	Janau ...	Murum ...
Behind ...	Unao ...	Pase ...	Loan ...
Who ...	Saro ...	Chan ...	To ...
What ...	Mah ...	Atawa ...	Shu ...
Why ...	Mano ...	Atani ...	Shumat ...
And ...	......	......	(La)ik ...
But ...	......	......	Gorung ...
If ...	......	Jodi ...	Thendok ...
Yes ...	Ongo ...	Han ...	Ak,Euk ...
No ...	Ongah ...	Era ...	Moin ...
Alas ...	Hai hai ...	......	Ha i u ...
A father ...	Bifa shacheh ...	Awa gasak ...	Abo kut ...
Of a father ...	Shacheh bifano ...	Awani ...	Abo so ...
To a father ...	Aplano ...	Awana ...	Abo so ...
From a father ...	Aphanefreh ...	Awajikin ...	Abonan ...
Two fathers ...	Bifa shaneh ...	Awa duita ...	Abo nyet ...
Fathers ...	Rifa gobang ...	Awa bren, awa bujun ...	Abo song ...
Of fathers ...	......	Awa bienni ...	Abo song so ...
To fathers ...	......	Awabrenna ...	Abo songlo ...
From fathers ...	......	Awa brennijikin ...	Abo songso ...
A daughter ...	......	Magjusasa ...	Ta u kup kath ...

Nepalese Languages.—(Continued.)

Nepalese.	Newar.	Limboo.	Magur.	English.
Ut ...	Oont ...	Oont ..	Oont ..	Camel.
Chara ...	Jhanga ...	Poo ..	Gwaja (small birds.)	Bird.
Heero ...	Hoon ...	Peg ma ..	Gnoongna ..	Go.
Khao ...	Noh ...	Chama ..	Jya ki ..	Eat.
Basa ...	Phatoo ...	U gna ..	Gnoo ki ..	Sit.
Aija ...	Wo ah ...	Phara ..	Rah ni ..	Come.
Kuta ...	Da ...	Hipma ..	Doong ki ..	Beat.
Ubho ...	Dong ...	Pima ..	Soki ..	Stand.
Moro ...	Seeta ...	Sha ..	Seki ..	Die.
Dey ...	Bi-u ...	Yea ba ..	Yaki ..	Give.
Doogro ...	Bwanhu ..	Lokma ..	Kher ki ..	Run.
Mathi ...	Cho-a ...	Tho ..	Dhenam ..	Up.
Muni or tolo ...	Ko-a ...	Yo ..	Mhaka ..	Down.
Astee or agher ...	Nhapa ...	Koodoo ma ..	Aghyer ..	Before.
Nujeek ...	Suttee ...	Neetang ..	Kherep ..	Near.
Tauro ...	Tāpa ...	Nang kha ..	Los ..	Far.
Puchke ...	Lipa ...	Egang ..	Gnoongla ..	Behind.
Ko ...	Soo ...	Hatia ..	Swale ..	Who.
Ke ...	Chu ...	Thebe ..	Hyale ..	What.
Keno ...	Chya ...	Thyang sa ..	Hyake ..	Why.
Ra ...	Nang (Doubtful) ...	Yang mo ..	Ra (Doubtful)	And.
Purunto ...	Puruntoo ...	Sang } (Doubtful)	Tara " ..	But.
......	......	Kucha } (Doubtful)	Dehreng " ..	If.
Auh ...	Ho (Doubtful) ...	Ah ..	Hau ..	Yes.
Nahee or hoyna ...	Moroo ...	Na ..	Mahla ..	No.
Aha or babyne. ...	Hai hai (Doubtful)	Kajang sama ..	Hai ..	Alas.
Egota babu. ...	Chhomho booba ...	Ambah *or* pa lopthik	Kat bai ..	A father.
Egota babu ko ...	Chhomho booba yia	Lopthik palen ..	Kat baiyo, baikoong.	Of a father.
Egotu bubu ko ...	Chhomho booba yia ta.	Lopthik pailen ..	Kat baiki	To a father.
Egota babu seteh ...	Chhomho booba napong.	Lopthik payonoo ..	Kat baile thing	From a father.
Duigota babu hero ...	Nemho booba ...	Pa neche ..	Nis bai puttoko	Two fathers.
Aabu hero ...	Booba poong ...	Paha ..	Boi puttako ..	Fathers.
Babu hero ko ...	Booba poong yia ...	Paha len ..	Boi puttoko koong.	Of fathers.
Babu hero ko ...	Booba poong yia ta	Pahailen ..	Boi puttoko ki	To fathers.
Babu hero seteh ...	Booba poong napong	Paha yonoo ..	Boi puttiko tething.	From fathers.
Egota chhoree ...	Chhomho mha ...	Lopthik menchema sa	Kat mushto mija.	A daughter.

English.	Mech.	Cooch.	Lepcha.
Of a daughter ...	......	Magjusasain ...	Ta u kup kath neu ...
To a daughter ...	......	Magjusasani ...	Ta u kup kat ko ...
From a daughter ...	......	Magjusasa jikin ...	Ta u kup kat so ...
Two daughters ...	......	Magjusasa duijon ...	Ta u kuep neth ...
Daughters ...	......	......	Ta u kup song ...
Of daughters ...	......	Magjusasagatani ...	Ta u kup song so ...
To daughters ...	......	Magjusasagatani ...	Ta u kup songlo ...
From daughters ...	......	Magjusasagatani-jikin ...	Ta u kup song so ...
A good man ...	Shacheh manshi mojang...	Murg penim ...	Moroaryumkath ...
Of a good man ...	......	Murg penimni ...	Moroaryum kathso ...
To a good man ...	......	Murg penimni ...	Mora aryum kuthka ...
From a good man ...	......	Murgpenimnijikin ...	Moroaryum kathso ...
Two good men ...	......	Murgduijonpenim ...	Moro aryum neth ..
Good men ...	......	Murg penim gata ...	Moro aryum song ...
Of good men ...	......	Murg penim gatani ...	Moro aryum songka ...
To good men ...	......	Murgpenimgatani ...	Moro aryum songlo ...
From good men ...	......	Murgpenim gatani jiken ..	Moro aryum song so ...
A good woman ...	Shacheh hinjao mojang ...	Magju penim ...	Ta u aryum kath ...
Good women ...	......	Magju penun gata ...	Tau dryum song ...
A bad boy ...	Shacheh Oodiah Bisha ...	Magju sasa gasak nagta ...	Tadi kup ozyen ...
A bad girl ...	Shacheh bisha hinjas oodia shama.	Sasa gasak nagta ...	Tau kup ózyen ...
Good ...	Mojang ...	Penim ...	Aryum ryumbs ...
Better ...	Mojancho mojang ...	Ujanichay ia penim ...	Dub ryumbs ...
Best ...	Shubshin ...	Sab se ia penim ...	Nejak ryumbs ...
High ...	Gujao ...	Chua punda ...	Atho ...
Higher ...	Bineebojow shong ...	Ujani chayia chau ...	Dop thobo ...

Nepalese Languages.—(Continued.)

Nepalese.	Newar.	Limboo.	Magur.	English.
Egota chhore ko ...	Chhomho mha yia	Lopthik mench ma-sa len.	Kat mushto mi-ja koong.	Of a daughter.
Egota chhore ko ...	Chhomho mha yia ta	Mench ma sailen ...	Mushto mija ki	To a daughter.
Egota chhore dekhi...	Chhomho mha na-pong.	Mench ma sa yonoo...	Mushto mija lething.	From a daughter.
Duigota chhoree ...	Gnee mha ...	Menchma sa nechi ...	Nis mushto mija	Two daughters.
Chhoree hero ...	Mah poong ...	Menchma sa ha ...	Mushto mija páttáko.	Daughters.
Chhone hero ko ...	Mah poong yia ...	Menchma sa ha len...	Mashto mija pottokoong.	Of daughters.
Chhore hero ko ...	Mah poong ta ...	Menchma sa hailen...	Mashto mija pattakki.	To daughters.
Chhoree hero dekhi...	Mah poong napong	Mench ma sa yonoo...	Mushto mija palla lething.	From daughters.
Egota jathi manchi ...	Chhomho bheng monoo.	Lopthik noba gname...	Kat jathe bhar-mi.	A good man.
Egota jothi manchi ko.	Chhomho bheng monoo yia.	Lopthik noba gname-len.	Kat jathe bhar-mi koong.	Of a good man.
Egota jathi manchi ka.	Chhomho bheng monoo yia ta.	Lopthik noba gname-i-len.	Kat jathe bhar-mi ki.	To a good man.
Egota jathi manchi songa.	Chhomho bheng monoo napong.	Lopthik noba gname yonoo.	Kat jathe bhar-mi lething.	From a good man.
Duota jathi manchi ...	Gnee mho bheng monoo.	Nechi noba gname. ...	Nis jathe bhar-mi.	Two good men.
Jathi manchi sabai ...	Bheng monoo poong	Noba gname ha ...	Jathe bharmi pattaka.	Good men.
Jathi manchi hero ko.	Bheng monoo poong yia.	Noba gname ha len...	Jathe bharmi patta koong.	Of good men.
Jathi manchi hero ka.	Bheng monoo poong yia ta.	Noba gname hailen...	Jathi bharmi pattaki.	To good men.
Jathi manchi hero sanga.	Bheng monoo poong napong.	Noba gname yonoo...	Jathi bharmi patta lething.	From good men.
Egota jathi aimai ...	Chhomho bheng meesa.	Lopthik noba menchma	Kat jathe mash-to bharmi.	A good woman.
Jathi aimai hero ...	Bheng meesa ta ...	Noba menchma ha ...	Jathi mashto bharme potta-ko.	Good women.
Egota naramro chhora	Chhomho-mohemah-mocha.	Lopthik men noba hen-ja.	Kat masecho jaja.	A bad boy.
Egota naramro chharee	Chhomho mohemah mha.	Lopthik men noba chook poosa keti.	Ka masecho mashtoja.	A bad girl.
Jathi ...	Bheng ...	Noba ...	Jathi, secho ..	Good.
Kub jathi ...	Sung bheng ...	Konnoole noba ...	Hos denang se-cho.	Better.
......	Khoob bheng, or Thakke sung bhing.	Kakmandhe noba ...	Patta denang secho.	Best.
Algo ...	Cho-a ...	Kaimba ...	Ghang cho ..	High.
......	Sung cho-a ...	Kon noole Kaimba ...	Hos denang ghang cho.	Higher.

English.	Mech.	Cooch.	Lepcha.
Highest ...	Boinobojow shang ...	Sab se ia chua ...	Nyak thobo ...
A horse ...	Gorai macheh ...	Ghora gasak ...	Oon bu kath ...
A mare ...	Goraijo macheh ...	Ghori magju ...	Oon moth kath ...
Horses ...	Gorai gobang ...	Ghora gata ...	Oon song ...
Mares ...	Goraijo gobang ...	Ghori magju gata ...	Oon moth song ...
A bull ...	Damrah macheh ...	Damra machu gasak ...	Long kath ...
A cow ...	......	Machu gai ...	Beegu kath ...
Bulls ...	......	Machu damra gata ...	Long song ...
Cows ...	......	Machu gai gata ...	Beegu song ...
A dog ...	Chhaimah ...	Kwai gasak ...	Kuzu bu kath ...
A bitch ...	Chhaimahjo ...	Kwai magju gasak ...	Kuzu month kath ...
Dogs ...	......	Kwai gata ...	Kuzu bu song ...
Bitches ...	......	Kwai magju gata ...	Kuzu moth song ...
A he-goat ...	Brama panta ...	Purun panta gasak ...	Sa ar bu kath ...
A female goat ...	......	Puran panti gasak ...	Sa ar moth kath ...
Goats ...	Brama pantee also bramajo	Purun gata ...	Sa ar song ...
A male deer ...	Moi shingul jola ...	Machuk panta ...	Sako bu kath ...
A female deer ...	Moijo ...	Machuk pantí ...	Sako moth katte ...
Deer ...	......	......	Sako ...
I am ...	Aug doug ..	An donna ...	Go gum ...
Thou art ...	Nooug dong ...	Ni don ...	Ho gum ...
He is ...	Obeh manshee dong ...	Ua don ...	Ha u gum ...
We are ...	Jong dong ...	Nun donna ...	Ko u gum ...
You are ...	Noong charo dong ...	Nirun don ...	Ha u pong gum ...
They are ...	......	Ujarun don ...	Ho u gum ...
I was ...	......	An tonba ...	Go nee ...
Thou wast ...	......	Ni tonba ...	Ho nee ...
He was ...	......	Ua tonba ...	Ha u nee ...
We were ...	......	Nun tonba ...	Ka u pong nee ...
You were ...	......	Nirun tonba ...	Ha u pong nee ...
They were ...	......	Jirun tonba ...	Ho u pong nee ...
Be ...	......	Dona ...	Khew ...
To be ...	......	Dona ...	Khew man ...
Being ...	......	Done ...	Chha bam mo ...

Nepalese Languages.—(Continued.)

Nepalese.	Newar.	Limboo.	Magur.	English.
......	Thukke sung cho-a	Kak mandhe kaimba	Patta denang ghang cho.	Highest.
Egota ghora ...	Chhomho sonla ..	On lopthik ...	Kat ghora ...	A horse.
Egota ghuri ...	Chhomho meesa mah sonlo.	Koomma on lopthik ...	Kat ghori ...	A mare.
Ghora sabai ...	Sonlo ta ..	On ha ...	Patta ghora ...	Horses.
Ghuri sabai ...	Meesa mah sonlo ta	Koomma on ha ...	Patta ghori ...	Mares.
Egota jura goru ...	Chhomho donhon	Bohor lopthik ...	Kat tor ...	A bull.
Egota gai ...	Chhomho sah ..	Pima lopthik ...	Kat gnet ...	A cow.
Jura goru sabai ...	Donhon ta ..	Bohor ha ...	Patta tor ...	Bulls.
Gai sabai ...	Sah ta ..	Pima ha ...	Patta gnet ...	Cows.
Egot kukur ...	Chhomho khecha ..	Khyaba lop thik ...	Kat chu chaura	A dog.
Egota chhaori kukur...	Chhomho meesa mah khecha.	Koomma khya lopthik	Kat chu chauree.	A bitch.
Kukur sabai ...	Kecha ta ..	Khya ba ha ...	Patta chaura	Dogs.
Chhaori kukur sabai..	Meesa mah khecha ta.	Koomma khya ha ...	Patta chauree	Bitches.
Egota bokra ...	Chhomho doogoo ..	Mentak lop thik ...	Kat rah ...	A he-goat.
Egota bokri ...	Chhomho choleh ..	Koomma mentak lop thik.	Kat mima rah	A female goat.
......	Choleh poong ..	Mentak ha ...	Patta rah ...	Goats.
Egota harin ...	Chhomho chunlleh	Pengwa lopthik ...	Kat kheshia ...	A male deer.
Egota harini ...	Chhomho meesa mah-chunlleh	Koomma pengwa lopthik.	Kat mima kheshia.	A female deer.
Mirga ...	Chunlleh poong ..	Pengwa-ha ...	Patta kheshia..	Deer.
Mo chha ...	....	Anga wa ...	Gna le ...	I am.
Timi chha ...	....	Kheneake wa ...	Nang le ...	Thou art.
U chha ...	....	Nakhen wa ...	Hos le ...	He is.
Hami hero chha ...	....	Ania wa ...	Kankoorika le	We are.
Timi hero chha ...	....	Kheneake wa ...	Nakoorika le...	You are.
Oon hera chha ...	....	Nakhen ha mewa ...	Hos koorika na le.	They are.
Mo theo ...	Jeedoo ..	Anga weyang ...	Gna le yia ...	I was.
Timi theo ...	Chha-doo ..	Kheneake weye ...	Kankoorika le yia.	Thou wast.
Thia thio ...	Wo-doo ..	Nakhen weye ...	Hos le yia ...	He was.
Hami hero theo ...	Jee poong doo ..	Ania weye ...	Kankoorika le yia.	We were.
Timi hero thio ...	Chha poong doo ..	Khenia ke weye ...	Nakoorika le yia.	You were.
Theo hero thio ...	Wo poong doo ..	Nakhen ha meweye ...	Hos koorika na le yia.	They were.
Hoa. ...	Joo ..	Poge } (Doubtful.)	Chhana ...	Be.
Hunu ...	Joo-e ..	Poung nia } (Doubtful.)	Chhanki ...	To be.
......	Joo-a-chona ..	Pokheyang } (Doubtful.)	Chhan nang ...	Being.

English.	Mech.	Cooch.	Lepcha.
Having been ...	......	Douimon ...	......
I may be ..	......	......	Go khen mo ...
I shall be ...	......	......	Go ong mo ...
I should be ...	......	......	Go khew pu ...
Beat ...	......	Tok ...	Bak ...
To beat ...	......	Tokni ...	Bak ka ...
Beating ...	......	Toke ...	Bak bam mo ...
Having beaten ...	......	Tokemon ...	Bak long ...
I beat ...	......	An toktu ...	Go bak ...
Thou beatest ...	......	Ní toktu ...	Ho bak to ...
He beats ...	......	Ua toktu ...	Ha bak bam ...
We beat ...	......	Nun toktu ...	Ka u pongbakto ...
You beat ...	......	Nírun toktu ...	Ho bak ka ...
They beat ...	......	Ujarun toktu ...	Ho u bak bam ...
I am beating ...	......	Aû tokna ...	Go bak bam ...
I was beating ...	......	An tokunba ...	Gobak bum ma ...
I had beaten ...	......	An tokbamun ...	Gonen bakma ...
I may beat ...	......	An tokniba toa ...	Go bak kheu ...
I shall beat ...	......	Aû tokna ...	Go baa sho ...
I should beat ...	......	Aû toknamun ...	Go nen baksho ...
I am beaten ...	......	Aû tokmausasí ...	Kas am bak mo ...
I was beaten ...	......	Au tok masapaisi ...	Kasam bak fat ...
I shall be beaten ...	......	Au tok mansana ...	Kasam baklong ...
I go ...	Aug thang aiseh ...	Au laina ...	Go no ong sho ...
Thou goest ...	Uoong thangdo ...	Ní laitù ...	Ho nong ...
He goes ...	Beathangaiseh ...	Ua laitu ...	Ha u nondat ...
I went ...	Aug thanaiseh ...	An laisí ...	Go no ong ma ...
Thou wentest ...	Nooug thanga ...	Ní laisí ...	Ho non nong ...
He went ...	......	Ua laisí ...	Hu non nong ...
Go ...	......	Lai ...	Non ...
Going ...	......	Lainiyai ...	Non det. ...
Gone ...	......	Laimun ...	Non thopa ...
What is your name?...	Noonguee moonga mamoong	Nini ata mun? ...	Hado breang shologo ...

Nepalese Languages.—(Continued.)

Nepalese.	Newar.	Limboo.	Magur.	English.
......	Jooa dhoonkclo ...	Pokhe yange ..	Chhanno ..	Having been.
Mo hunu sakeo ...	Jee doh then ...	....	Gna chhanki higley.	I may be.
Mo hun chhu • ...	Jee jooa ...	Anga pongha ..	Gna chhanni	I shall be
......	Jee jooa mah ...	Anga pongla ..	Gna ki chhanki pardele.	I should be.
Kutnu ...	Dah ...	Hiptia ..	Doongo ..	Beat.
Herkanu ...	Dai ...	Hipma ..	Doong ki ..	To beat.
Kutsa ...	Dala tena ...	Mi hiptooang ..	Doong nang ..	Beating.
Kuti kanna ...	Dai dhoonka ...	Mi hiptoole ..	Doongh no ..	Having beaten.
Mo kutsa ...	Jeen daitena ...	Anga Hiptoong ..	Gna doong le	I beat.
Timi kutsa ...	Chhan da ...	Kheniaki hiptoo ..	Nang doong le	Thou beatest.
Tesla kutsa ...	Won da la ...	Nakhen le hiptoo ..	Hos doong le..	He beats.
Hame hero kutsa ...	Jee mee sung da ...	Ania hipma ..	Kan koorika doongle.	We beat.
Teme hero kutsa ...	Chhamee sung da...	Kheneaki hiptoong ..	Na koorika doongle.	You beat.
Theo hero kutsa ...	Womee sondala ...	Nakhen hale mehiptoo.	Hos koorika doongle.	They beat.
Mo kutdesa ...	Jeen dia chona ...	Anga hiptoong ..	Gna doong le..	I am beating.
Mo kut de theo ...	Jeen dia tena ...	Anga hiptoong lapachang.	Gna ki doongle	I was beating.
Myla kuta ko theo ...	Jeen dia thaka ...	Anga hiptoong thang	Gna doong nya	I had beaten.
Myla kutna sekso ...	Jeen dia phoo ...	....	Gna doongi yeogle.	I may beat.
Mo kutsa ...	Jeen dia ...	Anga hipne ..	Gna doong nya	I shall beat.
Mo kutula ...	Jeen dia then ...	Anga hipma pong ..	Gna ki doong ki pardile.	I should beat.
Mo kutu kye ...	Jeeta dalan ...	Anga me hippa ..	Gna doongo nyele.	I am beaten.
Mo kuta kye theo ...	Jeeta dala ...	Anga me hiptoong lapache.	Gna doongo duma leya.	I was beaten.
Mo kuta khanso ...	....	Anga me hiptoong pa.	Gna doongo nyéhe.	I shall be beaten.
Mo jao ...	Jee wona ...	Anga peka ..	Gna noong le.	I go.
Temi jao ...	Chha hoon ...	Khenea ki peki ..	Nang noong le.	Thou goest.
Theo jao ...	Wo wonatena ...	Nakhen pek ..	Hos noong le.	He goes.
Mo gya ko theo ...	Jee wona wa ...	Anga pegang ..	Gna noo wa ..	I went.
Temi gya ko theo ...	Chha wona ana ...	Khenea pege ..	Nang noo wa.	Thou wentest.
The gyoko theo ...	Wo wono ...	Nakhen pege ..	Hos noo wa ..	He went.
Ja ...	Hoon ...	Pege ..	Noong ha ..	Go.
Janchha ...	Woni ...	Pekmayang ..	Noong le ..	Going.
Gyo ...	Wona dhoncla ...	Mepege ..	Noong cho ..	Gone.
Tero nawkeho ...	Chhan nam chhoo?	Ke ming the? ..	Nakoong myermin hyale?	What is your name?

English.	Mech.	Cooch.	Lepcha.
How old is this horse?	Goraini boishah beseh thaugbai?	Ighoror koi bosorni? ...	Oon ora nam suteh nong go?
How far is it from here to Kashmir?	Beneefra Kashmira beseh gajan?	Kashmir bísín jana? ...	Abanun Kashmir suteh ru?
How many sons are there in your father's house?	Nomphanee naw bisha besehbang dang?	Níní awaní nogai koy join murg sasa?	Hado bobka akup sulebth gni?
I have walked a long way to-day.	Ang gajaneefrah thabaibadang.	Tíní anpanais durníjíkia lajumpaisi.	Gomarum kor nong ma ...
The son of my uncle is married to her sister.	Augnee biftenee bisha binauoo baha khalan dang.	Anni uantini sasa wa magjuni janau buja raksi.	Kasak u tigri kup ora saing so bri thikpa.
In the house is the saddle of the white horse.	Obeh naw gorai gooful jin dong.	Nok bhiture ghara bokniyani jiatoa.	Oon a dum so go li araka ni.
Put the saddle upon his back.	Gorai bekhoong jin kha.	Uani kunjuai jin lakhau ...	Ora changa plong ka gotho
I have beaten his son with many stripes.	Bin bishako raidong jong shooha.	Uani sasawaa an banai toka suksi.	Gohu kupka agap bak ma..
He is grazing cattle on the top of the hill.	Obeh manshee hajo gajo mosho goomdung.	Hakan karaway machu datautu.	Tham chiaugzad bam hlo plong.
He is sitting on a horse under that tree.	Obeh manshee tomg pang joodaihai gorai kanahueejoietha dong.	Uapanchunaighurawai dongi tuntu.	Ho u oau plong ka ni kungsu gram ka.
His brother is taller than his sister.	......	......	......
The price of that is two rupees and a half	......	......	......
My father lives in that small house.	......	......	......
Give this rupee to him	......	......	......
Take those rupees from him.	......	......	......
Beat him well and bind him with ropes.	......	......	......
Draw water from the well.	......	......	......

Nepalese Languages.—(Continued.)

Nepalese.	Newar.	Limboo.	Magur.	English.
Kethi borkha au ghora kabhya?	Tho sonlo gola data?	Kon onin akhen barka pokhba?	Is ghora koo-rik baras chana?	How old is this horse?
He a dekhi Kashmir kethi tarosa?	Kashmir Thanna naug goolee ta tapa?	Ka-u-noo Kashmir akhen yarik mengba?	Itai Kashmir sumni koorik los le?	How far is it from here to Kashmir?
Tera babuka gharo kethe chhora chha?	Chhame booba yia chhen-go mha mo-chata doo?	Kembale kohemmo akhen sa muwabe?	Nakoong boi-o-imang lenja nuja koorika le?	How many sons are there in your father's house?
Aju mo taro dulla ...	Thong-jee apa law-gna dhoo no.	Anga ain mankha pegong.	Gna chini los noo wa.	I have walked a long way to-day.
Mira kancha babu kochhora oska boini seta bia gorro.	Jeemee kakayia-kai lesa waya kenhen beha yia ta.	Menchiala koonoo sa in noo ambhanga la koosanoo beha jogesi.	Gnou kancha boio lenja nuja-hoskoong banai khata biya jata.	The son of my uncle is married to her sister.
Gorma sito ghora ko jin chha.	Too-u-mha sonlo yia zin posh-chhen-doo.	Pho keloba onle jin himmo wa.	Bocho ghoran jin imang le.	In the house is the saddle of the white horse.
Jin uska pithu ma charadeo.	Weh mha zin posh tee.	Khenle kuekeyo jin phachhe.	Hocheo nuzang jin dao.	Put the saddle upon his back.
Usko chhora lyi dhur markyo.	Jeeng woa kai yiata kache kan dia dhoono.	Anga khenle koosa yalik hiptoong.	Gnai hocheo mizaki saro doongle.	I have beaten his son with many stripes.
Tella goat bhirko tuppa ma charaain chha.	Woa purbat cho-a sah ma-joa chona.	Nakhenle thigoo sam thang goru pit ba komosi.	Paharoong nan-gi yang hos gnet tor arch-hamne.	He is grazing cattle on the top of the hill.
Teo ghora mo basi ruk-kamoni baia ka chha.	Sheema qua sonlo gya chono.	Nakhen singaile koo-bungo nakhen-on yo yung.	Hos singho mer-toong gnang hos ghora take gnoo moo ne.	He is sitting on a horse under that tree.
......	Tata yia shemang khija torree.	Khunea noole-koo-noosa ken.	Hocheo banai denang hocheo bhai ghang-cheo le.	His brother is taller than his sister.
......	Weh mhoo-nirkatya	Nakhenle-koomaltoong nosi mohor-waa.	Hocheo mol banga mohar le.	The price of that is two rupees and a half.
......	Jeemee booba che-kee kha goo chhen chona.	Ambuh nakhen-chook-pa himmo yong.	Gnau boi hos marcheo im-ang dale.	My father lives in that small house.
......	Taka wo-a-ta bu ...	Kau angain nakhen phirea.	Is rupia hoski ya nhi.	Give this rupee to him.
......	Thoogoo taka woa ka ka.	Na angaha nakhe yonoo phettee.	Hos rupia hos lething la ni.	Take those rupees from him.
......	Wo a ta koob pian da khiptan-chu.	Na khene in yarik hipte yong thak pale khekse.	Hos ki bes khatta doongo atio hoski dorie chhyakni.	Beat him well and bind him with ropes.
......	Toonthi loh sa ..	Kooa gonoo chua late	Kooing di donni.	Draw water from the well.

English.	Mech.	Cooch.	Lepcha.
Walk before me ...	......	......	......
Whose boy comes behind you?	......	......	......
From whom did you buy that?	......	......	......
From a shop-keeper of the village.	......	......	......

Nepalese Languages.—(Concluded.)

Nepalese.	Newar.	Limboo.	Magur.	English.
......	Jee ho na Iroo theroo joo.	Anga adagayo langhege.	Gnun aghyer hwani.	Walk before me.
......	Soo mochata chung lena woala?	Hale koosa egang phembi?	Soowa mija gnoongle rachyo?	Whose boy comes behind you?
......	Soo lesa chung gne nah?	Hale yonoo nakhen keingoo?	Soo lething nakoi hos lowa?	From whom did you buy that?
......	O gaon-yia chugoo pasleh-lesa.	Pang pheyo thik modi yonoo.	Bustyoo pasale lething.	From a shop-keeper of the village.

11.

Assam languages.

LIST OF WORDS AND PHRASES

SHOWING

SHAN AND CACHAREE DIALECTS OF ASSAM.

List of English words and phrases with their corresponding words

English.	Assamese.	Ahom.	Khampti.
One ...	Ek ...	Leng ...	Langa ...
Two ...	Dui ...	Sang ...	Chhanga ...
Three ...	Tini ...	Sam ...	Chám ...
Four ...	Chári ...	Si ...	Si ...
Five ...	Pánch ...	Há ...	Há ...
Six ...	Chay ...	Ruk ...	Huk ...
Seven ...	Sát ...	Kit ..	Yeo ...
Eight ...	At ..	Pet ...	Peo ...
Nine ...	Na ...	Káu ...	Kan ...
Ten ...	Dah ...	Sip ..	Chhip ...
Twenty ...	Kuri ...	Sáu ...	Cháno ...
Fifty ...	Panchás ...	Sang sau sip ...	Háchhip ...
Hundred ...	Eksa ...	Pák ...	Pak ...
I ...	May ...	Káu ...	Kánt ...
We ...	Ami ...	Ráng ráu ...	Du ...
Thou ..	Apuni ...	Mou ...	Mátang ...
You ...	Tumi ...	Moule ...	Mán ...
He ...	Si ..	Feu ...	Kháng ...
They ..	Sihata ...	Feuluk ...	Kánlá ...
Of me, mine ...	Mor ...	Kaure ...	Háng kán ...
Of us, our ..	Amálokar ...	Raure ...	Kháng luh ...
Of thee, thine ...	Teor ...	Moule ...	Kháng khán ...
Of you, your ...	Tomár .	Mou-se ..	Kháng mán ...
Of him, his ...	Tár ..	Feu-le ..	Kháng máo ...
Of them, their ...	Sihatar ...	Feu-lukle ...	Kháng pan ...
Mine ...	Mor ...	Kau-re ...	Háng kan ...
Our ...	Amálokar ..	Rau-re ...	Kháng luh ...
Thine ...	Apanár ...	Mou-le ...	Kháng mán ...
Your ...	Tomár ...	Mou-se ...	Kháng mán ...
His ...	Tár ...	Feu-le ...	Kháng cho ...
Their ...	Táhatar ...	Feu-lukle ...	Kháng pán lá ...
Hand ...	Hát ...	Mo ...	Man ...
Foot ...	Bhari ...	Tin ...	Kádil ...
Nose ...	Nák ...	Dáng ...	Huláng ...
Eye ...	Chaku ...	Tá ...	Oyá ...
Mouth ...	Mukh ...	Sup ...	Shungpa ...
Tooth ...	Dant ...	Kheu ...	Khen ...
Ear ...	Kán ...	Pik ...	Hu ...

in Assamese, Ahom, Khampti, Aiton, Cacharee, Hojai, and Mikir.

Aiton.	Cacharee.	Hojai.	Mikir.	English.
Lung ...	Moonsa ...	Se ...	Eci ...	One.
Chhayang ...	Thaniai ...	Kini ...	Hini ...	Two.
Chaum ...	Thaithum ...	Katham ...	Kethum ...	Three.
Chhi ..	Thaileri ...	Biri ...	Phili ...	Four.
Han ...	Thaiba ...	Poa ...	Phungo ...	Five.
Hauk ...	Thairo ...	To ..	Thrak ...	Six.
Chet ...	Thaisini ...	Sini ...	Throkei ...	Seven.
Pet ...	Thaijat ...	Tehai ...	Nerkep ..	Eight.
Kau ...	Moonjee ...	Soko ...	Serkep ...	Nine.
Chhipalung ...	Manjat ...	Je ...	Kap ...	Ten.
Chhaulung ..	......	Bisosi ...	Inkoi ...	Twenty.
Hachip ...	......	Thodon ...	Phungokap ...	Fifty.
Paklung ..	......	Arjosee ...	Pharrow ...	Hundred.
Kau ...	Anug ...	Ang ...	Nai ...	I.
Hau ...	Joongphur ...	Jing ...	Nali ...	We.
Mau ..	Nong ...	Nisi ...	Nangli ...	Thou.
Chhun ...	Nong ...	Nisi ...	Nangli ...	You.
Maun ...	Be ...	Po ...	Hala ...	He.
Mainkhau ...	Bisur ...	Ponisi ...	Halatum ...	They.
Hanghau	Augmi ...	Oni ...	Ni ...	Of me, mine.
Hanghau tang lung ..	Joongphurni or Joongoni.	Jini ...	Ni ...	Of us, our.
Chhutang lung ..	Naugni ...	Nini ...	Naug ...	Of thee, thine.
Hangchu ..	Naugni ...	Nini ...	Naug ...	Of you, your.
Hangsun ..	Naugni ...	Nini ...	Naug ...	Of him, his.
....	Bisurni ...	Ninisini ...	Halatum ...	Of them, their.
....	....	....	....	Mine.
....	....	....	....	Our.
....	....	....	....	Thine.
....	....	....	....	Your.
....	....	....	....	His.
....	....	....	....	Their.
Mun ...	Ankhai ...	Eao ...	Ari ...	Hand.
Tin ...	Anthang ...	Eka ...	Akeng ...	Foot.
Lang ...	Youthong ...	Gong ...	Enokari ...	Nose.
Tan ...	Magun ...	Moo ...	Amak ...	Eye.
Chhap ...	Khooga ...	Khoo ...	Inghoe ...	Mouth.
Kheu ...	Hathai ...	Hethai ...	Eso ...	Tooth.
Pinghun ...	Khoma ...	Khamow ...	Enno ...	Ear.

List of English words and phrases with their corresponding words

English.	Assamese.	Ahom.	Khampti.
Hair ...	Chuli ...	Frum ...	Kam ...
Head ...	Mur ...	Ru ...	Hun káo ...
Tongue ...	Jibhá ...	Lin ...	Lin ...
Belly ...	Pet ...	Tang ...	Onga ...
Back ...	Pithi ...	Láng ...	Láng ...
Iron ...	Lo ...	Lik ...	Lek ...
Gold ...	Son ...	Kham ...	Khám ...
Silver ..	Rup ...	Nán ...	Ngal ...
Father ...	....	Pa ...	....
Mother ..	....	Me ...	....
Brother ...	....	Nang ...	....
Sister ...	....	Náng ning ...	....
Man ...	....	Kun ...	....
Woman ...	....	Funing ...	....
Wife ...	....	Mi ...	....
Child ...	....	Lok ...	....
Son ..	....	Luk-chái ..	....
Daughter ...	....	Luk-ning ...	....
Slave ...	....	Tukhá ...	....
Cultivator ...	....	Recná ...	....
Shepherd ...	....	Palic ...	....
God ...	....	Furá ..	....
Devil ...	....	Lung sut ...	....
Sun	....	Bán ...	....
Moon ...	..	Den ...	....
Star ...	....	Dáu ...	....
Fire ..	....	Fie ..	....
Water ..	....	Nam ...	....
House ...	....	Rán ...	....
Horse ...	....	Má ...	....
Cow ..	....	Hume ..	....
Dog ...	....	Semá ...	....
Cat ...	....	Meu ...	....
Cock ...	....	Ki ...	....
Duck ...	....	Pitnoy ...	....
Ass ...	....	Tung ...	....
Camel ...	....	....	....
Bird ...	....	Nuk ...	....
Go ...	Já ...	Ká ...	Ka ...
Eat ...	Khá ...	Kin ...	Kin ...

in Assamese, Ahom, Khampti, Aiton, Cacharee, Hojai, and Mikir.

Aiton.	Cacharee.	Hojai.	Mikir.	English.
Kaum ...	Khanai ...	Khanai ...	Eechoo ...	Hair.
Hunun ...	Khorro ...	Khoro ...	Ephoo ..	Head.
Lin ...	Salai ...	Salai ...	Eddai ...	Tongue.
Tattang ...	Udai ...	Pho ...	Eppuk ...	Belly.
Lang ...	Bikhoong ...	Sima ...	Enong ...	Back.
Lik ...	Sur ..	Ser ..	Inchin ...	Iron.
Kham ...	Durbi ...	Cogow ...	Sim ...	Gold.
Nu-eng-lip ...	Thaka ...	Kufoo ...	Rup ...	Silver.
Ponu ...	Affa ...	Baba ...	Po ...	Father.
Meu ...	Ai ...	Mama ..	Pi ..	Mother.
Pilang ...	Agai ...	Angphewng ...	Emar ..	Brother.
Nangchau ...	Agoi ...	Andow ..	Ingjerpee ...	Sister.
Kona chai ...	Hooasa ...	Sibung ...	Arling ...	Man.
Kunajing ...	Hinjao ...	Mosaijoo ...	Arlosa ..	Woman.
Mi ...	Beehi ...	Bihi ..	Peso ...	Wife.
Luklang ...	Phissa ...	Arsa ..	Osa-arlosa ..	Child.
Lukchai ...	Gotho ...	Pasa ...	Aso ..	Son.
Lukchau ...	Hinjaosa ..	Pusu ..	Asapi ...	Daughter.
Khaon ...	Leng ...	Leng ..	Ban ...	Slave.
Hidaihirna ...	Khetiak ...	Dongiaba ...	Sai-ketkee ..	Cultivator.
Chhauling-pe ...	Moorkhia ...	Gorokhia ..	Chimung, kibi-abang.	Shepherd.
Chau-phro ...	Issor ...	Issor ..	Arnam ..	God.
Phiphu ...	Modai ...	Soko ..	Hie e ..	Devil.
Bhan ...	San ...	Sai ...	Arni ..	Sun.
Neun ...	Okhaphoo ...	Dai ..	Cheklo ...	Moon.
Nao ...	Hathorkee ...	Hothrai ..	Cheklolanso ..	Star.
Kai ...	Oth ...	Oai ..	Me ..	Fire.
Nam ...	Dey ...	Di ..	Lang ..	Water.
Hun ...	Nan ...	Na ..	Hem ..	House.
Man ...	Gorai ...	Goroi ..	Lose ...	Horse.
Dau ...	Moson ...	Mossu ..	Chaino ..	Cow.
Ma-wan ...	Cimma ...	Cissa ...	Methang ..	Dog.
Me-u-e ...	Mousi ..	Alu ..	Meng ...	Cat.
Kai ...	Dan ...	Towno ..	Bhogomi ..	Cock.
Peheta ...	Hangse ...	Taflanda ..	Bhoka ..	Duck.
La ...	Gorai ...	Gada ..	....	Ass.
....	Ut ...	....	....	Camel.
Naokhan ...	Dow ...	Kow ..	Bho ..	Bird.
Paeka ...	Thang ...	Thangbo ..	Damai ..	Go.
Killa ...	Ja ...	Chiba ..	Chanai ...	Eat.

List of English words and phrases with their corresponding words

English.	Assamese.	Ahom.	Khampti.
Sit ...	Bah ...	Nang ...	Langa ...
Come ..	....	Mále ...	....
Beat ..	....	Dheksi ...	....
Stand ..	....	Chán ...	....
Die ..	....	Ti ...	....
Give ..	....	Hansi ...	....
Run ..	....	Len ...	....
Up ...	Upar ...	Nu ...	Kan lan ...
Near ...	Ochar ...	Khanpi ...	Kan tah ...
Who ...	Kone ..	Kanfreu ...	Nábi kháráo ...
And ...	Aru ...	Anbá ..	Khun láng káo ...
Yes ...	Hai ...	Changnái ...	Jáoh ...
Down ..	....	Teu ...	....
Far ..	....	Reu ...	....
What ..	....	Khamsang ...	....
But ..	....	....	....
No ..	....	Fang ...	....
Before ..	....	Ná ...	....
Behind ..	....	Lang láng ...	....
Why ..	....	Khamfi ...	....
If ..	....	Fátta ...	....
Alas ..	....	Mi-mi ...	....
A father ...	Bopái etá ...	Leng pa ...	Pan áláng ...
Two fathers ...	Bopái dutá ...	Sang-pa ...	Chhanga pan ...
Fathers ...	Bopái sakal ...	Pa-bat ...	Pán khán ...
Of a father ...	Etá bopáir ...	Pa-se ...	Háng pan khán ...
Of fathers ...	Bopái sakalar ...	Pa-sambat ...	Háng pan khán ...
To a father ..	Etá bopái lai ...	Pa-mán ...	Háng pan háon ...
To fathers ...	Bopái sakalak lai ...	Pa-sali ...	Hang pan hánt ...
From a father ...	Etá bopáir pará ...	Pa-mána ...	Ján khán pena má ...
From fathers ...	Bopái sakalar pará ...	Pa-mán báte ...	Jáu kháu pen má ...
A daughter ...	Ji ejani ...	Leng ning luk ...	Luk cháu ...
Daughters ...	Ji bilak ...	Luk-ning-bát ...	Luk cháu ...
Of a daughter ...	Ji ejanir ...	Luk-ning leng ...	Háng luk cháu nái kháu ...
Of daughters ...	Ji bilákar ...	Luk-ning-bat-se ...	Háng luk cháu nái kháu ...
To a daughter ...	Ji ejani lai ...	Luk-ning leng-se ..	Háng kung luk cháu kháu
Two daughters ...	Dujani ji ...	Sang luk-ning ...	Luk ying sangak ...
From a daughter ...	Ji ejanir pará ...	Luk-ning leng-sewá ...	Náu luk cháu nái kháu ...
To daughters ...	....	Luk-ning-bat-seá ...	....
From daughters ...	Ji bilákar pará ...	Luk ning bat sewá ...	Náu luk cháu nái kháu ...

in Assamese, Ahom, Khampti, Aiton, Cacharee, Hojai, and Mikir.

Aiton.	Cacharee.	Hojai.	Mikir.	English.
Nangla ...	Jo ...	Khamba ..	Minai ...	Sit.
Masa ...	Phai ..	Phaiba ..	Bengnai ..	Come.
Pahaga ...	Bubai ...	Towba ..	Chonnai ...	Beat.
Takuchan ...	Gosongdong ..	Songba. ..	Thornai ..	Stand.
Tai ...	Thaiba ..	Thiba. ..	Kithi ..	Die.
Hauma ...	Ho ..	Riha. ..	He ..	Give.
Lem ...	Khatdong ..	Khailong ..	Karnai ..	Run.
Luk la ...	Sa ..	Posow ..	Atha ..	Up.
Kaucha ...	Khathi ..	Sampha. ..	Adu ..	Near.
Kaune ...	Shur ..	Seri ...	Mor ..	Who.
Khuncham ...	Aru ...	Aru ...	Apar ..	And.
Chan ...	Noonggo ..	Gibi ..	Ta ..	Yes.
Keta-u ...	Singgao ..	Phokla ..	Abel ..	Down.
Kaite ...	Gojan ..	Kejing ..	Kehelo ..	Far.
Kechang ...	Ma ..	Sunang ..	Pe ..	What.
Huncham ...	Kintoo ...	Pimifising ..	Lahe ..	But.
Nangchau ...	Noonga ...	Nia ..	Koli ..	No.
Ananna ...	Siggongo ...	Sugeeho kedoha ..	Hafranghelong	Before.
Kallang ...	Oonou ..	Tanaha ..	Nefi ..	Behind.
Kangchhang ne ...	Mano ..	Simune ..	Kapee ..	Why.
....	Jodi ...	Thikade ..	Lahe ..	If.
Hai uh pibachangne...	Hai hai ..	Hai-hai ..	Cheche ..	Alas.
Paulung ...	Khasi afa ..	Baba sowse ..	Enguro po ..	A father.
....	Khanoi afa ..	Baba gini ..	Dohoni po ..	Two fathers.
Patanglu ...	Affa fore ..	Baba row ..	Aportu ..	Fathers.
....	Affani ..	Babani ..	Apo ..	Of a father.
......	Affa foreni ..	Baba rowni ..	Apoato ..	Of fathers.
Hang-po-lung ...	Affanen ..	Bohantha ..	Apale ..	To a father.
Hao-po-haon ...	Affamono ..	Boba rowtha ..	Apo artule ..	To fathers.
Lai-po-lung ...	Affaiya ..	Babani fereng ..	Nepopeng ..	From a father.
Lai-po-hau ...	Affa-forni-fry ..	Babarow fereng ..	Apo atumpen...	From fathers.
Chhau lung ..	....	....	....	A daughter.
Lukchhau nam ...	....	....	....	Daughters.
Lukchhau lung ...	....	....	....	Of a daughter.
Lukchhau khau ...	....	....	....	Of daughters.
Hang-luk-chau ...	....	......	....	To a daughter.
Hang luk chau tang lung	....	......	....	Two daughters.
Puluk chhau pulang...	....	......	....	From a daughter.
....	....	....	....	To daughters.
Lai puluk chau tang lung.	....	....	....	From daughters.

List of English words and phrases with their corresponding words

English.	Assamese.	Ahom.	Khampti.
A good man ...	Etá bhal mánuha ...	Leng di kun ..	Kal áloni lángo mái ...
Two good men ...	Dutá bhál mánuha ...	Sang kun di ...	Kalni chhang kang ...
Good men ...	Bhál mánuha bor ...	Di kun bat ..	Phan ni kháu ...
Of a good man ...	Etá bhal mánuhar ...	Leng di kun-se ..	Kal áloni lángo me ...
Of good men ..	Bhál mánuha borar ...	Di kun-batse ...	Phanui kháu ...
To a good man ...	Etá bhal mánuhalai ...	Leng di kun-sen ...	Hang kal ni mái ...
To good men ...	Bhál mánuha bilák lai ...	Kun di batsen ...	Káng phanni kháu mai ...
From a good man ...	Etá bhál mánuhar para ...	Leng di kun-sewá ..	Kal áloni náu ...
From good men ...	Bhál mánuha bilákár pará.	Di kun-batsea ...	Phanni hángui kháu nán ...
A good woman ...	Ejani bhál máiki ..	Funing di leng ...	Meh kal ni piying ...
Good women ..	Chikan máikibor ...	Di funing ...	An chen piying kháu ...
A bad boy ...	Etá beyá lará ...	Luk leng chayá ...	Toán mini lang ...
A bad girl ...	Ejani beyá choáli ...	Luk ning leng chya ...	Mini piying an lang ...
Good ...	Bhál ...	Di ...	Nioh ...
Better ...	Aru bhál ...	Lung di ..	Khun kángani ...
Best ...	Bhálat kai bhál ...	Long sang di ..	Nile tile te lang ...
High ...	Okh ...	Ren ..	Chhongá ...
Higher ...	Aru okhará ...	Then ren ..	Phá khun káng chhongá ...
Highest ...	Okhat kai okh ...	Nuchyan ..	Chungná mái chung lang má.
A horse ...	Ghorá etá ...	Má leng ..	Mah on lang ...
A mare ...	Ejani ghori ...	Mami ..	Máh dume langa ...
Horses ...	Ghorá bilák ...	Mábat ...	Máh ne kháu ...
Mares ...	Ghori bilák ...	Mami-bat ...	Máh dume kháu ...
A bull ...	Etá sár garu ...	Huba ..	Ngá pái anlang ...
A cow ...	Ejani gái garu ...	Mehn ...	Ngá dume lang ...
Bulls ...	Bhátara garubor ...	Hubá-bat ..	Ngán nái kháu othang ...
Cows ...	Garu bor ...	Mehn-bat ..	Dume lang kháu ...
A dog ...	Kukur etá ...	Semá ..	Mámáon ...
A bitch ...	Máiki kukur ejani ...	Mesemá ...	Máh me lang ...
Dogs ...	Kukur bor ...	Semábat ...	Mánái kháu ...
Bitches ...	Máiki kukur bor ..	Mesema-bat ...	Dume má nái kháu ...

in Assamese, Ahom, Khampti, Aiton, Cacharee, Hojai, and Mikir.

Aiton.	Cacharee.	Hojai.	Mikir.	English.
Khunni kulang ...	Khanoi-goham ..	Sowsi subon hambee..	Mesen arlung..	A good man.
....	Gaham manse ..	Hamba subon row ..	Banghini mesen arlung.	Two good men.
Khunni kau ...	....	....	Kadow kowa..	Good men.
Khunni-kuli-kolang...	Khase gohan mansein	Hamba sikonsini ..	Anut kemesen arlong.	Of a good man.
Khunni nena kha-um	Gaham manseeni..	Hamba siban rowsini	Kemesen arlong	Of good men.
Hang khunni kulang	Gaham manse lage	....	Anee mesent..	To a good man.
....	Gaham manse ferra	....	Lajukta mesen angoler.	To good men.
Hang khunni tang lung.	Khase gaham ningas	....	Kemesen arlong pensy relong-ta.	From a good man.
Laipu khunni kulang	....	....	....	From good men.
Pijingane kolang ...	Gaham hurjao ..	....	Anut kemesen apiso.	A good woman.
Miuni khao ...	Khasi hainagotho..	....	Tajukta mesen apiso.	Good women.
Lukhai kolang ...	Lase haina gotho..	....	Aneet kahingo aosa.	A bad boy.
Luk lau hau ...	Lase hama jousa ..	....	Anut kahigo krlosa.	A bad girl.
Ni uga ...	Bar gaham ..	....	Mesen ..	Good.
....	Be gabam ..	....	Lame musut..	Better.
Chhena-de ...	Goozon ..	....	Lame meechat lang.	Best.
Chhau ..	Bor goozon ..	....	Kangtoi ..	High.
....	Be goozon ..	....	Kangtaipar ..	Higher.
Chhong-te ...	....	....	Bi kangtozpar	Highest.
Matu lang ...	Khase ghorai ..	....	Ajun losai ...	A horse.
Mame tulang ...	Jo gorai ..	....	Ajun losai api	A mare.
Mathuk nam ...	Gorai fra ..	....	Losai atum ...	Horses.
Mame nama ...	Gorai bima ..	....	Losai api atum	Mares.
Buthuk lung ...	Bolud musan ..	....	Ajun . alowchi-nong.	A bull.
Utme o-lang ...	Gai-mosow ..	....	Ajun chinong api.	A cow.
Utthok kung-lang ...	Bhotora mosan ..	....	Chinnung alow atum.	Bulls.
Ume kung lang ...	Moosow bima. ..	....	Chinnung api atum.	Cows.
Mawan lung ...	Saym jala ..	....	Methan alow..	A dog.
Mawan melung ...	Sayma jo ..	....	Methan api ..	A bitch.
Mawan kang lung ...	Sayma fra ..	....	Methan alow atum.	Dogs.
Mawan me kang lung	Sayma jo fry ..	....	Methan api atum.	Bitches.

List of English words and phrases with their corresponding words

English.	Assamese.	Ahom.	Khampti.
A he-goat ...	Etá motá chhágali ...	Fupenga leng ...	Beyá dume lang ...
A female goat ...	Ejani máiki chhágali ...	Mipengá leng ...	Beyá thak lang ...
Goats ...	Chhágali bilák ...	Penga-bat ...	Beyá nan kháu ...
A male deer ...	Etá motá pahu ...	Tungifu leng ...	Naong thak lang ...
A female deer ...	Ejani pahu ...	Tungimi leng ...	Nang dume lang ...
Deer ...	Pahu bilák ...	Tungi-bat ...	Nang nái kháu ...
I am ...	May achho ...	Kau-e ju ...	Kánmái yángoh ...
Thou art ...	Apuni achha ...	Mou-eju ...	Mán jáoh ...
He is ...	He achhe ...	Feu-man ju ...	Mán khán yangongke ...
We are ...	Ami achho ...	Rang-rau ju ...	Duong mái ong ...
You are ...	Tumi áchha ...	Moule juse ...	Man yáng ong ...
They are ...	Teo bilák áchhe ...	Feu-luk rang ju ...	Kántá yáng than ...
I was ...	May áchhilo ...	Kau-e ju-mang ...	Kánt má yan ...
Thou wast ...	Apuni áchhile ...	Mou-e ju-koi ..	Matang jaoh ...
He was ...	Si áchhile ...	Feu ju-se ...	Kháng má yán ...
We were ...	Ami áchhilo ...	Rang rau juman ..	Duong máiong ...
You were ...	Tumi áchhila ...	Moule ju-sakoi ...	Máu máyán ...
They were ...	Teo bilák áchhile ...	Feu-luk rang-juse ..	Khán kang yáng ong ...
Be ...	Hay ...	Ju ...	Jáo ...
To be ...	Habole ...	Ju-man-se ...	Jaoya ...
Being ...	Hai pelái ...	Ju-klang ...	Jaoya oah ...
Having been ...	Hai pelai ...	Ju khan tang ..	......
I may be ...	May habo paro ...	Kau ju-toi ...	Káu pen ong ...
I shall be ...	May ham ...	Kau-e bai-ju ...	Kau pen ong ...
I should be ...	Haba lage ...	Kau-e folaiju ...	......
Beat ...	Mare ...	Dheksi ...	Pang ke ...
To beat ...	Maribalai ...	Dhekpasi ...	Mi pang ke ...
Beating ...	Marichhe ...	Dheksi ...	Pang nam ...
Having beaten ...	Mara hai pelai ...	Dhekpasi lung ...	......
I beat ...	May marichho ...	Kau-e dhek ...	Kau pang ka ...
Thou beatest ...	Apuni marichho ...	Moue dheksi ...	Matang pangma ...
He beats ...	Teo marichhe ...	Feu kon dhek ...	Maupang ma ...
We beat ...	Ami marichho ...	Rang rau dhek ...	Dupang nam ...
You beat ...	Tumi márichha ...	Mouledhek ...	Mau pung ke ...
They beat ...	Sihate marichhe ...	Feu luk dhek ...	Khan pang ma yau ...
I am beating ...	May marichhe ...	Kau-e dheksi dheksi ..	Kau mai pang ma ...
I was beating ...	May marichhilo ...	Kau-e dheksi lung ...	......
I had beaten ...	May marilo ...	Kau-e dheksile ...	Kau mai pang ma yau ...

in Assamese, Ahom, Khampti, Aiton, Cacharee, Hojai, and Mikir.

Aiton.	Cacharee.	Hojai.	Mikir.	English.
Pe thuk lung ...	Bormafantha mase	Bronjola mase ..	Bailo eyan ..	A he-goat.
Pe me lung ...	Burma bima manse	Bronboojoo manse ..	Biapi eyan ..	A female goat.
Phung-pe ...	Borma fur ..	Bronsi bangbie ..	Biatum ..	Goats.
Nithuk-lung ...	Moifanthi mase ..	Mijela masi ..	Thiakals ..	A male deer.
Nime lung ...	Moifanthi mase ..	Mi boojoo ..	Thoiapi ..	A female deer.
Kung ni ...	Moifur ..	Mi kabaug ..	Thiokatum ..	Deer.
Ka-ucha ...	Aung noongo ..	Ang jadoo ..	Nephanjee ..	I am.
Mauna ...	Noong moongo ..	Noong jadoo ..	Nangphanghon	Thou art.
Munacha ...	Be noonga ..	Boo jadoo ..	Kali hala ..	He is.
Ha-ucha ...	Jungphur noonga..	....	Netaplang-doonjiari.	We are.
Chhuna ...	Noongee noonga ..	Joong jadoo ..	Nangtoplang-douon.	You are.
Mun khauna ...	Aungh thathengmon	Poonsi jadoo ..	Kalonglo hala	They are.
Ka-u-jangcha ...	Noong thathengmon	Ang dangba ..	Nedolo ..	I was.
....	Be thathengmon ..	Namdi dangba ..	Nang dol ..	Thou wast.
Munajam ...	Jungphur thatheng-mon.	Noong dangba ..	Hala dolo ..	He was.
Hau tang lung jang...	....	Joong dangba ..	Nelli dolo ..	We were.
Chhutang lung jang...	Noongsur thatheng-mon.	Namai rowdungba ..	Nangtum dolo	You were.
Khau taka lung jang	Besur thathengmon	Poonisi doongbo ..	Halatum dolo	They were.
....	Noomgo ..	Jadoo ..	Phanglo ..	Be.
....	Namais ..	Jamah ..	Eapo ..	To be.
....	....	Jakha ..	Cee or see ..	Being.
....	....	Jakha ..	Cee or see ..	Having been.
Kupi nuchang ..	Aung jane hago ..	Aug jafooree ...	Netaplangton-gee.	I may be.
....	Aung jagon ..	Aug jamang ..	Ne-epo ..	I shall be.
....	....	Aug jafooree ...	Nedoijee ..	I should be.
....	Boo ...	Doh ...	Kochok ..	Beat.
....	Boono ...	Toma ..	Chokjee ..	To beat.
....	Boonaiow ...	....	Cho-pallo ..	Beating.
....	Boonaiow ...	....	Cho-pallo ..	Having beaten.
Kau thuppa ..	Aung boonee ...	....	Ne choknon ..	I beat.
Manpo ..	Noong boo ...	....	Nang choknon	Thou beatest.
Main-po ..	Be booro ...	....	Halla choknon	He beats.
Hau thuppa ..	Jung boonee ...	....	Nellee choknon	We beat.
Chhopama ..	Noongsur boo ...	....	Nangtum chok-non.	You beat.
Khau thopo ..	Besur booro ...	....	Hallatum chok-non.	They beat.
....	Aung boodung ...	....	Ne choklo ..	I am beating.
....	Aung boodungmon	....	Ne choktanglo	I was beating.
....	Aung boodungmon	....	Ne choktanglo	I had beaten.

List of English words and phrases with their corresponding words

English.	Assamese.	Ahom.	Khampti.
I may beat ...	May mariba paro ...	Kau-e dheksiloi ...	Kau pang pen ong ...
I have beaten ...	....	....	....
I shall beat ...	May marim ...	Kau-e dhek-boi ...	Kau pang ma yahe ...
I should beat ...	May marila hate ...	Kau-e dhek-falai ...	......
I am beaten ...	Mok marile ...	Kau-ke dheki ..	Khau mai pang ma yau ...
I was beaten ...	May mara halo ...	Kau-ke dheksi-lung ..	Kau mai pang ma yau ...
I shall be beaten ...	May mara ham ...	Kau-ke dheksipasi ..	......
I go ...	May jao ...	Kau-e ka ...	Kau ka kao ...
Thou goest ...	Apuni gaichhe ...	Mou-e ka ...	Mat jaumah ...
He goes ...	Teo jae ...	Feu ka ...	Káng máh ...
I went ...	May gailo ...	Kau-e paika ...	Káu máh ...
Thou wentest ...	Apuni gaichhile ...	Mou-e kase ...	Mátjánká yáo ...
He went ...	Teo gail ...	Feu ka-fai ...	Máuká yáo ...
Go ...	Ja ...	Ka ...	Ká ...
Going ...	Jam ...	Kafaile ..	Kálá ...
Gone ...	Gal ...	Ka-hau ..	Ká yáo ...
What is your name?...	Tor ki nam ...	Moule su kham sang ...	Yáng mán kácháng ...
How old is this horse?	Ei ghorar kiman bayas haichhe.	Ma tu pi le ...	Anái máh ki áchák thán ong.
How far is it from here to Kasmir?	Iar para Kasmir lai kiman dur.	Tinái mung ban Kasmiri theureu.	Luksi nái Kásmir mái khán kái.
How many sons are there in your father's house?	Tor baperar gharat kiman lora achhe.	Moule pamán rán luk chyang.	Hanpang mau mai luk an kha ratang.
I have walked a long way to-day.	May aji bahu dur phuri ahilo.	Kau-e menai fai mung faiban.	Kau mandaih tikai mai lechhi pang ka ma khun le pha.
The son of my uncle is married to her sister.	Tair chaniek more dadair puteke biya karichhe.	Kau-re áu chau luk feu-le ning-nang ning kákán.	Nang chau man mai luk pang au kau au heo meh yau.
In the house is the saddle of the white horse.	Gharar bhitarat thakajin khanbaga ghorator hayne	Ma fak ankham ran khau ju	Ong kana han mai naih anma phak naih yan ung ke.
Put the saddle upon his back.	Jinkhan tar pithat de ...	Feu-le lang bai ankham khutsi.	Au man oang kalang mau mai tah.
I have beaten his son with many stripes.	Tar putekak may bahut kob maricho.	....	Lukman ma ih kau jau thipa ya oh.
He is grazing cattle on the top of the hill.	Si parbatar tingat garu charaichhe.	Fen doilung ru hukin nya	Mau phang lang yik nae maih leng nga ong.
He is sitting on a horse under that tree.	Sei gachar talat si ghorat uthichhe.	Tun ten malang feu nang	Kanau hang nana man khi mah si ong yan.
His brother is taller than his sister.	Tar kakaek tar chaniyk kai okh.	Feu-le nang-ning feu man ki lung nu.	Piyái mán lang cháu mán mái kang chhong lang ma yán

Aiton.	Cacharee.	Hojai.	Mikir.	English.
Kaup tipino ..	Aung boonahago ...	....	Ne chokaon ..	I may beat.
....	....	....	....	I have beaten.
....	Aung boogun ...	....	Ne chokjee ..	I shall beat.
....	....	....	Ne choknangpo	I should beat.
Kau ken khawan ..	Aungtho booio ...	....	Ne kachok ..	I am beaten.
....	Aungtho boobai ...	....	Ne choklo ..	I was beaten.
....	Aungtho boogun ...	....	Ne chokpo ..	I shall be beaten.
Kau thopai ..	Aungthangni ...	....	Ne dampo ..	I go.
Mau pai ma ..	Noong thang ...	....	Nang dammon	Thou goest.
Mun paiga ..	Be thangtheng ...	....	Haladamtanglo	He goes.
Kapaima ..	Aung thangbai ...	....	Ne damtanglo	I went.
Ma paima ..	Noong thangbai ...	....	Nang dampo..	Thou wentest.
Mun paika ..	Be thangbai ...	....	La damtanglo	He went.
Paiga ..	Thang ...	....	Da ..	Go.
Paiuka ..	Thangdoong ...	....	Dambomlo ..	Going.
Paigao ..	Thangoai ...	....	Damtanglo ..	Gone.
Chiuma chiuchang ..	Noonghi nowama now.	....	Nangman kopoo	What is your name ?
Achhak-ma khelau lung ?	Be goraia bosur pisa jadoong.	....	La losai ning-kan kowanlo.	How old is this horse ?
Uthai hau thung Kasmir khelai lung ?	Bainifry Kashmere basa gojan.	....	Ladakpen Kashmere koando kahila.	How far is it from here to Kasmir ?
Hunapa mau luen imang khelau lung ?	Noongni noompa ni noton gotho khapsa dongo.	....	Ahen koando nang somar.	How many sons are there in your father's house ?
Kauka tang kaima teho.	Diniang nama gojan thabai bai.	....	Pinine kahilopar kafooridom.	I have walked a long way to-day.
Punung chau mun luk chai au kau pin hun.	Angni fodoini ficho-dla bini binoxnow-fo boba kulambai.	....	Naponoo aso asopi ponang kedo.	The son of my uncle is married to her sister.
Lau hun naima kuk an mun jangna.	Goorai goofootuijuna bai no dong.	....	Losai aklok jin halahem sido.	In the house is the saddle of the white horse.
Nulang muna kupana mun.	Binibi khwang jima khooai.	....	La amoi jin arboongum.	Put the saddle upon his back.
Hang luk mun kau thuk hau.	Augbini fisajala ko ghanimai boobai.	....	Ne labangso aso jasemet chuklo.	I have beaten his son with many stripes.
Nulae mun pai ning bu.	Be hojani sai awha moosow goonedong.	....	Englong apo chaimning kebi dam.	He is grazing cattle on the top of the hill.
Kun bulang tautun mainang nungma.	Bi bongfang singon gorai uthibai tha-dong.	....	Hala thaughi abinlosaiatha ingnisoo sido.	He is sitting on a horse under that tree.
Hang nang chau mun, nang chaimun khen chhang.	Bini bifunga bini bina nanikho goo-jan.	....	La amoo ang jirpi afan amoo dingmoo.	His brother is taller than his sister.

English.	Assamese.	Ahom in Roman character.	Khampti.
The price of that is two rupees and a half.	Tar dam du taka ek adhuli hay.	Feu khat sang tak faleng	Thang mán chhangta thuli yán yán.
My father lives in that small house.	Mor bopai seito saru gharete thake.	Kau-le pa ran noy ju-se ...	Pung kán yá jau kán hang la ana ná.
Give this rupee to him.	Eirup taka tak dibi ...	Feu-man tak leng housi ...	Ngá na trá nai mán mái hátang dah.
Take those rupees from him.	Tar para seir up khini anibi.	Feu se tak-bat ...	Lukman ma ih nga nanai khau aong ma dah.
Beat him well and bind him with ropes.	Tak bhalkai maribi aru jarire bandhi thubi.	Feu-man di dheksi anba feu-man si khat.	Pang mini oah khun lang kau chài phuka oai tah.
Draw water from the well.	Nadar para pani tol ...	Khum pen nam au ...	Nam mang mai nam oak tah.
Walk before me ..	Mor agat phur ..	Kau-le na khanpai khanma	Na kau mai ledah ..
Whose boy comes behind you?	Tor pachhat kar lara ahichhe.	Kanai lukman moule khen-lang mase.	Kalang mau mau luk kau laima.
From whom did you buy that?	Kar para seito kini lali ..	Kon feu-bat mou ansu ankhrai.	Luk kau mai an mau chhang ma kah.
From a shop-keeper of the village.	Gaor eta beparir para ..	Mung ban katram ansu ...	Mau mai lai pang pang ka án lang na ih.

in Assamese, Ahom, Khampti, Aiton, Cacharee, Hojai, and Mikir.

Aiton.	Cacharee.	Hojai.	Mikir.	English.
Khan annai chhang tahai thule.	Binidama rupgotnai adlisa.	....	Lahang son adur sika hini adobaug.	The price of that is two rupees and a half.
Pukai uhun annai ...	Augni afaia binour udniow thaio.	....	Nepo ha hemso sido.	My father lives in that small house.
Inguna ennai hau hang mun.	Bathakakho binaha	....	Ladhun lapinne	Give this rupee to him.
U-eng numu mu-ina auga.	Bathaka frookhanta	....	Lapen dhun anem.	Take those rupees from him.
Hang mun pani nila auchhai huk ninila.	Bikhan ghaminoboo didoong jung kha.	....	Lachuk mesen, armi le cog-num.	Beat him well and bind him with ropes.
Unam-mo-tak-ma ...	Hakhurnifra deg dikhang.	....	Langtook penla taug chugnum.	Draw water from the well.
Kai pang na ...	Aungin sigang an thabai.	....	Nefraug damun	Walk before me.
Kallang mau lu-an kaulema?	Noongni tinow than-gnaia sini gotho.	....	Naugfee mot aooso sinan-kidoom.	Whose boy comes behind you?
....	Sinifra bai nai ..	....	Labaugso mot pensa nanka-nam.	From whom did you buy that?
Lai-poka thai kalang	Jemini dokhani sasinifora bai nai.	....	Rong agulot-pensa nang kenam.	From a shop-keeper of the village.

CACHARI LANGUAGE.

NUMERALS.

One	...	Sei.	Six	...	Ran.
Two	...	Noi.	Seven	...	Sim.
Three	...	Tham.	Eight	...	Sikho.
Four	...	Bri.	Nine	...	Zat.
Five	...	Bá.	Ten	...	Zi.

Twenty ... Zan-khai-ba.

N.B.—There are no distinct words to express numerals above ten. There is however a collective word, "zan khai" = four; which, when followed by two other numbers, is to be multiplied by the *former*, while the second is to be added to the product so obtained. In this way the Cacharies can enumerate up to forty; beyond which they resort to the practice of counting objects into separate groups of fire.

Zan-khai-tham = four × three = 12.

Zan-khai-tham-(sa)—tham = four × three + three = 15.

Prepa-sa implies men, *e.g.*, sä-tham = three (men).

Ma, lower animals, ma-tham = (goats).

Mun, lifeless objects, mun-tham = bamboos.

The vowels in the above words are all pronounced with a short, sharp, clicking sound, not at all easy to catch or to imitate.

PRONOUNS.

Singular.			*Plural.*		
Ang	...	I.	Zung phoor	...	We.
Ang-ni	...	Of me.	,, ni	...	Of us.
Ang-nan	...	To me.	,, nan	...	To us.
Ang-kho	...	Me.	,, phoor pho	...	Us.
Ang-ni-phorai	...	From me.	,, niphorai	...	From us.
Ang-ni-on	...	In me.	,, ni-an	...	In us.
Nung	...	Thou.	Nung-soor	...	You.
Nung-ni	...	Of thee, &c., &c.	,, ,, ni	...	Of you, &c., &c.
Bi	...	He.	Bi-soor	...	They.
Bini	...	Of him, &c., &c.	,, ,, ni	...	Of them, &c., &c.

By means of these terminational affixes all personal pronouns, nouns, &c., are regularly declined in the genitive, dative, accusative, ablative, locative cases.

The adjective, when combined with a noun, sometimes precedes, sometimes follows it; but does not change its termination when declined, *e.g.*—

A good man	...	Gaham-man-soi.	Hair	...	Khe-nai.
Of a good man	...	Gaham-man-soi-ni.	Mother	...	Ai.
To a good man	...	Gaham-man-soi-nan.	Brother	...	A-goi.
Hand	...	A-khai.	Sister	...	Bi-na-non.
Foot	...	A-pha.	Man	...	Man-soi.
Nose	...	Gan-thung.	Woman	...	Hing zao.
Eye	...	Me gun.	Head	...	Khan-ran.
Mouth	...	Kha-ga.	Tongue	...	Ta-lai.
Tooth	...	Ha-thai.	Belly	...	Oo-doi.
Ear	...	Khoo-ma.	Back	...	Bi-khung.

Iron	... Sir.	Infant	... *Male*—ho-a-sa. *Female*—hing-za-sa.
Gold	... Hoo-na-der-lie.	Daughter	... Phi-sa-zan.
Silver	... Ror-pha-(roop).	Slave	... Banda (hindoo).
Sun	... Shan.	Cultivator	... Baiz-zen.
Moon	... A-kha-phur.	Shepherd	... Go-ra-khezia, men-da-gooni-nan.
Star	... Ha-thant-khi.	God	... Iswaree (hindoo), gan-thai-ya.
Fire	... Ant.	Devil	... Mo-dai.
Water	... Doi.	Ass	... Go-rai-gum-boo.
House	... Nan.	Camel	... Goi.
Horse	... Go-rai.	Bird	... Dao.
Cow	... Mo son.	Egg	... Dao-de.
Dog	... Soi-ma.	Go	... Thang-nan.
Cat	... Man zee.	Eat	... Za-nan.
Cock	... Don-la.	Sit	... Zan-nan.
Duck	... Hang-soopha-the.	Come	... Phai-nan.
Father	... A-pha.	Beat	... Boo-nan.
Wife	... Hing-zao.	Stand	... Gan-sung-nan.
Child	... Gan-than.		
Son	... Gan-than-ho-a-sa.		

Die ... ... Thoi-nan.
Give ... ... Han-nan.
Run ... ... Khat-nan.

These verbs are given in the Infinitive mood, the terminational affix of which is "nan" pronounced very short. The root of the verb as in the other aggluhuative languages undergoes no change in conjugation, combination, &c.

Up	... Sa-o.	Who	... Sur.
Down	... Sing-ao.	What	... Ma.
Before	... Si-gang-ao.	Why	... Ma-noo.
Near	... Kha-the-ao.	And*	... A-ru.
Far	... Ga-zam.	But*	... Khinto (kintoo).
Behind	... Oo-nao.	If*	... Zo-di.
Yes	... Mungo.	Alas*	... Hái? hái!
No	... Mang-a.		

Declensions.

A father	... Bipha.	A man	... Man soi.
Fathers	... Biphaphoor.	Men	... Man soiphoor.
Of a father	... Biphani.	Two men	... Sá sei.
Of fathers	... Biphaphooni.	Good	... Gáhám.
To a father	... Biphanan.	Better	... Gáhamsin.
From a father	... Biphani phorai.	Best	... Boi nan sari gáhám sin.
A good man	... Ga-ham mansoi	High	... Ge-zon.
A good woman	... Gaham bing-záo-sá.	Higher	... Gezon sin.

* These words are obviously corruptions of the Assamese forms in common use; the Cacharies often aspirate an initial consonant in such cases, *e. g.* as above Khintoo-kintoo!

Highest	.. Boi nān sari gezān sin.
I am	.. Ang. } Dung.
Thou wast	.. Nusy.
He is	.. Be.
We	.. Zung phoor
You	.. Nungsoor.
They	.. Bisoor.
I was	.. Ang. } Dung man.
Thou wast	.. Nung.
He was	.. Bi.
We were	.. Zung phoor.
You were	.. Nung soor.
They were	.. Bisoor.
Be	.. Zā.
To be	.. Zanān.
Being	.. Zavānān.
Having been	.. Zānān.
I may be	.. Angza nan hagon.
I shall be	.. Ang za gun.
I should be	.. Ang zā nan logiyāzādung.
To beat	.. Boo nān.
Beat	.. Boo.
Beating	.. Booni aio.
Having beaten	.. Boo za nai.
I beat	.. Ang boo dung.
We beat	.. Zang phoor boo ding.
Thou beatest	.. Nung boo ding.
You beat	.. Nung soor boo ding.
He beats	.. Bi booding.
They beat	.. Bisoor booding.
Horse	.. Go rāi.
Mare	.. Go rāi bi mā.
Horses	.. Go rāi phoor.
Mares	.. Go rāi bi ma phoor.
Bull	.. Mās son pa loo ā.
Cow	.. Mos son bi ma gai kindoo.
Bulls	.. Mas son ba loona phoor.
Cows	.. Mas son gāi phoor.
Dog	.. Soi mā.
Dogs	.. Soi mā phoor.
Bitch	.. Bi mā.
Bitches	.. Soi mā bimāphoor.
He-goat	.. Boor ma sagla.
He-goats	.. Boor ma saglaphoor.
She-goat	.. Boor ma phānthi.
She-goats	.. Boor ma phanthiphoor.
A male dear	.. Moi phān thā.
A female dear	.. Moi phān thi.
Male deer	.. Moi phan thā phoor.
Female deer	.. Māi phan thi phoor.
I am beating	.. Ang boo dung.
I had beaten	.. Ang boo dung man.
I shall beat	.. Ang boo gūn.
I am beaten	.. Ang boohoo dung.
I shall be beaten	.. Ang boohoo nar za gun.
I was beating	.. Ang boo hi thā dung mān.
I may beat	.. Ang boo nān ha gon.
I should beat	.. Ang boo nān logya dung man.
I was beaten	.. Ang boo hoo dung mān.
Go	.. Thang.
Going	.. Thang ni on nan.
Gone	.. Thang bāi.
I go	.. Ang thang ni dung.
Thou goest	.. Bing thang dung.
He goes	.. Bi thang dung.
We go	.. Zung phoor thāng ni dung.
You go	.. Nung soor thāng dung.
They go	.. Bi soor-thang dung.

What is your name	Mung ni nāo mā.
How old is this horse	Ber go-nā ya bese boyas za dungo.
How far is it from here to Kashmir? ..	Ber ni pherae Kashmir-on be se.
How many sons are there in your father's house?	Nang ni mung nao ni non on be se bang phi saod-ta dung.
I have walked a long way to-day.. ..	Diniang gāzān nā mā tha bāe bāe.
The son of my uncle is married to his sister	Ang nia-dae ni phi sād-tazabi nibi nānās-kho bā bā khān-nā bāe tā bāe.

In the house is the saddle of the white horse	Bio tran on goo phootgo rāe ni zim dang.
Put the saddle upon his back	Bini bi khāng on zim bān.
I have beaten his son with many stripes ...	Ang bini phi sād-la kho gan bangor nan boo bāi.
He is grazing cattle on the top of the hill ...	Bi yan ha zor-sao moson gum dung.
He is sitting on a horse under that tree ...	Bi yan bei bong phang sing ās go rāe ni-sāouth-i-nā noe tha-dung.
His brother is taller than his sister ...	Bini bigi yā bini binā-nāo nan sangazan sindung.
The price of that is two rupees	Bini dā mā thāe noe adlāi sei.
My father lives in that small house ...	Ang in a pha ya bei un dāe poe ān thāio.
Give this rupee to him	Buthākha khobi-nāu bān.
Take those rupees from him	Bei thākha phoor khobini phra etā.
Beat him well and bind him with ropes ...	Biphogā bu-māi nāu boi ārū diding zūng khā.
Draw water from the well	Hākhor-ni phrāe-dāe kho di khang.
Walk before me	Angni si gāng on thā bāi lāng.
Whose boy comes behind you?	Lurni gān thāu nūng ni-oonoo phāi gung.
From whom did you buy that?	Nung bikho māo ni phrāi bāi nā nyta dūng.
From a shop-keeper of the village... ...	Gāmi nida khān ni phrāe bāi nāi.

MEMORANDA.

The people known as Cacharies never speak of themselves under that name, but call themselves the "Boro," or more commonly "Boroni phisā," *i.e.* children of the Boro; but what idea may be conveyed by this term "Boro," I have never been able to ascertain.

From long intercourse with the Assamese, the Cacharies have adopted many words of Sanskrit or Hindu origin; but words so adopted always undergo certain changes in the mouth of a Cachari, *e.g.*—

1. Simple consonants are generally aspirated—"taka" (rupee) becomes tha-kha; "kintoo" becomes khin-thoo.
2. The sibilant letters, so common in Bengali, become very strong guttural aspirates, *e.g.*, "sokol" (all) becomes hokhol.

The prevalence of these gutturals becomes more marked in the neighbourhood of the mountains forming the northern boundary of Assam, the dooms lying at the foot of which are peopled mainly by Cacharies. The prevalence gutturaly among the people being near the mountains, or compared with the dwellers in the interior of the valley, is probably to be accounted for by the difference of climatic conditions, the same phenomenon being observed in other parts of the world, *e.g.* in the German of Hanover as contracted with that of Switzerland. The limits within which the Cachari language is spoken have never been exactly determined; but it is understood from a point west of Biznie (probably near Darjeeling) to the eastern extremity of the Assam valley. Eastwards of Sudze, throughout the whole of this district scattered Cachari communities exist.

LIST OF WORDS AND PHRASES

SHOWING

DIALECTS OF THE TIPPERAH, CHITTAGONG,

AND

CACHAR FRONTIER.

List of words and phrases showing dialects of the

English.	Cachari.	Garo.	Tipperah Hill.
Numerals.			
One ..	Thaisa ..	Cha ..	Kysa ..
Two ..	Thaina ..	Gali ..	Konye ..
Three ..	Thaitham ..	Gatham ..	Ka-htam ..
Four ..	Thaibre ..	Bri ..	Baroy ..
Five ..	Thaiba ..	Bonga ..	Ba ..
Six ..	Thairo ..	Dof ..	Dok ..
Seven ..	Thaisna ..	Suii ..	Tscinni ..
Eight ..	....	Chet ..	Tchyt ..
Nine ..	....	Sokhu ..	Tchiku ..
Ten ..	....	Sakhong ..	Tchi ..
Twenty ..	....	Gang Chiklung ..	Khul ..
Fifty ..	....	Bichagri Sokhung ..	Kornai tchee ..
Hundred ..	....	Rachhatta ..	Ra-ja-ha ..
Pronouns.			
I ..	Aug ..	Auga ..	Aong ..
We ..	Jongforno ..	Changa ..	Tchung ..
Thou ..	Nong ..	Na ..	Nung ..
You ..	Nongsorno ..	Nasma ..	Narowk ..
He ..	Bi ..	Sang Anga ..	Oba ..
They ..	Bisor ..	Oamang ..	Obarowk ..
Mine, *or* me ..	Augni ..	Augni ..	....
Our, *or* of us ..	Jongfoni ..	Suigni ..	....
Thine, *or* of thee ..	Naugni ..	Nangni ..	....
Your, *or* of you ..	Nongsorforni ..	Nosmangni ..	....
His, *or* of him ..	Bini ..	Wani ..	....
Their, *or* of them ..	Bisorui ..	Wamaugni ..	....
Mine ..	....	....	Ainee ..
Our ..	....	....	Tchini ..
Thine ..	....	....	Ninui ..
Your ..	....	....	Narowkni ..
His ..	....	....	Binni ..
Their ..	....	....	Obarowkni ..
Hand ..	Akhye ..	Jake ..	Yak ..
Foot ..	Atheng ..	Jafa ..	Yak-pha ..
Nose ..	Kanthom ..	Gongtheng ..	Rung htai ..
Eye ..	Mogon ..	Mokrong ..	Makoy ..
Mouth ..	Khuka ..	Khusuke ..	Baku ..
Tooth ..	Hatai ..	Wagam ..	Bu-a ..
Ear ..	Khama ..	Nashel ..	Kun-ju ..
Hair ..	Khanai ..	Khinni ..	Ka-nai ..

Lushai (of Chittagong Hills).	Khumi (of Chittagong Hills).	Mro (of Chittagong Hills).	Mugh of Chittagong.	English.
Pakat ..	Ha ..	Leux ..	Toi ..	One.
Pa-ni ..	Nue ..	Preh ..	Nhoi ..	Two.
Pa-tam ..	Toom ..	Choom ..	Soong ..	Three.
Pali ..	Pellue ..	Tullee ..	Ley ..	Four.
Pa-nga ..	Pang ..	Tunga ..	Gnah ..	Five.
Pa-rok ..	Turro ..	Turro .	Khrow ..	Six.
Pa-tsa-ri ..	Sherrue ..	Hvunneen ..	Khonoi ..	Seven.
Pa-ri-ek ..	Taiya ..	Riya ..	Shu ..	Eight.
Pa-kwa ..	Tukkor ..	Tukkoo ..	Roh ..	Nine.
Tschom ..	Ho ..	Humooi ..	Ychay ..	Ten.
Tschom-ni ..	Apoom ..	Pirmee ..	Nhoi tchay ..	Twenty.
Ischom-nga ..	Ooipang ..	Ngakom ..	Gna tchay ..	Fifty.
Ja ..	Kioongwie ..	Kom ..	Ta-ra ..	Hundred.
Koyma ..	Kai ..	Ang ..	Gna ..	I.
Koyma-ho ..	Kai chey ..	Ang een ..	Gna (roh *or* dok) ..	We.
Nangma ..	Nang ..	En ..	Sang ..	Thou.
Nangma-ho *or* ni ..	Nang chey ..	En een ..	Nang ..	You.
Ama ..	Hoo ..	Paimee ..	Soo ..	He.
Amani ..	Hooni chey ..	Haikuboa ..	Toh-soo-roh ..	They.
....	....	....	Gna-ay ..	Mine, *or* me.
....	....	....	Gna-roh-ay . ..	Our, *or* of us.
....	....	....	Sang-ay ..	Thine, *or* of thee.
....	....	....	Nangay ..	Your, *or* of you.
....	....	....	Sooay ..	His, *or* of him.
....	....	....	Soo-doh-ay ..	Their, *or* of them.
Koyma-ta ..	....	....	Gna ay ..	Mine.
Koyma-ho-ta ..	....	....	Gna-roh-ay ..	Our.
Nungma-ta ..	....	....	Sangay ..	Thine.
Nowkma-ho-ta ..	....	....	Nangay ..	Your.
Ama-ta ..	....	....	Soo-ay ..	His.
Mi-ta ..	....	....	Soodohay ..	Their.
Kut ..	Koo ..	Roo ..	Lak ..	Hand.
Ke ..	Kow ..	Kopa ..	Khree ..	Foot.
Nak ...	Nòturrung ..	Nakong ..	Nakhong ..	Nose.
Mith ..	Mey ..	Meen ..	Mea-tsee ..	Eye.
Mel ..	Lubbong ..	Nor ..	Kha-nang ..	Mouth.
Ha ..	Ho ..	Yeung ..	Soa ..	Tooth.
Beng ..	Kunnong ..	Purram ..	Nah ..	Ear.
Tscham ..	Sham ..	Cham ..	Chien-bang ..	Hair.

List of words and phrases showing dialects of the

English.	Cachari.	Garo.	Hill Tipperah.
Head ...	Khoro ...	Shokha ...	Ba-kro ...
Tongue ...	Shalai ...	Sra ...	Tsalai ...
Belly ...	Udi ...	Ok ...	Baho ...
Back ..	Bikhom ...	....	Ba-kung ...
Iron ...	Chor ...	Chhil ...	Tsur ...
Gold ...	Hona ...	Shona ...	Rangaja ...
Silver ...	Rupa ...	Rupa ...	Rupai ...
Father ...	Apha ...	Bapa ...	Amon ...
Mother ...	I ...	I ...	Apa ...
Brother ...	Ada ...	Ada ...	....
Ditto (elder) ...	....	....	(Elder) Ata ...
Ditto (younger) ...	....	....	(Younger) Amphai yung ..
Sister ...	Binanao ...	Abi ...	Aibi ...
Man ...	Manshai ...	Manda ...	Bro ...
Woman ...	Hinjao ...	Jake ...	Bruie ...
Wife ...	Augni Hinjao ...	Jake ...	Bihi ...
Child ...	Kotho ...	Doh ...	Ba-tsala ...
Son ...	Phisa ...	Manda Pisla ...	Batsa ...
Daughter ...	Phisa Hinjao ...	Mishik Bisha ...	Ba-tsa-juk ...
Slave ...	Golam ...	Nokhol ...	Isileng ...
Cultivator ...	Choklam Najane ...	Batal ...	....
Shepherd ...	Gurkhia ...	Rakhol ...	....
God ...	Ishar ...	Ishor ...	Matai ...
Devil ...	Mudai ...	....	Buraha matai ...
Sun ...	Chand ...	Chal ...	Tsal ...
Moon ...	Okhabor ...	Jah ...	Ial ...
Star ...	Atorki ...	Aski ...	Atukroi ...
Fire ...	Ot ...	Wol ...	Hor ...
Water ...	Dai ...	Si ...	Toey ...
House ...	No ...	Noke ...	Nok ...
Horse ...	Tangna Ghorai ...	Gura ...	Rori ...
Cow ...	Gai Mukhao ...	Masha ...	Masoo ...
Dog ...	Chaina ...	Achake ...	Tsoey ...
Cat ...	Monji ...	Mango ...	Billai ...
Cock ...	Toajla ...	....	Tow-la ...
Duck ...	Hongso ...	Dagop ...	Tow-kom ...
Ass ...	Gadha ...	Salja ...	....
Camel ...	Ut ...	Ut ...	....
Bird ...	Dow ...	Dow ...	Toksa ...
Go ...	Thang ...	Oaugbo ...	Thangdee ...
Eat ...	Jab ...	Chhabo ...	Tchadee ...

Lushai (of Chittagong Hills).	Khumi (of Chittagong Hills).	Mro (of Chittagong Hills).	Mugh of Chittagong.	English.
Lo ...	Loo ...	Loo ...	Gong ...	Head.
Le ...	Pellai ...	Die ...	Shea ...	Tongue.
Pum ...	Kuyow ...	Moong ...	Wyn ...	Belly.
Dum-le ...	Neetoom ...	Koom ...	Nouwkoon ...	Back.
Thir ...	Tamong ...	Longha ...	Syn ...	Iron.
Sona ...	Mukkoo ...	Koo ...	Rhooe ...	Gold.
Tanka-boan ..	Tunka ...	Tunka ...	Gnoay ...	Silver.
Ranu ...	Ng-ai ...	Apha ...	Apha ...	Father.
Rapa ...	Ng-oi ...	A-oo ...	Ahmee ...	Mother.
Tsapui ...	....	....	Ahpa ...	Brother
....	Yai ...	A-tai ...	....	Ditto (elder).
....	Beux ...	Now-ma ...	Ahko ...	Ditto (younger).
Pharnu ...	Toicho ...	Toama ...	Nhama ...	Sister.
Mi ...	Koomi ...	Mro ...	Do ...	Man.
Hmai tscier ...	Nongpui ...	Muchcheewa ...	Mama ...	Woman.
Nowpui ...	Ayoo ...	Muchchee ...	Mayah ...	Wife.
Nao ...	Dongdee ...	Ngiowa ...	Soognay ...	Child.
Phapa ...	Chennow ...	Ungcha ...	Sha ...	Son.
Sarnu ...	Chennue ...	Ungchumma ...	Samee ...	Daughter.
Boi ...	Mushong ...	Nar ...	Ruen ...	Slave.
Nga-tok-mi ...	Hlawo ...	Chairwa ...	Ley-loop-sah ...	Cultivator.
....	....	....	Soh-gwn-sah ...	Shepherd.
Rawvang *or* patien	....	....	Phovah ...	God.
....	Na ...	Na ...	Nat tcho ...	Devil.
Ni ...	Kunnee ...	Cha ...	Neeng ...	Sun.
Ha ...	Hlo ...	Ama ..	La ...	Moon.
Arshey ...	Kashee ...	Kreh ...	Kray ...	Star.
Moey ...	Hmai ...	Mai ...	Mee ...	Fire.
Tui ...	Tooi ...	Tooi ...	Ree ...	Water.
Een ...	Eem ..	Keem ...	Eing ...	House.
Isakur ...	Kong-o ...	Kor-nga ...	Mrang ...	Horse.
Isopey ...	Shirar ...	Chirma ...	Noa ...	Cow.
Ui ...	Ooi ...	Kooi ...	Khwee ...	Dog.
Jawtey ...	Mingcheux ...	Mar ...	Krong ...	Cat.
Ar Rong ...	A-looi ...	Waklang ...	Krakpa ...	Cock.
Varak ...	Rumpie ...	Oompie ...	Bey ...	Duck.
....	....	....	Mrey ...	Ass.
....	....	....	Kolaoopa ...	Camel.
Sava ...	Tawoh ...	Wah ...	Gnhak ...	Bird.
Rul-rok ...	Takoh ...	Koimang ...	Lalee ...	Go.
Oi-rok ...	Cho ...	Cha ...	Tchah ...	Eat.

List of words and phrases showing dialects of the

English.	Cachari.	Garo.	Hill Tipperah.
Sit ..	Job ..	Asangbo ..	Atsowkdi ..
Come ..	Phai ..	Mri ..	Phaidi ..
Beat ..	Bugone ..	....	Budi ..
Stand ..	Kosong ..	Chhadeb ..	Bachadi ..
Die ..	Haibai ..	Shib ..	Thoydi ..
Give ..	Ho ..	Walob ..	Rudi ..
Run ..	Khat Khat ..	Chakhadobo ..	Khaido ..
Up ..	Sao ..	Khasaf ..	Tsaka ..
Near ..	Khathio ..	Safang ..	Tsampa ..
Who ..	Chorbilai ..	Chaora ..	Sabho ..
And ..	Ar ..	Abong ..	Tarey ..
Yes ..	Naugo ..	Angbha ..	....
Down ..	Singao ..	Nang ..	Khama ..
Far ..	Gojan ..	Sola ..	Hakchal ..
What ..	Ma ..	Mai khoto cham ..	Toma ..
But ..	Bangai ..	Kintu ..	Asikley ..
No ..	Nanga ..	Ougja ..	Arey-pa ..
Before ..	Sagan ..	Khamba ..	Sikong ..
Behind ..	....	....	Yagul ..
Why ..	Mano ..	Maina ..	Tomana ..
If ..	Jodi ..	Oda ..	....
Alas ..	Hai Hai ..	Hani ..	....
A father ..	Afa Khasa ..	Cha afa ..	Apa ..
Of a father ..	Afanis ..	Baparni ..	Apa ni ..
To a father ..	Afano ..	Bapaky ..	Apa na ..
From a father ..	Afanefrai ..	Baparoni ..	Apa-ni-tinnee ..
Two fathers ..	Thama Afa ..	Goli afa ..	Krok-nyeapa ..
Fathers ..	Afa far ..	Afa amna ..	Apa-song ..
Of fathers ..	Afa manimi ..	Afa amnani juncke ..	Apa-song-ni ..
To fathers ..	Afa mamas ..	Afa aumna abo ..	Apa-song-na ..
From fathers ..	Afa fannifri ..	Afa nitho abora ..	Apa-song-ni-tini ..
A daughter ..	Khasa phisa hinjas ..	Chamisik bisa ..	Basajuk ..
Of a daughter ..	Phisa hinjas khasani ..	Misik bisani ..	Basajuk-ni ..
To a daughter ..	Phisa hinjaoni khasano ..	Mishiky bisaniky ..	Basajuk-na ..
From a daughter ..	Phisa hinjaoni fri ..	Mishiky bisanikara ..	Basajuk neetini ..
Two daughters ..	Haina phisa hinjas ..	Gali mishik bisa ..	Basajuk konye *or* krok-nye
Daughters ..	Phisa hinjas far ..	Mishik bisamaugni ..	Basajuk song ..
Of daughters ..	Phisa hinjas mansar ..	Mishiky bisasidaugni ..	Basajuk-song-nee ..
To daughters ..	Phisa hinjas manno ..	Mishiky bisaniky maugni	Basajuk-song-na ..
From daughters ..	Phisa hinjas fanifri ..	Mishiky bisamaugnara ..	Basajuk-song-ni-tini ..
A good man ..	Ghamansi khasa ..	Mandanama ..	Bro kaham ..

Tipperah, Chittagong, and Cachar Frontier.—(Continued.)

Lushai (of Chittagong Hills).	Khumi (of Chittagong Hills).	Mro (of Chittagong Hills).	Mugh of Chittagong.	English.
Htu-rok ..	Teux ..	Chum ..	Toing ..	Sit.
Horok ..	Ngy-yow ..	Wang ..	La ..	Come.
Bedrok ..	Pukkow ..	Tep ..	Syt bao ..	Beat.
Dmgrok ..	Undoh ..	Young ..	Ryt ..	Stand.
Ti-rok ..	Deux ..	Kung-kai ..	See ..	Die.
Pey-rok ..	Pœih ..	Peh ..	Pee ..	Give.
Tlandrok ..	Leux ..	Peuf ..	Bree ..	Run.
Tsaka ..	Hooling-bang ..	Choot-koi ..	Atak ..	Up.
Tlunga ..	Kung-sha ..	Athon ..	Anee ..	Near.
Tu ..	Meemo ..	Miacheux ..	Asoo ..	Who.
Dang ..	Wai ..	Awai ..	Ley gong ..	And.
Ni ..	Nain ..	Na ..	Hootaj ..	Yes.
Tlung lam ..	Ka-hlong-wa ..	Kuddum ..	Owkma ..	Down.
Hla ..	Kumlo-wa ..	Alama ..	Awee ..	Far.
Engey ..	Atee-mo ..	Tong-cheux ..	Jahley ..	What.
....	Nuhai ..	Alowey ..	Tho thawley ..	But.
Ni-loh ..	Na-eux ..	Na-dœi ..	Mahoop ..	No.
Amasa ..	Mowa ..	Poorgœi ..	Rheega ..	Before.
Mungloi ..	Neytoon ..	Koong-kœih ..	Howk-a ..	Behind.
Enga ..	Tenea-mo ..	Tomboka ..	Japrylo ..	Why.
....	Beleux ..	Punneux ..	Hliang ..	If.
Ajiley ..	Ng-ayiex ..	Apa-oh ..	....	Alas.
Rapa ..	Ai-harey ..	Apa-leux ..	Apa tayouk ..	A father.
Kapa-ta ..	Ai-meux ..	Apa-ga ..	Apa tayoukay ..	Of a father.
Kapa-vang ..	Ai-do ..	Apa-do ..	Apa tayoukgo ..	To a father.
Kapa-hneyna ..	Ai-bang-e ..	Apa-heun ..	Apa tayowkga ..	From a father.
Kapa-hni ..	Ai-nurerey ..	Apa-preya ..	Apa nhoiyao ..	Two fathers.
Kapa-ni ..	Ai-umpo ..	Apa-komma ..	Apa mea ..	Fathers.
Pa-ni-ta ..	Ditto ..	Ditto ..	Apa mea-ay ..	Of fathers.
Kapa-ho-vang ..	Ditto ..	Ditto ..	Apa-mea-go ..	To fathers.
Kapa-ho-hneyna ..	Ditto ..	Ditto ..	Apa-mea-ga ..	From fathers.
Sarnu ..	Chenneie-havey ..	Chumma-leux ..	Same-ta-yao ..	A daughter.
Sarnu-ta ..	Ditto ..	Ditto ..	Same-ta-yas ay ..	Of a daughter.
Sarnu-vang ..	Ditto ..	Ditto ..	Sametayas-go ..	To a daughter.
Sarnu-hneyna ..	Ditto ..	Ditto ..	Sametayas-ga ..	From a daughter.
Sarnu-pahnit ..	Ditto ..	Ditto ..	Same-nhoi-ya-o ..	Two daughters.
Sarnu-ho ..	Ditto ..	Ditto ..	Samu-meah ..	Daughters.
Sarnu-ho-ta ..	Ditto ..	Ditto ..	Samee-meahay ..	Of daughters.
Sarnu-ho-vang ..	Ditto ..	Ditto ..	Samee-mean go ..	To daughters.
Sarnu-ho-hneyna ..	Ditto ..	Ditto ..	Samee-meah-ga ..	From daughters.
Nu-hta ..	Khumi-hoi ..	Mro-yoong ..	Loogongtayas ..	A good man.

List of words and phrases showing dialects of the

English.	Cachari.	Garo.	Hill Tippera h.
Of a good man ...	Ghamansi khasani ...	Mandanama ninoky ...	....
To a good man ...	Khasa ghamansano ...	Mandanama namshong ...	....
From a good man ...	Khasa ghamansi fri ...	Mandanamani ...	....
Two good men ...	Thaina ghamansi ...	Gali mandama ...	Brokaham kroknyne ...
Good men ...	Ghaimansi far ...	Mandanam lijat ...	Brokaham rowk ...
Of good men ...	Ghamansi manui ...	Manda namli gukhaky baw	Brokaham rowkni ...
To good men ...	Ghamansi manno ...	Manda nama gumakho ...	Brokaham rowkna ...
From good men ...	Ghamansi fanni fri ...	Manda namli ...	Brokaham rowkni tine ...
A good woman ...	Gham hinjai khasa ...	Manda namni jaky ...	Brine kaham ...
A bad boy ...	Khasa hama gotto ...	Manda hisa namja ...	Batsa hamya ...
Good women ...	Ghani hinjas far ...	Ani choknamah ...	Brine raham rouk ...
A bad girl ...	Khasa haina phisa hinjo ...	Manda bisha namja ...	Shikla hamya ...
Good ...	Gham ..	Nama ...	Raham ...
Better ...	} Gham far ...	{ Nama ..	Tarey raham ...
Best ...		Nambia ...	....
High ...	Sao ...	Chua ...	Kachuk ...
Higher ...	} Sao far ...	{ Dano ...	Tarey kachuk ...
Highest ..		Changro bia ...	....
A horse ...	Masa ghorai sangua ...	Gura ...	Korai tchala ...
A mare ...	Masa ghorai sangui ...	Gura bima ...	Korai-bruie ...
Horses ...	Ghorai tangua far ...	Gura sadaug ...	Korai-rouk ...
Mares ...	Ghorai tangau far ...	Khonong ...	Korai-bruie rouk ...
A bull ...	Masa damra mokhow ...	Mashu ...	Masuk tchala ...
A cow ..	Gai mokhow ...	Mashu ...	Masukma ...
Bulls ...	Damra mokhow far ...	Khanang ...	Masuk tchala rowk ...
Cows ...	Gai mokhow far ...	Arbima ...	Masukma rowk ...
A dog ...	Saima bangra ...	Ashoky bima ...	Tsoey-la ...
A bitch ...	Saima bangri ...	Ashaky bima ...	Tsoey ma ...
Dogs ...	Bangra far ...	Ashak bima bang ...	Tsoey-la-rowk ...
Bitches ...	Bangri far ...	Ashay bima bikan jamakha	Tsoey-ma-rowk ...
A he-goat ...	Masa borma chhagla ...	Daboky bifa ...	Puin-jua ...
A female goat ...	Masa borma fanti ...	Daboky bima ...	Puin-ma ...
Goats ...	Borma chhagla far ...	Dabok rang ...	Puin-rowk ...
A male deer ...	Masa mui fanti ...	Mashoky bifa ...	Matsoi-tchala ...
A female deer ...	Masa mui fanti ...	Mashoky bima ...	Matsoi-ma ...
Deer ...	Mui fanti ...	Mashok rang ...	Matsoi-rowk ...
I am ...	Aug domo ...	Anga galong ...	Aong-tongo ...
Thou art ...	Naug domo ...	Nakho gilang ...	Nung-tongo ...
He is ...	Bi domo ...	Oa galang ...	Oba-tonga ...
We are ...	Jang forni domo ...	Singa galang ...	Tchung-tongo ...

Tipperah, Chittagong, and Cachar Frontier.—(Continued.)

Lushai (of Chittagong Hills).	Khumi (of Chittagong Hills).	Mro (of Chittagong Hills).	Mugh of Chittagong.	English.
....	....	....	....	Of a good man.
....	....	....	....	To a good man.
....	....	....	....	From a good man.
Mi-pahnit-hta ...	Long-nure-hoi ...	Mro yoong preya ..	Loogong nhoiyao .	Two good men.
Mi-hta-ho ...	Khumi-hoi ...	Mro yoong ...	Loogong meah ...	Good men.
Mi-hta-ho-ta ...	....	....	Loogong meahay...	Of good men.
Mi-hta-ho-vang ...	....	....	Loogong mea-go ...	To good men.
Mi-hta-ho-hneyna ..	....	....	Loogong mea-ga ...	From good men.
Honaitscier-hta ...	Nong-pui-hoi ...	Muchchee yoongleux	Meemagong-tayao	A good woman.
Nowpany-hta-lo ...	Chennow-hoi-eux..	Ngia-woa yoong dœi	Loobeasheay-tayao	A bad boy.
Hmaitscier-ho-hta ..	Nong-pui-hoi ...	Muchchee yoongleux	Meemagongmeah...	Good women.
Hmatscier-tey-hta-lo	Nong-pui-cheux-hoi-eux	Ung chumma yoong dœi	Tcho than meema gneay tyao	A bad girl.
Ahta ...	Ahoi ...	Yoong ...	Akong ...	Good.
....	Noihoi ...	Mummeela yoong...	Salo akong ...	Better.
....	Hoi-nahoi ...	Yoong-ma ...	Akong tchoon ...	Best.
Atchoi ...	Ashinag ...	Akvo-ma ...	Amrang ...	High.
....	Hoo-tlong-ashiang..	Mummeela akvo ma	Salo Amrang ...	Higher.
....	Hoo-ashiang-be ...	Kong kong kro ...	Amrang tchoon ...	Highest.
Tsuk-kur ...	Kong-o ...	Kor-nga ...	Mrang-tagong ...	A horse.
Tsuk-kur-nu ...	Kong-o-noo ...	Kor-nga-ma ...	Mrangniatagong ...	A mare.
Tsuk-kur-ho ...	Kong-o-bang ..	Kor-nga komma ...	Mrang-meah ...	Horses.
....	Kong-o-bang ...	Kor-nga komma ...	Mrangma-meah ...	Mares.
Tchofey-tsal-ho ...	Sheera puttai ...	Chealla ...	Noadee-tagong ...	A bull.
Tchofey-nu ...	Noo ...	Cheama ...	Noama-tagong ...	A cow.
Tchofey-tsal-ho ...	Noo bang ...	Cheama komma ...	Noadee-meah ...	Bulls.
Tchofey-nu-ho ...	Noo bang ...	Cheama komma ...	Khweedee tagong...	Cows.
Ui tsal ...	Ooi ...	Kooi ...	Khweema tagong...	A dog.
Ui-nu ...	....	....	Khweema tagong...	A bitch.
Ui-tsal-ho ...	....	....	Khwee meah ...	Dogs.
Ui-miho ...	....	....	Khweema meah ...	Bitches.
Kel-pa ...	Me-e ...	Roala ...	Teikbo tagong ...	A he-goat.
Kel-nu ...	Me-e-noo ...	Roama ...	Tseikma tagong ...	A female goat.
Kel-ho ...	Me-e-bang ...	Roama komma ...	Tseikmeah ...	Goats.
Tsaki-pa ...	Takee ...	Ng-kee ...	Darey thee tagong..	A male deer.
Tsaki-nu ...	Takee noo ...	Ng-keema ...	Dareyma tagong ...	A female deer.
Tsaki-ho ...	Takee bang ...	Ng-komma ...	Darey ...	Deer.
Koyma-om ...	Kai om ...	Ang-wey ...	Gnah heerey ...	I am.
Nangma-om ...	Nang om ...	En wey ...	Sang heerey ...	Thou art.
Ama om ...	Hoo om ...	Mro wey ...	Soo heerey ...	He is.
Roymanee-om ...	Kaichey om ...	Angeen wey ...	Ghnorok heerey ...	We are.

List of words and phrases showing the dialects of the

English.	Cachari.	Garo.	Hill Tipperah.
You are ..	Nongsorni domo ..	Darongara galong ..	Narowk tongo ..
They are ..	Bisor domo ..	Mui galong ..	Obarowk tongo ..
I was ..	Aug domon ..	Singa yalang cham ..	Aong-tong-kamo ..
Thou wast ..	Nong domon ..	Galang cham ..	Nung-tong kamo ..
He was ..	Bi domon ..	Oa galang cham ..	Oba-tong-kama ..
We were ..	Jonforui domon ..	Galangcham ..	Tcahung-tong kamo ..
You were ..	Nangsorui domon ..	Naia galangcham ..	Narowk-tong kamo ..
They were ..	Bisor domon ..	Oabaha galangcham ..	Obarowk tong kamo ..
Be ..	Nongo ..	Hangaonga ..	Una ..
To be ..	Jananong dong ..	Hangaonga ..	Ungnee ..
Being ..	Jananong dong ..	Nang ..	Ungo ..
Having been ..	......	Nang ..	Ungotsey ..
I may be ..	Angnongo ..	Singaonguama ..	....
I shall be ..	Augjaghon ..	Augaonguaumam ..	Ungwano ..
I should be ..	Augjaghon ..	Augaonguaumam ..	....
Beat ..	Bemi ..	Dokop ..	Bu ..
To beat ..	Bemi ..	Dokop ..	Bunani ..
Beating ..	Buidong ..	Dokai ..	Bu-o ..
Having beaten ..	Buidong ..	Dokacham ..	Bu-ey ..
I beat ..	Aug buni ..	Singadokna ..	Aong-bu-o ..
Thou beatest ..	Nong buni ..	Nadokor ..	Nang-bu-o ..
He beats ..	Bibuni ..	Oadoka ..	Oba-bu-o ..
We beat ..	Jongforno buni ..	Singadoknahoi ..	Tchung-bu-o ..
You beat ..	Nonsorno buni ..	Nasomang dokob ..	Narowk bu o ..
They beat ..	Bisor buni ..	Oamang doka ..	Obarowk bu-o ..
I am beating ..	Augbunidong ..	Singa dokai ..	....
I was beating ..	Augbunain ..	Augadokacham ..	Aong bu kamo ..
I had beaten ..	Augbudong ..	....	....
I may beat ..	Augbuna Hogon ..	....	....
I shall beat ..	Augbugon ..	Augadokanom ..	Aong bu ano ..
I should beat ..	Ditto ..	Augadokanom ..	....
I am beaten ..	Augbujadong ..	Auga jagenman ..	Aong-bu-jak-o ..
I was beaten ..	Augbaja domon ..	Augadoka khanacham ..	Aong-bu-jakamo ..
I shall be beaten ..	Augbujaghon ..	Auga jagen maulam ..	Aong bu jakano ..
I go ..	Augthangna ..	Singa Angloha ..	Aong thangni hna ..
Thou goest ..	Naugthang ..	Naiangho ..	Nung thangni hna ..
He goes ..	Bithang ..	Oaang chong ..	Oba thangni hna ..
I went ..	Augthangdomon ..	Singa aonghachem ..	Aong thang kha ..

Tipperah, Chittagong, and Cachar Frontier.—(Continued.)

Lushai (of Chittagong Hills).	Khumi (of Chittagong Hills).	Mro (of Chittagong Hills).	Mugh of Chittagong.	English.
Nungmanee-om ..	Nangohey om ..	Euee wey ..	Mangrok heerey ..	You are.
Amanee-om ..	Hooniohey om ..	Kubboa wey ..	Tosoorok heerey ..	They are.
Royma-om-don ..	Kai kuchehey ..	Aug wey beux ..	Gnahee poorey ..	I was.
Nungma-om don..	Nang kuchehey ..	Eu wey beux ..	Sanghee poorey ..	Thou wast.
Ama om-don ..	Hoonai kacheboh..	Pamiee beux ..	Soohee poorey ..	He was.
Roymanee on don	Kaiche kacheboh ..	Aug-een beux ..	Gnorokhee poorey..	We were.
Nungmani om dom	Nangche kacheboh..	En-een beux ..	Nangrokhee poorey	You were.
Amanee om don ..	Hooniche kacheboh	Kubboa beux ..	Tosoorokhee poorey	They were.
....	Non-tramlatavee ..	....	Prythey ..	Be.
....	Om ..	Wey ..	Pryfo ..	To be.
....	Not tramlatavee ..	....	Pry heerey ..	Being.
....	Eux ..	Wey boh ..	Pry roay ..	Having been.
....	Kaibeleux om eux..	Aug woy boh wey	Gnapry Rong pry-mey.	I may be.
....	Kai om kubbon ..	Aug dumg ..	Gn prymey ..	I shall be.
....	Not translavee ..	....	Gnapry po heerey..	I should be.
Vel ..	Pukkow ..	Tep ..	Bao ..	Beat.
Veltur ..	Pukkow che ..	Kuttep ba ..	Baopo ..	To beat.
Avelta ..	Pukkow boh ..	Te-tukkreux ..	Baonerey ..	Beating.
Vel-in ..	Pukkow bon ..	Tep-tukkreux ..	Baoroay ..	Having beaten.
Royma-vel ..	....	....	Gnabao they ..	I beat.
Nungma-vel ..	....	....	Sang bao they ..	Thou beatest.
Ama vel ..	....	....	Soo bao they ..	He beats.
Roymani-vel ..	....	....	Gnorok bao they ..	We beat.
Nungmani vel ..	....	....	Nang bao they ..	You beat.
Amani vel ..	....	....	Soodo-bao-they ..	They beat.
Koyma velta ..	....	....	Nga-bao-neerey ..	I am beating.
Koyma avel don-ta	....	....	Nga-bao-neelerey .	I was beating.
....	....	....	Nga-baole-poorey .	I had beaten.
....	Kai pukkow piyow	Aug-ya-tep ..	Nga-bao-rong-baomey.	I may beat.
Royma vel don ..	Kai pukkow neuh ..	Aug kuttep-beux ..	Ngabaomey ..	I shall beat.
....	Non translatavee ..	....	Nga baopp heerey .	I should beat.
....	Kai pukkow ..	Aug kai tep tunkai	Nga abaokhynrey .	I am beaten.
....	Kai pukkow ..	Aug kai tep tunkai	Nga abaokhynbrey	I was beaten.
....	Kai pukkow mo uma eux.	Uttep ang beux ..	Nga abaokhynra-eemey.	I shall be beaten.
Koyma akul ..	Kai ungyo kuobo..	Ang wang beux ..	Nga lah rey ..	I go.
Nungma rul ..	Nang ..	En wang beux ..	Sanglahrey ..	Thou goest.
Ama akul ..	Hooni ..	Paunee wang beux	Soolahrey ..	He goes.
Royma rulta ..	Kai ungwe both ..	Ang koi kreux ..	Gnalah Rheerey ..	I went.

List of words and phrases showing the dialects of the

English.	Cachari.	Garo.	Hill Tipperah.
Thou wentest ...	Nangthangdomon ...	Na aongchama ...	Nung thangkha ...
He went ...	Bithangna ...	Soambo ..	Oba thangka ...
Go ...	Thang ...	Eangbo ..	Thangdee ...
Going ...	Thangnonangon ...	Eangha ..	Thango ...
Gone ...	Thangdon ...	Eangha ..	Thangkha ...
What is your name?	Nangninamama? ...	Nangbimamai? ..	Nine ba nung toma? ...
How old is this horse?	Baghoria basa boikho jodong?	Eagura baita bolchi? ..	Ba rorai bursi ba shuk unkha?
How far is it from here to Kashmir?	Banafri Kashmir basa gojan?	Ani inkhal baita chala Kashmir bunaba?	Aroni by Kashmere bashuk tchal?
How many sons are there in your father's house?	Naugani nong fanninon fisa jala khapsadom?	Nangfa innoko baita golangdicha?	Napa nokwa batsatchala krok basuk tong?
I have walked a long way to-day.	Augna bhini gobaugnama thahaidong.	Anga bohut hoaman ..	Aong tini tchawha hak-tchal hinkha.
The son of my uncle is married to his sister.	Augniodin fisa jala rabini-bina nokhon hoba khalam-dom.	Adni maachadana dachhia Unjakho ahi.	Aini mamani batsala obin bibi juk na bihi lakha.
In the house is the saddle of the white horse.	Nouno ghorai guformi jini dongo.	Noke gurain khochha fo jin golang Madangja.	....
Put the saddle upon his back.	Bini bikhoao jin hu ...	Jimkho gubainjang golga-thop.	....
I have beaten his son with many stripes.	Augnobini fisa jalaklon busa karbai.	Oali miachba bishaks doks biha.	Obani batsalana bacham bacham rujey-bu-kha.
He is grazing cattle on the top of the hill.	Bis hajo thinagho kumai-dong.	Oa nabomo mash rakhia..	....
He is sitting on a horse under that tree.	Bishibangfang sinao ghorai chao jodong.	Oa bolnama khamo gura gokha dalong donga.	....
His brother is taller than his sister.	Bini bina naona thora bida jousan.	Oni adathan nogpan ujan bata.	Bini bibi jukni salai ba phaiyung tchuwo.
The price of that is two rupees and a half.	Bini dama thainai khassa	Ani daina fo baina ...	Bini baseng rang rowk nai matsa ong-o.
My father lives in that small house.	Augna afara hino uda thaio.	Oomoke bichas baba thua	Obanok shite apani rok tsey.
Give this rupee to him	Bataka binahu ..	Oathang khako ona oangho	Obana ba rang row ha rude
Take those rupees from him.	Bataka frakon bini fri la..	Oa gamoke udugui unthang hareba.	Obani-tini rang jata tsey ladi.

Tipperah, Chittagong, and Cachar Frontier.—(Continued.)

Lushai (of Chittagong Hills).	Khumi (of Chittagong Hills).	Mro (of Chittagong Hills).	Mugh of Chittagong.	English.
Nungma rulta ...	Nang ungwe boh...	Eu koi kreux ...	Sanglah Rheerey...	Thou wentest.
Ama kulta ...	Honi ungwe boh ...	Paimee koi kreux...	Soolah Rheerey ...	He went.
Kuldrok ...	Tukko ...	Kamang beux ...	Lah ...	Go.
Kul-don-ta ...	Tukko ...	Kamang beux ...	Lah neerey ...	Going.
Rulta ...	We-boh ...	Kamang kreux ...	Lah bea ...	Gone.
Nungma engmi ngey?	Nang amœin mee mo?	En meeng mia cheux?	Nangnamey jaley?	What is your name?
Hee sukkur rum engja ngeyani?	Hee kongo shinnee maeye vimmon?	Mummee kornga enning moonka cheux?	Dey mrangasak mea loathee bea ley?	How old is this horse?
Heta-om-in Kashmere enja ngeyhla?	Hee Kashmir keux rummang pullopie?	Mahoom Kashmir moonkha cheuxla?	Deh aroiga Kasmere go mea laowee reley?	How far is it from here to Kashmir?
Nungma pa eem-a-fa pha-eng-ja ngey om?	Umpo eem ma cheimou ma yere omoh?	Enpah keem la koi moomia cheux?	Nangapa eingma sah meayao heerey ley?	How many sons are there in your father's house?
Voina Royma akul chuk-em kahata.	Wai nee pullo pai kai puwai.	Unnee alla kœih ungullen.	Nga go neing lien amea rao yaong lakheerey.	I have walked a long way to-day.
Royma kapa-pha ama farnu nopwi anei ta	Kai muprang chennow ayoo la hooni e toicho.	Ang turrang cha chong mushee paunee toa ma.	Naaooree sahma soo nhoima go nee joirey.	The son of my uncle is married to his sister.
....	Eeru ma (no word for saddle) kangloong kong-o.	Kum koi akan kornga.	Mrangphrooma koongnee eingtey ma heerey.	In the house is the saddle of the white horse.
....	(No word for saddle) *back is* neetoon.	*Back is* koom (no word for saddle).	Koongnee go mrang takma tang.	Put the saddle upon his back.
Ama pha royma vel tochyemtin.	Hooni e chennow kai pukkow nung nung.	Mro cha koi aug augtep kong kong.	Gna soosah go akheak amea bao ley bea.	I have beaten his son with many stripes.
Flang pi-a tsalai alenta.	Moi shelloo tey-chapey paino.	Choo-ke e pey uacha	Sootong takma noa keong neerey.	He is grazing cattle on the top of the hill.
Hting hnoya atuh reynta.	Hooni ungteux kong klunga hooding keng akooya.	Mro chum kornga lookai pai shindaw e.	Toh apang owma soo mrang tak-ka tieng neerey.	He is sitting on a horse under that tree.
Ama tsapwi sarnu ai tsow jowk.	Hooni yai toicho klonga ashiang om.	Mro atai toa ma sharumkrow wey.	Soo-oiko soo nhoima tak awi rheyrey.	His brother is taller than his sister.
Ama mun takhaley ardali mun.	Hee nahai wang clap nurey adulli om.	Mummee choom prilap unqui wey.	Toh oochor apotienga nhoipra Rhoay.	The price of that is two rupees and a half.
Roymakapa tsaw een tey-a-om.	Kai rig-ai hoo eem cho om.	Ang pa paikeim chum cha pawey.	Toh eingsheay ma gna apa weingrey.	My father lives in that small house.
Tanka ama pey rok	Hee tunka hoonai pœih.	Mummee tunka paunee keux peh.	Soog-o-deh tienga peeloi.	Give this rupee to him.
Ama hneyna tanka ho larok.	Hoonai tunka thoui tayeux lo.	Paya tunkah mro tood e poh.	Toh teinga ahtee go soo baga yooloi.	Take those rupees from him.

List of words and phrases showing the dialects of the

English.	Cachari.	Garo.	Hill Tipperah.
Beat him well and bind him with ropes.	Eighon ghama bunana duruong jong khasna nadong.	Nama dokur bhagichaklah	Obana kamkey bu wey badu by khadee.
Draw water from the well.	Bahakoni fridai thang ...	Sia kolsi khobs ...	....
Walk before me ...	Augni khugao thabailong	Augni mokhangha amih ..	Aini sikong a hindi ...
Whose boy came behind you?	Nongui, nuao, chhorni fisa jala fidong?	Nashmang jamanoo chanda habiba?	Nini yagula sabhoni batsala phai?
From whom did you buy that?	Anni fri bikho? ...	Banuikhababa nakna aba?	Nung sabho ni tini pai? ...
From a shop-keeper of the village.	Gamini dokani gori fri ...	Chang chafsa briba ...	Parani dukan ni tini pai yu.

Tipperah, Chittagong, and Cachar Frontier.—(Concluded.)

Lushai (of Chittagong Hills).	Khumi (of Chittagong Hills).	Mro (of Chittagong Hills).	Mugh of Chittagong.	English.
Amakha vel tschem ròk-hnangin hny rok.	Hooni ai nung nung pukkow noomou koi akkom.	Paimi ke kong kong teba tomma leng hai.	Soogo krakroi bao-bea kroma khieng.	Beat him well and bind him with ropes.
Tui pin a (river) twi tschoyrok.	Tooi angom adoon tang beux.	Tooi kwam nuttung tooi.	Ree dwangga ree-gnang.	Draw water from the well.
Koyma nen kul dun drok.	Kai e mowa tukko.	Aug poor ke e mang	Gnarheega lah ...	Walk before me.
Nugnma hnunga tu now pang ngeyni?	Nang e naitoo na tukko uai leux mee ee chennow nah ?	En koonge amia cha cho. mang mee ?	Nang naoka asso sah lareyley ?	Whose boy comes behind you?
Tu tangey lei? ...	Hoo nahai mee tay wann moh ?	Paya mee ke e amia tood e choh erana?	Toh oocha go nang asso baga woay rey ley?	From whom did you buy that ?
Ama rua beypari ta alei.	He awaun dokan she waunahai.	Kooa kœi ka dookain ke e arana.	Roama tchoing say tayao baga.	From a shop-keeper of the village.

Further

LANGUAGES FROM TIPPERAH AND CACHAR.

English.	Kukee of Cachar.	Kukee of Tipperah.	Hallamee of Tipperah.	Hill Tipperah.
Numerals.				
One	Khát	Khat	Aukhat	Káichhá
Two	Ni	Ní	Auní	Kúnúí
Three	Tám	Thúm	Authúm	Káthám
Four	Li	Lí	Mánli	Búrñi
Five	Ngá	Rauga	Ráuga	Bá
Six	Gúp	Rúk	Arúk	Dok
Seven	Sági	Sharíh	Sharíh	Chhini
Eight	Gid	Ret	Ariet	Chár
Nine	Ku	Kúo	Akúo	Chukúk
Ten	Som	Sôm	Som	Chi
Twenty	Somini	Sômní	Somauni	Khol
Fifty	Somugá	Somranga	Somranga	......
Hundred	Jákhát	Razáka	Rázákhat	Rájsá
Pronouns.				
I	Kei	Keima	Keima	Áng
We	Keiha	Keimáni	Keima	Chúng
Thou	Nángin	Nangma	Nangma	Núng
You	Nángma	Nangmáni	Nangma	Norok
He	Ámá	Ma, Anni	Ama, Sava	Bo
They	Ámáo	Aumáni	Ama or Sava	Borok
Of me	Keimán	Keima	Keima	Áni
Of us	Keihám	Keimáni	Keima	Chini
Of thee	Nángmán	Nangma	Nangma	Nini
Of you	Nángmáha	Nangmáni	Nangma	Norokni, or Noroni
Of him	Ámáha	Auni	Ama or Sava	Bini
Of them	Ámáhao	Anmáni	Ama or Sava	Borongni
Mine	Keimu	Keima	Keima	Áni
Our	Kéiha	Keimáni	Keima	Chini
Thine	Nángmá	Nangma	Nangma	Nini
Your	Nángha	Nangmám	Nangma	Norokni or Noroni
His	Ámá	Auni	Ama or Sava	Bini
Their	Ámáo	Aumáni	Ama or Sava	Borongni
Hand	Khut	Kút	Nakhút	Iyák
Foot	Keng	Pheypá	Kakhey	Iyákúng
Nose	Ná	Nár	Guár	Kúng or Bukúng
Eye	Mit	Míth	Míth	Mokol
Mouth	Mu	Múr	Múr	Khúk
Tooth	Há	Há	Há	Oyá
Ear	Kul	Kor, Beng	Makúr	Khúmjú

Muneepooree.	Mikir.	Angamee Naga.	English.
Aunná	I see	Po	One.
Auni	Hinee	Kenná	Two.
Ahum	Kéthom	Sé	Three.
Mari	Phili	Dá	Four.
Manga	Phunga	Péngú	Five.
Tarúk	Thrak	Súrú	Six.
Tarét	Throree	Théná	Seven.
Nipal	Nerkep	Théthá	Eight.
Mápal	Sirkep	Thékú	Nine.
Tara	Kep	Kerr	Ten.
Kul	Inkoi	Mékú	Twenty.
Yángkhe	Plumgo-kép	Lhi-péngú	Fifty.
Chámá	Plear-isee	Krá	Hundred.
Yáki	Ngé	Á	I.
Akhoi	Ngétum	Héko	We.
Nang	Náug	No	Thou.
Nakoi	Nángli	Néko	You.
Másí	Hálánglí	Po	He.
Mokhoi	Hálútum	Lúko	They.
Yáki	Nge-ké	Á	Of me.
Akhoigi	Ngetum-án	Á	Of us.
Nangi	Náng ké	No	Of thee.
Nakhoigi	Náugle-ké	Néko	Of you.
Mahaki	Hálútum	Lú	Of him.
Mokhoigi	Hálátum-ké	Lúko	Of them.
Yáki	Ngé-ke-má	Á	Mine.
Akhoigi	Nge-tum	Héko	Our.
Nangi	Lákhe-náng	No	Thine.
Nakhoigi	Lákhe-nángli	No	Your.
Moháki	Hálá-bangpee	Lú, po	His.
Mokhoigi	Hálátum-án	Lúko	Their.
Khut	Ri	Bi or bhi	Hand.
Khongpák	Kéng	Phi	Foot.
Náthúon	Nukán	Nhitchá	Nose.
Mith	Mik	Mhi	Eye.
Chin	Engho	Tá	Mouth.
Yá	So	Hú	Tooth.
Nakhong	No	Nié	Ear.

Languages from

English.	Kukee of Cachar.	Kukee of Tipperah.	Hallamee of Tipperah.	Hill Tipperah.
Hair ..	Sam ...	Chám or Tsám ..	Chhám, Tsham ..	Khanai ..
Hair of man ..	......	......	......	......
Hair of animal ..	......	......	......	......
Head ..	Lu ...	Lú ..	Lú ..	Khorok ..
Tongue ..	Léi ...	Léy ..	Miley ..	Chhelái ..
Belly ..	Oé ...	Von ..	Von or Phúng ..	Ok ..
Back ..	Túngtún ..	Dár also rúong ..	Ruong ..	Phikúng ..
Iron ..	......	Thir ..	Thir ..	Tshar ..
Gold ..	Sáná ...	Rangachák ..	Rangachak ..	Rángchák ..
Silver ..	Danká ...	Sum or tanká (corruption of Persian *tankwah.*)	Súm ..	Rúfái ..
Father ..	Nápá ...	Pá ..	Kapá ..	Phá ..
Mother ..	Nánu ...	Núh ..	Kanúh ..	Má ..
Brother ..	U' ...	U'náo ..	Kichángpá ..	Pháiúng ..
Elder brother ..	......	U'pá ..	Káúpá ..	......
Younger brother ..	......	Naibung or kichang	Amilái, or korkhem	......
Sister ..	Á ...	Farnúh ..	Farnúh ..	Hâno ..
Elder sister ..	......	U'núh ..	Káúnúh ..	......
Younger sister ..	......	Farnúh ..	Kánáinúh ..	......
Man ..	Pasal ...	Mipá ..	Amánai, or savanai	Chálá ..
Woman ..	Numái ...	Núhpang ..	Núhpang ..	Burúi ..
Wife ..	Ji ...	Núhpui ..	Kádongma ..	Hik ..
Child ..	Chápá ...	Naú or nái ..	Naìpang ..	Chha ..
Son ..	Chápá ...	Náípá ..	Kánái ..	Chhájálá ..
Daughter ..	Chánu ...	Nainúhpang ..	Kachánúh ..	Chhájúk ..
Slave ..	Su ...	Bóy, cheloh (Rajah's)	Kasuokpa ..	Chhelong ..
Cultivator ..	Loubalá ...	......	......	......
Shepherd ..	Sil ...	......	......	......
God ..	Páthion ...	Patiyan ..	Patiyan ..	Mátáy ..
Devil ..	Thilá ...	Kóríh ..	Kóríh ..	Chhekal mátáy ..
Sun ..	Nisa ...	Ni ..	Mioha ..	Sál ..
Moon ..	Thlá ...	Thlá ..	Thá ..	Tál ..
Star ..	Ási ...	Archi ..	Archi ..	Athukúri ..
Fire ..	Méi ...	Méy ..	Mey ..	Hor ..
Water ..	Tui ...	Tui ..	Túi ..	Túi ..
House ..	In ...	Beng In ..	In ..	Nok ..
Horse ..	Sákar ...	Chakor ..	Chakor ..	Korái ..
Cow ..	Sirát ...	Cherát ..	Cherat ..	Músúk ..
Dog ..	Ui ...	Ui ..	Ui ..	Húi ..

Tipperah and Cachar.—(Continued.)

Muneepooree.	Mikir.	Angamee Naga.	English.
Chám Tsám ..	Chu ...	......	Hair.
......	......	Tha ..	Hair of man.
......	......	Ma ..	Hair of animal.
Kog ..	Téháng ...	Tsú ..	Head.
Léy ..	De ...	Mélla ..	Tongue.
Púk ..	Pok ...	Vádi, Váká ..	Belly.
Nangan ..	Nung ...	Nákú ..	Back.
Yôt ..	Ing chin ...	Thézé ..	Iron.
Sana ..	Ser ...	Sona ..	Gold.
Lúpa or tangá ..	Rup ...	Rákájé ..	Silver.
Ipá ..	Pu ...	Pú, Apú ..	Father.
Imá ..	Páé ...	Ázo, Zo ..	Mother.
Zámá ..	Né-ik ...	......	Brother.
Zamahal ..	......	Zoráo ..	Elder brother.
Inás ..	......	Sázéo ..	Younger brother.
Ichal ..	Néugzir ...	Alápoo ..	Sister.
Ichem ..	......	......	Elder sister.
Ichal ..	......	.....	Younger sister.
Nípá ..	Pincho ...	Théppromá, or Thémmá ..	Man.
Núhpi ..	Arloso ...	Thénúmá ..	Woman.
Itú ..	Piso ...	Kimá ..	Wife.
Ichá ..	Chupo ...	Nichúmá ..	Child.
Ichánípá ..	Chupi-nochu ...	No ..	Son.
Ichánúpí ..	Chupi ...	Nopvú ..	Daughter.
Mái ..	Bán ...	Théké ..	Slave.
Máibá ..	Kátiki-árteng ...	Létimá ..	Cultivator.
Záo sénba ..	Kévi ...	Thú-khwé-má * ..	Shepherd.
Apôkpá ..	Arnám kéthé ...	Terrho-diu ..	God.
Tamnăbá ..	Arnám ...	Terrho-kesho or bholo ..	Devil.
Numith ..	Arnee ...	Náki ..	Sun.
Thá ..	Chiklow ...	Khrr ..	Moon.
Tháwáínúchá ..	Chika longu ...	Thémú ..	Star.
Mey ..	Me ...	Mi ..	Fire.
Ising ..	Láng ...	Dzú ..	Water.
Yúm ..	Hem ...	Ki ..	House.
Chagôl ..	Losei ...	Kwirr ..	Horse.
Chhêl ..	Cháinong ...	Thúkr ..	Cow.
Siu ..	Máthán ...	Tefoh ..	Dog.

* Cowherd.

English.	Kukee of Cachar.	Kukee of Tipperah.	Hallamee of Tipperah.	Hill Tipperah.
Cat ...	Mengte ..	Meng ...	Meng ...	Aming ..
Cock ...	Ár ..	Ár ...	Ár ...	Táo ..
Duck ...	Váta ..	Borák or Báták ...	Botak ...	Tákhum ..
Ass ...	......	....	....	......
Camel ...	......	....	....	......
Bird ...	Vá ..	Sava ...	Vá ...	Táosá ..
Go ...	Chin ..	Kálro	Phero ...	Tháng-di ..
Eat ..	Neu ..	Pákro ...	Nero ..	Chádi ..
Sit ...	Touvin ..	Túngro ...	Auchuro, Thoiro ...	Achukdi ..
Come ...	Hang-in ..	Hongro ...	Hongro ...	Phaidi ..
Beat ...	Chákin ..	Hemro ...	Jemro ...	Budi ..
Stand ...	Ding-in ..	Tháúro, Nirro ...	Anthúiro, Nirro ...	Báchádi ..
Die ...	Thin ..	Tíro ...	Tíro ...	Thúidi ..
Give ...	Epin ..	Pero ...	Napíro ...	Rudi ..
Run ...	Klajin ..	Rângrâugnikalro ...	Inrángro ...	Káichikdi ..
Up ...	Váncháng ..	Chúngá ...	Chúng ...	Sáká ..
Near ...	Áhingá ..	Anaitha ...	Anaitha ...	Sám ..
Who ...	Kaihám ..	Thúmi ...	Thú ...	Sábo ..
And ...	Adáng ..	Adang ...	Adang ...	Tái ..
Yes ...	Uhm ..	Chang ...	Annih ...	Ayo ..
Down ...	Nái ..	Noya ...	Noy ...	Khámá ..
Far ...	Gám cheng ..	Állá ...	Áhlá ...	Hák-chál ..
What ...	Jhám ..	Imo ...	Imo ...	Tamo ..
But ...	Eé ..	....	....	......
No ...	Één Éen ..	Changmak ...	Mímak ...	Mang ..
Before ...	Máchánga ..	Máncha ...	Maton ...	Chhákáng ..
Behind ...	Nug cháng ..	Núnga ...	Núngá ...	Ulo ..
Why ...	Iding-niném ..	Idingmo, Ihángmo	Ilohrangmo ...	Tángmoy Tamani ..
If ...	Chute ..	....	....	......
Alas! ...	Áh-áh-áh ..	Augáithá ...	Augáíthá ...	......
A father ...	Nápá khát ..	Pá ...	Pá or kápá ...	Phákáichá ..
Of a father ...	Nápá ..	....	....	Phákáichání ..
To a father ...	Nápá-hingá ..	....	....	Phákáicháná ..
From a father ...	Nápá-hingá-pádin	....	....	Phánithani ..
Two fathers ...	Nápá ni ..	Pání ...	Pá anni ...	Phákunui ..
Fathers ...	Nápá-ugai ..	Páthamka (many fathers).	....	Phárok ..
Of fathers ...	Nápá-ugai-si ..	....	....	Pha-rokni ..
To fathers ...	Nápá-ugai-hingá ..	....	....	Phárokna ..
From fathers ...	Nápá-ugai-hingá-padin.	....	....	Pharoknithání ..
A daughter ...	Chá nu khát ..	Náinúkpáng ...	Kachánúh ...	Chhájúk khoroksá ..

Tipperah and Cachar.—(Continued.)

Muneepooree.	Mikir.	Angamee Naga.	English.
Háúdong ...	Ming ..	Núnno ...	Cat.
Yel ...	Vo ..	Votzú ...	Cock.
Gnánu ...	Bukák ..	Tophá ...	Duck.
Lolá ...	......	......	Ass.
......	......	......	Camel.
U'chek ...	Engnám-áro ..	Pérá ...	Bird.
Chalu ...	Kedám ..	Totáché ...	Go.
Cháo ...	Kichu ..	Chi-ché ...	Eat.
Phamum ...	Kánguí ..	Bale che ...	Sit.
Lao ...	Vánguon ..	Vor ché ...	Come.
Zéyú ...	Kichok ..	Vu che ...	Beat.
Lebú ...	Kárjáp ..	Thá-lé ché ...	Stand.
Chaknu ...	Kitho ..	Sátá ché ...	Die.
Pío ...	Piji-áré ..	Chú-ché ...	Give.
Pháo ...	Kikát ..	Tá-shi che ...	Run.
Matuktă ...	Ethák ..	Kérékré ...	Up
Mamakta ...	Nekíngri ..	Képénó ...	Near.
Kannáno ...	Khumát ..	......	Who.
Athái ...	Tánké ..	Ri ...	And.
Hói ...	To ..	U'wé U' ...	Yes.
Makhádá ...	Kángdeí ..	Pésú ...	Down.
Lápná ...	Káhílu ..	Shá-chá ..	Far.
Karíno ...	Pí ..	Keziki ...	What.
Kărígúmbá ...	Pénsethá ..	Kénno ...	But.
Năthé ...	Kálee ..	Mo ...	No.
Mamangdá ...	Chidbo-hedlo ..	Mohzu ...	Before.
Matúngda ...	Népi ..	Ṡa ...	Behind.
Kăridămăk ...	Pemá ..	Keziú, Ki ...	Why.
Kărigi ...	Tauké ..	......	If.
Zámnawáre ...	Po-hám ..	Hah ...	Alas !
Măpá ămma ...	Po ..	A'pú ...	A father
Măpá ămăgí, Măpá ămădu	Ne-po ..	......	Of a father.
Măpá ămădăgi ...	Né-po-álong ..	......	To a father.
Măpá adu-dăgi ...	Ne-po-alongpen ..	Apú-kino ...	From a father.
Măpá ănni ...	Po-hinee ..	A'pú Kénná ...	Two fathers.
Măpá káyáno ...	....	A'púnoko ...	Fathers.
Măpá átháigi ...	Po-átum-án ..	......	Of fathers.
Măpá athái-dagi ...	Po-má-álonkhē ..	......	To fathers.
Măpákibigthági ...	Po-atum álong pén ..	A'púnoko kino ...	From fathers.
Ichánupi ...	Nimchu ..	Nopvu ...	A daughter.

English.	Kukee of Cachar.	Kukee of Tipperah.	Hallamee of Tipperah.	Hill Tipperah.
Of a daughter ..	Chánu ..	....	....	Chhájukni ..
To a daughter ..	Chá-nu-hingá ..	....	....	Chhájuk khorok náini
From a daughter ..	Chá nu hingá pádin	....	....	Chhájuknitháni ..
Two daughters ..	Chá nu ni ..	Nái núhpangni ...	Káchánúh anni ..	Chhájúk, khoroknoí ..
Daughters ..	Chá nu ha ..	Nái nuhpáng thamka.	Kachá núh thamka	Chhájúk rok ..
Of daughters ..	Chá nu ha ..	....	....	Chhájúk rokni ..
To daughters ..	Chá nu hinga ..	....	....	Chhájuk roknoini ..
From daughters ..	Chá nu hinga padin	....	....	Chhájuk rokni tháni..
A good man ..	Pasál khát áfá ..	Mipá atthá ...	Amánái assá ..	Borok káhám ..
Two good men ..	Pasál ni áfá ..	Mipá atthá ni ...	Amánái assá anni..	Borok khorok nui káhám.
Good men ..	Pasál áboueen áfá	Mipá atthá thamka	Amánái assá thamka	Borok káhám rok ..
Of a good man ..	Pasál khát áfá pá chu.	....	....	Borok káhám ni ..
To a good man ..	Pasál khát áfá pá hingá.	....	....	Borok káhám no ..
From a good man ..	Pasál khát áfá pá hingá pádin.	....	....	Borok káhámni tháni
Of good men ..	Aboná pásal áfá ha	....	....	Borok káhám rokni..
To good men ..	Pasál ábouá hahingá	....	....	Borok káhám rokno..
From good men ..	Pasál áfá ha hingá pádin.	....	....	Borok káhám rokni tháni.
A good woman ..	Numái khát áfá ..	Núhpang atthá ...	Núhpáng assá ..	Káichá búrúi káhám
Good women ..	Áfá numái ha áboneen.	Núhpang-atthá thamka.	Núhpáng assá thamka.	Búrúi káhám rok ..
A bad boy ..	Chápángpá khát áfá lon.	....	....	....
A bad girl ..	Chápángnee khát áfá lon.	....	....	....
Good ..	Áfá ..	Átthá ...	Ássá ..	Káhám ..
Better ..	Haú pádin áfái ..	Manek atthá ...	Mánekia-ássá ..	....
Best ..	Áfá changnung pé-he	Reng kánek atthá...	Anreng kánekan ássá.	....
High ..	Ácháng ..	Ú'lien (tall, great) ancháng (high) ...	Ú'lien ..	Kúchúk ..
Higher ..	Áchánga ..	Manek úlien ...	Máneka úlien ..	....
Highest ..	Áchúng chungnung pene.	Reng kánek úlien...	Aurenkánek úlien..	....
A horse ..	Sákar khát ..	Chákôr pachál ...	Chákor a chál ..	Korái chálá má chhá
A mare ..	Sákar khát ánu ..	Chakor púi ...	Chákor, apúi ..	Korái búrúi má chhá
Horses ..	Sákar áboneen ..	Chakor pachál thamka.	Chákor pachál thamka.	Korái chala rok ..
Mares ..	Sákar ánu áboneen	Chakor pui thamka	Chákor apúi thamka	Korái burui rok ..

Tipperah and Cachar.—(Continued.)

Muneepooree.	Mirkir.	Angamee Naga.	English.
Ichánupiamagi ...	Nĕchupi ...	......	Of a daughter.
Ichánupiamadagi or amadu	Ấbá-álongpén ...	......	To a daughter.
Ichanupi mahakidămăk, or adúdagi.	Ấchupi-álonpén ...	Nopvu kino ..	From a daughter.
Machánupi anni ...	Ấlochi-bángní ...	Nopvú kénná ..	Two daughters.
Ichánupi káyáno, or kya subage nupi.	Ấrlasu-már ...	Nopvú-noko ..	Daughters.
Nupigi dămăk ...	Chupi-átum ...	......	Of daughters.
Nupigi maramgi ...	Nimchu-átum-álongpēn ...	......	To daughters.
Nupi adúdagi ...	Nimchu-átum-ákingri-pēn	Nopoo-noko-kino ..	From daughters.
Ama zámna paba mi ...	Pinso-ákmé ...	Thémmá kévi or kevimá ..	A good man.
Zámna paba mi anni ...	Pinso-áké-mēbángni ...	Thémmá kénná vi, or má vi kenna.	Two good men.
Miapăba măigám ...	......	Themma keviko ..	Good men.
Zámna paba mi amagi ...	Pinso-ákmesi ...	......	Of a good man.
Zámna paba mi amagi damak	Pinso-ákme-si-álom ...	......	To a good man.
Zámina paba adúdagi ...	Pinso-ákmesi álongpen ...	Kevima kino ..	From a good man.
Zámna paba migi maramgi	Pinso-pumár-álongpen ...	......	Of good men.
Zámna paba mi adúdagi ...	Pinso-pumár-ákmési-álong pén.	......	To good men.
Zámna paba mi adúsing dagi.	Pinso-pumár-ákmé-atum ..	Kevima kino ..	From good men.
Zamna paba nupi ...	Arlosu ákmesi ...	Thenu kévi ..	A good woman.
Anni ahúng zámna paba nupí.	Ấrlasu-átum-ákme ...	Thénu kéviko ..	Good women.
Naha achhe zámna phăte ...	Usu áké-ning-u ...	Nichú késho ..	A bad boy.
Nupi machha achhe zámná phăte.	Ấrloso áke-ning-u ...	Thénú késho ..	A bad girl.
Phéy ...	Ấkme ...	Kevi, vi ..	Good.
Ấdudăgi ătésu phéy ...	Me-ong-lo ...	Ki-kevi ..	Better.
Guămnă măktăgi phéy ...	Ấkme-si-lá-tāl ...	Kevi-tho or vishivé ..	Best.
Awángba ...	Kángtoi ...	Békré ..	High.
Adúdăgi hen awángba ...	Kángtoi-muchat ...	Ki-rékrí ..	Higher.
Gnamna maktagi hen ăwángba.	Lápár-ákúngtoi-ábeto ...	Rékréshivé ..	Highest.
Chagol amma ...	Losăē isce ...	Kwirr ..	A horse.
Chagol amôm amma ...	Losăē-ijon ...	Kwirr-kee ..	A mare.
Chagol manga tarúk ...	Kádu káne-álosăē ...	Kwirrko ..	Horses.
Chagol amôm mauga taruk	Losăe ápí-kádu kávē ...	Kwirrkrrko ..	Mares.

English.	Kukee of Cachar.	Kukee of Tipperah.	Hallamee of Tipperah.	Hill Tipperah.
A bull ..	Sirát chál khát ...	Cherát pachál ...	Cherát, achal or ate	Músúk chálá máchhá
A cow ..	Sirát ánu khát ...	Cherát pui ...	Cherát núhpang ..	Musuk burui máchhá
Bulls ..	Sirát chál áboneen	Cherát pachál thamka.	Cherát achál thamka	Musuk chálá rok ...
Cows ..	Sirát ánu áboneen	Cherát púi thamka	Cherat nuhpang thamka.	Musuk burui rok ...
A dog ..	U'i khát ...	U'i pachál ...	U'iácál ..	Sinjálá máchhá ...
A bitch ..	Uinu khát ...	U'i púi ...	Uipúi ..	Suima machha ...
Dogs ..	Ui áboneen ...	U'i pachál thamka...	U'iachál thamka ..	Súijálá rok ...
Bitches ..	U'inu áboneen ...	U'i púi thamka ...	U'ipúi thamka ..	Sui márak ...
A goat ..	......	......	....	....
A he-goat ..	Kel chál khát ...	Kel pachal, kel chal	Kel chál ..	Púnjnoyá máchhá ...
A female goat ..	Kel ánu khát ...	Kel pui ...	Kel púi ..	Púnjúk máchhá ...
Goats ..	Kelna aboneen ...	Kel thamka ...	Kel thamka ..	Púnjnoyá rok ...
A male deer ..	Sázu áchál khát ...	Sachal ...	Achál ..	Musúim chálá má chhá.
A male deer (large)	......	Chájúk ...	Chájúk ..	......
A male deer (small)	......	Chakki ...	Chakki ..	....
A female deer ..	Sázu ánu khát ...	Chájúk púi, chakki púi	Chajúk nuhpang, chakki nuhpang.	Musúi búrui máchhá
Deer ..	Sázu áboneen ...	Chájúk thamka, Chakki thamka	Chajuk thamka, chakki thamka.	Musúi rok ...
I am ..	Kei Káma náe ...	Keima om ...	(Much the same throughout as the Kukee).	Angong ...
Thou art ..	Nángmá ná umé ...	Nangma ommo ...	......	Núng ong ...
He is ..	Ámá á-ume ...	Anni ommo ...	......	Bo-ong ...
We are ..	Kēha Káum náé ...	Keimáni om ...	......	Chúng ong ...
You are ..	Nángba ná umē ...	Nangmáni ommo	......	Norok ong ...
They are ..	Ámabá-á-umē	Anmáni ommo ...	......	Borok ong ...
I was ..	Kēijin ká umēi ...	Keima om ...	......	Ong tonkhá ...
Thou wast ..	Náng-ná umin ...	Nangma ommo ...	......	Nung tonkhá ...
He was ..	Amá á umin ...	Anni ommo ...	......	Bo-tonkhá ...
We were ..	Kēha ká umēi ...	Keimáni ommo ...	......	Chung tonkhá ...
You were ..	Nángha-ná-umin ...	Nangmáni-ommo...	......	Norok tankhá ...
They were ..	Ámáha á-umin ...	Anmáni ommo ...	......	Borok tonkhá ...
Be ..	Áhije ...	Om ...	......	Ong ...
To be ..	Áhite ...	Omna ...	......	Ong náni ...
Being ..	Áhitáe ...	Omthá ...	......	Ongoi ...
Having been ..	Áhijon táe ...	Omthá ...	......	......
I may be ..	Kēi hinánge ...	......	......	Áng ong náni mán ...
I shall be ..	Kēima hingkáte ...	......	......	Ángong ánu ...
I should be. ..	Kei hiding kahin ...	......	......	......
Beat ..	Chákin ...	Hem ...	......	Búyo ...

Tipperah and Cachar.—(Continued.)

Muneepoore.	Mikir.	Augamee Naga.	English.
Sandāmba amma ..	Chainong állu-áktē ...	Thúdo ...	A bull.
Salámôm amma ..	Chainong ápi-ijon ...	Thúkrr ...	A cow.
Sandamba anni hum ..	Chainong állú-kádu-kávē...	Thúdoko ...	Bulls.
Salamôm anni hum ..	Chainong ápi-kádu kávē...	Thúkrrko ...	Cows.
Hui amma ..	Máthán ijon ...	Téfoh ...	A dog.
Hui amon amma ..	Máthán ápi-ijon ...	Fohkrr ...	A bitch.
Hui mayam-amma ..	Máthán-állu kádu kávē ...	Tefohko ...	Dogs.
Hui amôm mayam amma..	Máthán ápi kádu kávē ...	Fohkrrko ...	Bitches.
......	......	Taneu ...	A goat.
Hámeng lábá ámmá ..	Bi ijon ...	Néúdô ...	A he-goat.
Hámeng ámom ámmá ..	Bi-ápi-izan ...	Neukrr ...	A female goat.
Hámeng anni hum ..	Bi-álu-kádu káve ...	Taneuko ...	Goats.
Khorsá lábá ámmá ..	Thiok állu izon ...	Chă chă ...	A male deer.
......	......	......	A male deer (large).
......	......	......	A male deer (small).
Khorsá ámom ámmá ..	Thiok ápi-izon ...	Ch-krr ...	A female deer.
Khorsá ..	Thiok-pi kádu kávē ...	Chă-chăko ...	Deer.
Yahak léy ..	Ngē tádo ...	A bá ...	I am.
Nang su léy ..	Náng tádo ...	No bá ...	Thou art.
Masu léy ..	Abang duma ...	Po bá ...	He is.
Akhoi kibig suléy ..	Ngē tum tádo ...	Héko bá ...	We are.
Nokhoi kibig suléy ..	Nángee tum tádo má ...	Néko bá ...	You are.
Mokhoi kibig suléy ..	Hállátum-tádo ...	Lúko bá ...	They are.
Yahak sulé rammi ..	Ngĕ zok tádo ...	Á bárr ...	I was.
Nahak sulé rammi ..	Náng zok tádo má ...	No bárr ...	Thou wast.
Mahak sulé rammi ..	Hállá bángpu zok tádo ...	Po bárr ...	He was.
Okhoi kibig sulé rammi ..	Nge tum badu tádo ...	Héko bárr ...	We were.
Nokhoi kibig sulé rammi..	Náng tum zok tádo má ...	Néko barr ...	You were.
Mokhoi kibig sulé rammi..	Hállá báng-po-tádo ...	Lúko bárr ...	They were.
Oyu ..	Chákpo ...	Bá ...	Be.
Oyga damak ..	Chákji ...	Bá ...	To be.
Oyrá dana ..	Thangpo ...	......	Being.
Oygrabā matung da ..	Chaktánglo ...	Bité ...	Having been.
Óyri ..	Nge thaukzi ...	Á chiléto ...	I may be.
Oybatári ..	Nge chakzi-avi ...	Á chito ...	I shall be.
Oyre ..	Ngé-pár-áke-thik áve longé-ánhel.	Á chilotowel ...	I should be.
Yéyua ..	Kisoko ...	Vú ché ...	Beat.

English.	Kukee of Cachar.	Kukee of Tipperah.	Hallamee of Tipperah.	Hill Tipperah.
To beat ...	Ácháte ...	Hemna ...	......	Búnáni ...
Beating ...	Áchákin ...	......	......	Búoi ...
Having beaten ...	Áchánái ...	Hemtha ...	......	Búkha ...
I beat ...	Kēijin káchá ...	Keima nin hem ...	......	Ong búyo ...
Thou beatest ...	Nángin cháin ...	Nángma nin hem...	......	Nung búyo ...
He beats ...	Ámán áchain ...	Áuni nin hem ...	......	Bo búyo ...
We beat ..	Ke-han káchá-un	Keimáni nin hem ...	......	Chúng búyo ...
You beat ...	Nánghan náchá-un	Nang mani nin-hem	......	Norok búyo ...
They beat ...	Ámáhan áchá-un ...	Anmani nin hem ...	......	Borok búyo ...
I am beating ...	Keijin káchákẃ áhije	Keima nin hem ...	......	......
I was beating ...	Keijin káchákálé ...	......	......	......
I had beaten ...	Keijin káchákẃ ...	......	......	Ong búkhá ...
I may beat ...	Keijin chathái jinge	......	......	Ong búnáni mán ...
I shall beat ...	Keijin chá inge ...	Keima hem ding ...	Keima chém kati...	Áng búyáno ...
I should beat ...	Keijin káchádíng áhain.	......	......	Áng bunani chay ...
I am beaten ...	Keimá ei chá-ei ...	......	Keima anni chémtha	Áng bújág ...
I was beaten ...	Kei-ei-chá-in-áhin	......	......	Áng bújág kha ...
I shall be beaten ...	Keima ei-chá-in tei	......	......	Áng bújág ánú ...
I go ...	Keima chitánge ...	Keima nin kál ...	......	Ang thangyo ...
Thou goest ...	Nángmá chitán ...	Nangma nin kál ...	......	U'núg thángyo ...
He goes ...	Ámá chin ...	Anni nil kál ...	......	Bo-thangyo ...
I went ...	Keimá káchin ahije	Keima kin kálthá...	......	Áng tháng ká ...
Thou wentest ...	Nángmá náchin áhije	Nangma kil káltha	......	Núng tháng ká ...
He went ...	Ámá áchin áhije ..	Anni nin kaltha ...	......	Bo-tháng ká ...
Go ...	Áchi ...	Kálro ...	......	Thángo ...
Going ...	Áchin áhije ...	Kin kál ...	......	Thángoí ...
Gone ...	Áchi tei ...	Káltha ...	......	Tháng ká ...
What is your name?	Námin nam? ...	Nang ma imô ming?	Nagnma nirhming imô?	Nini mung tám? ...
How old is this horse?	Sákar kum i-ját hiján?	Ma chákor chuôkna kum izaka chang-tha? [let that horse's birth (being born) years now may (ago) happen-ed?]	Ma chakor kúm jámo chuôkna?	I korái (chála) bisi busúkni?
How far is it from here to Kashmir?	Hikamá pádin Kash-mir i-chan gám-lam?	Mátha hin Kashmir zán izáka lám, [Let from here Kash-mir days how many journey?] *or* Mátha omhin Kashmir enthen-boni?	Hethaká om hín Kashmir idormol allallhá?	Arni Kashmir musúk chal?

Tipperah and Cachar.—(Continued.)

Muneepooree.	Mikir.	Angamee Naga.	English.
Yeyga damak ...	Kichok-thik-dun-má ..	Vú lé ...	To beat.
Yeyna ...	Chok thánglo ávé ..	Vúé ...	Beating.
Yeyra dana ...	......	Vúrr ...	Having beaten.
Yahak yeygedaure ...	Nge thábokzi ..	Á vú ...	I beat.
Nang yeyga daurebra ...	Náng choknon ..	No vú ...	Thou beatest.
Ma yeyge daurebra ...	Káchi chok ..	Po vú ...	He beats.
Okhoi yeyge daure ...	Nge tum badu sokzi ..	Héko vú ...	We beat.
Nokhoi su yeyge daurbra ...	Nanglitum choknon ..	Néko vú ..	You beat.
Mokhoi na yeyge nairibra	Hállátum kéchi chok ..	Lúko vú ...	They beat.
Yakbo yéyni ...	Nge ke choklo ..	Á vú ...	I am beating.
Yakpo yeyram gani ...	Chílo chi chakzi ..	Á vú bágo ...	I was beating.
Mábo yey rammi ...	Nge chokzi dak-daklo ..	Á vúiágo ...	I had beaten.
Mábo yeyba grammi yeyni	Nge chok-hái-ávi ..	Á vúléto ...	I may beat.
Yahak yeyni ...	Nge náng chokzi ..	Á vúto ...	I shall beat.
Yahakpo yeyge dauri ...	Pio-pio-nge-chokzi áví ..	Á vúshito ...	I should beat.
Yahak chey chare ...	Náng-pán-náng kichok ..	Á vú vé ...	I am beaten.
Yahak cheycháredo ...	Áku nge choklo ..	Á vúé ...	I was beaten.
Yahak chey chágo daba mali.	Nge-dum-dene chok dezi ..	Á vúté ...	I shall be beaten.
Yahak chale ...	Nge kédám ..	Á toté ...	I go.
Mang su challabra ...	Náng dám non ..	No toté ...	Thou goest.
Masu chale ...	Hállá bángpo-nang thik má.	Po toté ...	He goes.
Yahak chu chale ...	Nge tákedám ..	Á totéwé ...	I went.
Nang suchal ammi ...	Náng táng dámá ..	No totéwé ...	Thou wentest.
Ma suchal ammi ...	Hállá bángpu-dámlo-má ..	Po totéwé ...	He went.
Chalu ...	Dám non ..	Toté ...	Go.
Chasí ...	Dámlo ..	Kétoki ...	Going.
Chakre ...	Dám táng lo ..	Totá ...	Gone.
Nangi naming kárino? ...	Náng men konpumá? ..	Un zá sopo? ...	What is your name?
Chagôl asi chahi kayá súre?	Lábáng so á-lo sae koián áning-khándo pumá?	Kwirr háo chi kichú? ...	How old is this horse?
Asidagi Kashmir kayá thabe bage?	Ládák penhá Kashmir kal-ándumá-káil?	Hánúnú Káshmir kéji thir	How far is it from here to Kashmir?

English.	Kukee of Cachar.	Kukee of Tipperah.	Hallamee of Tipperah.	Hill Tipperah.
How many sons are there in your father's house?	Nángmá nápá i-ná-i-ját chápángpá umám?	Nangma pá iná nái izáka om?	Nipá iná nái ijámo a om?	No phá ni nau aibchhfa khorok busúk?
I have walked a long way to-day.	Keimá tunin gamcheng káki choune.	Keima hongna, von lám álláh chángtha. [My coming today path-far has been]	Avuon nakin hongna lám allah.	Tini áng rúmchha nimkhá.
The son of my uncle is married to her sister.	Keimá kápángá chápá ámá chánuta ákhi chengé.	Ma núhpang farnúh keima pánghánk náipá núhpúi neitha.	Ma núhpáng farnúh keima pánghánk nái dongmá alláktha.	Ani kákáni báchha jolá báha nau no káijákha.
In the house is the saddle of the white horse.	Sákar ángon jin iná a-um náe.	Chákôr-ngau chúngá chúngá tutmun ina om [Horse white upon-to-sit-seat in the house is.] (No word in kuki or Hallami for saddle).	Chákor-angoi chúnga chungna toimun ina om.	Inog korái kuforni jin long-o (*jin*, Bengali, no word in Tipperah for saddle).
Put the saddle upon his back.	Ámáchangá jin kámin.	Mádár chúnga tutmun semro.	Adár chunga tuimun shinro.	Korái sákáy jín bok shádi.
I have beaten his sons with many stripes.	Ámá chápá chu kei mán káchá in ting pumin.	Mahá náile keima thukmutin hem.	Ámá náile keima thokmol ajem.	Ang bono chomsá búkhá.
He is grazing cattle on the top of the hill.	Ámán chingláng chungá sirát áchingin.	Thúng chúnga ma cheerát hol.	Thúng chúnga (or thieng) keng cherát ahol.	Bo musúk no háchuk o sám cháru náni náng khá.
He is sitting on a horse under that tree.	Ámá hiche thing bul noiá sákar changá átowvin.	Má thíng noya chákor chúnga thúng mái.	Má thíng noya chákor chúnga athoi mái.	U bufáng khámá o bo korái sáká o achug o tong-o.
His brother is taller than his sister.	Ásu pina sángin ásupipá achange.	Má farnúh nína amá unáo mánekúlien.	Anní únái nekin amá farnúh úlien.	Báhá nau ni sánái bofáyung hám.
The price of that is two rupees and a half.	Áhimonhi chenguile ake mon ahije.	Ma aman cheng ní le duli.	Amá man dár ní le áduli.	U' moni dam khok núi mámá.
My father lives in that small house.	Kapa hiche in ne ucha anme.	Keima pá ma ina thé ompui.	Keima kapá ma ina thé a ompui.	U' nau kiste o phá tong o.
Give this rupee to him.	Hiche dankahi ama chupin.	Má som amále péro	Amá súm dár khút amálé pero.	I ráng bon rúdí ...
Take those rupees from him.	Hiche danka aboneen ama hinga lan.	Má som anni khútle juláro.	Má súm ni khút in lé juláro.	Bini thánini u ráng tánángdi.
Beat him well and bind him with ropes.	Ámáhi phátá in chá in chute khávin kánin.	Málé thatakin hémro hemjoyin rúyín phirro.	Amálé achatakin jémro nijémjoile ruyín khitro.	Bon kâhám khánái oi búdi tái dug-húi boi khádi.
Draw water from the well.	Teepuma tee thálin	Túi kúi nienga túi juláro.	Túi kuongáneng túi ju choiro.	Kowáni túi ti shádi...
Walk before me ...	Keima máchángá chida in.	Keima mánoha kálro	Keima matona pheng kiti.	Áni sákáng o himdi...
Whose boy comes behind you?	Nángmá nungá kai chápong hungám?	Nangma núnga thú nái mo hong?	Nangma núnga ka thú nái mo hong?	Nini uno sábáni báchha kái?
From whom did you buy that?	Nángin hichehi kohingá nacha hizam?	Thú nienga ma nen chok?	Amaka thú kuonga nirchokmo?	Nung sábáni tháni páikha?
From a shop-keeper of the village.	Hiche koá dukándár pahingá.	Boma múdí nienga kin chok.	Boma mudí kuonga nenun kiner chok.	Bárí múdí ni tháni páikhá.

Tipperah and Cachar.—(Continued.)

Muneepooree.	Mikir.	Angamee Naga.	English.
Nahakki napá mayúm da macha kayáno ?	Nángpo á-hem ásopinso bangkoán-má ?	Un pú ki nú nono kichúro ?	How many sons are there in your father's house ?
Asi yámna lápna lákle ...	Mini nge ke ákáhilo dámlo	A thá to shwéwé ..	I have walked a long way to-day.
Yahakki kuragi machá na núpi asagi mana núpi luhonggre.	Nepunn ásopuke ángzir pi-che-en.	A néno nowé po lúpoo penhubá.	The son of my uncle is married to her sister.
Chágôl angobagi sábal imda le bane.	Lasáé kélls ájin hém-árlo sedo.	Kwirr kécháo chijé kinú zá wé.	In the house is the saddle of the white horse.
Magi matúkta sábal nabo	Athák jin árthág non ..	Chijeú po nákú gi shiché...	Put the saddle upon his back.
Magi macha bo yámna yeyre.	Lábángcho-áchop-jongh nge chokol.	Po no á vúshwévé ..	I have beaten his son with many stripes.
Ching matukta chhál cheli	Juglong kángtoi háná chái-nong birechá báp chube.	Kizikhrúgi po thú hokhothá	He is grazing cattle on the top of the hill.
Upal begi makáda chágôl matukta ley.	Thingpi árum hálá bánchu losae áthák ingui kok sido.	Lú sikhr khro kwirr gi bázo.	He is sitting on a horse under that tree.
Mági machémdagi mapu-wana hena wángi.	Angzirpi áfán áchik ktepo kéding.	Po sázeo po lúpooki rékré..	His brother is taller than his sister.
Magi mathauna léy badi lípá anni makai.	Lávángso ánám siká hinee rá-áduli.	Pomá ráká kénnári dúli po	The price of that is two rupees and a half.
Im changai machad ipá phamdan léy.	Hemsu-ngepu si-kido ..	Apú ki kéchi nú báiá ..	My father lives in that small house.
Lúpa ase mangoda pío ..	Hálá bángsu-ásiká-hálá bángpu-pidámnon.	Háú ráká potsúché ..	Give this rupee to him
Adúdagi lúpa láwo ..	Lá vángso ásiká hálá bángpu áking ri-pu-non.	Ráká háko lélé ..	Take those rupees from him.
Mábo yámna yéyraga pun-dana thamo.	Hálá bángpu chokmé chénrá ári pen kok non.	Po vúshwédi phálé ché ..	Beat him well and bind him with rope.
Kohadagi ising so-o ..	Lángtukso áláng sok-non..	Dzu khú no dzu lúlé ..	Draw water from the well.
Yaki imángda chalo ..	Ngephrang dám bom non..	A mhozu tolé ..	Walk before me.
Kanagi macha no matángda lá ibá asíde ?	Nángphimát-ánso náng ki-dunmá ?	So po nono únsá toga ? ..	Whose boy comes behind you ?
Adu kanadagi ley bage ?	Mát ákéngré si-kénám ? ..	Haú kezi ki nó khrléloi ? ..	From whom did you buy that ?
Kulgi poy yomba dagi leyye.	Rang árlo dukándár ákeng-risi.	Réná po théli-kéchi-ma ki nó khrléwé.	From a shop-keeper of the village.

LIST OF WORDS AND PHRASES SHOWING LANGUAGES

OF THE

HILLS SURROUNDING ASSAM AND CACHAR.

List of English words and phrases with their corresponding words

English.	Manipuri.	Kuki.	Khasi.
One ...	Ama ...	Khatka ...	Uwei, kawei, or wei, without the article.
Two ...	Ani ...	Nika ...	Ar ...
Three ...	Ahum ...	Thumka ...	Lai ...
Four ...	Mari ...	Lika ...	Saw ...
Five	Manga ...	Rangaka ...	Saw ...
Six ...	Taruk ...	Rukka ...	Hinriw, hynriw ...
Seven ...	Taret ...	Sarika ...	Hiniew ...
Eight ...	Nipal ...	Riekka ...	Phra ...
Nine ...	Mapal ...	Kokka ...	Kliyudai ...
Ten ...	Tara ...	Somka ...	Shiphew ...
Twenty ...	Kul ...	Somnika ...	Arphew ...
Fifty ...	Jyankai ...	Somrangaka ...	San-phew ...
Hundred ...	Cha-ama ...	Riza ..	Shi-spab ...
I ..	Ai ...	Kaima ...	Nga, or manga ...
We ..	Ikhoi ...	Kaimani ...	Ngi, or ma-ngi ...
Thou ..	Nang ...	Nangma ..	Me, or ma-me ...
You ..	Nang ...	Nangmani ...	Phi, or ma-phi ...
He ..	Mana ..	Anmanihi ...	U, or ma-u ...
They ..	Makhoina ..	Anmanihe thamka ..	Ki, or ma-ki ...
Of me, mine ...	Jyakbo ...	....	Na nga (1). ... Shapang jong nga (2). Jong nga (3.)
Of us, our ...	Ikhoibo ..	....	Na ngi (1) ... Shaphang jong ugi (2). Jong uqu (3).
Of thee, thine ...	Nang ..	....	Na me (1) ... Shaphang jong me jong me.
Of you, your ...	Nakhoida ...	....	Na phi (1) ... Shaphang jong phi (2). Jong phi (3).
Of him, his ...	Makhoida ..	....	Na u (1) ... Shaphang jong u (2). Jong u (3).
Of them, their ...	Makhoida ..	....	Na ki (1) ... Shaphang jong ki (2). Jong ki (3).
Mine ..	Jyaki ..	Kaimatha ...	Jong uga la ka jong. ...
Our ..	Ikhoiki ..	Kaimanitha ...	Jong ugi ...
Thine ..	Nangi ..	Nangmatha ...	Jong me ...
Your ..	Nakhoigi ..	Nangmanitha ...	Jong phi ...
His ..	Mahaki ..	Anmani-hi-tha ...	Jong u ...
Their ..	Makhoigi ..	Anmani-hi-thamka-tha ...	Jong ki ...

Singpho.	Naga of Luckimpore.	Naga of Seebsaugor.	Miri.	English.
Ai ...	Oyán thek ...	Etta ..	Abakka ...	One.
Oukhanga ...	Oyáni ...	Ani ...	Anyika ...	Two.
Muchom ...	Oyán ram ...	Ajam ...	And mak ...	Three.
Pili ...	Belli ..	Alli ...	Appik ...	Four.
Pándá ...	Bangá ...	Agá ...	Auka ...	Five.
Kro ...	Irak ...	Arak ...	Aukek ...	Six.
Sinit ...	Ingit ...	Anák ...	Kinitkang ...	Seven.
Máyát ...	Ichhat ...	Aset ...	Pinibank ...	Eight.
Yikhu ...	Ikhu ...	Apu ...	Kanák ...	Nine.
Si ...	Ichhi ...	Ván ...	Inká ...	Ten.
Khon ...	Rangi ...	Chá ...	Uin akhink ...	Twenty.
Mángasi ...	Rak bangá ...	Punihunai Khavan ...	Uin ánka ...	Fifty.
Láyá ...	Sáthe ..	Poga ...	Ing ink ...	Hundred.
Nái ...	Mi ..	Kuoí ...	Nga ...	I.
Náng ...	La ...	Kukhí ...	Nga lu ...	We.
Lii ...	Lánga ...	Nange ...	Aune ...	Thou.
Láni ...	Lángá ...	Házám ...	Nabut ...	You.
Khiná ...	Nángá ...	Si ...	Bye ...	He.
Khini ..	Chemin ...	Hukhi ...	Kyen ...	They.
Nainá ...	Niya ...	Kuku ...	Ngabek ...	Of me, mine.
Chánáná ...	Hái hái ...	Kemku ...	Ngalubká ...	Of us, our.
Khiliná ...	Irepá ...	Nangpu ...	Byan baká ...	Of thee, thine.
Náná ...	Lánga ...	Hazamku ...	Nabek ...	Of you, your.
Khila ...	Irep ...	Chiku ...	Khubek ...	Of him, his.
Khiliná ...	Chemin ...	Hamku ...	Byalukhe ...	Of them, their.
Náiná ...	Niya ...	......	Ngabek ...	Mine.
Chánáná ...	Hái hái ...	......	Ngalubká ...	Our.
Nana ...	Lengá ...	......	Byubek ...	Thine.
Lángalá ...	Nángá ...	......	Nanke ...	Your.
Khiná ...	Ire ...	......	Bukke ...	His.
Mácháná ...	Chemin ...	......	Pyaluk ...	Their.

List of English words and phrases with their corresponding words

English.	Manipuri.	Kuki.	Khasi.
Hand ...	Khut ..	Niban ...	Ka kti ...
Foot ...	Khang ..	Pai ...	Ka sla jat ..
Nose ...	Naton ..	Nar ...	Kakhmut ..
Eye ...	Mith ..	Mith ...	Kakhymat ..
Mouth ...	Chil ..	Mur ...	Ka shintur ..
Tooth ...	Jya ..	Niha ...	Ka byniat ..
Ear ...	Nakong ..	Nikur ...	Kashkor ..
Hair ...	Chham ..	Sam ...	U shniuh ..
Head ...	Kok ..	Looh ...	Ka khlih ..
Tongue ..	Lei ..	Lai ...	Ka thyllied ...
Belly ..	Puk ..	Phoong ...	Kakypoh ..
Back ..	Nangan ..	Roong ...	Ka ing dong ..
Iron ...	Jyat ..	Thhir ...	U nar ..
Gold ...	Chhana ..	Rangkachak ...	Ka ksiar ..
Silver ..	Lopa ..	Tangka ...	Ka rupa (B) ..
Father ...	Pa ..	Pa .	U kypa ..
Mother ...	Ma ..	Noo ...	Ka kaymi ..
Brother ...	Iyama (elder), Inao (younger).	Keoo, Kinaiboong (younger).	U hynmen (elder), u hynbew (younger), u para (in general.)
Sister ...	Ichim (elder) ..	Kifarnoo ...	Ka hynmen (elder), ka hynbew (younger), ka para (in general).
Man ...	Nipa ..	Ipa ...	U briw ...
Woman ...	Nupi ..	Nupang ...	Ka briw ...
Wife ...	Nupi ...	Nupni ...	Katynga, ka skaw ...
Child ...	Macha ...	....	I khynnah ...
Son ...	Cha ...	Ipathey ...	U khun ...
Daughter ...	Ichanupi ...	Nupangthey ...	Ka khun ...
Slave ...	Minai ...	Boy ...	U or ka mraw ...
Cultivator ...	....	Karin-faennat ...	U nongrep ...
Shepherd ...	Semba ...	Rakhal ...	U nongap langbrot.
God ...	Athai-ba-lai ...	Pathhiang ...	U blei ...
Devil ...	Lamai-thambí ...	Karhi ...	U ksuid ...
Sun ...	Numith ...	Soom ...	Ka sugi ..
Moon ...	Tha ...	Thla ...	U bynai ..
Star ...	Thaa macha ...	Arsi ...	U khlur ..
Fire ...	Mai ...	Mai ...	Ka ding ..
Water ...	Ichhing ...	Thui ...	Ka um ..
House ...	Jum ...	In ..	Ka ing ..
Horse ...	Sagol ...	Sakar ...	U kulai (B) ..

in Manipuri, Kuki, Khasi, Singpho, Naga, and Miri.

Singpho.	Naga of Luckimpore.	Naga of Seebsaugor.	Miri.	English.
Latah ...	Dák ...	Sák ...	Anáng ...	Hand.
Longang ...	Dá ...	Sya ...	Nepabyeng ...	Foot.
Nádi ...	Khan ...	Nako ...	Inebyon ...	Nose.
Mih ...	Mit ...	Nik ...	Amik ...	Eye.
Ningop ...	Thun ...	Bikha ...	Nápán ...	Mouth.
Oya ...	Pá ...	Bá ...	Ai ...	Tooth.
Ná ...	Ná ...	Ná ...	Eron ...	Ear.
Kárá ...	Khich chhu ...	Kha ...	Dumit ...	Hair.
Ngerang ...	Khau ...	Khang ...	Mittop ...	Head.
Chingleo ...	Thelli ...	Lay ...	Aiya ...	Tongue.
Kán ...	Oyak ...	Wok ...	Akheye ...	Belly.
Sing mang ...	Tám ...	Tak ...	Amirá ...	Back.
Ikri ...	Ján ...	Jan ...	Iyagire ...	Iron.
Jah ...	Kám ...	Sen ...	Aine ...	Gold.
Kom krang ...	Ngun ...	Nun ...	Morkang ...	Silver.
......	......	Hopá ...	......	Father.
......	......	Hunu ...	.. .	Mother.
......	......	Honao ...	....	Brother.
......	......	Sikau honao ...	....	Sister.
......	......	Mi ...	....	Man.
......	......	Sikau ...	....	Woman.
......	......	Husenu ...	....	Wife.
......	......	Sisi ...	....	Child.
......	......	Hosá ...	....	Son.
......	......	Sikau hosa ...	....	Daughter.
......	......	Dá ...	....	Slave.
......	......	Majrimi ...	....	Cultivator.
......	......	....	....	Shepherd.
......	......	Rangbao ...	....	God.
......	......	Bau rang ...	....	Devil.
......	......	Ranghan ...	....	Sun.
......	......	Letnu ...	....	Moon.
......	......	Letsee ...	....	Star.
......	......	Bau ...	....	Fire.
......	......	Ti ...	....	Water.
......	......	Hám ...	....	House.
......	....	Mán ...	....	Horse.

List of English words and phrases with their corresponding words

English.	Manipuri.	Kuki.	Khasi.
Cow	Sal-amum	Chherrad-jel	Ka massi
Dog	Hui	Oohi	U ksew
Cat	Handang	Meng	Ka miaw
Cock	En	Arkhong	U siar
Duck	Enganu-macha	Varak	Ka haw (B)
Ass	Lala	......	Ka gadda (B)
Camel	....	......	U ut(B) উষ্ট্র
Bird	Uchek	Bah	Ka sim
Go	Chappar chala (in general.)	Kalro	Leit
Eat	Chao	Faro	B am
Sit	Fama	Thhungro	Shong
Come	Lao	Hungro	Wan
Beat	Jyaio	Varoh	Shoh
Stand	Leba	Nierroh	(y) Jeng
Die	Chhiba	Jthie	(y) Jap
Give	Pia	Pero	Ai
Run	Chela	Thloiro	Phet
Up	Mathakda	Choongah	Halor
Near	Nakna	Kinihanga	Hajan
Who	Konanu	Thumoh	Mano
And	......	Rek	Rub, bad, de
Yes	Hai	Oh	Haoid
Down	Mokha	Nooaha	Shat y bian
Far	.....	Ahlah	Jing nqai or Ji nqai
What	Kari	Imoh	Kaba, or aiuh ?
But	Kariki	....	Hinrei, te
No	Mai	Changmok	Em-em
Before	Mathakda	Mansaroh	Shiwa
Behind	Itungda	Noongthiang	Shadin
Why	Karigi	Imothoh	Balei
If	....	Achang choon	Lada
Alas	Hae	Eh-eh	Waw ! or Wa !
A father	Mapa-ma	Khatka pa	U kypa
Two fathers	Mapa-ni	Nika pa	Arngut ki hypa
Fathers	Napa-iamha	Thhamka pa	Ki hypa
Of a father	Mapa-ma-amagi	....	Na u kypa (1), shaphang u kypa (2), jong u kypa (3).
Of fathers	Napa-iamagi	....	Na ki kypa (1), shaphang ki kypa (2), jong ki kypa (3).

Singpho.	Naga of Luckimpore.	Naga of Seebsaugor.	Miri.	English.
......	....	Mihu ...	....	Cow.
......	....	Hi ...	....	Dog.
......	....	Mesa ...	....	Cat.
......	....	Upang ...	....	Cock.
......	....	Upák ...	....	Duck.
......	....	....	....	Ass.
......	....	....	....	Camel.
......	....	Fauo ...	....	Bird.
Chal ...	Kán ...	Paulá ...	Gekáng ká ...	Go.
Cháh ...	Cháon ...	Lesa ...	Dát ...	Eat.
Dungo ...	Táng ..	Nahai ...	Dutang ...	Sit.
....	....	Homanhu ...	....	Come.
......	....	Maithan ...	....	Beat.
......	....	Ajanghai ...	....	Stand.
......	....	Jile ...	....	Die.
.....	....	Láko ...	....	Give.
......	....	Riklá ...	....	Run.
Ling cháng ...	Rankha ...	Dingta ...	Taleng ...	Up.
Nih dái ...	On thek ...	Sonlay ...	Anene ...	Near.
Jangining rái háh ...	Hánná ...	Abe ...	Chyekan ...	Who.
Gálái ..	Dákka ...	Athasu ...	Tapaná ...	And.
Ráikon ...	Idangele ...	Changle ...	Eddu ...	Yes.
......	....	Tang ...	....	Down.
......	....	Atai lay ...	....	Far.
......	....	Bole ...	....	What.
....	....	Hafima ...	....	But.
....	....	Manchang ...	....	No.
....	....	Thamá ...	....	Before.
....	....	Fima ...	....	Behind.
....	....	Bole-thaipu ...	....	Why.
....	....	Hebamá ...	....	If.
....	.....	Nabang ...	....	Alas.
Oáh áimá ...	Oyánthe ibbá ...	Tá hopa ...	Abaká ábbut...	A father.
Onkhanga oáh ...	Ibbá oyáni ...	Ani hopá ..	Anyiká ábbut	Two fathers.
Oáh ni ...	Ibbá he ...	Hopa-lai ...	Abbu bajek ...	Fathers.
Oáh niná ...	Oyánthe ibban ...	Hopáku ...	Abak ábbut ...	Of a father.
Oáh ni ná ...	Ibbá henáng ...	Hopa-hámku ..	Abbu bajeke...	Of fathers.

List of English words and phrases with their corresponding words

English.	Manipuri.	Kuki.	Khasi.
To a father ...	Mapa-amada ...	Khatkapa nihanga ..	Ha u kypa ..
To fathers ...	Napa-iamada ..	.....	Ha ki kypa (1), sha ki kypa (2).
From a father ...	Mapa-amadegi ...	....	Na u kypa ...
From fathers ...	Napa iamadegi ...	....	Na ki kypa ..
A daughter ..	Macha-nupi-ama ..	Khatka nupangthey ...	Ka khun ..
Daughters ..	Macha-nupi-iamaba ...	Thamka nupangthey ...	Ki khun kynthei ...
Of a daughter ...	Macha-nupi-amagi ...	....	Jong ka khún ..
Of daughters ..	Napa-iamagi ..	....	Jong ki khun kynthei (1), shaphang ki khun kynthei (2), na ki khun kynthei (3).
To a daughter ...	Macha-nupi-amada ...	....	Sha ka khun, ha ka khun..
To daughters ..	Macha-nupi-iamada ...	.....	Ha ki khun kynthei (1), sha ki khun kynthei (2).
From a daughter ..	Macha-nupi-amadegi ...	....	Na ka khun ...
Two daughters ..	Machanupini ..	Nika nupangthey ..	Arngut ki khun ..
From daughters ..	Macha-nupi-iamadegi ...	....	Na ki khun kynthei ..
A good man ...	Mi-afaba-ama ..	U briw uba bha ...	U briw uba bha ...
Two good men ...	Mi-afaba-ani ...	Nika atah ipah ...	Arngut ki briw kiba bha ..
Good men ...	Afaba-mi-khibik ...	Thamka atah ipa ...	Ki briw kiba bha ...
Of a good man ...	Mi-afaba-amagi ..	....	Na u briw uba bha (1), shaphang u briw uba bha (2), jong u briw uba bha (3).
Of good men ...	Afaba-mi-khibikgi ...	....	Na ki briw kiba bha (1), shaphang ki briw kiba bha (2), jong ki briw kiba bha (3).
To a good man ...	Mi-ama-afabada ..	....	Sha u briw uba bha (1), ha u briw uba bha (2).
To good men ...	Afaba mikhibikda ...	....	Sha ki briw kiba bha (1), ha ki briw kiba bha (2).
From a good man ...	Mi-ama-afabadegi ...	....	Na u briw uba bha. ...
From good men ..	Afaba-mi-khibikdegi ...	.....	Na ki briw kiba bha. ...
A good woman ...	Afaba-nupi-ama ...	Khatka atahnupang ..	Ka briw kaba bha, ...
Good women ...	Afaba-nupi-khibik ...	Khamka atah nu pang ...	Ki hynthei kiba bha ...

Singpho.	Naga of Luckimpore.	Naga of Seebsaugor.	Miri.	English.
Oáh niá jái ...	Oyánthe ibbá karáng	Hopá-ku ...	Abbuter neká kámár.	To a father.
Oyáh ni á jái ...	Ibbá henáng kak ...	Hopá-kulai ..	Abbu bane bajek.	To fathers.
Oáh niá gailá ...	Oyánthe ibbá iyákbá	Hopam ...	Abbak ábbut nengáng.	From a father.
Oyáh duo áni gailá ...	Ibbá hengerá ...	Hopa-aupa ..	Abbu bane kanek.	From fathers.
Chiya cháni bak ...	Itchhá oyánthe ...	Sikau ...	Umme ábak ...	A daughter.
Chlyi chánibak ...	Chenná kámin ...	Sikou ham ...	Umme bajek...	Daughters.
Chá chhiyi máng niná	Itchá oyánthe thimákbá.	Sikou-ku ..	Umme ábakka	Of a daughter.
Chá chiyi mánga ni theng ájái.	Chhi nángá ...	Sikau-homenpa ...	Umme kidinábká	Of daughters.
Chá chhiyi mángani...	Itchhá oyánthe therákbá.	Sikou ...	Umme ábkán	To a daughter.
......	......	Sikau-hamku ..	....	To daughters.
Chá chhiyi mánganiá	Oyánthe itchhá iyák-bá.	Sikou hosa ...	Abká umme ke negáng.	From a daughter.
Chidi máng okhang...	Itchhá oyáni ...	Ani-sikou ..	Anyek umme	Two daughters.
Chá chhiyi mángani gáilán.	Itchhi ngábá ...	Sikau-homenpani ...	Umme gánge	From daughters.
Yomaphah gájá áimá eán.	Oyánthe michhen...	Etta mi my ...	Abká áinámne	A good man.
Ongkhanga yomaphah	Oyáni áchhen ...	Mi my ni ...	Anyekchim máine amme.	Two good men.
Yo maphah gájá ...	Mi iyán chhen ...	Mi my ham ..	Máine ámiki bichi áibdá.	Good men.
Yomaphah gájábak ...	Oyanthe mián chen	....	Abká ainamnek	Of a good man.
Yo maphah gájá ...	Mi iyán chhen ...	Mi my hamenpa ...	Máine ámiki bichi áibdá,	Of good men.
Yomaphah gájá ámájai.	Mioyán chen oyán therák.	Etta mi my hamku ...	Abká áinám nená.	To a good man.
Yo maphah gájá baka jái.	Mián chenhi nángá	Mi my hamenpa ku...	Aine kin dingká	To good men.
Yo maphah gailán ...	Itchhi michhen ...	Etta mi my anpá ...	Ainámne gange	From a good man.
Gájá yo tho má yo maphah ningái nán.	Mián chhenhi ngeo yábá.	Mi my hamenpa ...	Aine ne ugánge	From good men.
Lomchá gájá áimá lom chá.	Bániá ...	Etta chya mi ...	Abká áine nenge.	A good woman.
Gájá lomchá baka ...	Dihiák chen ...	Chya mi ...	Nenge ibe kane káng kene.	Good women.

List of English words and phrases with their corresponding words

English.	Manipuri.	Kuki.	Khasi.
A bad boy ...	Phattaba-angangama ...	Khatka talai ipathey ...	Ukhyn nah uba liymman, or U khynnah liymman.
A bad girl ...	Angangmacha-ama ...	Khaka talai nupangthey	Ka khynnah kaba liymman, or Ka khynnah liymman.
Good ...	Afaba ...	Atah ...	Babha ...
Better ...	Iam-afaba ...	Atah thak thak ...	Bakhambha ..
Best ...	Iam-afaba ...	Atah thak thak hilthing umok.	Babha tam ...
High ...	Aange ...	Ansang ...	Halor jerong, Ba jerong ..
Higher ...	Iamaange ...	Ansang thak thak ...	Ba kham jerong ..
Highest ...	Iamaange ...	Ansang thak thak hithing umok.	Ba jerong tam ...
A horse ...	Sagol-ama ...	Khatka sakor ...	U kulai ...
A mare ...	Sagol-amum-ama ...	Khatka sakar nupang ...	Ka kulai, or ka kulai kynthei
Horses ...	Sagol-khibik ...	Thamka sakor ...	Ki kulai ...
Mares ...	Sagol-amum-khibik ...	Thamka sakor nupang ...	Ki kulai kynthei ..
A bull ...	Sal-laba-ama ...	Khatka serrah til loiloi....	U massi kyrtong, or U massi.
A cow ...	Sal-amum-ama ...	Khatka cherrad-jel ...	Ka massi, or ka massi kynthei.
Bulls ...	Sal-labo-khibik ...	Thamka Serrah-til loiloi ...	Ki massi kyrtong ...
Cows ...	Sal-amum-khibik ...	Thamka cherrad-jel ...	Ki massi kynthei ...
A dog ...	Hui-laba-ama ...	Khatka oohi ...	Ksew ..
A bitch ...	Hui-amum-ama ...	Khatka oohi pooi ...	Ka ksew ..
Dogs ...	Hui-laba-khibik ...	Thamka oohi ...	Ki ksew ..
Bitches ...	Hui-amum-khibik ...	Thamka oohi pooi ...	Ki ksew kynthei ...
A he-goat ...	Haeng-laba-ama ...	Khatka kel-chal ...	Ubtang soh moh ...
A female goat ...	Haeng-amum-ama ...	Khatka-kelpooino ...	Ka blang ..
Goats ...	Haeng-khibik ...	Thamka kel chal ...	Ki blang ..
A male deer ...	Saji-laba-ama ...	Khatka Sajook chal ...	U'kei rang ..
A female deer ...	Saji-amum-ama ..	Khatka Sajook pooi ..	Ka skei ...
Deer ...	Saji-khibik ..	Sajook ..	Ki skei ..
I am ...	Iyak-leiri ..	Ken nooi ..	Uga long ...
Thou art ...	Nang-leirilira ..	Nen nooi ..	Pha long (female), Me long (male.)
He is ...	Ma-leiri ..	An nooi ..	U long ...

Singpho.	Naga of Luckimpore.	Naga of Seebsaugor.	Miri.	English.
Aimá máng ongái dái.	Báng chhi ...	Etta misi newsa ...	Abká áimá ne kává.	A bad boy.
Ong gájá lomchá áimá	Dihiák chhá pháng chhi.	Etta misi faví ...	Aimá ne neng ábakká.	A bad girl.
Gájá ...	Achhen ...	My ...	Aidák ...	Good.
Khá áng khup gájá ...	Dakmachhen ...	Amy ...	Anying ák ...	Better.
Gájá dái ong lang gájá dái.	Achhen chhenná ...	Amypa ...	Aidak anying ák.	Best.
Jadái ...	Achho yáng ...	Haha ...	Ayábe ...	High.
Khaang khup jadái ...	Dak áchhoeng ...	Háho ...	Ayábek ...	Higher.
Yádái lathang yáh dái	Achang lekechang	Hafa ...	Apping ken pe námái ádbak.	Highest.
Gombáng áimá ...	Mak oyánthe ...	Etta mán ...	Abakká godee	A horse.
Gombáng numá ..	Oyánthe mak ngiyáng.	Etta mán hunu ...	Abká gobechi neng ká.	A mare.
Gombáng ...	Makkhi ...	Inu mán ...	Gobeye bak ...	Horses.
Gombang am ...	Mak ngiyánghi ...	Inu-man hunu ...	Gobechi neng bak.	Mares.
Koncho chokang áimá	Oyanthe mán chhám reká.	Horan pang ...	Abká bátaru nagabimne.	A bull.
Koncho go numá ...	Mániyáng oyánthe	Myh-hunu ...	Abká unnek nengká.	A cow.
Koncho choáng bak ...	Láng chán bak mán pang.	Inu-horanpang ...	Bhatar nagar ábakka.	Bulls.
Numá bak ...	Maniyáng lang ...	Inu myhu hunu ...	Unnek nengká	Cows.
Goi áimá ...	Oyánthe hulá ...	Hilá ...	Abbaká ikie ...	A dog.
Goi go numá ...	Oyánthe huyang ...	Hinu ...	Abaká ikineng-ká.	A bitch.
Goini kon ...	Huh he ...	Hirem ...	Ekiye bajek ...	Dogs.
Goye goi bak ...	Huh niyáng he ...	Hinu rem ...	Pabká báng ne bajek.	Bitches.
Báinám ái áimá ...	Oyánthe keyen ..	Ran-pang ...	Abakká chabene	A he-goat.
Báinám ái áimá ...	Oyánthe kenang ...	Rannu ..	Abakká chaben nengká.	A female goat.
Báinám bak ...	Ken he ...	Ran hurem ...	Chaben bajek	Goats.
Chan chánlá áimá ...	Oyánthe ngám pang	Mikhi pang ..	Abakká chibin minank.	A male deer.
Báinám ái áimá ...	Oyánthe khehinang	Mikhi hunu ..	Abakká chibin nengká.	A female deer.
Chánani bak ...	Ngám he ...	Chenu mikhi ...	Chinine bajek	Deer.
Ngái lang gai ...	Mi tangian ...	Ku tai lay ...	Ngá dunká ...	I am.
Nángá án khá ...	Nang ne ..	Nang lay ...	Na dune ...	Thou art.
Khining ngá ákháh ...	Phang tang mátangá	Si lay ...	Bandue ...	He is.

English.	Manipuri.	Kuki.	Khasi.
We are ...	Ikhoi-leiri ...	Kennin nooi ..	Ugi long ..
You are ...	Nang leirilira ..	Nennin nooi ..	Phi long ..
They are ...	Makhoi-leiri ..	Annin nooi ..	Ki long ..
I was ...	Iyak-leirem-me ...	Kehoom kennoi ...	Uga la long ...
Thou wast ...	Nang-leirem-me ..	Nehoom nennooi ..	Me pha la long ...
He was ...	Ma-leire ..	Anihom Armoi ...	U la long ...
We were ...	Ikhoileirem-me ..	Kennin nooi augarha ...	Ugi la long ...
You were ...	Nakhoi-leirem-me ..	Nennin ooni augarha ...	Phi la long ...
They were ...	Makhoi-leire ...	Amin nooi augarha ..	Kilalong ...
Be ...	....	Thunin ...	Long, don ...
To be ...	....	....	Ba'n long, ban don ...
Being ...	.....	Thunin changati. ...	Da long (1), kaha long (2), kaha don (3).
Having been ...	......	Thuninachangka ...	'Yuda la long ...
I may be ...	Iyak-leirangami ..	Kaihum chongthaithennim	Nga lah lean long, nga lah lean down.
I shall be ..	Iyak-leini ..	Kaiham Chongthaithennim	Nga'n long, nga'n don ...
I should be ...	Ikhoina-laideaonatikae ..	In khilloivalin changkaithie	Ka da lea ngan long, ka du lea ng'an don.
Beat ..	Ieiba ...	Varho ...	Shoh ...
To beat ..	......	....,	Ba'n shoh ...
Beating ..	......	Reuokinning ...	Kaba shoh (1), da shoh (2).
Having beaten ..	....	Revok thk ...	'Ynda la shoh ..
I beat ..	Iyak ieige ...	Vong kaithee ...	Nga shoh ...
Thou beatest ..	Nangieio ...	Nanghom varoh ...	Me or pha shoh ...
He beats ..	Ma-eeire ...	Anmani-hi varoh ...	U shoh ...
We beat ..	Ikhoi ieige ...	Kaimani varoh ...	Ngi-ia-shoh ...
You beat ..	Nang ieio ...	Naugmani varoh ...	Ngi-ia-shoh, phi ia shoh ..
They beat ..	Makhoi-ieire ...	Anmani-hi thamka varoh.	Ki shoh, or ki ia-shoh ...
I am beating ..	Iyak ieiri ...	Kaima vokthing ...	Nga dang shoh ...
I was beating ..	Iyak-eiram-me ...	Kaima ken-vok-ning ..	Nga la dang shoh ...
I had beaten ..	Iyakna ieirame ...	Kaima ken-vok ...	Nga la lah shoh ...
I may beat ..	Iyak ieingami ...	Kaima homin-ningkeuon-gohm.	Nga lah ba'n shoh ...
I have beaten ..	.....	....	Nga dang lah shoh ...
I shall beat ..	Iyak-ieini ...	Kaima homin-ningkeuon-gohm.	Nga'n shoh ...
I should beat ..	Iyakna-ieiba-matikoe ...	Kaima vong keti ...	Ka dei ba nga'n da shoh ...
I am beaten ..	Ai-ieiba-fangale ...	Kehom—anevok ...	La dang shoh ia nga ...
I was beaten ..	Ai-ieiba-fangle ...	Kehom-anevokthey ...	La lah shoh ia nga ...
I shall be beaten ..	Ai-ieiba fangni ...	Kaima-nen-voh—ning ..	Yn sa shoh ià nga ...
I go ..	Iyak-challe ...	Kaicho kal kehti ..	Nga leit ...

Singpho.	Naga of Luckimpore.	Naga of Seebsangor.	Miri.	English.
Ináng gáiá áng dai ...	Lahu thang ...	Kem lay ...	Ngá lu dungáyá	We are.
Nanga akha ...	Náng mahu tháne .	Hazam lay ...	Ná dungái ...	You are.
Khini akha oah ...	Chenin thán ...	Humtai lay ...	Kyengdungá	They are.
Ngai oabin dai ...	Mi mátang taya ...	Ku nâ lay ...	Ngá dungái ...	I was.
Li ni aukha ...	Langa neah ...	Nang nâ lay ...	Aune dune ...	Thou wast.
Khini oabin dai ...	Ire matang taya ...	Si nâ lay ...	Bukke dingái	He was.
Inang gaia ang dai ...	La huthang	Kem nâ lay ...	Ngálu dungáyá	We were.
Nang oabin dai ...	Nang mahu thane ..	Hazam nâ lay ...	Nádungái ...	You were.
Khini thing monga dai.	Jeheme thangta ...	Ham nâ lay ...	Byaluc dungáne	They were.
Raiah ...	Madanga ...	Nâ hay ...	Gide ...	Be.
Raidai ...	Madangaleh ...	A chang ...	Gide há ...	To be.
Raidaia ...	Madanga ta ...	Usua ...	Gidengá ...	Being.
......	......	......	......	Having been.
Nái tái ngoá ...	Ngái tá dáng ...	Kuachange ...	Ngá ippá eppe	I may be.
Nái tái gá ...	Ngai dang and ...	Kuachangai ...	Ngá uppe ...	I shall be.
......	......	Kuachangtaibu ...	......	I should be.
Ni ...	Anang ...	Mithan ...	Pái ...	Beat.
Nai dup ái ...	Mábát iká ...	Mia ...	Pákáp ...	To beat.
Dup dái ...	Oyat ikang ...	Milay ...	Pádung ...	Beating.
......	......	Midenpu ...	......	Having beaten.
Ngái dup há ...	Inga me batah ...	Kumia ...	Ngá chung padung.	I beat.
Lii dup dái ...	Langa oyatikang ...	Nange milay ...	Aune pádák ...	Thou beatest.
Khi dup dái ...	Atana oyat ika ...	Si-emilay ...	Byu padak ...	He beats.
I dup há ...	Inga me bat ikong .	Keme mia ...	Ngá lu padung	We beat.
Langi ni dup ...	Langa maba ika ...	Hazam mia ...	Nabub pakane	You beat.
Khni dupha dai ...	Chennin maba ika .	Ham mia ...	Byulun pakane	They beat.
Ngai phe dupdai ...	Inga nang batah ...	Kuamilay ...	Ngam padung	I am beating.
......	Inga oya thenga ...	Kuafitlay ...	......	I was beating.
Ngaiphe dup ha dai...	Inga la oat thang .	Kuafitlay ...	Ngam pat ...	I had beaten.
Ngai dup ngot oa ..	Nga ma ita bibatang	Ku mitouke ...	Nga pape eppe	I may beat.
......	......	......	......	I have beaten.
Ngai duppe ...	Inga thenga ah ...	Kuamia ...	Nga pat ka ...	I shall beat.
......	......	Kuamaupa ...	.....	I should beat.
Ngai phe dup hadai...	Ingala oat thang ...	Kuta atha milay ...	Ngam pat ...	I am beaten.
Ngai phe dup hadai...	Ingala oat thang ...	Kutu fit lay ...	Ngam pat ...	I was beaten.
......	......	Kutu mi ta ...	......	I shall be beaten.
Ngai chang ...	Kikang ...	Ku paue ...	Nga gip ...	I go.

List of English words and phrases with their corresponding words

English.	Manipuri.	Kuki.	Khasi.
Thou goest ...	Nang-chala ...	Naugma kalro ...	Me leit ...
He goes ...	Ma-chale ...	Anmanihi kalro ...	U leit ...
I went ...	Iyak-challame ...	Kai-kenhanga ...	Nga la leit ...
Thou wentest ...	Nang-chalabda ...	Nangma nehanga ...	Me la leit ...
He went ...	Ma-chakre ...	Anmani-hi-nehanga ...	U la leit ...
Go ...	Chala ...	Kalro ...	Khie leit ...
Going ...	Chappa ...	Kathing ...	Da leit (1), aba leit (2) ...
Gone ...	Chalare ...	Kehanga ...	Ba la leit, ba la lah leit ...
What is your name?..	Nangi-naming-karikauge ?	Niriming-ee-mochang? ...	Ka kyrteng jong phi ka long ainh ?
How old is this horse ?	Achhi chhogolgi chehi kaya sure ?	Ma-sakor-hi-kom jakamo ?	Une u kulai ula katno snem, or Une u ku-lai u la don katno snem.
How far is it from here to Kashmir ?	Achhidegi-Kashmirleipak-kaya-labe ?	Mathaka omin-Kashmir ithen-kamoalat ?	Naugne hadub ka shnong Kashmir ka jing ngaikat-no ?
How many sons are there in your father's house ?	Nangi-napagi-macha-kaya-poi ?	Nangma-pa ija kamo ipa om ?	Ha ing utrypa jong phi don katnongut ki khun shinrang ?
I have walked a long way to-day.	Achhi iyakna iom miang koyare.	Khirong kehang ...	Nga la iaid nadub jing-ngai niyuta.
The son of my uncle is married to her sister.	Iyaki khuragimacha nipana may machem laure.	Kifang hak na-hen kifarnoo auai.	U khun u kyn-gi jong nga u la shong kurim bad ka para jong ka.
In the house is the saddle of the white horse.	Ium-achhida chhagol an-ganbagi chhaban.	Sakor-ongoi ke-ina ahom-they roh-homaoni.	Haing don ka jin jong u kulai lib.
Put the saddle upon his back.	......	Sakor choongah they roh pierroh.	Buh ka jui balor jong u ...
I have beaten his son with many stripes.	Iyakna mai macha nipab licheina ieire.	Thunahn ina nabi nium-vokim kevok.	Nga la sympatka u khun jong u da ki bun ki jing sympot.
He is grazing cattle on the top of the hill.	Chingi mathakta mana chhal chhendenaleire.	Pahar choongah cherrad-in luia fah.	U pynbam phlang-ia ki jing ri halor lum.
He is sitting on a horse under that tree.	U-achhigi makhada chha-gol gi mathakda lei.	Thing-nuhuia sakor choon-gah atung then.	U shong halor u kulai hapoh kato ka ding.
His brother is taller than his sister.	Magi manaona machem degi ayange.	Ania boongalier un-unekin	U para jong u, u kham jerong (or san) ia ka para jong u.*

* (Literal and ambiguous.) But when the two " his 's" mean

Singpho.	Naga of Luckimpore.	Naga of Seebsaugor.	Miri.	English.
Nii rang dái ...	Lang tha ...	Nang paw la ...	Aoye giniá ...	Thou goest
Khin ráng dái ...	Ire tha ...	Si pawl a ...	Bye giniá ...	He goes.
Ngái oáráng dái ...	Aoang thang ...	Ku jale ...	Ngá gini ...	I went.
Nii há dái ...	Lang thanta ...	Nang jale ...	Aoye gikáp ...	Thou wentest.
Khi chá há dái ...	Atela thangta ...	Si jale ...	Bye gikáp ...	He went.
Chal ...	Kau ...	Paula ...	Gikáng ká ...	Go.
Chákan ...	Chhebka ...	Jale ...	Giep ...	Going.
Chá ha dai ...	Thanta ...	Pau e na ...	Gikáp ...	Gone.
Nángá ming mákhái	Mamin marva ...	Nang bule manpu ...	Nangá minángká.	What is your name?
Idái gom ráng oá pit khe deh duhá.	Emak iye pa chhenta rang pa madanga.	Abi rang heman pu ...	Go ráije chabak ditáge eddek edung.	How old is this horse ?
Náng gái nan Kásmir ge deh yán.	E Kasmira la pa chhet janga.	Ete khange abe inlam Kasmiri kapang.	Chákke Kásmire e anappa edi ke dung.	How far is it from here to Kashmir ?
Na lang oah na ontá gai mang gedeh ngah dai.	Maba hu ma nanga neta chhenta.	Nang hanpama hamma abitaibu sisi neusa.	Nanga bukke enchamla kaoe edikke dung.	How many sons are there in your father's house ?
Nga dai nih saba dudam di oah rang dai dam hang dai.	Nga theiya bala nang phang tak.	Ku ani asule ham dawa	Nga chin ai rup gigatta.	I have walked a long way to-day.
Khia ganau kenge oah dai na kachai khung ran ha.	Iremi an ire iyang teying didi chama kap ika.	Ku apali husa usua hunau toi zingle.	Byu gamma paike aomma midamat.	The son of my uncle is married to her sister.
Aug tha tukhaih nga dai pak paa gomrang yikrang oana raya	Humiyo khan oya jin mak papanang ma danga.	Man tha zinhamma tai le.	Chide gaduchi gobere pudak amirna tam lik namme.	In the house is the saddle of the white horse.
Pang kap oa khina sing mangeh khrat dioh.	Atmanang khakka	Siku takma zim khaley	Gadu chimbik amirda tam likt.	Put the saddle upon his back.
Khi kacha pheh ngai siba khin dio ha.	Achanang iya ranga aoyatak.	Ku-e fid deua asule siku hosan.	Byung ang demai rupa pat.	I have beaten his son with many stripes.
Khi bom bum ding ngai siyah remdai.	Haha nang mau bamika.	Mihu ni ele ha hutu.	Byu adi tanen inne gae bar dem kang su dung.	He is grazing cattle on the top of the hill.
Sidai ong tah katah i gom rang jatang dinga dai	Iman khanang maktam nang chang ika.	Sieman takma nale panu tangma rang khunma jakle.	Byu inne gae bar kei kau gore dem change dung.	He is sitting on a horse under that tree.
Khina ko phu gah khina ganan ong lah yah ga tang.	Anang tei yang nama anang te achho yang.	Chiku hanau fai chiku sikou hanas lale.	Byuk chache byung birme dem penam áiare dák.	His brother is taller than his sister.

the same person it will be—*Ja la ka para kham san u para jong u.*

English.	Manipuri.	Kuki.	Khasi.
The price of that is two rupees and a half.	Achhigi maman lopani-makhae.	Mathero munnhi chengnika nindooli	Ka dor kato kalong ar tyng ka pia.
My father lives in that small house.	Iyaki pabna ium apichha-fada leire.	Khipa ma in the-asun a-om	U kypa jong uga u shong ha kato ka ing rit.
Give this rupee to him.	Achhi lopa maba pia ...	Thanka enaka pero ...	Ai kane ka tyngka ia u ...
Take those rupees from him.	Achhi lopa khibik mangan degi looro.	Ma nihanga thanka taro ...	Shine noh-ia kito ki tyng ka na u.
Beat him well and bind him with ropes.	Maba iyam ieiro khaurina pulla	Nieon thunkinthu kinla ruin pierroh.	'Yuda shoh eh ia u, teh da ki tyllai.
Draw water from the well.	Kua degi icching laura ...	Thin thuka thui choiro ...	Tongune naka pukri ...
Walk before me.	Iyaki iyanagda kaero ...	Kimo-kinna kalra ...	Jaid sha shiwa jong nga ...
Whose boy comes behind you ?	Achhi angang macha ko-nana nangi natung indna lai ?	Thu na imo niengah ahung ?	U khynnah jong no ub a wan na shadin jong phi ?
From whom did you buy that ?	Konadegid achchi bi rui ?...	Ma thero kathey thu nihangah ni chogmo ?	Nangno phi la thied ia kato ?
From a shop-keeper of the village.	Kulgi dukandar degi ...	Ke chogna kua maha jonina kencho.	Na u nong die jong die ha shnong.

Singpho.	Naga of Luckimpore.	Naga of Seebsaugor	Miri.	English.
Khina monu dala ong khang thuli reh.	Phani khath heh athapa.	Usna nun khaomi athati	Edak atang kange anyi kaná tebakka.	The price of that is two rupees and a half.
Nge oah sidai ong tah kiyi gai nga dai.	Iba pahuma chane rang tanga.	Ku apa usua ham sama anokle.	Ngá ke ábbu ádaye kamu dud.	My father lives in that small house.
Ong dai kom krang dala khiphe yan.	Un phathepa kak...	Ea nun khau usua ang laka.	Chimbarakang ábár chim bum bibi taká.	Give this rupee to him.
Khi thang gai lan kom phrang theng latang na.	Angeya ngun hi ugaba kar.	Usu anpa nun pai jan hai.	Bik kanak ede mbá rakang dembande koen.	Take those rupees from him.
Aidi dupunah galai sing rü khang dau.	Jarang obad ate ruma khák chhen.	Usua maile maithen athasu usua lunge khadu.	Byum air pát rabike ená.	Beat him well and bind him with ropes.
Khabang gailan i yin jah ong.	Ja nad khan ma jakhan.	Takai anpa tikha hai	Chibonák achi getka.	Draw water from the well.
Nge man idamo ..	Jma karang phang khama.	Ku pam thoma aham hai.	Nga ka ne dun-gig min nang ka.	Walk before me.
Nana ning dim iga-dai na mang cha dai	Madinang han chao yang ira.	Nang faima oham pu	Nak nedung chek kaoe gidang	Whose boy comes behind you ?
Gadai nan sidai oa miri laba dai.	Hange oya rita oya irepa.	Oma sapu ...	Chekka lak retang bibke nak.	From whom did you buy that ?
Mereng na pa ga oa aima gailan.	Haoya tha chang te neoya.	Tinkha unpa hat ...	Dalung kabe mannanak na-tang ni.	From a shop-keeper of the village.

LANGUAGES OF THE NORTH-EAST OF ASSAM.

English.	Aka.	Duffla.	Miri.
Numerals.			
One	Un	Akin	Áka
Two	Guni	Ani	Anyeka
Three	Gethan	Am	Áunaka
Four	Bli	Apli	Ápika
Five	Buṅgu	Ango	Ánaka
Six	Re	Akia	Ákanaka
Seven	Mia	Kanug	Kinitaka
Eight	Sige	Plognug	Painika
Nine	Esthen	Kyo	Kananka
Ten	Len	Rungchung	Eünaka
Twenty	Genelen	Chamni	Kuri
Fifty	Buṅgolen	Chamuo	Áraikuri
Hundred	Boloṅun	Cham-rungchung	Eha
Pronouns.			
I	Niang	Ngo	Na
We	Ani	Ngolu	Na-lu
Thou	Pho	Noh	Na
You	Pho	Noh	Na-lu
He	Thang	Asi	Bi
They	Phoi	Mige	Bu-lu
Of me	Niang	Ngokue	Nak
Of us	Anithe	Anga	Na-lukke
Of thee	....	Asoko	Na-kke
Of you	....	Asoko	Na-lugike
Of him	Nunathai	Alokoa	Bi-kke
Of them	Numan-nathai	Alopanga	Bu-lukake
Mine	Niang	Ngokue	Nak
Our	Anithe	Anga	Na-lukake
Thine	Phoithai	Asoko	Na-kke
Your	Phoithai	Asoko	Na-lukike
His	Nunathai	Alokoa	Bi-ki
Their	Numan-nathai	Alopanga	Bu-lukike
Hand	Gi	Lake	Álák
Foot	Gle	Leh	Ále
Nose	Nubiong	Nyopom	Iëbung
Eye	Mre	Nyegh	Ámịde
Mouth	Neug	Gām	Nappang
Tooth	Thu	Fi	Atreu

Abor.	Sulikátá Mishmees.	Digarú Mishmees.	English.
Ákka ...	Ékhé ..	Ékhing ..	One.
Anikka ...	Káni ..	Káeng ..	Two.
Ánmak ...	Kásh ..	Kácháng ..	Three.
Ápio ...	Káppi ..	Kápi ..	Four.
Pilanka ...	Mángá ..	Mángá ..	Five.
Akkeko ...	Ahe ..	Anhrá ..	Six.
Kililák ...	Joh ..	Uré ..	Seven.
Palik ...	Ilú ..	Ilum ..	Eight.
Kanengka ...	Khili ..	Kaeling ..	Nine.
Iongka ...	Hush ..	Halang ..	Ten.
Iengnie ...	Anihush ..	Kachiling ..	Twenty.
Eingpilank ...	Mangalon ..	Mángáháláng ..	Fifty.
Lingka ...	Malú ..	Malum ..	Hundred.
U'lú ...	Ngialúmbro ..	Ning or Há ..	I.
Milúm ...	Ehundna ..	Taji ..	We.
Ngo ...	Ngio ..	Nga ..	Thou.
Ngolo ...	Ehund ..	Nga ..	You.
Ngo-bolu ...	Ngio-ápu ..	Ngoeláng ..	He.
Milúme ...	He-aibu ..	Ngoelang-tha .	They.
Ngolona ...	Nge-ehunde ..	Lomening ..	Of me.
Ulukke ...	Ngaji-appo ..	Ningoge ..	Of us
Buluke ...	Newji ..	Uagé or nega ..	Of thee.
Buluke ...	Newji ..	Uagé or nega ..	Of you.
Bukke ..	Mimút or Mit ..	Dege ..	Of him.
Búlúke-upek ...	New-ipo-máya ..	Uaga-lánge ..	Of them.
Ngolo ná ...	New-ehunde ..	Lomening ..	Mine.
Ngolo-apekap ...	Ngialadu ..	Ningoge ..	Our.
Nalukke or buluke ...	Newji ..	Nega ..	Thine.
Nalukke or buluke ..	Newji ..	Nega ..	Your.
Bukke ...	Mimut or mit ..	Dege ..	His.
Búlúke-upek ...	New-ipo-maya ..	Uaga-lánge ..	Their.
Áláge ...	Akhmo ..	Hattia ..	Hand.
Leppia ..	Byápá ..	U'groká ..	Foot.
Ngyabung ...	Enabo ..	Heliagom ..	Nose.
Ámik ...	Elábyá ..	Molom ..	Eye.
Nappang ...	Ekabe ..	Takkay ..	Mouth.
Ïpang ...	Támbyá ..	Lá ..	Tooth.

English.	Aka.	Duffla.	Miri.
Ear ..	Jho ...	Nyorung ...	Nerung ..
Hair ..	Hupshe ...	Dumpo ...	Dumit ..
Head. ..	Tokiang ...	Demeg ...	Tukko ..
Tongue ..	Jakse ...	Ro ...	Yaper ..
Belly ..	Lon ...	Kopo ...	Áki ..
Back ..	Gebang ...	Lamko ...	Lámka ..
Iron ..	Sen ...	Rogdur ...	Yogir ..
Gold ..	Shen ...	En ...	Áin ..
Silver ..	Lemen ...	Dumpin ...	Mulkang ..
Father ..	Aboa ...	Abo ...	Ábba ..
Mother ..	Ane ...	Ane ...	Ánne ..
Brother ..	Nu ...	Abung, Tete, Boro ...	Burra ..
Sister ..	Nie ...	Ame, Burme ...	Birme ..
Man ..	Nu ...	Bangni ...	Ámme ..
Woman ..	Nimre ...	Nyame ...	Neng ..
Wife ..	Zi ...	Nyafung ...	Miäng ..
Child ..	Guli ...	Anga ...	Koue ..
Son ..	Zu ...	Kao ...	Áüa ..
Daughter ..	Zue ...	Nyameka ...	Omma ..
Slave ..	Nullo ...	Nyara ...	Pakba ..
Cultivator ..	Nimiang ...	Kedeh ...	Árigija ..
Shepherd ..	Khen ...	Rakhidono ...	Rakhine ..
God ..	Nitchao ...	Oiu ...	Isor ..
Devil ..	Tehimu ...	Kencha-deo (evil spirit)..	Bhut ..
Sun ..	Jho ...	Doni ..	Daäniá ..
Moon ..	Lu ...	Polo ..	Pala ..
Star ..	Litsoṅ ...	Taker ..	Tákáre ..
Fire ..	Meh ...	Emeh ..	Umme ..
Water ..	Vza ...	Esi ..	Átse ..
House ..	Nen ...	Ou ..	Ákume ..
Horse ..	Gorra ...	(No Duffla equivalent) ..	Gure ..
Cow ..	Shufshe ...	Hene ..	Inne ..
Dog ..	Shazi ...	Eki ...	Ikiä ..
Cat ..	Khushu ...	Ase ...	Mendári ..
Cock ..	Dublang ...	Porok ...	Parak ..
Duck ..	Ngosa ...	Hāṅ ...	Pajap ..
Hen ..	Done ...	....	....
Ass ..	Shubabu ...	(No Duffla equivalent) ...	Gádhá ..
Camel ..	....	(Ditto ditto.) ...	Ut ..

East of Assam.—(Continued.)

Abor.	Sulikátá Mishmees.	Degará Mishmees.	English.
Nyerung ...	Akuná ...	Nakra ...	Ear.
Damude ...	Thámbyá ...	Tháng ...	Hair.
Ugke-takku ...	Eku-ekura ...	Hamkuru ...	Head.
Ayah ...	Lina ...	Thalingna ...	Tongue.
Áki ...	Khiapu ...	Kitápung ...	Belly.
Lámku ...	Erambo ...	Ipring ...	Back.
Ukdin ...	Si ...	Si ...	Iron.
Ebane ...	Pidi ...	Pádi ...	Gold.
Murkang ...	Pau ...	Páwe ...	Silver.
Ábo ...	Nábá ...	Nábá ...	Father.
Nál ...	Náni ...	Námá ...	Mother.
Ániánge ...	Áliá ...	Pamro ...	Brother.
Burme ...	Athepoá ...	Nábi ...	Sister.
Milange ...	Meya ...	Máwá ...	Man.
Mienga ...	Iáh ...	Miawá ...	Woman.
Ome mienga ...	Áku ...	Miawa (" Wife" not used)	Wife.
Anjineka ...	Áwu ...	Áblayá ...	Child.
Ounga ...	Ábro ...	Ua ...	Son.
Pápie ...	Amyau ...	Ayá ...	Daughter.
Pákbo ...	Eppo ...	Umpo ...	Slave.
Agre-gerurau ...	Ári ...	Bayah ...	Cultivator.
Soben-kyane ...	Maji-halu ...	Babi-hosuá ...	Shepherd.
Dane-talenge ...	Ini-huná ...	Ring ...	God.
Ayu ...	Daen ...	Taliah ...	Devil.
Dani ...	Ini ...	Ringdá ...	Sun.
Pala ...	Elá ...	Haluda ...	Moon.
Takar ...	Ádikro ...	Káding ...	Star.
Emme ...	Amihú ...	Naming ...	Fire.
Áse ...	Maji ...	Maji ...	Water.
Ekúm ...	Uka ...	Áng ...	House.
Guré ...	Geera ...	Gouri ...	Horse.
Ánek ...	Majookru ...	Kru-majoo ...	Cow.
Iki ...	Ikú ...	Lookui ...	Dog.
Kadari ...	Majari ...	Majari-dá ...	Cat.
Porok ...	Eto ...	Mityo ...	Cock.
Pejábo ...	Dekibu ...	Krembú Oálá ...	Duck.
....	....	....	Hen.
(None in this District) ...	(None in this District) ...	(None in this District) ...	Ass.
Ditto ...	Ditto ...	Ditto ...	Camel.

English.	Aka.	Duffla.	Miri.
Bird ..	Buzzu ..	Pata ..	Patáng ..
Go ..	Phokhame (" you go.") ..	Ngiku ..	Gikapen ..
Eat ..	Sune ..	Dutto ..	Datta ..
Sit ..	Iongme ..	Dungto ..	Dota ..
Come ..	Hademe ..	Ngtoku ..	Sapagalá ..
Beat ..	Lubrokheme ..	Jungto ..	Páttaká ..
Stand ..	Giume ..	Dokto ..	Dáktaka ..
Die ..	Thidamun (" to die") ..	Siktaribo (" to die.") ..	Si-a ..
Give ..	Bime ..	Keh ..	Bitpaná ..
Run ..	Zougme ..	Furrto ..	Duktaka ..
Up ..	Meliviang ..	Aopa ..	Táleng ..
Near ..	Mani ..	Genekto ..	Aninsa ..
Who ..	Ṭhiu ..	Helo ..	Sekan ..
And ..	Aio ..	Angneba ..	Áru ..
Yes ..	Mivi ..	Eh ..	Agi ..
Down ..	Melenen ..	Arungpa ..	Ámang ..
Far ..	Maren ..	Adopo ..	Mateng ..
What ..	Ṭhen ..	Hogue ..	Akkan ..
But ..	....	(No Duffla equivalent) ..	Kintu ..
No ..	Ngoa ..	Moh ..	Má ..
Before ..	Nivia ..	Atokto ..	Ananná ..
Behind	Manen ..	Koyungto ..	Ledda ..
Why ..	Thurede ..	Hogobo ..	Akapa ..
If ..	Saio ..	Hobolape ..	Jadi ..
Alas! ..	Aia! ..	Tah! ..	Yá yá ..
A father ..	Aboa ..	Abo ..	Ábátere ..
Of a father ..	....	......	Ábbatere-loke ..
To a father ..	....	......	Ábba-kan-kepe ..
From a father ..	....	......	Abba-kan-lákum ..
Two fathers ..	Guni aboa ..	Abo ani ..	Abba-anyeka ..
Fathers ..	Ani aboa ..	Abo arukpa ..	Ábbu-kading ..
Of fathers ..	....	......	Ábbu-kading-ke ..
To fathers ..	....	......	Abbu-kading-kepe ..
From fathers ..	....	......	Abbu-kading-lakke ..
A daughter ..	....	Nyameka ..	Ommá-terak ..
Of a daughter ..	....	......	Ommá-teroke ..
To a daughter ..	....	......	Ommá-ter-dakkepe ..
From a daughter ..	....	......	Ommá-ter-kakke ..
Two daughters ..	....	Nyameka anigo ..	Omma-anyeka ..

East of Assam.—(Continued.)

Abor.	Sulikátá Mishmees.	Digarú Mishmees.	English.
Peotáng ...	Pya ...	Om-pya ...	Bird.
Giká ...	Báná ...	Buná ...	Go.
Doyo ...	Há ...	Thana ...	Eat.
Dootká ...	Jibá ...	Diná ...	Sit.
Kájo ...	Ebalibi ...	Hánáná ...	Come.
Ditka ...	Hoop ...	Hoo-íná ...	Beat.
Dáktolá-dákot ...	Deva ...	De-dena ...	Stand.
Hikáng ...	Hiba ...	Hina-hibo ...	Die.
Bito ...	Hábá ...	Hángná ...	Give.
Dookáng ...	Dobo ...	Chou ...	Run.
Teung ...	Etúdú ...	Taji ...	Up.
Mungiá ...	Ánomá ...	Ungya ...	Near.
Uma ...	Á-áya ...	Cha-kádá ...	Who.
Biánge ...	Ámá-má ...	Oago ...	And.
Eda ...	Áya ...	Oaú ...	Yes.
Roongkinge ...	Ripoma ...	Hálá ...	Down.
Motunge ...	Mralo ...	Dá ...	Far.
Ingkok ...	Esia ...	Umja ...	What.
Byánge ...	Ámámá ...	Roypinge ...	But.
Kámáng ...	Ngybo ...	Áyum ...	No.
Nápáyápo ...	Áhyá ...	Hioya ...	Before.
Melám ...	Epindolu ...	Hamyo ...	Behind.
Dekeku ...	Ejap ...	Uajá ...	Why.
Dem-ma-moolo ...	Ejamigo ...	Roiping ...	If.
Ah! Ah! ...	Akh! akh! ...	Eh! eh! ...	Alas!
Ábo-átaluk ...	Ekke-nábá ...	Khinge-nábá ...	A father.
Ataluk-ábo kepá ...	Ekke-nábá-juibo ...	Khinge-nábá-lánke ...	Of a father.
Ataluk-ábo-kepe ...	Ekke-nábá-ji ...	Khingi-nábábá ...	To a father.
Ataluk-ábo-lenne ...	Ekke-nábá-kepowji ...	Khingi-nábá-egu leá ...	From a father.
Ánikka ábo ...	Káni-nábá ...	Káeng-nábá ...	Two fathers.
Ábo-búlú ...	Nábá-ejá ...	Nábáláng-nábá ...	Fathers.
Ábo-búlú-kepá ...	Nábá-juibo ...	Nábá lánke ...	Of fathers.
Ábo-búlú-kepe ...	Nábá-ji ...	Nábáláng-ombá ...	To fathers.
Ábo-búlú-keluk ...	Nábágá-juibo ...	Nábáláng-duná ...	From fathers.
Átaluk-ome or papie ...	Kepate-amyau or ayah ...	Khinge-aya ...	A daughter.
Ome ataluk len ...	Aya páte ah ...	Aya-egoge ...	Of a daughter.
Omeke ataluk ...	Aya-ji ...	Aya-úabá ...	To a daughter.
Ataluk ome lábum ...	Patela-aya ...	Khingi-aya ...	From a daughter.
Ánikka óme ...	Kani-aya ...	Kaeng-aya ...	Two daughters.

English.	Aka.	Duffla.	Miri.
Daughters ..	....	Nyame arukpa ..	Omma-kading ..
Of daughters ..	....	......	Omma-kading-ke ..
To daughters ..	....	......	Omma-kading-kapa ..
From daughters ..	....	......	Omma-kading-lagane ..
A good man ..	Nu mevi ..	Alepa ..	Áka íne ámme ..
Of a good man ..	....	......	Áka íne ammi-ke ..
To a good man ..	....	......	Áka íne ammi-kapa ..
From a good man ..	....	......	Áka íne ammi dekke ..
Two good men ..	....	Ani alepa ..	Ine amme anyeka ..
Good men ..	Nu mevihaṅ ..	Alepa arukpa ..	Ámme íne kiding ..
Of good men ..	....	......	Ámme íne kiding kakke.
To good men ..	....	......	Ine amme kiding-kapa ..
From good men ..	....	......	Ine amme kiding lagang.
A good woman ..	Nimre mevi ..	Nyame anyapa ..	Aka ine neng ..
Good women ..	Nimre mevihaṅ ..	Nyame pang alepa ..	Ine neng-kiding ..
A bad boy ..	Nu meni ..	Kao karu ..	Aka ímane kauá ..
A bad girl ..	Nimre meni ..	Nyameka karu ..	Aka imáne kanauka ..
Good ..	Mevi ..	Alepa ..	Ine ..
Better ..	Honte mevi (Than that good.)	Humpe humpe alepa (*i.e.*, More more good.)	Eda-ine ..
Best ..	Ditto	Ditto ..	Eda-íru-dung ..
High ..	Miphiang ..	Aopa ..	O-dak ..
Higher ..	Honte miphiang (Than that high.)	Humpe humpe aoiyopa, (*i.e*, More more high.)	Oddur-dak ..
Highest ..	Ditto	Ditto ..	Od-bun-dak ..
A horse ..	....	No Duffla equivalent. "Horses" are called ghoras, and "mares" ghoris or maiki ghora.	Gure-adarka ..
A mare ..	Gorra-mene ..		Gure renaka ..
Horses ..	....		Gure kiding ..
Mares ..	....		Gure rene kiding ..
A bull ..	Mubze ..	Hebo ..	Garu ettum tuma namme
A cow ..	Mene ..	Hene ..	Garu-inne-ádárk ..
Bulls ..	Mubze-menou ..	Hebo arukpa ..	Ettum-tuma-namme kiding.
Cows ..	Mene-menou ..	Hene arukpa ..	Guru-inne-adark ..
A dog ..	Shazi ..	Eki kibo (*i.e.*, a male dog)	Iki-ádark ..
A bitch ..	Shazi-mene ..	Eki kine (*i.e.*, a female dog.)	Iki-kine-adark ..
Dogs ..	Shazi-menou ..	Eki kibo arukpa ..	Iki-kiding ..
Bitches ..	....	Eki kine arukpa ..	Iki kine-kiding ..

East of Assam.—(Continued.)

Abor.	Sulikátá Mishmees.	Digarú Mishmees.	English.
Ome-kiding ..	Aya-dolumbro ..	Ah-láng ..	Daughters.
Ome kidinke ..	Aya-jipo ..	Ah lánge ..	Of daughters.
Ome kidi-lukke ..	Aya lumbro ..	Ah lang-báge ..	To daughters.
Ome kidiluk ..	Ah lumbro ..	Ah lang dogo ..	From daughters.
Átaluk ayne ámya ..	Khenge premupo ..	Khinge-prao-náme ..	A good man.
Ataluk ayne mil ..	Khenge premuji ..	Khinge-prao-náme úage..	Of a good man.
Ataluk ayne-miem ..	Khenge premujiá ..	Khinge-prao-náme gao ..	To a good man.
Kidiluk ayne ámya ..	Khenge-premu-polumbro	Khinge-prao náme dogo..	From a good man.
Anikka-ayne-ámya ..	Kani-praya-premu ..	Kaeng-prá-máeh ..	Two good men.
Ámya-ayne-ápoya ..	Prá-lumbro ..	Pra-máeh-oeláng ..	Good men.
Ayne-ámy-kidinge ..	Prá-imo-dolumbro ..	Pra-maeh-lángure ..	Of good men.
Ayne-amy-kidilukke ..	Prá-imo-dolumbroji ..	Pra-máeh-lángbá ..	To good men.
Ayneji-amya-kidilukke ..	Pra-imola-pradoibu imo dolumbroji.	Pra da pragomoh maeh roilangdo.	From good men.
Ataluk ayrunek mienga..	Khenge pradu-aya ..	Khinge-pra-miawa ..	A good woman.
Ayru mimen-kidinge ..	Pradu-aya ..	Pra-mia ..	Good women.
Ataluk ay támá ah ..	Kepate (or, khenge) nápá khi ah.	Khinge práúm ah ..	A bad boy.
Ataluk ayma-mimek ..	Khenge-mipathy áku ..	Khinge-prayam-mia ..	A bad girl.
Ayrunek or aydo ..	Pradu or praijah or athopra	Prá ..	Good.
Aidák-edem pesin-aiadak	La praibo pradaibo ..	Prá uagra prá ..	Better.
Apúng kempe aiadak ..	Tapum praibo ..	Jomme-oú tagre prá ..	Best.
Bodod ..	Ruendo ..	Uaji ..	High.
Uwitdak apung kem pun námá bodoiadak.	Ruendo ji iruendo ..	Uaji gáme uaji ..	Higher.
Apung kempune bodod..	Tapume ji ruendo ..	Jomme uaji ..	Highest.
Ataluk gúre ..	Kepate geera ..	Khinge gouri ..	A horse.
Rele gúre ..	Kepate geera ápi ..	Uapi gouri ..	A mare.
Gure kidinge ..	Geera pajaibon ..	Gouri lánge ..	Horses.
Gure kidarde, or gure bodok	Geera apidr ..	Gouri láng ..	Mares.
Ataluk mepakut chowoo..	Kepáte áheprá ádeva máju	Khinge liakobo maju ..	A bull.
Ataluk chownek chow ..	Kepate majú kro ..	Khinge maju kro ..	A cow.
Mepakutá chow bodok ..	Majú áhe pelá doi-ebon..	Maju láng, or maju lánge	Bulls.
Chow nek kidinge ..	Maju dolombro ..	Maju láng-bá ..	Cows.
Ataluk ekki ..	Kepate ekú ..	Khinge lukui ..	A dog.
Ataluk kinek ekki ..	Kepate ekú kro ..	Khinge uápikro lukui ..	A bitch.
Ekki kidinge ..	Ekú pájá, or ekú dú ..	Lukui láng ..	Dogs.
Ekki kinek kidáre ..	Api ekú doi-ebon ..	Uapikro lukui roilang ..	Bitches.

English.	Aka.	Duffla.	Miri.
A he-goat ..	Shubshen-mubze ..	Sabin Binpo ..	Saven-adurk-Benba ...
A she-goat ..	„ mene ..	Sabin Bine ..	Saven-benne-adark ...
Goats ..	Shubshen-mubro ..	Sabin arukpa ..	Saven-kiding ...
A male deer ..	Shu-mubze ..	Sodum dombo ..	Domsong-sabo-adark ...
A female deer ..	Shu-mene ..	Sodum domne ..	Domsong-sone-adark ...
Deer ..	Shu-mubro ..	Sodum arukpa ..	Domsong-kiding ...
I am ..	......	......	Na-dong ...
Thou art ..	......	......	Na done ...
He is ..	......	......	Bido ...
We are ..	......	......	Nâ-lu do ...
You are ..	......	......	Nalusin done ...
They are ..	......	......	Buludo ...
I was ..	......	......	Nâlu doai ...
Thou wast ..	......	......	Nasin dongka ...
He was ..	......	......	Bisin dongai ...
We were ..	......	......	Nâlusin dongai ...
You were ..	......	......	Nâlusin dongai ...
They were ..	......	......	Bulusin dongai ...
Be ..	......	......	Ipane ...
To be ..	......	......	Kaiepa ...
Being ..	......	......	......
Having been ..	......	......	Katidainap ...
I may be ..	......	......	Nâmolap ...
I shall be ..	......	......	Nâîpa ...
I should be ..	......	......	Nâiparnne ...
Beat ..	......	......	Pattaka ...
To beat ..	......	......	Pakaso ...
Beating ..	......	......	Pagoiala ...
Having beaten ..	......	......	Panaka ...
I beat ..	......	Ngo jungto ..	Nâpasa ...
Thou beatest ..	......	......	Napáta ...
He beats ..	......	......	Bipata ...
We beat ..	......	......	Nâlupata ...
You beat ..	......	......	Nâlupata ...
They beat ..	......	......	Belupalu ...
I am beating ..	......	......	Nâpatidungdo ...
I was beating ..	......	......	Nâpatidaná ...
I had beaten ..	......	......	Nâpatara ...
I may beat ..	......	......	Nâpalap ...

East of Assam.—(Continued.)

Abor.	Sulikátá Mishmees.	Degares Mishmess.	English.
Ataluk ohoben ..	Kepate maji ..	Khinge mábi (or maji) ..	A he-goat.
Ataluk mime ohoben ..	Kepate api akro maji ..	Khinge uapi mábi kro ..	A she-goat.
Choben benne kidare ..	Maji dolombro ..	Mabi lángbá ..	Goats.
Ataluk ábuk ohimone ..	Kepate áron májo ..	Khinge kari máju ..	A male deer.
Ataluk ohonne ohimone..	Kepate ápi májo ..	Khinge uapi máju ..	A female deer.
Chimone ..	Majo ..	Maju ..	Deer.
Ulu dúnede ..	Ngia lumbro la ji ji ..	Ha majo or Ning majo ..	I am.
Ngo andra duneá ..	Ngio muji gá ..	Ngá ja mago idi ..	Thou art.
Ngo bolug dúnede ..	Ngio apuji ..	Ngleelang májo ..	He is.
Milum dunede ..	Ehundna jigá ..	Tojí máj ..	We are.
Ngolo dunea ..	Ehund ji ji ..	Nga idigé ..	You are.
Mi-lu-mé dunede ..	He-aibu ia ji jigá ..	Ngoe lang-tha idi máj ..	They are.
Ulu dúneá né ..	Ngia lumbro igápo ..	Ning idi má ..	I was.
Ngo dúneá né ..	Ngio jigjá ..	Nga iappa or gna idi má..	Thou wast.
Ngo-bolu bomáde dúneáb	Ngio-ápu mujiji ..	Ngoe lang iappa ..	He was.
Milum tená dungáné ..	Ehundna jiga ..	Taji lang idimá ..	We were.
Ngolo du ngáné ..	Ehund mujiga ..	Nga iáppá ..	You were.
Milu má búlú du ngáné..	He-aibu mujiga ..	Ngoelangtha iáppá ..	They were.
Al rúné dópé ..	Aibo ah ápá ..	Emago esábo ..	Be.
E derung ..	Aji poyá ..	Chabon ..	To be.
Ngá ná ..	Ngá-é ..	Hachadima ..	Being.
Bomjáh ..	Eja jipo mijah ..	Muja mang chabo ..	Having been.
Ulu ipebo ..	Ngialumbro eyokachna ..	Ning chanane ..	I may be.
Ulu ippe ..	Ngialumbro kachna ..	Ning chóendé ..	I shall be.
Ulu dejie ..	Ngialumbro mumota ápá	Ning ichabo ..	I should be.
Pyepé, papebo or ditaké..	Nupá áhu prá wá ..	Hui huiboing ..	Beat.
Pyepé papebor ..	Núpá áhú prá wá ..	Hui huiboing ..	To beat.
Ditala ..	Ahú lyáh ..	Huiah mo ..	Beating.
Ditálá ná ..	Ahi lyah ..	Hui ámá ..	Having beaten.
Ulu pyepe papebo ..	Ngialumbro ahi lyah ..	Ning hui huiboing ..	I beat.
Ngo ditaké ..	Ngio ahu lyah ..	Nga huiah ..	Thou beatest.
Ngo bolu ditané ..	Ngio-apu ahu lyah ..	Ngoelang hui ámá ..	He beats.
Milum páduné ..	Ehundna apu prálá ..	Tajihindé ..	We beat.
Ngolo ditane ..	Ehund ahu lyah ..	Nga huiah ..	You beat.
Milume bolú ditá ..	He-aibu ahulyah ..	Ngoelang-tha huiah ..	They beat.
Ulu ditálá ..	Ngialombro mujiji lyah	Ning majo mo huiah ..	I am beating.
Ulu dita ..	Ngialombro igapo muja	Ning idimah nuiah ..	I was beating.
Ulu padúlal ditá ..	Ngialombro ahu muja lyah	Ning huiah miag ..	I had beaten.
Ulu haidup dita ..	Ngialombro padunépya ahu.	Ning huiah háné-ing ..	I may beat.

English.	Aka.	Duffla.	Miri.
I shall beat ..	......	......	Nâpápa ..
I should beat ..	......	......	Nâpaperune ..
I am beaten ..	......	......	Nâm pata ..
I was beaten ..	......	......	Nâm páká ..
I shall be beaten ..	......	......	Nâm pápa ..
I go ..	......	Ngo ngbo ..	Nâ gikape ..
Thou goest ..	......	......	Na gikálá ..
He goes ..	......	......	Bigiá ..
I went ..	......	Ngo ngpane ..	Nâgika ..
Thou wentest ..	......	......	Nagikan ..
He went ..	......	......	Bigikan ..
Go ..	......	Ngniku ..	Gikapen ..
Going ..	......	Ngne Kobobo ..	Gila ..
Gone ..	......	Ngne Koba ..	Gikang ..
What is your name? ..	Nimre za tenthene (Your name what is called?)	Hogo mangmina (what name.)	Nakke amine akkon ..
How old is this horse? ..	......	......	Ide gure detakpe idi-ka-idun
How far is it from here to Kashmir?	......	......	Sakke kasmir bapa idika mate dáng.
How old are you? ..	Nidren kunia (Your age what is?)	......	......
How far is it from Tezpore to your house?	......	Tezporiso noubo hodugo adopa (From Tezpore your home how far is.)	......
How many sons are there in your father's house?	Ni aboaner kunia zu due? (Your father how many sons has?)	Nao aboga kaoa akupa (Father's house sons how many.)	Nakke abbaterloke a-kum-nak ana idekan.
I have walked a long way to-day.	Hungu meringi dene (To-day a long way have come.)	Ngo adobo angena solo (I far have walked to-day)	Nâ sila abaka giga tai ..
The son of my uncle is married to his sister.	......	Ngo piega kao maga bor-mem sebedodona (My uncle's son his sister has married.)	Nâke paike ane bikke bir-mina midangem mola langka.
In the house is the saddle of the white horse.	Neme lonru mugrang gorra zimduene (In the house the white horse's) (saddle is.)	......	Kampane gureke zim em-akum árála dong.
Put the saddle upon his back.	......	......	Bike lamkula zim emrag-lukta.
Put the saddle upon the horse's back.	Zime gorra mugubang rome (The saddle the horse's back place on.)	......	......
I have beaten his son with many stripes.	Ezu muno vegune (His son severely have beaten.)	Magę kaom ale jungpene (His son well I have beaten).	Bikke anem na abaka pa-bita.

East of Assam.—(Continued.)

Abor.	Sulikátá Mishmees.	Degaree Mishmees.	English.
Ulu ding kape dita ..	Ngialombro ahu prawa ...	Ning hui giji bandé ..	I shall beat.
Ulu dita pone ..	Ngialombro ahu proa jiva	Ning hui bandé ..	I should beat.
Ulu padune dita ..	Ngialombro ahu lai ...	Ning hiwa huiah. ..	I am beaten.
Ulu mo padulal dita ..	Ngialombro ahu proa lyah	Ning huiah mag ..	I was beaten.
Ulu mo di abo dita ..	Ngialombro na-ahu pra wa.	Ning hui ing tia ..	I shall be beaten.
Ulu gikappe ..	Ngialombro bapra wayah	Ning hoende. ..	I go.
Ngo giappe ..	Ngio banalah ...	Nga hayá ..	Thou goest.
Ngo bolu gieppo ..	Ngio-apu balyah ...	Ngoelang habo ..	He goes.
Ulu gikubo jigidrakané..	Ngialombro babyah ...	Ning hoya ..	I went.
Ngo homade gikang ..	Ngio banabah ...	Nga re habo ..	Thou wentest.
Ngo bolu gikang ..	Ngio apu belaga edya .	Ngoelang mahabo ..	He went.
Gipeji giepé ..	Bala uji *or* baladra ...	Bonende *or* habo ..	Go.
Aikabbo ..	Bamiah ...	Bande ..	Going.
Aikang ..	Babya ...	Habo ..	Gone.
Nakke ingko á mune ..	New siládrá ámu ...	Na mujá ámáng ..	What is your name.
Esigure adit ditakaji ..	Heya geerámag phiáhá ...	E gourikadening saba ..	How old is this horse.
Sak kidi Kashmir bolopé edit dadi?	Ejaniba ba kashmir ajige mag fiaha?	Eg kashmir kadego daeng	How far is it from here to Kashmir?
......	......	......	How old are you?
......	......	......	How far is it from Tezpore to your house?
Nakké aho ekumel editke kud dulé.	New hábá ah ji ji gá ...	Na nábá ángo kadago ah i ieng.	How many sons are there in your father's house?
Nga sil bajerengkagigay eka giku ji gigayeka.	Nga etani mala guge mya la aghuha.	Ha tahing dá dániágá khiep hana hada humobo.	I have walked a long way to-day.
Bukke burme demukke paieke adeya mané mét.	Heya athi ebo ah yabi gyah.	Umjagé mathi hage naba you ige wa sabo.	The son of my uncle is married to her sister.
Ekku máráb dune gatad yasile gure delak pima myah.	Nga kua andye lapna geera ayah jiji payá.	Nga tia ieh dipa la gouri gé roi ságé.	In the house is the saddle of the white horse.
Gátad dem lángku put ..	Andaye lamra puru ...	Dip takhengre umja umpling há dáná.	Put the saddle upon his back.
......	......	......	Put the saddle upon the horse's back.
Bakke ádé mángá bajek.. *ditto.*	Newa nga midu hulá pata	Mujake ah ha da limbo..	I have beaten his son with many stripes.

English.	Aka.	Duffla.	Miri.
He is grazing cattle on the top of the hill.	Shufshekhun (the cattle the keeper) phong (the hill) mud or (top on) khenru (is grazing).	Alo bangnia modi aoa seh rakido (That person the hill-top cattle is grazing on).	Aditai ata bi garam menjagam nesin domolá dágáne.
His brother is taller than his sister.	Enu (his brother) enie (his sister) mudome (is taller than).	Alo bormeam boroa aoiopa (His sister than his brother is shorter).	Bikke birmeden penem bikke birâde o-dak.
He is sitting on a horse under that tree.	......	......	Ellu ising rumkingola gure taleda sálá dung.
He is sitting on a stone under that tree.	Thou (that) gunne (tree) molonrun (under) golong (a stone) nu (the man) unduru (is sitting on).	Sengne lakinga elengava dungpa (That tree under stone top of he is sitting).	......
The price of that is two rupees and a half.	......	Aso kere baringola adoligo (That thing's price is two rupees and a half).	Ellekem barnika adhalika.
The price of this is 2 or 3 rupees.	Tankha-ruphu (rupees) guni (two) [*or*] gothen (three) jonkhane (is worth.)	......	......
What is the price of that thing?	Hunso (that thing) khenia (how much) jonkhane? (is worth).	......	......
My father lives in that small house.	Nia (my) aboa (father) nen (a house) muzuru (small) dionru (is living in).	Ngo abo alo oupenchungalo dodona (My father that small house lives in).	Nake babubi amene akumala doda.
Give this rupee to him ...	Tankha-ruphu (the rupee) phon (his) igiru (hand in) bime (place).	Sotungka barsom alo bikto (This one rupee him give).	Edem murka abarsemlim bitaka.
Take this rupee from him	Thankha-ruphu (the rupee) phon (his) igiru (hand in) khalune (take).	Aloke tunga noto (From him the rupees take).	Bik kalukem markang kidingem lotak.
Take those rupees from him.	......	......	......
Beat him well and bind him with ropes.	......	......	......
You beat him well and bind him well with ropes	Thou (you) ero (him) mivi (well) vem (beat) oddu (with ropes) mivi (well) jome (bind).	Amalebo jungto usolo nolo leto (Him well beat, rope bring and bind).	Bim aipa pataka aru bim soriku eaaka.
Draw water from the well.	......	......	......
Draw water from this hollow.	Vze (water) thong (the hollow) lubime (bring from).	Kal soko esilo tokto (From this hollow water draw).	Sirang aralak asika talaka.
Walk before me ...	So (go) niang (me) mivia deme (in front of [and] walk.)	Ngo atokbo oke (My front go).	Nak kárása gidong gitak taka.
Whose boy comes behind you?	Theu (whose) zu (son) ni (you) nerun (behind) dehou (is walking?)	Hygia kao nokoionga angdona (Whose boy behind you is going)?	Nak leduda sek ane gidang.
From whom did you buy that?	Hunzo (that thing) khio lune (who from [you] have bought)?	Nao ejia hogolukko raepena (Your cloth where from did you buy)?	Edem sekelak na rakan.
From a shop-keeper of the village.	Gibiang (the village) nu (a man) untsonru (a shop-keeper from) lune (have bought).	Hogoga gola aloko rengaena (The village a shopkeeper from I brought).	Daulolak dokanloke.

East of Assam.—(Concluded.)

Abor.	Sulikátá Mishmees.	Degaroo Mishmees.	English.
Ba aditeya tel chow uh ráki dúng.	E heiá tá áng gupu maju halni.	Reja thiago maju hugura	He is grazing cattle on the top of the hill.
Bukke ábung nge bukke hurmé dem hodoya dung.	Ah heia apía aheya athi a roind.	Rage napung rega mathe lágé májá dáring chábo.	His brother is taller than her sister,
Ah eching rung king elba gúre la chá lá dung.	Heia aganuah dábo é heiá geera ja jigya.	Re masang halag reja gouri chohá.	He is sitting on a horse under that tree.
......	......	......	He is sitting on a stone under that tree.
Bukke aré barne halá abil ik odebá.	Aheya aji geya e mu káni atigé ayho.	Roige taju pla kaeng ahali chamag.	The price of that is two rupees and a half.
......	......	......	The price of this is 2 or 3 rupees.
......	......	......	What is the price of that thing?
Ukke ábuge tat yá já ede anjab ekum la dung.	Ngá nálá ná ah hi majia jigya.	Ha genábá nábá ringya roija úgyago iah.	My father lives in that small house.
Sim ábár sim bámdeh bitakkka.	Eja pro premé ha ala ...	E paring pla reba halang	Give this rupee to him.
......	......	......	Take this rupee from him
Bukke teluk morkung temo látká.	Ahaia e hemahé pow ahu hohá ágay.	Umja dogo paring re che-nna.	Take those rupees from him.
Ay rupé pátké ekung bome soruluk ya wáká.	Pre agay hoop jíbu eja al bion jiji abá.	Pralon howina roigum roi ja kowrig gowri chona.	Beat him well and bind him with ropes.
......	......	......	You beat him well and bind him well with ropes
Seringla achi utka ..	Eu poma ajia maji bogen	Toingo maji ryna ..	Draw water from the well.
......	......	......	Draw water from this hollow.
Ngaké keral apuné ..	Agu pragé lámá ..	Hajed hemna ..	Walk before me.
Nakke mela mal sekka ke kinge gidang ne.	Nas mita asia ah iga yaba	Na umplig cha ah bana ha	Whose boy comes behind you?
Sekkelak edem retanee ..	Esu ayga ne ayha isima loga lah.	Roida roiga chad brichia	From whom did you buy that.
Dalulák bakke karé bakke lak.	An ma kheng gé abi ji ehenia.	Mih matingo khing gé briadon brichia.	From a shop-keeper of the village.

LIST OF WORDS AND PHRASES

IN THE

LANGUAGE OF EACH OF THE Naga TRIBES

FOUND ~~WITHIN THE~~ on the borders of the

DISTRICT OF SIBSAGAR, ASSAM.

List of words and phrases in the Language of each of the Tribes found within the District of Sibsagar, Assam.

English.	Miklai Naga Dialect.	Hati Garya Naga Dialect.	Dop-darya Naga Dialect.	Abhay Purya Naga Dialect.	Tablungia Naga Dialect.	English.
One ...	Machunga ...	Ákhát ...	Ákhá ...	Ettá ...	Chhaáh ...	One.
Two ...	Ini ...	Ánek ...	Áná ...	Áni ...	Ih ...	Two.
Three ...	Etham ...	Áchám ...	Ásam ...	Ájám ...	Lum ...	Three.
Four ...	Mejo ...	Fli ...	Fezu ...	Álli ...	Pelih ...	Four.
Five ...	Manga ...	Fángá ...	Fungu ...	Ágá ...	Ngá ...	Five.
Six ...	Torok ...	Thorok ...	Thorok ...	Árák ...	Wak ...	Six.
Seven ...	Kin ...	Theni ...	Thenet ...	Ánát ...	Niat ...	Seven.
Eight ...	Tejá ...	Chet ...	Thí ...	Áset ...	Tát ...	Eight.
Nine ...	Toko ...	Thuku ...	Toko ...	Áku ...	To ...	Nine.
Ten ...	Táro ...	Therá ...	There ...	Ván ...	Pan ...	Ten.
Twenty ...	Muki ...	Meki ...	Mechu ...	Chá ...	Táh ...	Twenty.
Fifty ...	Najoá ...	Chámrá ...	Thenem ...	Punihunái shán ván ...	Tihjá bapan ...	Fifty.
Hundred ...	Thengá ...	Telengá ...	Teláng khá ...	Pogá ...	Ngá táh ...	Hundred.
I ...	Ákha ...	Ni ...	Ni ...	Kuoi ...	Táw ...	I.
Of me ...	Áche ...	Ilábá ...	Kame yang ...	Kuku ...	Teseí ...	Of me.
Mine ...	Áche ...	Kábá ...	Kame yang ...	Kuku ...	Tesei ...	Mine.
We ...	Hetku ...	Ilánching ...	Áják (or) ojanak ...	Kukhi ...	Tomán Ásseih ...	We.
Of us ...	Áche ...	Árogá ...	Áják meyang (or) ojanak meyang.	Kemku ...	Tomán Ásseih seih ...	Of us.
Our ...	Áche ...	Iláteláng ...	Ajak meyang (or) ojanak meyang.	Kemku ...	Tomán Ásseih seih ...	Our.
Thou ...	Álálá ...	Náng ...	Ná ...	Nánge ...	Náng ...	Thou.

Of thee	Inte	Bá	Ná meyang	Nángpu	Nang seih	Of thee.
Thine	Inte	Nebá	Ná meyang	Nángpu	Náng seih	Thine.
You	Andalla	Ninglá	Nának	Házám	Nomán	You.
Of you	Indese	Ninglábá	Nának meyang	Házámku	Nomán seih	Of you.
Your	Indese	Ninglábá	Nának meyang	Házámku	Nomán seih	Your.
He	Icha chalá	Chyuráj	Fái	Chhi	Ih-muh	He.
Of him	Achiche	Bábá	Pái meyang	Chiku	Ih-muh seih	Of him.
His	Achiche	Bábá	Pái meyang	Chiku	Ih-muh seih	His.
They	Chiyáng	Tohlá	Pái nak	Hukhi	Ih-muh ásseih	They.
Of them	Acháng iche	Bibá	Pái nak meyang	Hamku	Ih-muh ásseih seih	Of them.
Their	Acháng iche	Tohlábá	Pái nak meyang	Hamku	Ih-muh ásseih seih	Their.
Hand	Akhe	Dekhat	Teben (or) Teget	Chák	Yák	Hand.
Foot	Acha	Tejáng	Tomobu	Chia	Láfáh	Foot.
Nose	Khen	Tená	Teni	Náko	Ná siyáng	Nose.
Eye	Ahminik	Tinak	Tenak	Mik	Mik	Eye.
Mouth	Apang	Tebang	Tepáng	Bikha	Chhuh	Mouth.
Tooth	Ahah	Tefá	Tobo	Bá	Pháh	Tooth.
Ear	En	Tenaro	Teñarang	Ná	Ná	Ear.
Hair	Achán	Koá	Ku	Khá	Sángla	Hair.
Head	Kuri	Tekálok	Tokolák	Kháng	Sáng ching	Head.
Tongue	Nih	Temili	Temeli	Le	Yáih	Tongue.
Belly	Apak	Tepok	Tobok	Wok	Suh	Belly.
Back	Máng ku	Tenam	Torong Tong	Tak	Ngap	Back.
Iron	Unchak	Jáien	Insáng	Ján	Yán	Iron.

List of words and phrases in the Language of each of the Tribes found within the District of Sibsagar, Assam.—(Continued.)

English.	Miklai Naga Dialect.	Hati Garya Naga Dialect.	Dop-darya Naga Dialect.	Abhay Purya Naga Dialect.	Tablungia Naga Dialect.	English.
Gold ..	Tramnukh ..	Taro ..	Táribi ..	Sen ..	Khám ..	Gold.
Silver ..	Ichrang ..	Rop ..	Sen ..	Ngun ..	Nin ..	Silver.
Father ..	Apá ..	Abá ..	Tobo (or) Obá ..	Hopá ..	Páh ..	Father.
Mother ..	Áio ..	Áiá ..	Ojá ..	Hunu ..	Nyuh ..	Mother.
Brother ..	Ánga ..	Tongdati ..	Uti (or) Keno (or) Teno.	Honáo ..	Áchhai (or) Náwh ..	Brother.
Sister ..	Aila ..	Tanu ..	Teji (or) Teno ..	Sikou honáo ..	Ányah (or) a-Náwh..	Sister.
Man ..	Acham ..	Ábáo cháore ..	Nisung ..	Mi ..	Kátáh ..	Man.
Woman ..	Alai ..	Ánudi ..	Tesari ..	Sikou ..	Si-kah ..	Woman.
Wife ..	Enga ..	Kahín ..	Khibuchhu ..	Husenu ..	Si-kah ..	Wife.
Child ..	Ngara ..	Techáre ..	Tánuri ..	Sisi ..	Náháh ..	Child.
Son ..	Nchai ..	Kechápá ..	Toboro jari ..	Hosá ..	Nitau náháh ..	Son.
Daughter ..	Achalla ..	Kechálá ..	Tesari jari ..	Sikon hosá ..	Sikah náháh ..	Daughter.
Slaves ..	Nri ..	Eláre ..	Álári .	Dá ..	Áh ..	Slave.
Cultivator ..	Áliloai ..	Ájam ..	Álu áinákur ..	Mánráimi ..	Ká hamsi ..	Cultivator.
Shepherd ..	Mangchárákhi ..	Máchui nakre ..	Nábung nákur ..	Ránnicle ..	Yun yun si ..	Shepherd.
God ..	Pacha ..	Sing hram ..	Ánong chongbá ..	Rángbáo ..	Káw wáng páh ..	God.
Devil ..	Chengkhram ..	Nah chir ..	Nuh chhírrh ..	Báuráng ..	Máh ..	Devil.
Sun ..	Eng ..	Singhi ..	Ánu ..	Ranghán ..	Wang hih ..	Sun.
Moon ..	Chara ..	Látá ..	Jitá ..	Letnu ..	Lih ..	Moon.
Star ..	Chandeo ..	Chuin ..	Petinu ..	Letchi ..	Lithá ..	Star.

Fire	Amni	Meju	Mi	Ván	Áh	Fire.
Water	Achin	Áchi	Threr	Ti	Liyáng	Water.
House	Aki	Áki	Khi	Hám	Nak	House.
Horse	Ur	Kuri	Kror Tobong	Mán	Kai-eh	Horse.
Cow	Akin	Chillá	Náso	Máihu	Máhu ányuh	Cow.
Dog	Fra apung	Áhi	Ájo	Hi	Koi-háh	Dog.
Cat	Ali ara	Machi	Thanee	Mesá	Máhih	Cat.
Cock	Hámpun	Toro	Ántabong	Upang	Áw pang	Cock.
Duck	Pata Hángki	Tichi	Fáták	Upák	Páták ányuh	Duck.
Ass	(No term)	(No term)	(No term)	(No term)	(No term)	Ass.
Camel	(No term)	(No term)	(No term)	(No term)	(No term)	Camel.
Bird	Uro	Oájé	Ojo	Fáuo	Áwháh	Bird.
Go	Iyá	Oáu	Wáng	Páulá	Tái	Go.
Eat	Chowá	Cháo	Chungáng	Lesá	Háhsi	Eat.
Sit	Khop khethá	Milyang	Menáng	Nábai	So-chih	Sit.
Come	Roá	Roh	Árong	Homán	Pei-keih	Come.
Beat	Táwá	Vikra	Ásokáng	Máithán	Mátchih	Beat.
Stand	Panthia	Hulyang	Noktákáng	Ájaugháí	Tang si	Stand.
Die	Chethákå	Chio	Soku	Jeli	Lítikeh	Die.
Give	Piyá	Khángá	Ko-á	Láka	Yáfáh	Give.
Run	I-ungá	Chamu	Ásamáng	Riklá	Fassih	Run.
Up	Ai áki	Aning	Tamá	Dingt	Átak	Up.
Down	Akapi	Deching	Tolong	Fáng	Áfáng	Down.
Before	Abangi	Minang	Teják	Thamá	Saw saw	Before.

List of words and phrases in the Language of each of the Tribes found within the District of Sibsagar, Assam.—(Continued.)

English.	Miklai Naga Dialect.	Hati Garya Naga Dialect.	Dop-darya Naga Dialect.	Abhay Purya Naga Dialect.	Tablungia Naga Dialect.	English.
Near ...	Ngatanga ...	Anáná ...	Anessá ...	Chanley ...	Teffin ...	Near.
Far ...	Ekani ..	Telengá ...	Abighá ...	Atay lay ...	Hah sah ...	Far.
Behind ...	Chelani ...	Techi ...	Tesse ...	Fáimá ...	Fei máh ...	Behind.
Who ...	Chachalá ...	Chyá ...	Si ...	Abe ...	Awai ...	Who.
What ...	Untallá ...	Chyáha ...	Kiji (or) Kisi ...	Tem ...	Hángeih ...	What.
Why ...	Unto áda ...	Chubá ...	Káchho ...	Bole nyákpu ...	Háng neigh ...	Why.
And ...	Enung ahá ...	Chátá ...	Anu ...	Athásu ...	Efeimáh ...	And.
But ...	(No term) ...	(No term) ...	(No term) ...	Hefimá ...	(No term) ...	But.
If ...	(No term) ...	Chepá ...	(No term) ...	Hebamá ...	Hamáh ...	If.
Yes ...	Atata ...	Am ...	Hán ...	Chángle ...	Eiáh ...	Yes.
No ...	Mek ...	Nanga ...	Nougá ...	Máúchaúg ...	Yáh ...	No.
Alas ...	Aháhá ...	Aká áká ...	Khángá khángá ...	Nabáng ...	Ai si eheh ...	Alas.
A father ...	Machunga ápa ...	Abá átá ..	Tobo khá ...	Táhopá ...	Chháh páh ...	A father.
Two fathers ...	Apa ini ...	Abá áhnutu ...	Tobo áná ...	Ani-hopá ...	Ih páh ...	Two fathers.
Fathers ...	Apa initham ...	Abá kohálangá ...	Tobo áighá ...	Hopálái ...	Páh má ...	Fathers.
Of a father ...	Apa machunga ...	Abápá ...	Tobokhá meyang ...	Hopáku ..	Chháh páh seih ...	Of a father.
Of fathers ...	Apacha machunga	Abá riboá ...	Tobo áighá meyang ...	Hopáhámku ...	Páh má seih ...	Of fathers.
To a father ...	Apa machunga ...	Abá likhu ...	Tobo nam khá ...	Hopáku ...	Chhá páh to ...	To a father.
To fathers ...	Apa initham ...	Abárili khorák ...	Tobonam áighá ...	Hopáku lái ...	Pá má to ...	To fathers.
From a father ...	Apaná muchungá ...	Abánu khánu ...	Tobo khá táng nangági	Hopám ...	Páh mápu ...	From a father.
From fathers ...	Apaná initham ...	Abá riboá ...	Tobo aighá táng nan-gági.	Hopá ánpá ...	Páhmá mápu ...	From fathers.

A daughter ...	Uchum machungá...	Tánu adao, or kechelá ádáo.	Tesseri jari khá ...	Sikau ...	Chháh sikah náháh ...	A daughter.
Two daughters ...	Uchum ini ...	Kechelá áhnat ...	Tesseri jari áná ...	Áni-sikau ...	Ih sikah náháh ...	Two daughters.
Daughters ...	Uchum initham ...	Kechelá árogá ...	Tesseri jari áighá ...	Sikau-hám ...	Sikah náháh má ...	Daughters.
Of a daughter ...	Uchamcha machungá	Kechelá ájáo ...	Tesseri jari khá meyang	Sikau-hu ...	Chháh sikáh náhá seih	Of a daughter.
Of daughters ...	Uchumcha initham	Kechelá árogá ájáo ...	Tesseri jari áighá meyang.	Sikau-homenpá ...	Sikáh náhá má seih ...	Of daughters.
To a daughter ...	Ucham machunga...	Kechelá kho ...	Tesseri jari nam khá...	Sikau ...	Chháh sikiáh náhá to	To a daughter.
To daughters ...	Ucham initham ...	Kechelá árogá kho ...	Tesseri jari nam áighá	Sikau hamku ...	Sikáh náhá má to ...	To daughters.
From a daughter ...	Achalna machunga or uchumna machungá.	Kechelá fenu ...	Tesseri jari khátáng tang nangági.	Sikau hosá ...	Chháh sikáh náhá mapu.	From a daughter.
From daughters ...	Achalana initham or uchumna initham.	Kechela árogá fenu...	Tesseri jari áikhá táng nangági.	Sikau homenpáni ...	Sikáh náhá má mápu	From daughters.
A good man ...	Bhuná áchám muchungá.	Átá puyánu ...	Nisung tásung khátong.	Ettá mi my ...	Chháh kátáh ámey ...	A good man.
Two good men ...	Bhuná acham ini ...	Ami áhnat tipanga...	Nisung áná tásung ..	Mi my ni ...	Ih kátáh amey ...	Two good men.
Good men ...	Bhuná acham ...	Arogá ámi tipanga...	Nisung áighá tesung...	Mi my hám ...	Meyáng kátáh amey	Good men.
Of a good man ...	Bhuná achamcha machungá.	Ámi tipang bá ...	Nisung khátáng tasung meyang.	Ettá mi myku ...	Chháh kátáh amey seih.	Of a good man.
Of good men ...	Bhuná achamcha initham.	Ámi tipanga árogá...	Nisung áighá tásung meyang.	Mi my hámenpá ...	Kátá mámey seih ...	Of good men.
To a good man ...	Bhuná acham machungá.	Ámi tipanga likha ...	Nisung tásung khatong num.	Ettá mi my hámku ...	Chháh kátáh ámey to	To a good man.
To good men ...	Bhuná acham initham.	Ámi tipang khong ...	Nisung tásung áighái num.	Mimy hámku ...	Kátáh má amey to ...	To good men.
From a good man ...	Bhuná achamná machungá.	Ámi tipáng mátáng oáire bário.	Nisung tasung khá táng nungági.	Ettá mimy ...	Chháh kátáh amey mápu.	From a good man.
From good men ...	Bhuná áchamná initham.	Ámi tipang árogá nijkáno.	Nisung tásung áighá táng nungági.	Mimy hámenpá ...	Kátáh má ámey mápu	From good men.

List of words and phrases in the Language of each of the Tribes found within the District of Sibsagar, Assam.—(Continued.)

English.	Miklai Naga Dialect.	Hati Garya Naga Dialect.	Dop-darya Naga Dialect.	Abhay Purya Naga Dialect.	Tablungia Naga Dialect.	English.
A good woman	Bhuna elai muchungá.	Ami tipang kechela nájáti.	Tesseri khá tásung	Ettá chyá my	Chháh sikah amey	A good woman.
Good women	Bhuna elai	Ami tipang kechelá árogá.	Tesseri áighá tasung	Chyá me	Sikah má amey	Good women.
A bad boy	Omha	Mibong khá	Tuburu jáná	Ettá missi neusa	Chhah imeyh nitan náháh.	A bad boy.
A bad girl	Ichamha	Bárichári mibong khá	Tesseri jáná khá támá sung.	Ettá missi fabái	Chháh imeyh nitan sikah náhá.	A bad girl.
Good	Bhuná	Tipanga	Tásung	My	Amey	Good.
Better	Tantam bhuná	Bongánu	Tasung bá	Ámy	Cháh mynáng-kih	Better.
Best	Tantam bhunilá	Tasung bongánu	Khánga khángá tásung	Ámypá	Chháh enuh maynáng kih.	Best.
High	Lántu	Telengá	Lánger	Háha	Setáwh	High.
Higher	Tamtam chaná	Cháká lengánu	Lángerbá	Háho	Cháh setáwh	Higher.
Highest	Chongán chongán chaná.	Cháká cháká telengá	Khángá khángá lánger	Háfá	Cháh enuh setáwh	Highest.
A horse	Ur machungá	Áttá kori	Kror tobong khá	Ettá mán	Chháh kaieh	A horse.
A mare	Ur raki machungá	Kari techi	Kror techho khá	Ettá mán hunu	Chháh kaieh ányáh	A mare.
Horses	Urriá	Kari árogá	Kror tobong áighá	Inumán	Kaieh má	Horses.
Mares	Ur khachá	Kari techi árogá	Kror techho áighá	Inumán hunu	Kaieh ányáh má	Mares.
A bull	Mang chapu machungá.	Átá machu	Náso tobong khá	Horánpang	Chháh máhu apang	A bull.
A cow	Mang chaki machungá.	Chilá	Náso techho khá	Mighu hunu	Chháh máhu ányuh	A cow.

Bulls	Mang chiá	Máchu árogá	Náso tobong áighá	Inu horán pang	Máhu apang má	Bulls.
Cows	Mang chaki khachá	Chilá árogá	Náso techho áighá	Inu myhu hunu	Máhu ányuh má	Cows.
A dog	Apung muchungá	Áhi árá	Ájo tobong khá	Hilá	Chhá koi háh	A dog.
A bitch	Fra aping muchungá	Áhi techi árá	Ájo techho khá	Hinu	Chhá koi nyuh	A bitch.
Dogs	Khachá apung	Áhi árogá	Ájo tobong aighá	Hirem	Koiháh má	Dogs.
Bitches	Fra aping khachá	Áhi techi árogá	Ájo techho áighá	Hinurem	Koi nyuh má	Bitches.
A he-goat	Ngyá machungá	Nápung tápung árá	Nábung tubung khá	Ranpang	Chhá yán apang	A he-goat.
A female goat	Ngyá ngyá aki machungá.	Nápung techi árá	Nábung techho khá	Rann	Chhá yan enyuh	A female goat.
Goats	Ngyá ngyá khachá	Nápung árogá	Nabung áighá	Ranhurem	Yan má	Goats.
A male deer	Chepu machungá	Hariná tapung	Hariná tubung khá	Máikhi páng	Chhá tak apáng	A male deer.
A female deer	Uku Machungá	Hariná techi	Hariná techho khá	Máikhi hunu	Chha tak enyuh	A female deer.
Deer	Chepu khachá	Áchá harin	Hariná aighá	Chenu máikhi	Tak má	Deer.
I am	Áná awáná	Ni lyánu	Ni lirr	Kutáiley	Táw nángki	I am.
Thou art	Nao án chake	Náng lyáche	Ná lirr	Náng ley	Náng nángki	Thou art.
He is	Chi owáná	Chu baju lyáche	Pái lirr	Chi ley	Jhuh nángki	He is.
We are	Ete ene thamáná	Ilánching lyáche	Ojanak lirr	Kem ley	Tomán nángki	We are.
You are	Ete owán chuke	Ninglá lyáche	Nának lirr	Házám ley	Nomán nángki	You are.
They are	Cháng hafená	Tohla lyáche	Pái nak lirr	Hum tái ley	Jhuh mán nángki	They are.
I was	Áná owánle	Ñi ligechánu	Ni li áso	Kunáley	Táw ngapai	I was.
Thou wast	Na owán che	Náng ligechánu	Na li áso	Náng nga le	Náng nga ehei	Thou wast.
He was	Chihá owáná	Chureya ligechá nu	Paili áso	Chináley	Ih-muh nga ehei	He was.
We were	Owáná owán chukhá	Ilanching ligechánu	Ojanak li áso	Kem ná ley	Tomán nga pai	We were.
You were	Inte nowán chuke	Niláng ligechánu	Nának li áso	Házam ná ley	Nomán nga ehei	You were.
They were	Cháng habáná	Tohla ligechánu	Páinak li áso	Hám ná ley	Ih-muh nga ehei	They were.

List of words and phrases in the Language of each of the Tribes found within the District of Sibsagar, Assam.—(Continued.)

English.	Miklai Naga Dialect.	Hati Garya Naga Dialect.	Dop-darya Naga Dialect.	Abhay Purya Naga Dialect.	Tablungia Naga Dialect.	English.
Be ...	Mohaná ...	Liyá ...	Ā́ng ...	Ná hay ...	Nángki ehei ...	Be.
To be ...	Mohaná ...	Li ...	Ā́ng ...	Āchá́ng ...	Nángki ...	To be.
Being ...	Mohaná wáná ...	Lyá ...	Lirr áng ...	Usuá ...	Nangki ching ...	Being.
Having been ...	Mohanágá ...	Lyáole ...	Koko ...	Usuáley ...	Yángpu ...	Having been.
I may be ...	Mohaná chuku ku	Ni chámá .	Ni chámá ...	Kuá chánge ...	Jáwn akbak ...	I may be.
I shall be ...	Mohaná chaká ...	Ni cho ...	Ketak cho ...	Kuá chángai ...	Táwa láká ...	I shall be.
I should be ..	Mohana hom chuká	Ni ali ...	Ni áli ...	Kuá cháng táibu ..	Táwá che lak ...	I should be.
Beat ..	Tábá ...	Sikra ...	Ā́sok ...	Miáthán ...	Setchhi ...	Beat.
To beat ..	Talai jyálá ...	Sikra	Ā́sok ...	Máiá ...	Set ..	To beat.
Beating ...	Táwáná ...	Sikra áli ...	Ā́sokong ...	Mái ley ..	Set ching ching ..	Beating.
Having beaten ...	Tá tháká .	Sikra áole ...	Ā́sokoko ...	Mái usualey ...	Set yángpu ...	Having beaten.
I beat ...	Ā́ná táu i ...	Nini sikra ...	Ni ások ...	Ku mái	Táwa set nangki ..	I beat.
Thou beatest ...	Ná táwá ...	Nángni sikra ..	Ná ások ...	Nánge máiley ...	Náng set nangki ...	Thou beatest.
He beats ..	Chiná táthaká ...	Churaju sikra ...	Pái ások ...	Siá máiley ...	Iheh set puchá ...	He beats.
We beat ...	Etapu hemái tábá ..	Ilánching sikra ...	Ā́jonak asok ...	Kom mia ...	Tomán set nángki ...	We beat.
You beat ...	Inte nátábá. ...	Ninglá sikra ...	Nának asok ...	Hávám máiea ...	Noman set nángki ..	You beat.
They beat ...	Unte nátá thoká ...	Tohlá sikra ...	Painak ások ...	Hám máiea ..	Ih muh set nángki ..	They beat.
I am beating ...	Ā́ná tao ...	Sikran sikra ...	Ni ásokong lirr ..	Kuá máiea ...	Táw set ching chingele nga nángki.	I am beating.
I was beating ...	Ā́ná táchu ...	Nisikrá állie ...	Ni ásokong li áso ...	Kua fito ley ...	Táw set nga puyáh ..	I was beating.
I had beaten ...	Nátá tháka ...	Ni sikra áole ...	Ni Támásá ásokoko ...	Kua fit ley ..	Táw set nga puyáh nángki.	I had beaten.

I may beat ...	Ána takuku ...	Nini in sikra ...	Ni ások chámá ...	Kua máitoake ...	Táwa set akták ...	I may beat.
I shall beat ...	Ána táo ...	Ninu sikra ...	Ni ások chho ...	Kua máiea ...	Táw set láká ...	I shall beat.
I should beat ...	Ána táoo ...	Ninu sikra náli ...	Ni ások náli ...	Kua máinpá ...	Táw set chelák ...	I should beat.
I am beaten ...	Ni tá tháká ...	Niga sikraoa ...	Keták ásoktáki ...	Kuo áthá máile ...	Tetáw set nángki ...	I am beaten.
I was beaten ...	Acha chiná tá tháká	Niga sikraoale ...	Keták ásokoko ...	Kutu fit ley ...	Tetáw sat teke ...	I was beaten.
I shall be beaten ...	Átá·komámu ...	Ni sikraocho ...	Keták ásokoho ...	Kutu máiyá ...	Set fálák yáng ...	I shall be beaten.
I go ...	Ái hiya ...	Ni oáu ..	Ni uti ...	Ku poue ...	Jáw táinu ...	I go.
Thou goest ...	Náo á ...	Nángni oáu ...	Ná uti ...	Náng páulá ...	Nánga tachi ...	Thou goest.
He goes ...	Achu tháká ...	Chyráju oáu ...	Pai uti ...	Sipáu lá ...	Jheh táchi ...	He goes.
I went ...	Ánáo thaká ...	Ni oáok ..	Ni or ...	Ku jále ...	Táw tai nángki ...	I went.
Thou wentest ...	Ná othá chuke ...	Nángni oáok ...	Ná or ...	Náng jále ..	Náng tai nángki ...	Thou wentest.
He went ...	Itháká amba ...	Churáju oáok ..	Pái or ...	Si jále ...	Jheh tai nángki ...	He went.
Go ...	Iyá ...	Oa ...	Uti ...	Páulá ...	Tái shi ...	Go.
Going ...	Iwáuá ...	Aiá álile ...	Utáki ...	Jále ...	Tái tái ...	Going.
Gone ..	Ithaká ...	Oáok ...	Uku ...	Páuená ...	Tái nángki ...	Gone.
What is your name?	Nana ta minglá? ..	Nining chyáha? ...	Ná meyang tenungsi?	Nángbule mánpu? ...	Náng bángkei min pueih?	What is your name?
How old is this horse?	Ur chang chang thaká?	Karito kata ájánti?...	Kror iá kám koighá?...	Obi ráng he mán pu?	Táw kaich wáng pey-áng háng seng?	How old is this horse?
How far is it from here to Kashmir?	Hinachá Kashmi rala kuteng hárá la?	Bibhinu Kashmir ka fiá?	Iák nangági Kashmir átong chu ko bigha?	Ete khongea obe nilám Kashmir kápang?	Hámá puáh Kashmir háng seng?	How far is it from here to Kashmir?
How many sons are there in your father's house?	Nipacha ochai kotá-lá?	Nabá kiko Techaku háilyá?	Nabo khitáng tuburu jari koighá lirr?	Náng háupámá hama obi táibu sisi neusá?	Náng pá nak má áháh háng sing nga náng-ki?	How many sons are there in your father's house?
I have walked a long way to-day.	Inching iy a kon ráu á.	Tháni anti telenga ...	Ni tháni lemáng ábighá jájáuko.	Ku áni ásule hámdaoá	Tiniyáh táwá miyáng hái kem hákih.	I have walked a long way to-day.

List of words and phrases in the Language of each of the Tribes found within the District of Sibsagar, Assam.—(Concluded.)

English.	Miklai Naga Dialect.	Hati Garya Naga Dialect.	Dop-darya Naga Dialect.	Abhoi Purya Naga Dialect.	Tablungia Naga Dialect.	English.
The son of my uncle is married to her sister.	Áparu átál chowái thaká.	Ábá nujábá tanyu kibá chub áoá.	Koko tánobo jari pá teno ági.	Ku ápáli husa usuá hunáu toi zingle.	Apá suan ábá fáwnak sikah yá nángki.	The son of my uncle is married to her sister.
In the house is the saddle of the white horse.	Ure hum cháki yáná "jim."	Áki chinga karichá-bák khánu.	Kror tamassong nisung ámunbá khi enangji kháre.	Mán tho zim hámmá táiley.	Ataw nak kaich eheng tawmá hipu mahucha	In the house is the saddle of the white horse.
Put the saddle upon his back.	Mang kui ná changá "jim."	Tenem karichábák hangchába.	Pá meyang torong tong nisung ámenbá álen-áng.	Jiku tokmá zim kháley	Kaieh tawmá mahucha hechi.	Put the saddle upon his back.
I have beaten his son with many stripes.	At chungá ichung inetham echa ká.	Bácháriga árogá chiká	Ni pári jari ták rijáng ági khángá asá koko.	Kue fid deua asule usuá husân.	Ihahah taw set yangki taw eh.	I have beaten his son with many stripes.
He is grazing cattle on the top of the hill.	Fungá ni mángche ek málá.	Áhan jáng muchu han cháise.	Pá átáng num nási anakar.	Sie miehu niele háhutu	Jheh kátáfáw mámáhu yam nangki.	He is grazing cattle on the top of the hill.
He is sitting on a horse under that tree.	Atang chi anatang mángkui owáná.	Koriga nák tong chá mung chángu nyánu	Songtong jongtáng kror torongtong nong pá mená lirr.	Sie mán tokmá nále pannu tongmá iáng-khunmá jakle.	Taw pichangmá kaieh tang máh anágenga nángki.	He is sitting on a horse under that tree.
His brother is taller than his sister.	Api áocha ailá chi chipao chipaoe.	Tenu to tenu telangbá	Pá teno tesseri ı áteno tuburn tálang bá.	Chiku honou fái chiku sikou honáo lale.	Ih náw taw náhá taw setauh pu.	His brother is taller than his sister.
The price of that is two rupees and a half.	Hile echeráng che inichi athli.	Higo dobá áhnat áthliá.	Ibáji táchok áná adhalli lánger.	Usuá nun kháoui átholi	Taw tawá nginkha jheba ethuri.	The price of that is two rupees and a half.
My father lives in that small house.	Ápa kitu kárachila áná.	Ábá nujábá kikáliri...	Kobo khi tálá ibá-nunji lir	Ku ápá usuá hám sámá ánokle.	Tapá taw nak ahá má nga nángki.	My father lives in that small house.
Give this rupee to him	Echeráng chi piyá	Tebák báliko ...	Já táchok pánam áges-áng.	Eá nun kháu usuá áng-lák.	Taw ngin khawchá taw náhá taw fási.	Give this rupee to him.

Take those rupees from him.	Arángchi chiklulaniá hánchiyá.	Baibhinu baithung haneo.	Ibáji táchok áighá pa táng nángági penarwáng.	Usuá ánpá nun pai ján hái.	Taw ngin jyák mapu iyáchi.	Take those rupees from him.
Beat him well and bind him with ropes.	Mohaná táche chingi atá.	Krogá chiká áling rikáo.	Páták khángá ásokáng áno songjági álenáng.	Usua máile máithen áthásu usuá lenge khádu.	Taw ná set chi sá chi..	Beat him well and bind him with ropes.
Draw water from the well.	Aku chi fra achuá..	Khálat áchi hiniro ..	Khánglá táng nongági chho tátetáng.	Takai anpa tikh hoi ..	Taw yang pa mápu yang sawchi.	Draw water from the well.
Walk before me ..	Abhangi nábbá ..	Kitáng menáng cháo	Ka meyang teják jájá..	Ku pám thomá ahám hái.	Tessei sawmá kemchi	Walk before me.
Whose boy comes behind you?	Ni chalá nicha acha chailá?	Michingá chu cháre iátoko?	Ná meyang tesse seri jari árntági.	Náng fáimá ohompu..	Ata náng feima awhá wenkiki?	Whose boy comes behind you?
From whom did you buy that?	Na achathinge shi chalá?	Náng kutáng lia? ..	Ibáji sitáng ali ..	O má sápu ..	Nángá taw aw seih sák kichi.	From whom did you buy that?
From a shop-keeper of the village.	Kia aiyán shi cha..	Ai am ga tokáni hiano	Ki angarr me yang goládári táng nangogi	Tinok unpá hát ..	Ataw ching mápu taw náng mápu sák kai inkiki.	From a shop-keeper of the village.

DEKA HIMONG DIALECT (NAGA HILLS).

Numerals.

One	Áká.
Two	Áná.
Three	Áshum.
Four	Pojjo.
Five	Pongo.
Six	Torok.
Seven	Ténnétt.
Eight	Tee.
Nine	Toko.
Ten	Térr.
Twenty	Muttcho.
Fifty	Téném.
Hundred	Teleng, or nuklang.

Pronouns.

I	Nee.
We	Ónook.
You	Ná.
He	Pá.
They	Párénook.
Of me	Kou, or ko.
Of us	Ójjo.
Of you	Nnoo.
Of him	Párr.
Of them	Parre nook.
Mine	Kou.
Our	Ojjo.
Your	Nar.
His	Par.
Their	Parronook.
Hand	Téká.
Foot	Témoo-boo.
Nose	Ténee.
Eye	Tnok.
Mouth	Tebáng.
Tooth	Tépoo.
Ear	Ténárung.
Hair	Koo.
Head	Tukolák.
Tongue	Témélee.
Belly	Tubok.
Back	Trungtung.
Iron	In.
Silver	Tareebee in.
Father	Toboo.
Mother	Téttehé.
Brother	Ténoo.
Sister	Tennoo.
Man	Nishung.
Woman	Téttchér
Wife	Geenungchu.
Child	Téttcheer.
Son	Cheer.
Daughter	Ténnu.
Slave	Álár.
Cultivator	Álloo-eemér
Shepherd	Mér á cheebá
God	Loongkee-jeengbá.
Devil	Sungrum.
Sun	Anno.
Moon	Etá.
Star	Pétteenu.
Fire	Me.
Water	Chu.
House	Kee.
Horse	Koorr.
Cow	Nasee chulá.
Dog	Ájjo.
Cat	Tánnoo.
Cock	Án tooboong.
Duck	Pátták.
Ass	Have no such name in nga language.
Camel	Ditto ditto.
Bird	Ujjo.
Go	Wáng.
Eat	Jungáng.
Sit	Tá-mén.
Come	Arung.
Beat	Tájjok.
Stand	Té-nukták.
Die	Tásér.
Give	Ágéjáng.
Run	Tásém.
Up	Ájjoklen.
Near	Ánásá.

Who	... Seebá.
And	... Ánou.
Yes	... Áu.
Down	... Télung.
Far	... Táláng.
What	... Kétehee.
But	... Jookoo.
No	... Nungá.
Before	... Tejáklén.
Behind	... Tésélén.
Why	... Kásá.
If	... Aj ánglá.
Alas	... Ái-téi.
A father	... Tóboo.
Of a father	... Tóboo nong.
To a father	... Tóboo nong.
From a father	... Tóboo nóng-é.
Fathers	... Tóboo nong-ér.
Of fathers	... Tóboo nongér nung.
To fathers	... Tóboo nongér nung.
From fathers	... Toboo nonger nungé.
A daughter	... Ténno.
Of a daughter	... Tennolá nong.
To a daughter	... Tennola nong.
From a daughter	... Tennola nunge.
Daughters	... Ténnoolá nunger.
Of daughters	... Tennoolá nunger nong.
To daughters	... Tennoolá nungér nong.
From daughters	... Tennoola nunger nunge.
A good man	... Nishung tájung.
Of a good man	... Nishung tajung-nung.
To a good man	... Nishung tájung-nong.
From a good man	.. Nishung átjung nung-é.
Good men	... Nishung tajung nunger.
Of good men	... Nishung tajung nunger nong.
To good men	... Nishung tajung nunger nong.
From good men	... Nishung tajung nunger nung.
A good woman	... Téttcher tajung.
Good women	... Téttcher tajung tésé.
A bad boy	... Tanoor tám ájung.
A bad girl	... Téttchér jánoo tám ájung.
Good	... Tájung.
Better	... Kángá jung.
Best	... Tájung tubá.
High	... Táláng.
Higher	... Tálángbá.
Highest	... Táláng teeba.
A horse	... Koorr tooboongka.
A mare	... Koorr téttchéká.
Horses	... Koorr teluk.
Mares	... Koor téttchéluk.
A bull	... Náshee poongcheeká.
A cow	... Nashee chulaká.
Bulls	... Nashee poongcheeluk.
Cows	... Nashee chula luk.
A dog	... Ajjoká
A bitch	... Ajjo tetcheká.
Dogs	... Ájjo luk.
Bitches	... Ajjo tetcheluk.
A he-goat	... Náboongká.
A female goat	... Náboong tetchéká.
Goats	... Naboong luk.

Naga have not any name for deer, because in the mountain have no such animal.

I am	.. Ne are.
You are	.. Ná are.
We are	.. Onook are.
He is	.. Pa are.
They are	.. Parénook are.
I was	.. Ne leeásho.
We were	.. Onook leeásho.
You were	.. Ná leeásho.
He was	.. Pá leeásho
They were	.. Pasénook leeásho.
You were	.. Nénook leeásho.
Be	.. Leeá tom.
To be	.. Leeá tomcho.
Having been	.. Leeá tomasho.
I may be	.. Ne leeátom lábá.
I shall be	.. Ne leeátom-lár.
I should be	.. Ne leeátomlaba.
Beat	.. Tájok.
To beat	.. Tájokcho.
Having beaten	.. Ájok.

I beat	.. Ne ájok.	I am beaten	.. Ne ájok.
You beat	.. Ná ájok.	I was beaten	.. Ne joka leeásho.
He beats	.. Pá ájok.	I shall be beaten	.. Ne joklár.
We beat	.. Ónooké ájok.	I go	.. Ne odee.
You beat	.. Nenooké ájok.	Thou goest	.. Ná ódáge.
They beat	.. Parénooké ájok.	He goes	.. Pá autcher.
I am beating	.. Ne jodkage.	I went	.. Ne orr.
I was beating	.. Ne jokeeálee.	You went	.. Ná uká.
I had beaten	.. Ne joko leeasho.	He went	.. Pá uká.
I may beat	.. Ne jokter.	Go	.. Wáng.
I shall beat	.. Ne jokla.	Going	.. Odágé.
I should beat	.. Ne joklaha.	Goue	.. Ugo.

What is your name?	Nenong seeba?
How old is this horse?	Koorr yá kam kooyee?
How far is it from here to Kashmir? ...	Yung neengé Káshmir koopeegá?
I have walked a long way to-day ...	Ne tánno ápeegá senogo.
How many sons are there in your father's house?	Noboor keedangé tétcheer kooyeegá álé?
The son of my uncle is married to her sister	Ugalar cheere tenootu kéyé áv.
In the house is the saddle of the white horse	Koorr tamisung méndén jee kee dang lur.
Put the saddle upon his back	Koorr rungtung nung méndén álén lákáng
I have beaten his son with many stripes ...	Ne paro cheer dang áeebén jukokéhuá.
He is grazing cattle on the top of the hill	Attáng kulák nung pa nashee téluk jeeung. dak cho dagee.
He is sitting on a horse under that tree ...	Ábá sungjungnungjee, koorr rungtung nung suager pa méná leer.
His brother is taller than his sister ...	Paro ténoo dáng pá teno tálangbá.
The price of that is two rupees and a half ...	Ábá álángjee tátchak ana sér a doleéá.
My father lives in that small house ...	Obalabo ótjee kee tálába nung leer.
Give this rupee to him	Tatchak ebái panong ágéjáng.
Take those rupees from him	Pakét nunge sun jee honarong.
Beat him well and bind him with ropes ...	Pádák jung jungá tuper, leesho age séntéká yuáng chuboo nung chuda tétáng.
Walk before me	Kéják dáng já jáng.
Whose boy comes behind you?	Nésélén sire cheer ároodágee?
From whom did you buy that?	Na ajee seeba dang alee?
From a shop-keeper of the village ...	Kee a nung aleeba gula nunge alee.

The above is a list of words and phrases translated into the language spoken by the Deka Himong Nagas, and has been compiled by a Native Christian teacher attached to the Baptist Mission at Seebsaugor.

LIST OF WORDS AND PHRASES

IN THE

LANGUAGE OF THE TRIBES

INHABITING THE

KHASI AND JYNTEAH HILLS.

List of words and phrases in the Language of the Tribes inhabiting the Khasi and Jynteah Hills.

English.	Khasi.	Synteng.	Battoa dialect.	Amwee dialect.	Lakadong dialect.	English.
One ...	Wei ...	Wi ...	Wi ...	Mi ...	Bi ...	One.
Two ...	Ar ...	Ar ...	Ár ...	O ...	Á ...	Two.
Three ...	Lai ...	Lei ...	La ...	La ...	Loi ..	Three.
Four ...	Saw ...	So ...	So ...	Siá ...	Tháu ...	Four.
Five ...	San ...	San ...	Sán ...	Sán ...	Thán ...	Five.
Six ...	Hynriw ...	Ynru ..	Ynru ...	Thrau ...	Thro ...	Six.
Seven ...	Hyniew ...	Ynniaw ...	Yniá ...	Ynthla ...	Humthloi ..	Seven.
Eight ...	Phra ...	Phra ...	Phrá ...	Humpyo ...	Humpy á ...	Eight.
Nine ...	Khyndai ...	Khynde ...	Khynda ...	Hunsiá ..	Hunsuai ...	Nine.
Ten ...	Shiphew ...	Shiphaw ...	Shiphá ...	Shipho ...	Shipháі ...	Ten.
Twenty ...	Arphew ...	Ar phaw ...	Ar pha ...	Arphui ..	Ar phái ...	Twenty.
Fifty ...	Sanphew ...	Sanphaw ...	Sán pha ...	San phui ...	Zan phai ...	Fifty.
Hundred ...	Shispah ...	Shispah ...	Shispáh ...	Shi su wáh ...	Shi su wah ...	Hundred.
I ...	Nga ...	Nga ...	Ngá ...	Ná ...	Á ...	I.
We ...	Ngi ...	I ...	I ...	Ái ...	I ...	We.
Thou ...	Me ...	Me ...	Ma ...	I ám ...	Ám ..	Thou.
You ...	Phi ...	Phi ...	Shi ..	Áhi ...	Shi ...	You.
They ...	Ki ...	Ki ...	Ká ...	Ká ...	Ká ..	They.
Of me ...	Na nga ...	Na nga ...	Na ngá ...	Ná nga á ...	Ná nga a ...	Of me.
Of us ...	Na ngi ...	Na I ...	Ná I ..	Ná ái ...	Na I ...	Of us.
Of thee ...	Na me ...	Na me ...	Na ma ...	Ná I ám ...	Ná ma ...	Of thee.

Of you	Na phi	Na phi	Na phi	Ti I am	Na phi	Of you.
Of him	Na u	Na u o	Ná u	Ná aiu	Ti bá-u	Of him.
Of them	Na ki	Na ki	Ná ki	Ná ii	Ná ki	Of them.
Mine	Jong nga	Jong nga	Jong nga	Jong nia	Jong a	Mine.
Our	Jong ngi	Jong I	Jong Í	Jong u	Jong Í	Our.
Thine	Jong me	Jong me	Jong ma	Jung ám	Jung ma	Thine.
Your	Jong phi	Jong phi	Jong phi	Jong ahi	Jong phi	Your.
His	Jong u	Jong u o	Jong u	Jong ia u	Jung u hi	His.
Their	Jong ki	Jong ki	Jong ki	Jong ai ki	Jong ki	Their.
Hand	Kyti	Kti	Ká kti	Ká ta	Ká toi	Hand.
Foot	Kyjat	Kyjat	Ká kyját	Ká nia	Ká nau	Foot.
Nose	Khymut	Khymut	I khymut	Mur kong	Mur kong	Nose.
Eye	Khymat	Khymat	Ka khymát	Ká mát	Ka mát	Eye.
Mouth	Shintur	I kytin	I ktín	Í tykong	Í tykong	Mouth.
Tooth	Byniat	Ly mein	Ka lymaín	Ka lyman	Ká lyman	Tooth.
Ear	Shkor	Shkur	Ka shkur	Tárang	Tárang	Ear.
Hair	U shinuih	U shniuh	U synuíh	U sngúh	Ú súh	Hair.
Head	Khlih	Khlih	Í khlih	Ka khliá	Ka khlán	Head.
Tongue	U thyllied	U thyllied	Ú thylliad	Ú khlid	Ú khliad	Tongue.
Belly	Ka kypoh	U kypoh	Ú kypuoh	U poh	U poh	Belly.
Back	Ing dong	I ryng khi	Í kuméáng	I tháliáng	Í thaliang	Back.
Iron	U nar	U nar	U nár	U nar	Ú nar	Iron.
Gold	Ksier	I ksiar	Í kysiár	I ksi	Í ksi	Gold.
Silver	Rupa	I rupa	Í rupuá	I rupo	Í rupá	Silver.

List of words and phrases in the Language of the Tribes inhabiting the Khasi and Jynteah Hills.—(Continued.)

English.	Khasi.	Synteng.	Battoa dialect.	Amwee dialect.	Lakadong dialect.	English.
Go ..	Khie ...	Khai ...	Lá ..	Lia ..	Loi ..	Go.
Eat ..	Bam ...	Bam ...	Bám ..	Bo ..	Bá ..	Eat.
Sit ..	Shong ...	Shong ...	Shong ..	Skiá ..	Skán ..	Sit.
Up ..	Hajerong .	Ha jerong ...	Há jrong ..	Há korong ..	Há korong ..	Up.
Near ..	Jan ...	Jan ...	Háján ..	Hu ján ..	Ján ..	Near.
Who ..	U ei ...	U I ...	Ú Í ..	Ú a ..	U u ..	Who.
And ..	Bad ...	Bad ...	Bá ..	Bo ..	Bo ..	And.
Yes ..	Hoid ...	Oh ...	Ú úoh ..	Hu u ..	Áh ..	Yes.
A father ..	U kypa ...	U pa ...	Ú puá ..	Ú po ..	U pá ..	A father.
Of a father ..	Ńa u kypa ...	Na u pa ...	Ná u puá ..	Ná ú po ..	Ná ú pá ..	Of a father.
To a father ..	Ha u kypa ...	Ha u pa ...	Íá ú puá ..	I á ú po ..	Há u pá ..	To a father.
From a father ..	Na u pa ...	Na u pa ...	Ná ú puá ..	Ná u po ..	Ná ú pá ..	From a father.
A daughter ..	Ka khun kynthei ...	Ka khon kynthai ...	Ká huon kynthá ..	Ká huon kyntha ..	Ká hun hunthoi ..	A daughter.
From a daughter ..	Na ka khun kynthei ...	Na ka khon kynthai ...	Ná ká huon kynthá	Na ka huón yntha ..	Ná huon hun thoi ..	From a daughter.
A good man ..	U briw ba bha ...	U bru u ba bha ...	U bru ba bha ..	U jopru u la diam ..	U mursoi u bá iám ..	A good man.
Of a good man ..	......	......	Ná ú brú bá bhá ..	Ná újopraúba diám..	Na u mursoi u bá iam	Of a good man.
To a good man ..	Ha u briw ba bha ...	Ha u bru ba bha ...	Í á ú brú ú bá bhá..	Íá ú joprú bá diám..	Íá ú mursoi u bá iam	To a good man.
From a good man ..	Na u briw ba bha ...	Na u bru ba bha ...	Ná ú bru ú bá bhá	Ná u jopru ú bá diám	Ná ú mursoi u bá iam	From a good man.
A good woman ..	Ka briw ba bha ...	Ka bru ka ba bha ...	Ká kynthá ká bá bhá	Ká jopru ká bá diám	Ká hunthoi ká bá iam	A good woman.
A bad boy ..	U khynnah bymman...	U khonnah ba sib ...	Ú khynná bymán ..	Ú humbo u bá sniá ..	U humbo u ba sih ..	A bad boy.
Good ..	Bha ...	Bha ..	I bá bhá ..	Bá diám ..	Í ám ..	Good.

High	Jerong	Jerong	Jrong	Korong	Korong	High.
A horse	U kulai	U kule	Ká kula	Kuroi	Kurái	A horse.
A bull	U masi shinrang	U masi shinrang	Ú mássi	Ú mássan	U massan	A bull.
A dog	U ksew	U ksaw	Ú kysá	Ú ksiá	U ksán	A dog.
A he-goat	U lang shinrang	U lang shinrang	Ú blá ang shinrang	Ú blang tyrma	U blang tyrma	A he-goat.
A male deer	U bythong, u bythet	U ser, U bythong	Ú py thong shiurang	U pythong tyrma	U py thong tyrmoi	A male deer.
	U ser, u khiat	U rynjang, U skai	......	....	....	....
	U skei	......	......	....	....	....
I am	Nga long	Nga long	Ngá mán	Ngá long	Mán	I am.
We are	Ngi long	I long	Í mán	Ai ki	I mán	We are.
Father	Kypa	Pa	Ú puá	U pá	U pá	Father.
Mother	Kymei	Bei	Ká ba	Ká ma	Ká moi	Mother.
Brother	Para shinrang	Para shinrang	Ú pá in	Ú párọ	U láih	Brother.
Sister	Para kynthei	Para kynthai	Ká pá in	Ká páro	Ká laih	Sister.
Man	U briw	U bru	Ú bru	Ú jopron	Ú múrsoi	Man.
Woman	Ka briw	Ka bru	Ká kynthá	Ká yntha	Ká ynthoi	Woman.
Wife	Ka tynga	Ka shkaw	Kách kiá	Ká kynáng	Ka chybbi	Wife.
Child	Khynnah	Khon tlung	Ú khon bo	Ú humbo	Ú humbo	Child.
Son	Khun shinrang	Khon shinrang	Ú huon	Ú hun	U hun	Son.
Daughter	Khun kynthei	Khou kynthai	Ká khyn kynthá	Ká hun yntbá	Ká hun ynthoi	Daughter.
Slave	Mraw	Bro	Bro	Mo	Ma	Slave.
Cultivator	Nongrep	Nongrep	Ú bá lur	Á hi	U bá lur	Cultivator.
Shepherd	U nong-ap-langbrot	U nong-ap-longbrot	Ú nong shárai blang	U nong sharai blang	U nong sharai blang	Shepherd.
God	U blei	U blai	Í kysiár	Í ksi	Íksi	God.
Devil	Soitan	Soitan	U soi-tan	U soi-tan	Ú soi-tain	Devil.

List of words and phrases in the Language of the Tribes inhabiting the Khasi and Jynteah Hills.—(Continued.)

English.	Khasi.	Synteng.	Battoa dialect.	Amwee dialect.	Lakadong dialect.	English.
Come ..	Alé ...	Alé ..	Álla ..	Álla ..	Álla ..	Come.
Beat ..	Shoh ...	Bom ..	Bom ..	Bom ..	Shop ..	Beat.
Stand ..	Jeng ..	Jen ...	Í iain ..	Sain ..	Zain ..	Stand.
Down ..	Ha-ty-bian ..	Hatybian ...	Ha tyban ..	Ha ram ..	Ha ram ..	Down.
Far ..	Jing ngai ...	Kynjeh ..	Jong ngá ..	Shn ngoi ..	Zing ngái ..	Far.
What ..	Aiüh ...	I yee ..	Ká J'a ..	Í a ..	U a ..	What.
But ..	Hynrei ..	Katda ..	Maita ..	Í ..	Í ..	But.
No ..	Em ..	Oho ..	Ym am ..	A hon ahta ..	Ahta ..	No.
Two daughters ..	Ar hi khun kynthei ...	Ar ki khon kynthai ..	Árngut khon kyntba	Ár ba hun yntba ..	Arboi hun ynthoi ..	Two daughters.
Two fathers ..	Ar kypa ...	Arpa ...	Ar pua ..	Ar po ..	Arpa ..	Two fathers.
Two good men ..	Ar ngut ki briw ba bha	Ar ngut ki bru babha ..	Árngut kibru ba bhá	Arba ki jopru kiba diam.	Árboi ki mursoi ki bá iám.	Two good men.
Better ..	Kham bha .	Khambha ...	Rab bha ..	Rább diám ..	Rab ji ám ..	Better.
Higher ..	Kham jerong ..	Kham jerong ...	Rab jrong ..	Ráb korong ..	Ráb korong ..	Higher.
A mare .	Ka kulai ..	Ka koole ...	Ká kula kyntha ..	Ká kuroi yntba ..	Ka kurái ynthoi ..	A mare.
A cow ..	Ka masi ..	Ka masi ...	Ká mássi ..	Ká massan ..	Ká mássan ..	A cow.
A bitch ...	Ka ksew kynthei ...	Ka ksaw kynthai ..	Ka ksá kynthá ..	Ká ksiá yntha ..	Ka ksán yn thoi ..	A bitch.
A female goat ..	Ka lang kynthei ...	Ka lang kynthai ...	Ká blang kynthá ..	Ká blang yntha ..	Ká blang yn thoi ..	A female goat.
A female deer ..	Ka bythong, ka bythet, kaser, ka khiat, ka shei	Ka, ser, ka bythong karynjang, ka skai	Ka py thong kynthá	Ká py thong yntha..	Ka pythong ynthoi ..	A female deer.

Thou art	Me long	Me long	Má man	Á mán	Mán	Thou art.
You are	Phi long	Phi long	Phi mán	Í a mán	I a mán	You are.
Sun	Ka sngi	Ka sngi	Ká sngi	Ká jungá	Ká sngoi	Sun.
Moon	U bynai	U bynai	Ú byná	U punuo	U punoi	Moon.
Star	U khlur	Khlur	U khlur	U khlo chomán	U khlo choman	Star.
Fire	Ka düng	Ka deim	I din	Í choman	Í choman	Fire.
Water	Ka um	Ka oom	Ka um	Ká ám	Ká ám	Water.
House	Jing	Jüng	Í ung	Ka 1 sü	I snü	House.
Horse	Kulai shinrang	Kule shinrang	Ká kula	Ka kuroi	Ka kurái	Horse.
Cow	Masi kynthei	Masi kynthai	Ká mássi	Ká mássan	Ká mássan	Cow.
Dog	Ksew shinrang	Ksaw shinrang	U ksiá	Ú ksiá	U ksáw	Dog.
Cat	Miaw	Miaw	Ká miáw	Ká miw	Ka miáw	Cat.
Cock	Jar shinrang	Jar shinrang	U syi ar rungkuo	U syi runghoh	U syi runghoh	Cock.
Duck	Ka han	Ka rapassa	Ká ráp ásá	Ká rápásso	Ká rápásá	Duck.
Ass	Gada	Gadda	Ká gádá	Gáddá	Ká gádá	Ass.
Camel	Ut	Ut	Ka ut	Ká üt	Ká üt	Camel.
Bird	Ka sim	Ka sim	Ka sim	Ká ksam	Ká ksam	Bird.
Die	Jap	Jap	Í ap	Ip	Ip	Die.
Give	Ai	E.	A	Á	Oi	Give.
Run	Phet	Phet	Í ut	Rykew	Rykew	Run.
Before	Ha khymat	Ha phrang	Há phráng	Í phrang	Ná phrang	Before.
Behind	Sha dün	Sha dün	I dian	Putre	Putre	Behind.
Why	Balei	Ileh	Í leh	Kí a	Ti bá khi	Why.
Alas	Aha	Ooho	Ú hü	U hü	Ú hü	Alas.

List of words and phrases in the Language of the Tribes inhabiting the Khasi and Jynteah Hills.—(Continued.)

English.	Khasi.	Synteng.	Battoa dialect.	Amwee dialect	Lakadong dialect.	English.
If ..	Lada ..	Lada ...	Ngi dá ..	Ná ..	Ná ..	If.
Fathers ..	Ki kypa ..	Ki pa ...	Ki kypuá ..	Ki kypuo ..	Ki kypá ..	Fathers.
Of fathers ..	Na ki kypa ..	Na ki pa ...	Na ki kypna ..	Ná ki puá ..	Ná ki pá ..	Of fathers.
To fathers ...	Ha ki kypa ..	Ha ki pa ..	Sha ki pá ..	Shá ki po ..	Shá ki pá ..	To fathers.
From fathers ...	Na ki kypa ..	Na ki pa ..	Na ki pá ..	Ná ki po ..	Ná ki pá ..	From fathers.
Daughters ...	Ki khun kynthei ..	Ki khon kynthai ..	Ki khon kynthá ..	Ki hun yntha ..	Ki hun ynthoi ..	Daughters.
Of daughters ...	Na ki khun kynthei ..	Na ki khon kynthai ...	....	....	....	Of daughters.
To daughters ..	Ha ki khun kynthei ..	Ha ki khon kynthai ...	Shá ki khon kynthá	Shá ki hun yntha ..	Shá ki hun ynthoi ..	To daughters.
From daughters ...	Na ki khun kynthei ..	Na ki khon kynthai ...	Ná ki khon kynthá	Ná ki hun yntha ..	Ná ki hun ynthoi ..	From daughters.
Good men ...	Ki briw ba bba ..	Ki bru ba bba ..	Ki brú bá bbá ...	Ki jopru ki bá diám	Ki mursoi ki bá iam ..	Good men.
Of good men ..	Na ki briw ba bha ..	Na ki bru ba bba ..	....	....	....	Of good men.
To good men ...	Ha ki briw ba bha ..	Ha ki bru ba bha ..	....	....	....	To good men.
From good men ...	Na ki briw ba bha ..	Na ki bru ba bha ..	Ná ki bru kiba bha	Na ki jopru kibá diám	Na ki mursoi kibá iam	From good men.
Good women ...	Ki kynthei ba bha ..	Ki kynthai ba bba ..	Ki kyntha ki bá bbá	Ki yntha ki bá diám	Ki ynthoi kibá iám ..	Good women.
A bad girl ..	Ka khynnah bymman	Ka khon thong ka basih solon ..	Khynnáh kába sih...	Ká humbo ká bytah	Ka humbo kábá shi ..	A bad girl.
Best ...	Bhatam ...	Kaba miat tam ..	Ka bá miát tain ..	Kábá rymma tain ..	Ká ba iám tain ..	Best.
Highest ...	J-erong-tam ..	Jerong tam ..	Kábá jrong tain ..	Ká korong tain ..	Ká korong tain ..	Highest.
Horses ..	Ki kulai ..	Ki kule ...	Ki kula ...	Ki kuruo ..	Ki kurái ..	Horses.
Bulls ..	Ki masi shinrang ..	Ki masi shinrang ..	Ki mássi kyrtong ...	Ki massan kyrtong ..	Ki massan kyrtong ..	Bulls.
Dogs ...	Ki ksew shinrang ..	Ki ksaw shinrang ..	Ki ksia ...	Ki ksiá ..	Ki ksow ..	Dogs.

Mares	Ki kulai kynthei	Ki kule kynthai	Ki kula kynthá	Ki kuruo ynthá	Ki kurái ynthoi	Mares.
Cows	Ki masi kynthei	Ki masi kynthai	Ki mássi	Ki mássan	Ki mássan	Cows.
Bitches	Ki ksew kynthei	Ki ksaw kynthai	Ki ksiá	Ki ksiá	Ki ksow	Bitches.
Goats	Ki blang	Ki blang	....	... .	....	Goats.
Deer	Bythong, bythet, ser, khiat skei.	Ser, bythong, rynjang skai.	Pythong	Pythong	Pythong	Deer.
He is	U long	U long	Ú mán	U ju mán	U mán	He is.
They are	Ki long	Ki long	Ki mán	Iá mán	I ä mán	They are.
I was	Nga la long, nga ladon	Nga la long, nga la don	Ngá lá mán	Ngá dá mán	Ngá dá mán	I was.
We were	Ngi la don	Ngi da em	Dá am	Dá áh	Dá áh	We were.
Be	Long	Long	Mán	Mán	Mán	Be.
I may be	Lehse ngán long	Nga dang u ioh	Dá ú mán	Dá ú mán	Dá ú mán	I may be.
Beat	Shoh	Bom	Shuoh	Shoh	Shoh	Beat.
I beat	Nga shoh	Nga bom	Ngá shuoh	Ngá shoh	Ngá shoh	I Beat.
We beat	Ngi shoh	Ngi bom	Ngi shuoh	Ai shoh	Ai shoh	We beat.
I am beating	Nga dang shoh	Nga dang bom khyrngang.	Dáng shuoh	Dáng shoh	Dáng shoh	I am beating.
I may beat	Leh-se-nga-ioh-shoh	Bong da ioh bom	Bong ioh shuoh	Bong dá shohó	Bong di shuoh	I may beat.
I am beaten	Nga-dang-ioh-shoh	Nga dang ioh bom khyrngang.	Dáng ioh shuoh	Dáng judi shoh	Dáng judi shoh	I am beaten.
I go	Nga leit	Nga lai	Ngá lá	Ju liá	Ju loi	I go.
I went	Nga-la-leit	Nga da dep lai	Dá dap lá	Niá dá liá	Ngá dá loi	I went.
Go	Leit	Lai	Lá	Lia	Loi	Go.
Thou wast	Me-la-long	Da man mi	Ma dá mán	I ám dá mán	A má dá mán	Thou wast.
You were	Phi-la-long	Da dep man phi	Phi dá dap man	Phi dá dap man	A phi dá abmán	You were.
To be	Ban-long	Ba u man	Bá u man	Dá mán	Dá mán	To be.

List of words and phrases in the Language of the Tribes inhabiting the Khasi and Jynteah Hills.—(Continued.)

English.	Khasi.	Synteng.	Battoa dialect.	Amwee dialect.	Lakadong dialect.	English.
Being ..	Dang-long ..	Dang man ..	Dáng mán ..	Dáng mán ...	Dáng mán ...	Being.
I shall be ..	Ngan-sa-long ..	Nga dang u man ..	Ngá sá ú mán ..	Niá uju mán ...	A u ju mán ...	I shall be.
To beat ..	Ban-shoh ..	Ban bom ..	....	.. ..	....	To beat.
I beat ..	....	....	Ba u shuoh ..	Ju shoh ...	Ba u shoh ...	I beat.
Beating ..	Dang-shoh ..	Dang bom ..	Dáng shuoh ..	Dáng shoh ...	Dáng shoh ...	Beating.
Thou beatest ..	Me-shoh ..	Me bom ..	Ma shuoh ..	Aim shoh ...	Mi shoh ...	Thou beatest.
You beat ..	Phi-shoh ..	Phi bom ..	Phi shuoh ..	A hi shoh ...	Phi shoh ...	You beat.
I was beating ..	Nga-dang-la-shoh ..	Nga dang bom ..	Nga dang la shoh ..	Dang shoh ...	Dang shoh ...	I was beating.
I shall beat ..	Ngan-sa-shoh ..	Ngan bom ..	Ngá dáng ú shoh ..	Ngá dáng ju shoh ...	Ngá dáng ú shoh ...	I shall beat.
I was beaten ..	Dang-lah-shoh-ia nga	La bom ia nga ..	Dáng dap shoh ia ngá	Dáng dap shoh há niá	Dang dap shoh há-á...	I was beaten.
Thou goest ..	Me-leit ..	Me lai ..	Ma bu lá ..	I ám ju liá ...	A mi u ju loi ...	Thou goest.
Thou wentest ..	Me-la-leit ..	Me da dep lai ..	Ma dá dap lá ..	Am dá liám ...	Am dá dap loi ..	Thou wentest.
Going ..	Dang-leit ..	Dang lai ..	Dáng lá ..	Dáng lia ...	Dáng loi ...	Going.
He was ..	U-la-long ; u-la-don ..	Da dep em u ..	Ú da man, dá ám ..	Dá mán ú ...	Má dá mán ...	He was.
They were ..	....	....	Ki dá dap mán ..	A bi da dap mán ...	Ki dá dap mán ...	They were.
Having been ..	La lah don ..	Da dep em ..	Dap am ..	Dá dap am ...	Dá dapam ...	Having been.
I should be ..	Lehse ngan long ..	Dang u man nga ..	....	....	....	I should be.
I shall be ..	....	....	Bong u mán nga ..	Tra bong mán ...	Bong u mán ...	I shall be.
Having beaten ..	Dang shoh putet ..	Dang bom khyrngang	Dáng shuoh putit ia nga.	Dáng shoh ki ba nia...	Dáng shoh putet tibá	Having beaten.
He beats ..	U shoh ..	Ki bom ..	Ú shuoh ..	Ú shuoh ...	Ú shuoh ...	He beats.

They beat ...	....	....	Ki shuoh ..	A' shoh ki ...	Bá shoh ki ...	They beat.
I had beaten ..	Nga la-lah-shoh ..	Nga da dep bom ..	Ngá dá dap shoh ..	Niá dá dap shoh ...	A' dá dap shoh ...	I had beaten.
I should beat ..	Ngan shoh ..	Ngan bom ..	....	....	....	I should beat.
I shall beat ..	....	....	Ngá ü shoh ..	Niá ju shoh ...	A' ü shoh ...	I shall beat.
I shall be beaten ..	Yn shoh ia nga ...	Da u bom ia nga ..	U shuoh ia ngá ..	U ju shoh há niá ...	U shoh ba a ...	I shall be beaten.
He goes ..	U leit ..	U lai ..	U lá ..	U liá ...	U loi ...	He goes.
He went ..	U la leit ..	U la dep lai ..	U dá dap lá ..	Ú dá dap lia ...	Ú dá dap loi ...	He went.
Gone ..	La leit ..	Da dep lai ..	Dá dap lá u ..	Dá dap lia u ...	Dá dap loi u ...	Gone.
What is your name?	Kaeika kyrteng jong phi?	E pyrtuit phi? ...	I'ü I'purtuit phi ..	I'a i táwi ang phi ...	Tá i tiang phi ...	What is your name?
How old is this horse?	Katnoka ryta u ne u kulai?	Katnoon i ryta uni u koole?	Katnu iryta u ni u kula.	Shi bau ká ruta u na u kuruo u jong iau.	Shi bau i ryta u kurai jong u.	How old is this horse?
How far is it from here to Kashmir?	Jingngai katno nangne sha Kashmir?	Katwon ba kynjih na ini sha Kashmir.?	Kátno bajing ngái ná i ni shá Kashmir.	Shi hun bow ná chungoi nu na sha Kashmir,	Kat shi bau chungoi tina sha Kashmir.	How far is it from here to Kashmir?
How many sons are there in your father's house?	Katno ngut ki khun shinrang ha üng u kypa jongphi?	Katno ngut ki khon shinrang ha üng u pa phi?	Kátno ngut kikhuon shinrang ba am ha ung u pua phi.	Shi hun bow ba ki hun tyrma u po sha sniu	Shi baw boi ki hun tyrmoi tasni u pa phi.	How many sons are there in your father's house?
I have walked a long way to-day.	Myntaha kane ka sngi nga laiad jing ngai lynti.	Ha kani ka sngi jing ngai sang ka luti ba lai.	Nga la le jing nga myntu kana ka sngi.	Kana ka junga lia chungoi dang ia i ryhan.	Mynta ka sngoi jing ngai sang juloi i ryhan.	I have walked a long way to-day.
The son of my uncle is married to his sister.	U khun u kynü jongnga u shongkurim ia kapara jong u.	U khon u ma u la shong shkaw ha ka paiuh u.	U khuon u ma da la chikaha ka paiu u.	U hun u niáw lia kynang ta ka parow.	U hun u ma u loi chybbi tib a ka la ih.	The son of my uncle is married to his sister.
In this house is the saddle of the white horse.	Kajin u koolai lich kadon haüng.	Ka jin u koole ba lich ka em ha iung.	Há ká ung an ka jin u kula bá lah.	Li sni áh ká jin u kuruo ná slng.	Li sni bá áh ká jin ú kurai slang.	In the house is the saddle of the white horse.
Put the saddle upon his back.	Teh jin halor jong u ...	Kydoh ka jin ha jerong u.	Kuduoh ká jin há jrong ú.	Kut ka jin tiu korong u, or ti ka nau u.	Kydoh kajiu ha u korong u.	Put the saddle upon his back.

List of words and phrases in the Language of the Tribes inhabiting the Khasi and Jynteah Hills.—(Concluded.)

English.	Khasi.	Synteng.	Battoa dialect.	Amwee dialect.	Lakadong dialect.	English.
I have beaten his son with many stripes.	Nga la shoh bun thrü ia u khun jong u.	Nga la bom bun thrü ia u kyon u.	Ngá dá shuoh shibun thri ha u huon u.	Niá dá shoh lia u hun u she baw pla.	A ba shoh lia u hun u shibaw ploi.	I have beaten his son with many stripes.
He is grazing cattle on the top of the hills.	U ap blang, masi, halor lum.	U share blang, masi ha phdein lum.	Bá shara blang mássi-há jrong u lum.	Ba sharo blang máss-an ta ki na pydain.	Sharai blang massan borong pydain.	He is grazing cattle on the top of the hills.
He is sitting on a horse under that tree.	U shong kulai hopoh katai ka düng.	U shong koole hapoh katai ka düng.	U shong kula ha poh ka tia ka dain.	Skia kurou ta poh ka non ka ot.	Skau kuroi ta poh ka non ka ot.	He is sitting on a horse under that tree.
His brother is taller than his sister.	U para jong u kham jerong na ka para jong u.	U pain jong u kham jerong na ka paiuh.	Bá jrong u pa iu ná ka pá iu jong u.	Ba korong u parou ha ka parou.	Bakorong u la ü ha ka la ü u.	His brother is taller than his sister.
The price of that is two rupees and a half.	Ka dor katai long shi-tyngka-piah.	Ka dor katu shiluri piah.	I dor ká tia ar piah. .	I dor ka non opiah ...	I dor ka tun a piah ...	The price of that is two rupees and a half.
My father lives in that small house.	U kypa jong nga u shong haitai i üngrit.	U pa nga u shong ha itu i iung khian.	U pua shong lia itai i ung sy bait.	U po jong nia u skia ti hun sni ba sybiat.	U pa jong a skau ti sni sybbat.	My father lives in that small house.
Give this rupee to him	Ai kane ka tyngka ha u	E kani ka luri ia u ...	Á kana ka tyngko ia u.	A kana ka tyngko sha iau.	Oi kana ko tyngko ti ba u.	Give this rupee to him.
Take those rupees from him.	Shim noh kito ki tyng-ka na u.	Him noh ki tu ki luri na u.	Him kitu ki tyngka na u.	Tham ki tyngka na iau.	Tham ki tyngká ta ba u.	Take those rupees from him.
Beat him well and bind him with ropes.	Sympat ha ban da biang khum putet da ki tyllai.	Bom ia u jong heh, kydoh khyrnagng.	Shoh ia u ha ba jain kydoh putet dá u tylla.	Bom ia u tia san u, kut da u tarana.	Shoh ia u bái haba jain kut da uturai.	Beat him well and bind him with ropes.
Draw water from the well.	Tong um na ka pung	Pieh um na ka biar ...	Tong oom ná ká biár.	Pooh am ta biar ...	Pooh am ta biar.	Draw water from the well.

Walk before me ...	I ad ha shina jong nga	Pi lai ha phrang nga...	Phi ha phrang nga...	Hau ma phrang ngua.	Poi loi na phrang nguo	Walk before me.
Whose boy comes behind you?	U khun jong no u ba bud nadün jong phi.	U jong u tu u khon ba bud na dün phi.	Jong u khuon utia la na din.	Ú á jong hun u ba lia ta putra.	U tia jong hun ba loi shatroi.	Whose boy comes behind you?
From whom did you buy that?	Nang no phi thiod ia ka tai.	Na i won thied phi katu.	Na u ia thied phi ia kátu.	Ti u á kti bi ia ka tum.	Na u tia kti phi ia ka tum.	From whom did you buy that?
From a shop-keeper of the village.	Na u nong shong dukan ha shnong.	Na u ba shong dukan ha shuong.	Na u nong dá kynrá ha pyrdi shong.	Na u toon ba skia dukan ti pa a shnong.	Ti báh ba dai dukan ha paoi shnong.	From a shop-keeper of the village.

BURMESE LANGUAGES COMPARED WITH OTHERS.

English.	Shan of Burmah.	Mekir of Cachar.	Muneepooree.	Tonghtoo of Burmah.
Numerals.				
One ..	Neung ..	Ichi ..	Ámá ..	Ta-bâh ..
Two ..	Hsaung ..	Hini ..	Ánee ..	Nee-bâh ..
Three ..	Hsām ..	Ketham ..	Áhum ..	Thom-bâh ..
Four ..	Hsēe ..	Kli ..	Maree ..	Lit, *or* leet-bah ..
Five ..	Hah ..	Kuño ..	Mongá ..	Ngât-bâh ..
Six ..	Hok ..	Tharak ..	Taru ..	Thoo-bâh ..
Seven ..	Sit ..	Tharakachi ..	Taret ..	Noot-bâh ..
Eight ..	Pet ..	Nerkeb ..	Nipal ..	Thaut-bâh ..
Nine ..	Kow ..	Chirkeb ..	Mapol ..	Koot-bah ..
Ten ..	Hseep ..	Kep ..	Tárá ..	Tâh-tsee ..
Eleven ..	......	......	......	......
Twenty ..	Hsow ..	I kae ..	Kul ..	Nee-htsee ..
Fifty ..	Hah hseep ..	Kuaekep ..	Yenkai ..	Ngât-htsee ..
Hundred ..	Pāk ..	Unknown ..	Chámá ..	Taryah, *or* ta-reah..
Pronouns.				
I ..	Kow-khah ..	Ne ..	Ái ..	Khôay ..
We ..	How-khah ..	Nángthu ..	Ikhá ..	Nee-khô ..
Thou ..	Mul ..	......	Náng ..	Nâ ..
You ..	Hsoo ..	Nángthum ..	Náng khoi ..	Tsee, *or* thee ..
He ..	Man ..	Láke ..	Má ..	Weh ..
They ..	Khow ..	Haláke ..	Mákhoi ..	Weh-tsee ..
Of me ..	Kow-khah ..	Ne ..	Ingandá ..	Khoây-âkhrong ..
Of us ..	How-khah ..	Nangthum ..	Ikhodá ..	Nee-âkhrong ..
Of thee ..	Mul ..	......	Nángondá ..	Nâ-âkhrong ..
Of you ..	Hsoo ..	Nang ..	Nánghkoidá ..	Thee-âkhrong ..
Of him ..	Man ..	Bang ..	Mángandá ..	Weh-âkhrong ..
Of them ..	Khow ..	......	Makhoidá ..	Weh-tsee-âkhrong
Mine ..	Kow-khah ..	Ne ..	Áigi ..	Khôāy-tâ ..
Thy ..	......	......	......	......
Our ..	How-khah ..	Nángthum ..	Ikhoigi ..	Nee-tâ ..
Thine ..	Mul ..	......	Nángi ..	Na-ta ..
Your ..	Hsoo ..	Náng ..	Nángkhoigi ..	Thee-tâ ..
His ..	Man ..	Báng ..	Máigi ..	Weh-tâ ..
Their ..	Khow ..	......	Mákhoigi ..	Weh-tsee-tâ ..
Hand ..	Meu ..	Ibi ..	Khul ..	Tsoo, *or* tsu ..
Foot ..	Teen ..	Ikeng ..	Khong ..	Khâng ..
Nose ..	Hkoo-lang ..	Nakáng ..	Nátol ..	Nee-phoo ..
Eye ..	Tah, *or* māk-tah ..	I mek ..	Mit ..	Māi ..
Mouth ..	Hsop ..	Inghu ..	Chil ..	Phrong ..

Poi of Burmah.	Talain of Pegu (Burmah.)	Sonthali of Sonthal Pergunnahs, Western Bengal.	Moondaree of Chota Nagpore, Western Bengal.	English.
Pakar ..	Moä ..	Mit' ..	Míyad ..	One.
Punnai ..	Bä ..	Bārea ..	Bāria ..	Two.
Puttao ..	Pe ..	Péa ..	Apiā ..	Three.
Papulle ..	Paun ..	Pnéa ..	Upunya ..	Four.
Papar ..	P-sone, *or* m-sone	Moṛé ..	Moṇiān ..	Five.
Passeru ..	K-rou, *or* t-reou ..	Turui ..	Turúya ..	Six.
Passare ..	K-pauh, *or* ht-pauh	Eae ..	Eyá ..	Seven.
Passarea ..	K-cham, *or* t-cham	Irāl ..	Iralya ..	Eight.
Passaku ..	K-cheet *or* t-cheet	Āré ..	Áreya ..	Nine.
Parrar ..	Chauh ..	Gel ..	Gelya ..	Ten.
......	Chauh-moa ..	......	......	Eleven.
Pakke ..	Bä-cho ..	Mit'-isi ..	Míyad hisí ..	Twenty.
Sawpa ..	P-sone-cho ..	Bar-isi-gél ..	Bár hisí gelya	Fifty.
Yokor ..	Klaun ..	Moṛe-isi ..	Moṇi hisí ..	Hundred.
Kama ..	Oä ..	In ..	Aiñ or Iñ ..	I.
Hse er se ..	Pooey* ..	A-le-a-bon, a-b ..	Ale ..	We.
Nama ..	M-neh* ..	Am ..	Am ..	Thou.
Numai ..	M-neh-tau* ..	A-pe ..	Ape ..	You.
Amaya ..	Nyeh* ..	Ach' (ai:) ..	Iní ..	He.
Mee er se ..	Nyeh-tau* ..	A-ko ..	Ako ..	They.
......	......	In-ren, or'* reak' ..	Aiñya ..	Of me.
......	......	Ale-ren, or rea ..	Alea ..	Of us.
......	......	Am-ren, or reak' ..	Amá ..	Of thee.
......	......	Ape-ren, or rea ..	Apeá ..	Of you.
......	......	Ach'-ren, or reak' ..	Iniá ..	Of him.
......	......	Ako-ren, or reak' ..	Akoá ..	Of them.
......	......	Tin ..	Same as above	Mine.
......	......	Ta-m ..	......	Thy.
......	......	Ta-le ..	......	Our.
......	......	......	......	Thine.
......	......	Ta-pe ..	......	Your.
......	......	Ta-e ..	......	His.
......	......	Ta-ko ..	......	Their.
Ku ..	Toä ..	Ti ..	Tí ..	Hand.
Ape ..	Chung ..	Jaṅga ..	Kátá ..	Foot.
Nan pussu ..	Moo ..	Mu ..	Muṇ ..	Nose.
Mhay ..	Mote ..	Met' ..	Met ..	Eye.
Apakar ..	Paing ..	Mocha ..	Mochá ..	Mouth.

* *N.B.*—Cases distinguished by position.—Nominative precedes Verb; Objective follows Verb; Possessive placed after the thing possessed.

English.	Shan of Burmah.	Mekir of Cachar.	Muneepooree.	Tonghtoo of Burmah.
Tooth ...	Khyo ...	Icho ...	Yá ...	Tâ-ngâ ...
Ear ...	Hoo ...	Imo ...	Nákong ...	Nâ ...
Hair ...	Khoon ...	Ichhuu ...	Sam ...	Tâ-loo ...
Head ...	Ho ...	Iku ...	Kok ...	Ka-too ...
Tongue ...	Leen ...	Ide ...	Lei ...	Plee ...
Belly ...	Taung ...	Ipak ...	Puk ...	Hô ...
Back ...	Lang ...	Inung ...	Námgan ...	Ngâm ...
Iron ...	Lik ...	Ingchin ...	Yot ...	Pâthee ...
Gold ...	Kham ...	Cher ...	Sáná ...	Khâm ...
Silver ...	Ngeun ...	Rup ...	Rupá ...	Ron ...
Father ...	Pau ...	Po ...	Pá ...	Phâ ...
Mother ...	Mè ...	Pe ...	Má ...	Moo, *or* mu ...
Brother ...	......	Nekor ...	Muchimanán ...	......
Brother (elder) ...	Pee-sai ...	......	......	Wāi-kho ...
Brother (younger) ...	Naung-sai ...	......	......	Poo ...
Sister ...	......	Injurpi ...	Machal ...	......
Sister (elder) ...	Pee-nang ...	......	......	Wai-moo ...
Sister (younger) ...	Naung-yeeng ...	......	......	Poo-moo ...
Man ...	Ko on, *or* koon-sai, or hpoo-sai.	Pincho ...	Nipá ...	Loê ...
Woman ...	Koon-yeeng, or *or* hpoo-yeeng, *or* mè-yeeng.	Arnocho ...	Nupi ...	Loê-moo ...
Wife ...	May ...	Nepicho ...	Motu ...	Mâh ...
Child ...	Look ...	Uchhayár ...	Machá ...	Loê-pāi ...
Son ...	Look-sai ...	Uchho ...	Nipá machá ...	Poê ...
Daughter ...	Look-yeeng ...	Nechhapi ...	Nupi machá ...	Poê-moo ...
Slave ...	Khah ...	Bán ...	Mínái ...	Thon ...
Snake ...	......	......	......	......
Cultivator ...	Koon-hit-nah ...	Cháigátiki ...	Lon-noá mi ...	......
Shepherd ...	Koon-lăyng-hso ...	Bigabiyábáng ...	Shán silvá ...	......
God ...	Hprah ...	Arnámgete ...	Lái ...	Pârâh ...
Devil ...	Mah-nāt ...	Chelángo ...	Támnábá ...	Tâkiê, *or* tâkye ...
Sun ...	Kāng-wan ...	Arni ...	Numit ...	Mu, *or* moo ...
Moon ...	Leûn ...	Chekelá ...	Thá ...	......
Star ...	Low ...	Tiklángcho ...	Tháoál michák ...	Htsâ ...
Fire ...	Hpai ...	Me ...	Mái ...	Mai ...
Water ...	Nam ...	Láng ...	Ising ...	Htee ...
House ...	Heûn ...	Hem ...	Im ...	Lâm ...
Horse ...	Ma ...	Lochhái ...	Ságal ...	Thāi ...

compared with others.—(Continued.)

Poi of Burmah.	Talain of Pegu (Burmah.)	Sonthali of Sonthal Pergunnahs, Western Bengal.	Moondaree of Chota Nagpore, Western Bengal.	English.
Ahow ...	Gna-uk ...	Data ...	Dáṭá ...	Tooth.
Nakaw ...	K-to ...	Lutur ...	Lutur ...	Ear.
Asshur ...	Soke ...	Up' ...	Ub ...	Hair.
Lu ...	K-dou, *or* k-neep.	Boho ...	Bo ...	Head.
Pullai ...	L-tike ...	Alaṅ ...	Alañ or lee ...	Tongue.
Re ...	K-na-ou ...	Lach' ...	Lai ...	Belly.
Nowlir ...	Chä ...	Dea ...	Deyá ...	Back.
Tewaie ...	P-soä ...	Meṛhet' ...	Mened ...	Iron.
Noung ...	......	Sona ...	Samarum ...	Gold.
......	Saun ...	Rupa ...	Rupá ...	Silver.
Opar ...	Ma, *or* ma-auk ...	Apa, baba ...	Apu ...	Father.
Onor ...	Me *or* yai ...	Eṅga, ayo ...	Engá ...	Mother.
Antar ...	......	Boiha, bokot ...	Hagá ...	Brother.
......	Kou ...	......	......	Brother (elder).
......	Tā ...	......	......	Brother (younger).
Shirtanoung ...	......	Mis-cra ...	Misí ...	Sister.
......	Boä ...	......	......	Sister (elder).
......	Ta-pra-ow ...	......	......	Sister (younger).
Soirhar ...	M-neeh, *or* m-neeh-troo.	Herel ..	Hoṛo (generic), Koṛá.	Man.
Sanoung ...	M-neeh pra-ou ...	Maejiu ...	Kúṛí ...	Woman.
Alapenoung ...	Pra-ou ...	Era, aimai ...	Kúṛí ...	Wife.
Trasenoung ...	Knonè ...	Gidra ...	Hon ...	Child.
Harsepa ...	Kone-troo ...	Koṛa-hopon ...	Kora hon ...	Son.
......	Kone-pra-ou ...	Koṛi-hopon ...	Kúṛí hon ...	Daughter.
Hshay ...	Deik ...	Guti ...	Dási (hired) ...	Slave.
Purre ...	......	......	......	Snake.
......	Mneeh klone p-gnaer	Siok'-ich' ...	Kisán ...	Cultivator.
......	P-mong-soh ...	Gupi ...	Mahrá; gupitaní.	Shepherd.
......	Kyike ...	Thakur, boṅga ...	Sing bonga= sun spirit.	God.
......	K-lok mā-er	Maraṅ-buru ...	Bonga (all malicious spirits).	Devil.
Nai ...	T-gnoa ...	Ber-sin-chando ...	Singi ...	Sun.
Klapar ...	K-to ...	(Ninda) chando ...	Chandu ...	Moon.
Ase ...	S-nong ...	Ipil ...	Ipil ...	Star.
......	K-mote ...	Seṅgel ...	Sengel ...	Fire.
Te ...	Dike ...	Dak' ...	Dáa ...	Water.
Aem ...	S-gnee ...	Aṛ-ak' ...	Oṛaá ...	House.
......	Cheh ...	......	Sádom ...	Horse.

English.	Shan of Burmah.	Mekir of Cachar.	Muneepooree.	Tonghtoo of Burmah.
Cow ...	Woomè ...	Cháinong ...	Sullámon ...	Po-moo ...
Dog ...	Mah ...	Mátán ...	Whui ...	Htwee ...
Tiger ...	......	......	......	......
Cat ...	Meow ...	Meng ...	Háudang ...	Ngyoung ...
Cock ...	Kai-pau ...	......	Yét ...	Khya-tee ...
Hen ...	......	......	......	......
Duck ...	Pit ...	Bukák ...	Ngánu ...	Kam-piê ...
Ass ...	Lau ...	......	Lalá ...	......
Camel ...	Ka-la-ook ...	......	Ut ...	......
Bird ...	Nok ...	Bowo ...	Uchok ...	Wâh ...
Rice ...	......	......	......	......
Chillies ...	......	......	......	......
Bamboo ...	......	......	......	......
Plantain ...	......	......	......	......
Elephant ...	......	......	......	......
Go ...	Kwah ...	Dá ...	Cholo ...	Lôay ...
Eat ...	Keen ...	Chhanon ...	Cháo ...	Am ...
Sit ...	Nang ...	Ininan ..	Phámo ...	Ong-lâng ...
Come ...	Mah ...	Bángnun ...	Láku *or* Láo ...	Lon ...
Beat ...	Yen, *or* pau, *or* tayng.	Bágnun ...	Yeoi yu ...	Tway ...
Stand ...	Sook ...	Ár jápman ...	Lépu ...	Ong-htong ...
Die ...	Tai ...	Titánglo ...	Shiro ...	Thee ...
Give ...	Pan ...	Ke ...	Piu ...	Phāy ...
Buy ...	......	......	......	......
Kill ...	......	......	......	......
Drink ...	......	......	......	......
Run ...	Len ...	Kácháng chang ...	Chelu ...	Loâng ...
Sell ...	......	......	......	......
Up ...	Neû ...	Thurnan ..	Máthák ...	O-kyee ...
Down ...	Tul ...	Ininan ...	Mákhá ...	O-là ...
Before ...	Nah, *or* pah-nah ...	Aphrang ...	Mámáng ...	Thâ-ngâh ...
Near ...	Sam ...	Idung ...	Nák ...	Bau, *or* baw ...
Far ...	Kái ...	Akai hinapi ...	Árápá ...	Ngyâh ...
Behind ...	Lang *or* pah-lang...	Api ...	Tungdá ...	Tha-khya ...
Who ...	Hpul, *or* hpoo-lul...	Kamádamá ...	Kaná ...	Pâmiê ...
What ...	Kah-hsang, *or* hsang	Kapimá ...	Kari ...	Tamiê ...
Why ...	Hit-hèu-lè, or hit-hsang-lè.	Kapimá ...	Kariná ...	Poê-pyee-miê ...
And ...	Tang, or lè ...	......	Ásumná ...	Tom ...
But ...	Pāyk-hsam, or kwai-kah.	......	Tonvá kumbáshunag	Nujin-htwâ-pyee-now.

compared with others.—(Continued.)

Poi of Burmah.	Talain of Pegu (Burmah.)	Sonthali of Sonthal Pergunnahs, Western Bengal.	Moondaree of Chota Nagpore, Western Bengal.	English.
......	Kla-ou-booh ...	Gai ...	Gai ...	Cow.
E ...	Klur ...	Setak' ...	Setá ...	Dog.
Hsugge ...	......	......	......	Tiger.
......	P-koa ...	Pusi ...	Púsí ...	Cat.
Akawbir ...	Saing-k-mok ...	Saṇḍi ...	Sáṇḍi ...	Cock.
Anooar ...	......	......	......	Hen.
......	A-ta-er ...	Geḍe ...	Koṛo ...	Duck.
......	Mai ...	Gadha ...	Gádhá ...	Ass.
......	Oot ...	Uṭ ...	Unṭ ...	Camel.
Pawar ...	K-chame ...	Cheṛe ...	Cheṇe ...	Bird.
Bow ...	......	......	......	Rice.
Irhay ...	......	......	......	Chillies.
Remun ...	......	......	......	Bamboo.
May-pe ...	......	......	......	Plantain.
Hsuppir ...	......	......	......	Elephant.
Zer ...	Á ...	Sen, chala ...	Senomeṅ (imp.)	Go.
Guyar ...	Cheer ...	Jom ...	Iommeṅ ...	Eat.
......	K-cho ...	Daṛup' ...	Dubmeṅ ...	Sit.
Wewor ...	Kloong ...	Hejuk' ...	Elá; hijumeṅ...	Come.
Baw ...	Tok, *or* boong ...	Dal ...	Dálmeṅ (imp.)	Beat.
......	T-tou ...	Tiṅgun ...	Tingunmeṅ ...	Stand.
Adir ...	Chot ...	Gujuk' ...	Goi (root) ...	Die.
Pay ...	Ka ...	Em ...	Um ,, ...	Give.
Hsilasay ...	......	......	......	Buy.
Baw ...	......	......	......	Kill.
Nietay ...	......	......	......	Drink.
Row ...	Krape ...	Nir, daṛ ...	Nir (root) ...	Run.
Ye ...	......	......	......	Sell.
......	L-toe ...	Chetan ...	Sirma=sky; cheatan=upon.	Up.
......	A-hmau ...	Latar ...	Latar ...	Down.
......	K-tä ...	Laha, maṛaṅ samaṅ...	Aiar ...	Before.
......	Kraup ...	Sor ...	Náne ...	Near.
......	Gnoä ...	Saṅgin ...	Saññ ...	Far.
......	Lok-k-rou ...	Tayom ...	Táyom ...	Behind.
......	Nyeh-kawh-rou ...	Okae, chele ...	Okoî ...	Who.
......	Moo-kauh-rou ...	Chet' ...	Chikan, chinaá	What.
......	Moo-hät-rou ...	Chedat' ...	Chikaná mente, chia.	Why.
......	Kä ...	Ar, ado ...	Oṛo ...	And.
......	Htoo-tauh-sike-kauh (Lit.—*If it be not so.*)	Men-khan ...	Mendo, batkam	But.

English.	Shan of Burmah.	Mekir of Cachar.	Muneepooree.	Tonghtoo of Burmah.
If ...	Pau, *or* hsang ...	......	Badi ...	Myin ...
Yes ...	Sul-yow ...	Melo ...	Hoe ...	Moye, *or* moie ...
No ..	Am sul ...	Bángri ...	Náte ...	Môye-tow ...
Alas! ...	A lo ...	I-ing, hanang ...	He ...	Hein ...
A father ...	Pau (kau-neung) ...	Pumáboli ...	Pá ámá ...	Phâ-tâphrâ ...
Of a father ...	——Pau (kau-neung).	......	Pá ámági ...	Phâ âkhrong ...
To a father ...	Tee pau, *or* hang pau (kau-neung).	Hapo nepan pilákotá	Pá-dá ...	......
From a father ...	Kah-lee-pau (kau-neung).	Hánne-pu-pen ...	Pá-tagi ...	Phâ-dô ...
Two fathers ...	Pau hsaung kau ...	......	Pá-ánec ...	Phâ-nee-phrâ ...
Fathers ...	Pau lul ...	......	Pá-iámbá ...	Phâ-âh ...
Of fathers ...	——Pau lu ...	......	Pá-iámgi ...	Phâ-âh-âkhrong ...
To fathers ..	Tee pau lul, *or* hang pau lul.	Nipo chhido ...	Pá-pum numakdá...	......
From fathers ...	Kah tee pau lul ...	......	Pá-pum numaktagi	Phâ-âh-dô ...
A daughter ...	Look yeeng (kau neung).	Nechhapi innar ...	Nupi macháámá ...	Poê-moo-tâ-phrâ ...
Of a daughter ...	—— Look-yee n g (kau neung).	......	Nupi machági ...	Poê-moo-ah-âkhrông
To a daughter ...	Lee look-yeeng, *or* hang look-yeeng (kau neung).	Hope ponon ...	Nupi machádá ...	......
From a daughter ...	Kah tee look-yeeng (kau neung.)	Háne chhapi penchi kelang.	Nupi machádagi ...	Poê-moo-dô ...
Two daughters ...	Look-yeeng hsaung kau.	......	Nupi machá ánee...	Poê-moo-nee-phrâ..
Daughters ...	Look-yeeng lul ...	Nechhapi ák aukapi	Nupi machá-pum numak.	Poé-moo-âh ...
Of daughters ...	——Look-yee n g lul.	......	Nupi machá pum numakgi.	......
To daughters ...	Lee look-yeeng lul, *or* hang look-yeeng lul.	Háne chhapi ábid-ing.	Nupi machá pum numakda.	......
From daughters ...	Kah tee look-yeeng lul.	......	Nupi machá pum numakdagi.	Poê-moo-âh-dô ...
A good man ...	Koon lee (kau neung).	Arlingethe ...	Mí áfábá ámá ...	Loê-how-tâphrâ ...
Of a good man ...	——Koon tee (kau neung).	......	Mí áfábá ámági ...	Loê-how-âkhrông...
To a good man ...	Tee koon lee, *or* hang koon lee (kau neung).	Arling ethepen ...	Mí áfábá ámádá ...	......

compared with others.—(Continued.)

Poi of Burmah.	Talain of Pegu (Burmah.)	Sonthali of Sonthal Pergunnahs, Western Bengal.	Moondaree of Chota Nagpore, Western Bengal.	English.
......	Yäm ...	Khan ...	—— re or —— re do.	If.
......	Yuh ...	He ...	He ...	Yes.
......	Hoo-sā-ung (sit.—*Not so.*)	Baṅ ...	Ká, bano ...	No.
......	O yai (sit.—*Oh mother!*)	Haere ...	Helaiya, háe, oh	Alas!
......	Mā *or* mā-auk ...	Apa ...	Apu ...	A father.
......	......	Apa-ren ...	Apuá ...	Of a father.
......	......	Apa-ṭhen ...	Apu te ...	To a father.
......	Noo-mā ...	Apa-khon ...	Apu te ...	From a father.
......	Mā-bä ...	Apa-kin ...	Apukiñ ...	Two fathers.
......	Ma-tau, *or* ma km-lung (sit.—*All fathers.*)	Apa-ko ...	Apuko ...	Fathers.
......	......	Apako-ren ...	Apukoá ...	Of fathers.
......	......	Apako-ṭhen ...	Apu kote ...	To fathers.
......	Noo mā km-lung	Apako-khon ...	Apu kote ...	From fathers.
......	Kone pra-ọu ...	Hoponera ...	Kúṛí hom ...	A daughter.
......	......	Hoponera-ren ...	Kúṛí honá ...	Of a daughter.
......	......	Hoponera-ṭhen ...	Kúṛí honte ...	To a daughter.
......	......	Hoponera-khon ...	Kúṛí honte ...	From a daughter.
......	Kone pra-ou bä ...	Hoponerakin ...	Kúṛí honkiñ ...	Two daughters.
......	Kone pra-ou km-lung.	Hoponerako ...	Kúṛí honko ...	Daughters.
......	......	Hoponerako-ren ...	Kúṛí honkoá...	Of daughters.
......	......	Hoponerako-ṭhen ...	Kúṛí hon kote	To daughters.
......	......	Hoponerako-khon ...	Kúṛí hon kote	From daughtérs.
Sorrhar par ...	M-neeh käh ...	Bugi herel ...	Bugin hoṛo ...	A good man.
......	......	Bugi herel-ren ...	Bugin hoṛoá...	Of a good man.
......	......	Bugi herel-ṭhen ...	Bugin hoṛo te	To a good man.

English.	Shan of Burmah	Mekir of Cachar.	Muneepooree.	Tonghtoo of Burmah.
From a good man ...	Kah tee koon lee (kau neung).	Arling ethe ápáu ..	Mi áfábá ámádagi...	Loê-how-dô ...
Two good men ...	Koon lee hsaung kau.	......	Mi áfábá ánee ...	Loê-how-nee-phra..
Good men ...	Koon lee lul ...	......	Mi áfábá pum numak.	Loê-how-ah ...
Of good men ...	——— koon lee lul	......	Mi áfábá pum numakgi.	Loê-how-ah-âkhrong
To good men ...	Tee koon lee lul, *or* hang koon lee lul.	......	Mi áfábá pum numaktá.	......
From good men ...	Kah tee koon lee lul.	......	Mi áfábá pum numaktági.	Loê-hôw-âh-dô ...
A good woman ...	Koon-yeeng lee, *or* hpoo-yeeng lee, *or* mè-yeeng lee (kau-neung.)	Arling ikhe ápichho	Nupi áfábi ámá ...	Loê-moo-how-tâphra
Two good women ...	......	......	......	......
Good women ...	Koon-yeeng lee lul, *or* hpoo-yeeng lee lul, *or* mè-yeeng lee lul.	Arling ekhe ápichho	Nupi áfábi pum numak.	Loê-moo-how-āh ...
Of a good woman ...	......	......	......	......
To a good woman ...	......	......	......	......
From a good woman...	......	......	......	......
A bad boy ...	Look-sai-aun hai ...	Uchulángo ...	Áugongphátábá ámá	Loê-kiê-pai-taphra
A bad girl ...	Look-yeeng-aun hai	Aruchulángo ...	Phátábi nupi machá ámá.	Loe-moo-kiê-pāi-tâphrâ.
Good ...	Lee ...	Meechen ...	Áfábá ...	Ahow ...
Better ...	Khen tee, *or* lee hsay.	......	Okhák fábá ...	Aling-how ...
Best ...	Lee hsay peûn ...	Meelo ...	Yám ná fábá ...	Ahow-thoot ...
High ...	Hsoong ...	Ingtinang ...	Áoángbá ...	A-htô ...
Higher ...	Khen hsoong, *or* hsoong hsay.	......	Okhák áoángbá ...	Ating-htô ...
Highest ...	Hsoong hsay peûn	Akáng tuípi ...	Yámuá áongbá ...	A-htô-thoot ...
A horse ...	Ma-pau (to neung)	Lochái ejnád ...	Ságalámá ...	Thâi-tee-tâbah ...
A mare ...	Ma-mè (to neung)	Lochái ápi ejnád ...	Ságal ámom ámá ...	Thai-moo-tabah ...
Horses ...	Ma-pau lul ...	Lochái ákángpi ...	Ságol i ámbá ...	Thāi-tee-ah ...
Mares ...	Ma-mè lul ...	Lochái ápi ákángpi	Ságalámom iámbá	Thai-moo-ah ...
A bull ...	Wo-pau (to neung)	Cháinung animácho	Shállá ámá ...	Pô-tsam-deê-tabah
A cow ...	Wo-mè (to neung)	Chainang ánim panang ejnád.	Shál ámom ámá ...	Pô-moo-tabah ...
Bulls ...	Wo-pau lul ...	Animchho ákángpi	Shállabá iámbá ...	Pô-tsam-dee-ah ...

compared with others.—(Continued.)

Poi of Burmah.	Talain of Pegu (Burmah.)	Sonthali of Sonthal Pergunnahs, Western Bengal.	Moondaree of Chota Nagpore, Western Bengal.	English.
......	Noo m-neeh kah ...	Bugi herel-khon ...	Bugin hoṛo te	From a good man.
......	M-nee kah bä ...	Bugi-herel-kin ...	Bugin hoṛo kiñ	Two good men.
......	M-neeh-käh km-lung.	Bugi-herel-ko ...	Bugin hoṛoko	Good men.
......	......	Bugi-herel-ko-ren ...	Bugin hoṛokoá	Of good men.
......	......	Bugi-herel-ko-ṭhen ...	Bugin hoṛo kote	To good men.
......	Noo m-neeh käh km-lung.	Bugi-herel-ko-khon ...	Bugin hoṛo kote	From good men.
Sanoung parne (*pronounced like the Hindustani* pani, *for water.*)	M-neeh pra-ou kah	Bugi maejiu ...	Bugin kúṛí ...	A good woman.
......	......	Bugi maejiukin ..	......	Two good women.
......	M-neeh pra-ou kah km-lung.	Bugi maejiuko ...	Bugin kúṛíko...	Good women.
......	......	Bugi maejiu-ren ...	......	Of a good woman.
......	......	Bugi maejiu-ṭhen ...	......	To a good woman.
......	......	Bugi maejiu-khon ...	......	From a good woman.
......	Kone-troo tm-ruh	Barich' kora ...	Etkan koṛá ...	A bad boy.
......	Kone-pra-ou tm-ruh	......	Etkan kúṛí ...	A bad girl.
......	Käh ...	Bugi ...	Bugin ...	Good.
......	Käh lone ...	Arho bugi ...	—— te bugin	Better.
......	Käh at ...	Sanam-khon bugi *or* bugi.	Sobente bugin, *i. e.*, of all.	Best.
......	Hloong ...	Usul ...	Sálangí ...	High.
......	Hloong lone ...	Arho usul ...	(No comparative and superlative forms.)	Higher.
......	Hloong at ...	Sanam-khon usal or usul uttar.	(No comparative and superlative forms.)	Highest.
......	Cheh ka-mok ...	Aṇḍia sadom ...	Sánḍí sadom ...	A horse.
......	Cheh booh ...	Eṅga sadom ...	Engá sadom ...	A mare.
......	Cheh km-lung ...	Aṇḍia sadomko ...	Sánḍi sádom ko	Horses.
......	Cheh booh km-lung	Eṅga sadomko ...	Engá sádom ko	Mares.
......	Kla-ou k-mok ...	Daṅgra ..	Haḍá ...	A bull.
......	Klā-ou booh ...	Gai ...	Gai ...	A cow.
......	Klā-ou k-mok km-lung.	Daṅgrako ...	Haḍáko ...	Bulls.

English.	Shan of Burmah.	Merkir of Cachar.	Muneepooree.	Tonghtoo of Burmah.
Cows ...	Wo-mè lul ...	Chinang ápi ákángpi	Shálámom iámbá...	Pô-moo-ah ...
A dog ...	Mah-pau (to neung)	Mathan ijon ...	Whui ámá ...	Htwee-tee-tabah ...
A bitch ...	Mah-me (to neung)	Mathán ápi ejnad ...	Whui ámom ámá ..	Htwee-moo-tabah ..
Dogs ...	Mah-pau lul ...	Mathán ákángpi ...	Whui i ámbá ...	Htwee-tee-ah ...
Bitches ...	Ma-mè lul ...	Mathán ápi áhurak ákángpi.	Whui ámam i ámbá	Htwee-moo-ah ...
A he-goat ...	Pè-pau (to neung)	Bianu ijnád ...	Hámeng lává ámá	Beh-tee-tabah ...
A female goat ...	Pè-mè (to neung)...	Biápi ejnád ...	Hámeng ámom ámá	Beh-moo-tabah ...
Goats ...	Pè lul ...	Bi ákángpi ...	Hámeng ámom i ámbá.	Beh-ah ...
A male deer ...	Kwáng-pau (to neung).	Thiak álu ejnád ...	Shongái láiri ámá ..	Aphraing-tee-tabah
A female deer ...	Kwāng-mè (to neung).	Thiak ápi ejnád ...	Shongái ámom ámá	Aphraing-moo-tabah
Deer ...	Kwang lul ...	Thiak ...	Shongái i ámbá ...	Aphraing-ah ...
Gun ...	......	......	......	......
Pig ...	......	......	......	......
Koung (or drink from rice.)	......	......	......	......
I am ...	Kow-khah pin ...	Netám ...	Ái oé ...	Khôay-ow ...
Thou art ...	Mul pin ...	Nángho ...	Náng oé ...	Na-ow ...
He is ...	Mau pin ...	Hálánáng ...	Má oé ...	Weh-ow ...
We are ...	How-khah pin ...	Náng kido kábe ...	Ikhoi oé ...	Nee-ow ...
You are ...	Hsoo-pin ...	......	Nang khoi oé ...	Thee-ow ...
They are ...	Khow pin ...	......	Makhoi oé ...	Weh-thee-ow ...
I was ...	Khow-khah pin you	......	Ái oé rammi ...	Aree-khoay-ow ...
Thou wast ...	Mul pin you ...	......	Náng oé rammi ...	Aree-na-ow ...
He was ...	Man pin you ...	......	Má oé rammi ...	Aree-weh-ow ...
We were ...	How-khah pin you	......	Ikhoi oé rammi ...	Aree-nee-ow ...
You were ...	Hsoo pin you ...	......	Náng khoi oé rammi	Aree-thee-ow ...
They were ...	Khow pin you ...	......	Mákhoi oé rammi...	Aree-weh-thee-ow
Be ...	Pin *(to exist)*, *or* mee *(to be in some place or belonging to.)*	......	Oé bá ...	Ow ...
To be ...	(No independent form.)	......	Oe bádá ...	Ow ...
Being ...	Mee-yoo ...	......	Oé ri ...	......
Having been ...	Meē-yoo sang ...	......	Oé ramli ...	Ow-len-htoo ...
I may be ...	(No independent form.)	......	Ái oé yái ...	Khoay-ow-latam ...
I can be ...	Kow-khah pin lai...	......	......	....
I shall be ...	Kow-khah tak mè, *or* pin.	......	Ái oēgini, aioē gidábá mátikoe.	Khoāy-ee-ow
I should be ...	(No independent form.)	......	......	Khoay-ow-thang ...

compared with others.—(Continued.)

Poi of Burmah.	Talain of Pegu (Burmah.)	Sonthali of Sonthal Pergunnahs, Western Bengal.	Moondaree of Chota Nagpore, Western Bengal.	English.
......	Klā-ou booh km-lung.	Gaiko ...	Gai ko ...	Cows.
......	Klue ke-mok ...	Setak' ...	Sánḍí setá ...	A dog.
......	Klur booh ...	Eṅga setak' ...	Engá setá ...	A bitch.
......	Klur k-moh km-lung.	Setak' ko ...	Sanḍi setá ko	Dogs.
......	Klur booh km-lung	Eṅga setak' ko ...	Engá setá ko ...	Bitches.
......	K-bà k-mok ...	Merom-anḍia ...	Bakṛá ...	A he-goat.
......	K-bà-booh ...	Merom-eṅga ...	Engá merom...	A female goat.
......	K-bà-km-lung ...	Meromko ...	Merom ko (generic).	Goats.
......	Krai k-m-mok ...	......	Sándí jílu ...	A male deer.
......	Krai booh ...	......	Engá jílu ...	A female deer.
Sar ...	Krai km-lung ...	......	Jílu ko ...	Deer.
Metay ...	......	......	......	Gun.
Wow ...	......	......	......	Pig.
Psamar ...	......	......	......	Koung (or drink from rice.)
......	Oä noom ...	Menana, or kanan ...	Aiñ menaiñyá	I am.
......	M-neh noom ...	Menama, or kanam ...	Am menameá	Thou art.
......	Nyeh noom ...	Menaea, or kanae ...	Iní menaiyá ...	He is.
......	Pooey noom ...	......	Ale menaleá ...	We are.
......	M-neh tau noom ...	......	Ape menapeá	You are.
......	Kyneh tau noom ...	......	Ako menakoá	They are.
......	......	Tahekonan ...	Aiñ tainkenain	I was.
......	......	Tahekonam ...	Am tainkenam	Thou wast.
......	......	Tahekanae ...	Iní tainkenai...	He was.
......	......	......	Ale tainkenale	We were.
......	......	......	Ape tainkenape	You were.
......	......	......	Ako tainkenako	They were.
......	......	Hoyuk' mé ...	Akanmen ...	Be.
......	......	Hoyuk' ...	......	To be.
......	......	Hoyuk' ...	Akan ...	Being.
......	......	Hoeakan-khan ...	Jan ...	Having been.
......	......	Hoyuk'-gi-chon ...	......	I may be.
......	......	......	......	I can be.
......	......	Hoyuk'-an ...	Oá ...	I shall be.
......	......	Hoe-kok'-an ...	......	I should be.

English.	Shan of Burmah.	Mekir of Cachar.	Muneepooree.	Tonghtoo of Burmah.
Beat	......	Chak nun	Yáibá	Tway
To beat	......	......	Yáibádá	Tway
Beating	......	......	Yáiri	......
Having beaten	......	......	Yái rimi	Twāy-len-htoo
I beat	Kow-kah yen	Ne-náng chhagi	Ái yái	Khoāy-twāy
Thou beatest	Mul yen	Pináng chhapabebe-daná.	Náng yái yu	Na-twāy
He beats	Man yen	Hálá chichá gadera	Má yái	Weh-twāy
We two beat	......	......	......	......
You two beat	......	......	......	......
They two beat	......	......	......	......
We beat	How-khah yen	Nechi-chaga-bereno	Ikhoi yái	Nee twāy
You beat	Hsoo yen	Kida kábe chhagelo	Náng khoi yái	....
They beat	Khow yen	Hálá tum chigi chak	Má khoi yái	Weh-thee-twāy
I am beating	Kow-khah yen yoo	......	Ái yái ri	Khāoy-ow-tway
I was beating	......	......	Ái yái ramli	Khoāy-ow-tway ngathai.
I had beaten	Kow-khah yen yow yow.	......	Ái yái khare	Khoay-twāy-len-htoo.
We two are beating	......	......	......	......
We are beating	......	......	......	......
I may beat	(*No independent form*)	......	Ái yái bá yái	Khoay-twāy-nong
I shall beat	Kow-khah tak yen	......	Ái yái gani	Khoāy-tway-now
I should beat	(*No independent form*)	......	Ái yái gidábáoe	Khoāy-twāy-thāng
I am beaten	Kow-khah kham tang yen.	......	Ái bu yái	Khoāy-kham-bah-len-atway.
I was beaten	Kow-khah lai kham tāng yeng yow.	......	Ái bu yái ri	Khoāy-kham-bah-len-atway.
I shall be beaten	Khow-khah tak lai khām tāng yen.	......	Ái bu yái gani	Khoāy-ee-kham-bah-atway.
I go	Kow-khah kwah	Nedám po	Ái chatē	Khoay loay
Thou goest	Mul kwah	Náng dám nan	Náng chatē	Ha-loay
He goes	Man kwah	Náng naám khunan	Má chate	Weh-loay
I went	Kow-khah kwah you	Nedám táng-pu	Ái chalambu	Khoay-loay-leu
Thou wentest	Mul kwah you	......	Náng chalambu	Na-loay-leu
He went	Man kwah you	......	Má chalambu	Weh-loay-leu
Go	Kwah	......	Chálpá	Loay
Going	Kwah yoon	......	Chali	A-loay-tong
Gone	Kwah you-you	......	Chal khorē	Loay-len
What is your name?	Seu mul haung sen hen? (*Lit*, what do you call your name?)	Náng men kapimá?	Naming kari konĕ?	Na-myin pamiē?

Poi of Burmah.	Talain of Pegu (Burmah.)	Sonthali of Sonthal Pergunnahs, Western Bengal.	Mondaree of Chota Nagpore, Western Bengal.	English.
Baw ...	Tok, *or* boong (present and infinitive)	Dal-mé ...	Dálmen (2 p.s. imp.)	Beat.
......	......	Dal ...	Dálteá ...	To beat.
......	Tok-mong ...	Dadal, dal-ket-khan...	Dáltan ...	Beating.
......	Tok to-ey ...	......	Dálkedte ...	Having beaten.
......	Oa tok ...	Dal et'-an ...	Aiñ dáli aiñ ...	I beat.
......	M-neh tok ...	Dal-et'-am ...	Am dáli am ...	Thou beatest.
......	Nyeh tok ...	Dal-et'-ae ...	Iní dáli ai ...	He beats.
......	......	Dal-et'a lin ...	......	We too beat.
......	......	Dal-et'-aben ...	......	You too beat.
......	......	Dal-et'-akin ...	......	They too beat.
......	Pooly tok ...	Dal-et'-ale ...	Ale dáli ale ...	We beat.
......	M-neh tau tok ...	Dal-et'-ape ...	Ape dáli ape...	You beat.
......	Nyeh tau tok ...	Dal-et'ako ...	Ako dáli ako...	They beat.
......	Oa tok mong ...	Dal-et'-kan-an ...	Ain dáltanaiñ	I am beating.
......	Oa tok mong ...	......	Ain dáltan taikena.	I was beating.
......	Oa tok to-ey ...	......	......	I had beaten.
......	......	Dal-et'-kana-lin ...	......	We two are beating.
......	......	Dal-et'-kan-ale ...	......	We are beating.
......	(*No equivalent without circumlocution.*)	Dal-gi-chon ...	......	I may beat.
......	Oä tok rong ...	Dal-an ...	Ain daléaiñ ...	I shall beat.
......	Oa krike ka tok (*I ought to beat.*)	Dal-ke-an ...	......	I should beat.
......	Oä toong tok ...	Dal-ochok'-kan-an ...	(No passive form.)	I am beaten.
......	Oä toong tok to-ey	Dal-ocho-enan ...	......	I was beaten.
......	Oä toong tok rong (I must be beaten.)	Dal-ochok'-au ...	......	I shall be beaten.
......	Oä ā ...	Senok' konan ...	Aiñ senoaiñ ...	I go.
......	M-neh ä ...	Senok' konam ...	Am senoam ...	Thou goest.
......	Nyeh ä ...	Senok' konae ...	Iní senoai ...	He goes.
......	Oä a toey ...	Senenan ...	Aiñ senkenaiñ	I went.
......	M-neh a toey ...	Senenam ...	Am senkenam	Thou wentest.
......	Nyeh ä ...	Senenae ...	Iní senkenai ...	He went.
Zer ...	A ...	Sen ...	Senomeñ ...	Go.
......	A mong ...	Senok' ...	Senotan ...	Going.
......	A toey rä ...	Sen, or Senakan ...	Senojan ...	Gone.
......	Y-moo m-neh moo-kauh row ?	Chet' nutum-tama ?...	Ama nutum chikaná ?	What is your name ?

English.	Shan of Burmah.	Mekir of Cachar.	Muneepooree.	Tonghtoo of Burmah.
How old is this horse?	Ma to nai a-hsak lai lai pee?	Lábáng cho álochhi ning kán kowá nasa?	Ságal áshi cháhi koiá shurvá?	Thai-yô-phrâ-htoo không-miê?
How far is it from here to Kashmir?	Look kah tee nai kwah tee meûng Ka-sha-meera kai kah heu?	Dák pen há Káshmir kawán hilomá?	Áshi digi Kashmir koiá lápá?	Ow-yô-tôm Cash-mêre ângyâh không-mie?
How many sons are there in your father's house?	Nul heûn pau mul, mee look-sai lai kau?	Náng pe átu áhem kawán athumár angmá?	Nángi nápági machá koiá shuvá?	Nâ-phâ-lâm-pô-ŏw-không-miê-phrâ?
I have walked a long way to-day.	Meu nai, kow-khah lè kai tè tè.	Há ákáhi lopi pen-chi kibánglo.	Ashi nimit yámná lápuá chát liu.	Hâ-nié-khôay-lôay-len-tâpoo-ngyâh.
The son of my uncle is married to her sister.	Took-sai loong kow khah ownaung-yeeng koon-yeeng nan (that woman) lut may.	Nepuno áchho áng jin rapí biákari tánglo.	Áigi khurági machá ná mági machal louré.	Khôay-phâtân-pô-iê weh-poomoo.
In the house is the saddle of the white horse.	Nul heûn nai mee kaupma to pheûk nai eu.	Hálá bángsa áhem álo lochhái ákelak jin dumá.	Ságal ángonbági sábal imdálái.	Thai bwâh-kop-ow-lam-kô.
Put the saddle upon his back.	Hsul kaup-ma nêu lang man ta.	Lochái áthák jin ár báknan.	Ságal sábal liába ...	Weh-ngâng-lông-on-dâng kop.
I have beaten his son with many stripes.	Kow-khah la yen look-sai man hwai nam nah tè tè au.	Nehálá bángs-o in-glang á kingri chainang kiri.	Mági machábu áiná yámná yáire.	Weh-pô-khôay-tway âhtsang-âh.
He is grazing cattle on the top of the hill.	Man layng wó lul neû pai kong au.	....	Má ching thák tá shán shete.	Weh-ow-tee-pô-pânâ-kong-nâ.
He is sitting on a horse under that tree.	Man naug yoo neû ma to neung tul toon mai nan au.	Hálá báng chho árlèng theng pi árum lochái áthak innichha.	Máná ukhádá ságal tongdáná lái.	Weh-ow-on glang-thai-long-ow-o-thâ-ing moohait.
His brother is taller than his sister.	Pee-sai man khen hsoong hsay pee nang man au.	Hálá bángso árleng ákling le te akibi ding munák.	Machándági moi ámá uángi.	Weh-wai-khô-hto-len-weh-moo.
The price of that is two rupees and a half.	Kah an-nan tok teng-kah hsaung khep pai kheung neung.	Lábáng chho ám-már chiká hinirá ádhuli.	Másigi mal tángá ánuee makhái.	Tâ-thoo-â-ngôe-thambat.
My father lives in that small house.	Pau kow-khah mee yoo nul heun aun nan au.	Nepo hálá hem cho-chid.	Áigi ipá im ápisádá lái.	Khôay-phâ-ow-lâm-pai-now-kô.
Give this rupee to him.	Pan man teng-kah khep neung nai ta, *or* pau teng-kah khep neung nai hang man ta.	Hálá dhan pinan ...	Tángá si máugándá pio.	Tânkâ-yô-tabee-phay-weh-thoo.
Take those rupees from him.	Nook ow teng-kah seu nan-kah tee man ta.	Hálá dhan panan ...	Tángá i ámbá mán-gantagi lou.	Htoo-tânkâ-âh-ô-weh-thoo.
Beat him well and bind him with ropes.	Yen man tee tee lè ow mat man tang seuk lul ta.	Hálá jáchhene cha-ganan ári kaga-dangnan.	Mábu zámná yái yu shámná thouriná pulla.	Weh-thoo-tway-how-tsong-tom-taplwee.

compared with others.—(Continued.)

Poi of Burmah.	Talain of Pegu (Burmah.)	Sonthali of Sonthal Pergunnahs, Western Bengal.	Moondaree of Chota Nagpore, Western Bengal.	English.
......	Cheh woo äyook moo chee rou?	Noi sadom dò tin sermaren konae?	Ne sadom chimin sinua hobákaná?	How old is this horse?
......	Noo enau tur ka reah Cashmere bot lm-gnore row?	Noṇḍekhon Kashmir-te tin sangina?	Nea te Kashmír chiminañ sañiña?	How far is it from here to Kashmir?
......	P-dore s-gnee ma m-neh kone-troo noom mo che rou?	Apum oṛak're tinak' hopon menakoa?	Apumá oraá re chimin koṛá honko menákoá?	How many sons are there in your father's house?
......	T-gnore woo oä kwike gnore toey ra.	Teheṇ adi sangen in sentaṛamket'a.	Sisiñ aiñ asu sañiñá tein hijulená.	I have walked a long way to-day.
......	......	Mamonren hopon oniren miseratit' ṭhene capla akana.	Kakainyaá hon te koṛá iniá misé loo árandiakanai.	The son of my uncle is married to her sister.
......	Poon cheh p-taing noom p-doä sngee.	Poṇḍ sadomreak' palan oṛ ak're menak'a.	Oraá re punḍí sadomá jín mená.	In the house is the saddle of the white horse.
......	P-ton poon l-too chä deh.	Deare palan lade ae me.	Niá deyá re jín doimen.	Put the saddle upon his back.
......	......	Hopontit' adi dal in dal akadea.	Ain iniá hon koḍrá te isu hansakíya.	I have beaten his son with many stripes.
......	Nyeh ma-ung mong kla-ou l-too tur.	Buru chot chotte gaie atin et'ko kana.	Iní burn chetan re uri ko gupitanai.	He is grazing cattle on the top of the hill.
......	Nyeh k-cho mong ltoo cheh ä-hmau t-nome choo tä.	Hana dare butare sadomre e dech' akana.	En dáru súbá re iní sádom re dubakanai.	He is sitting on a horse under that tree.
......	Kou nyeh hloong lone noo boä nyeh ra.	Miseratit' khon, bokottit' e usula.	Inia hagá te iniá mísiáte sál-angíakanai.	His brother is taller than his sister.
......	Gnoo traup kauh tauh bä t-ka k-pät.	Anareak' gonoṅ tet' do bartaka tala.	Ená réa gonoñ bár taká adalí mená.	The price of that is two rupees and a half
......	Ma oä mong p-doä sngee dote ta.	Apundo hana hopon hopon oṛak're e tahen kana.	Apúiñ en huḍiñ oraá re taintanai.	My father lives in that small house.
......	Saun moa k-ta kauh ka nyeh nye.	Noa taka emae me.	Ne taká umai meṅ.	Give this rupee to him
......	Saun kauh kate noo nyeh.	Ma noako taka oni ṭhen khon ataṅ me.	En taká ko iní táte agúimeṅ.	Take those rupees from him.
......	Tok deh klung toey ta-uk ka chook.	Bugite dalepue or baberte tol kae me.	Khúb dálímen oro baiar te tholimeṅ.	Beat him well and bind him with ropes.

English.	Shan of Burmah.	Mekir of Cachar.	Muneepooree.	Tonghtoo of Burmah.
Draw water from the well.	Tek nam kah tee nam man ta.	Láng tuk álláng náng chhaganun.	Kubá dagi ising shak-u.	Bon-htee-ong ...
Walk before me ...	Kwah leè pah-nah kow-khah ta.	Áfráng áfráng dám bamnun.	Ái-mángdá challa.	Lôay-khôay tângâh
Whose boy comes behind you?	Look hpul mah pah-lang mul?	Nángki kanád ája-chho náng kiduna-má?	Nátungdá kánáke ángáng láe.	Pâmiê-pai lon nâ thâkhyâ?
From whom did you buy that?	Hseu an-nan kah tee hpul?	Mate penachi náng ke námmá?	Káná dagi lái?	O-tâ-thoo-nâ-phray-pamiê-dô?
From a shop-keeper of the village.	Kahtee koon khai-kho nul wan nai.	Hálá bángso dukán penachináng ke-nám.	Khungi dukán dar-dagi.	Dông-kô-htsai-thee-dò.

compared with others.—(Concluded.)

Poi of Burmah.	Talain of Pegu (Burmah.)	Sonthali of Sonthàl Pergunnahs, Western Bengal.	Moondaree of Chota Nagpore, Western Bengal.	English.
......	Took dike noo dike p-ting.	Kui khon dak' lo agui me.	Kuán te dáa uruñemen.	Draw water from the well.
......	Kwike k-tä oä.	In samaṅ samaṅte (*or* laha la hate) chalak' me.	Aiñya aiar re senomeṅ.	Walk before me.
......	Krone-troo m-kloong lek-a-row kauh tauh kone nyeh kaŭh rou?	Okoeren koṛa hopon am ta gomte e he juk'kana?	Okoiá koṛa hon amá tayomte hijutaná ?	Whose boy comes behind you?
......	Trope kauh m-neh ran nyeh kauh rou?	Oua do okoe then an kirin ket'a?	Enáam okai tá tem kiriñlaá.	From whom did you buy that?
......	Oa ran noo m-neeh p-neik p-doa quan.	Atoreṅ mit' ṭaṅ dokan ṭhen.	Hatu ren moy-ad dokanü tá te.	From a shop-keeper of the village.